The Philosophy of
Christian Religious Education

The Philosophy of Christian Religious Education

Jeff Astley

Religious Education Press
Birmingham, Alabama

Library of Congress Cataloging-in-Publication Data

Astley, Jeff.
    The philosophy of Christian religious education / Jeff Astley.
    Includes bibliographical references and indexes.
    ISBN 0-89135-093-4
    1. Christian education—Philosophy.   I. Title.
BV1464.A76   1994   93-43675
268'.01—dc20   CIP

Religious Education Press, Inc.
5316 Meadow Brook Road
Birmingham, Alabama 35242
10 9 8 7 6 5 4 3 2

Religious Education Press publishes books exclusively in religious education
and in areas closely related to religious education. It is committed to enhanc-
ing and professionalizing religious education through the publication of
serious, significant, and scholarly works.

PUBLISHER TO THE PROFESSION

Contents

PART IV: SOME KEY PHILOSOPHICAL ISSUES IN CHRISTIAN RELIGIOUS EDUCATION

Preface

This book has been written with the intention that it should be useful to, and therefore usable by, Christian religious educators of widely differing theological and educational outlooks. I hope that this is the case, for I am more eager to encourage other people to think through for themselves their own positions on Christian religious education than to persuade them of mine. What follows will inevitably present a particular view about a number of topics in Christian religious education, but it will also provide what I hope is a fair account of a range of other opinions.

Why a *"philosophy* of Christian religious education"? My understanding of philosophy and the philosophy of Christian religious education will be developed in Part I. I may anticipate here by saying that the book will be a philosophy of Christian religious education primarily in the sense that it will attempt to apply the clarifying, reflective, argumentative *method* of philosophy to various philosophically-interesting *issues* and *problems* in Christian religious education. In doing so the text will also on occasions reflect on and articulate various aims for, and understandings of, Christian religious education. It will thus also offer material for what is sometimes called, rather loosely, "a philosophy of"—or "(speculative) theory of"—Christian religious education. By illuminating Christian religious education in these ways with a searchlight that is directed by the philosopher, and by the philosopher's colleagues in the philosophy of education and the philosophy of religion, the book will provide what some may prefer to describe as a book on "philosophy *and* Christian religious education".

I appreciate that philosophy is not everyone's favorite subject. But philosophy cannot be avoided. We can hardly avoid having some sort of theory of the practice of Christian religious education: of acting and operating in ways that imply and ultimately rest on an understanding of what we are doing and why we are doing it. Such aims and understandings are often not explicitly recognized, but they are there none the less. Practice, unless it is totally chaotic and undirected, is built on the foundation of theory; and it is

1

often said that there is nothing so practical as a good theory. So we need to reflect on the theory of Christian religious education, and ultimately we shall need to do so with the tools of the philosopher. *Good* theories need to be thought-through, as well as empirically-grounded; analyzed and clarified, as well as tested out. Philosophy as a method is primarily an attempt to think clearly: to clarify concepts and to examine arguments. It is clear, reflective, critical thinking. Very many of the issues and problems in the theory and practice of Christian religious education need this sort of study, and it is my contention that they can be particularly illuminated by the work of philosophers, especially philosophers of religion and philosophers of education. Occasionally their work may appear to be somewhat technical and removed from the practicalities of the religious educator. But I hope that the discussion will not be ignored just because it sometimes becomes difficult, for a great deal of what these thinkers have to say is far too important to be passed over quickly or to be left solely in the hands of the professional philosopher.

What I attempt here, therefore, is a serious and indepth study of some of the philosophical issues relating to the theory and practice of Christian religious education. I hope that it will make some sort of contribution to future discussion about the nature of this most important activity of the Christian church.

Part I offers some introductory material about the nature of Christian religious education and what constitutes a philosophical examination of this field of endeavor.

Part II approaches the philosophy of Christian religious education through a study of the implications of the term "education": clarifying educational terminology before embarking on the major topics of indoctrination and the role of critical education in Christian religious education.

Part III approaches the subject through an analysis of the word "Christianity", particularly with reference to Christian attributes and Christian learning outcomes. Where Part II draws primarily on the literature in the philosophy of education, here the main contribution is from the philosophy of religion. This part includes discussion of the role of reason in religion and of the nature of religious understanding.

Part IV deals critically with other philosophical issues of a more complex nature that are raised by reflection on Christian religious education: i.e. the relativism debate and the particular problems posed by discussion about freedom of belief, the nature of morality, moral education, and the emotions and their education.

It is not easy to avoid the appearance of sexism, particularly when writing in English. Instead of constantly using such cumbersome phrases as "he or she" and "him/her", I have sometimes written about human beings in the feminine gender, and sometimes in the masculine. Therefore "she" usually implies "she or he" and "he" implies "he or she". I think it is proper to permit oneself this shorthand only if it is adopted in both forms.

A select *Glossary of Philosophical Terms* is provided at the end of the book. I hope that this will be of some use in clarifying philosophical terminology, particularly where terms are used rather differently by psychologists and philosophers.

I am grateful to the Society for Promoting Christian Knowledge for permission to quote from Basil Mitchell's Appendix on "Indoctrination" in *The Fourth R*, to the Macmillan Press for permission to quote from John Wilson's *A Preface to Morality*, and to the editors and publishers of *The Journal of Theological Studies, The Modern Churchman, Religious Education* and the *British Journal of Religious Education* for allowing me to incorporate some paragraphs, in a revised form, from my articles published in these journals.

I am most grateful for the support I have received from a variety of sources during my work on this book. The Management Committee of the North of England Institute for Christian Education (NEICE) allowed me a period of study leave during which much of the initial reading and writing was undertaken; particular thanks are due to my former colleague, Elizabeth Fisher, who served as Acting Director during my absence. Two secretaries of the Institute carried out the task of typing this text with considerable skill, patience and good humor. Norma Dent initiated the work and Dorothy Greenwell, her successor, bore most of the burden of the day as the book grew and went through countless revisions.

Many colleagues, friends and acquaintances have helped me in my thinking on the topics covered here. Members of NEICE's multidisciplinary Christian Education Seminar made a number of useful comments on early versions of these arguments. I am particularly grateful to two philosophers of education, Richard Smith of the University of Durham, England and Elmer Thiessen of Medicine Hat College, Alberta, Canada for many valuable suggestions about the arguments in the book. Unfortunately I cannot blame any of the above for the faults that remain.

In the end my deepest thanks must go to my wife, Helen, for her continuing support and encouragement, even when work on this project overflowed into times and spaces to which it had no right.

Part I

Philosophy
and
Christian Religious Education

CHAPTER 1

The Meaning of
Christian Religious Education

INTRODUCTION

The Problem of Terminology

At the outset of any study of this area some discussion about what it is to be called is inevitable. The problem is exacerbated if, as with the present text, literature and practices from both sides of the Atlantic are to be surveyed. It should be made clear at the outset (to both readers and librarians) that in the United States and Britain the same phrases often name radically different activities.[1]

In the United States "Christian education" has historically been a Protestant term. It is often claimed that it now has some rather negative connotations, carrying overtones of indoctrination or circumscribed and triumphalistic interpretations.[2] Primarily, however, it denotes the formative (usually including the evangelistic) activities of the church in developing Christian beliefs, attitudes and overt behaviors. As such its denotation is the same as that of the phrases "Christian education" and "Christian nurture" as used in Britain. Catholics, and more recently some others, often prefer to describe this activity as "catechesis",[3] but the more popular and ecumenical term for it (which

---

1. See Gabriel Moran, "Religious Education", in Mircea Eliade, ed., *Encyclopedia of Religion*, Vol. 12 (New York: Macmillan; London: Collier Macmillan, 1987); "Religious Pluralism: A U.S. and Roman Catholic View", in Norma H. Thompson, ed., *Religious Pluralism and Religious Education* (Birmingham, Ala.: Religious Education Press, 1988) and *Religious Education as a Second Language* (Birmingham, Ala.: Religious Education Press, 1989), p. 85, ch. 4 and *passim*.

2. See Thomas H. Groome, *Christian Religious Education* (San Francisco: Harper & Row, 1980), p. 24; James Michael Lee, *The Shape of Religious Instruction* (Birmingham, Ala.: Religious Education Press, 1971), p. 6.

3. For a summary of the different ways in which the term catechesis is used in the United States, and his own understanding of it, see James Michael Lee, "Catechesis Sometimes,

7

is in principle usable by members of other religions also, and in practice by Jews) is "religious education". Religious education in the United States, therefore, in its Christian redaction, is usually seen as a church sponsored and church oriented activity leading to the development of a wide range of Christian outcomes in the learners.

In British debate the activities outlined above are often described as "confessional". This does not imply a limited denominational objective, but merely formation in a religion—the (intentional) nurturing of a particular religious commitment.[4] The current British usage is broadly as follows. "Religious education" (often abbreviated to "RE") specifies a general educational activity, usually treated as a part of schooling—including nonsectarian publicly funded schooling, that educates children about religion. Currently this is usually taken to involve an empathic but nonevangelistic and nonformative (often described as "nonconfessional") educating activity focused on a variety of religions.[5] RE is often also regarded as having the additional functions of developing the learners' own religious or quasi-religious sensitivities, and their search for meaning and truth.[6]

"Christian education", on the other hand, is on the whole the term used in Britain for the confessional activity of teaching the Christian religion (but see pp. 14-18 below for a qualification of this claim). Many prefer the term "Christian nurture" for this activity; some (especially Catholics) retain the hallowed, but somewhat archaic term "catechesis"; others describe it as "confessional RE". The situation is complicated by the fact that in Britain many "church schools" (general educational establishments often originally founded and wholly funded by the church, but now supported mainly by public funding) see their work as "Christian nurture" rather than, or at least alongside, "religious education".[7] So we have a terminological problem at the

Religious Instruction Always: Another Roman Catholic Perspective", in Marlene Mayr, ed., *Does the Church Really Want Religious Education?* (Birmingham, Ala.: Religious Education Press, 1988), pp. 34-66.

4. The confessionalism group of words are normally used "to connote instruction in particular beliefs to the exclusion of all others". Robin H. Shepherd, "Confessionalism", in John M. Sutcliffe, ed., *A Dictionary of Religious Education* (London: SCM, 1984), p. 94. The use of these particular terms has been criticized, see John M. Hull, *Studies in Religion and Education* (Lewes, England: Falmer, 1984), p.180. On the use of the term "commitment" see Chapter 8 below.

5. See Michael Grimmitt, *What Can I do in RE?* (Great Wakering, England: Mayhew-McCrimmon, 1973), ch. 3; Ninian Smart, *Secular Education and the Logic of Religion* (London: Faber & Faber, 1968); Schools Council, *Religious Education in Secondary Schools* (London: Evans/Methuen, 1971); Peter Gardner, "Religious Education: in defence of non-commitment", *Journal of Philosophy of Education* 14: 2 (1980).

6. Bishop of Durham's Commission on Religious Education in Schools, *The Fourth R* (London: National Society/SPCK, 1970), ch. 4; Schools Council Project on Religious Education in Primary Schools, *Discovering an Approach* (London: Macmillan, 1977), chs. 6 and 7; Michael Grimmitt, *Religious Education and Human Development* (Great Wakering, England: McCrimmon, 1987), ch. 6.

7. In Britain Roman Catholic and Anglican church schools are part of the "maintained system", i.e. they are largely funded by local or central government. Most private or independent

outset! I intend in this book to follow some others[8] in using the somewhat cumbersome term "Christian religious education". As others have noted, the term avoids any hint of Christian empire building and "colonial dominance" of religious education, as well as being sufficiently generic to be ecumenical. Christian religious education is more or less the same as, or at least includes, what most readers will understand by the Christian church's task of "religious education", "Christian education" or "catechesis". The term Christian religious education has the advantage of being different enough from the term "religious education" to signal to those conversant with the British literature that I am *not* primarily writing about "religious education in secular schools", but rather about a confessional, churchly activity of evangelism, instruction and nurture. I shall, however, draw occasionally on the debate about the former in the course of my analysis of the nature of the latter.

Definitions

I shall adopt a fairly broad notion of Christian religious education and Christian learning in this book. Arguments for and against my understanding of these phrases will surface shortly, but for the moment perhaps the reader will be willing to take these definitions more or less on trust. I shall define *Christian religious education* as the process whereby Christian learning takes place. It often involves "teaching": that is, the intentional facilitation (promotion, enabling, aiding) of *Christian learning*. I understand Christian learning (spelling it out as "Christian religious learning" is surely unnecessary) to be the "learning of Christianity", in the sense of a person's learning to be Christian. Broadly speaking, it is the adoption and deepening of his or her Christian beliefs, attitudes, values, and dispositions to experience and act in a Christian way.

These are indeed very broad definitions. I think that they can be defended against critics who understand both "education" and "learning" more narrowly, and I will attempt to do so below in Part II. But even if they could not, we should need *some* terms to refer to those processes (and the results of those processes) by which people become Christian and come to be more Christian. Others will continue to prefer to speak of "Christian nurture", "Christian formation" or "catechesis"; but there is merit in retaining the language of education and learning, not least because it forces us to reflect on the relevance for our particular concerns of the more general philosophical and psychological discussions that deal with these topics.[9]

---

schools (which Britons still sometimes perversely call "public schools") also have a Christian foundation.

8. See Groome, *Christian Religious Education*, pp. 24-25 and James Michael Lee, "Christian Religious Education and Moral Development", in Brenda Munsey, ed., *Moral Development, Moral Education, and Kohlberg* (Birmingham, Ala.: Religious Education Press, 1980). See also John M. Hull, "RE, Nature of", in Sutcliffe, ed., *A Dictionary of Religious Education*, p. 284, and Gabriel Moran, *Religious Education Development: Images for the Future* (Minneapolis, Minn.: Winston, 1983), pp. 190-191.

9. Groome, *Christian Religious Education*, pp. 23, 27.

WHERE IS CHRISTIAN RELIGIOUS EDUCATION?

If this definition of Christian learning is permitted, then we may claim that it is something that is taking place all the time and everywhere. Wherever, whenever and however people become more Christian as a result of their experiences, there they are learning Christianity. Christians learn to be Christian *both* through and in the worship, spirituality, ministry and fellowship of the church, *and* through and in many and various other, apparently more "secular",[10] activities. The Christian life is learned in overtly Christian contexts and in those that carry no Christian labels. We are changing all the time, and some of these changes are changes in the direction of becoming in some sense more Christian.

Of course there is an implied evaluation here. To think of these changes as changes in a Christian direction is to make a normative judgment about what Christianity is, and what it is to be Christian. Different Christians will agree on a number of these judgments, but there will also be controversial areas. A group of Christians may argue about what constitutes Christian learning because they do not agree as to what constitutes Christianity. In my experience most important disagreements about Christian religious education are at base of this kind. Thus different Christians may all accept that Christian learning can happen anywhere and at any time, but dispute as to whether a particular occasion of learning is an example of *Christian* learning.[11]

If Christian learning is, in principle, a very widespread activity, what about Christian religious education? One distinction that is often made between learning and education is that the latter is intentional and deliberate.

---

10. I appreciate that the designation "secular" is itself the subject of debate. Some argue that the term secular only properly applies (like "secularism") to *anti*religious stances, experiences and educational approaches, but normal usage seems to predicate it of *non*religious positions and phenomena. I use it here to apply to activities that would not be explicitly labeled as "religious" by most people. The sociological phenomenon of secularization has been much discussed. Peter Berger offers a fairly noncontroversial definition: "by secularization we mean the process by which sectors of society and culture are removed from the domination of religious institutions and symbols". Peter L. Berger, *The Social Reality of Religion* (Harmondsworth, England: Penguin, 1973; = *The Sacred Canopy*, Garden City, N.Y.: Doubleday, 1967), p. 113.

11. See below Chapter 6. It should be clear from what I have said above that Christian learning here refers to the learning of Christian beliefs, attitudes, lifestyle etc., i.e. learning that results in Christian outcomes. The use of the phrase does *not* imply that there are learning faculties or processes that are specifically Christian. "Christian learning" (= "Christian religious learning") and "Christian learning outcomes" are simply phrases that are used here in the way that others have used the terms "religious learning" and "religious learning outcomes". See, for example, James Michael Lee, "The Authentic Source of Religious Instruction", in Norma H. Thompson, ed., *Religious Education and Theology* (Birmingham, Ala.: Religious Education Press, 1982), pp. 114, 138. The language must not be taken as suggesting the existence of a Christian learning that is to be paralleled by a "Christian dentistry" or a "Christian farming". Compare James Michael Lee, *The Flow of Religious Instruction* (Birmingham, Ala.: Religious Education Press, 1973), pp. 33, 59.

Another is that education, unlike learning, is systematic, structured and sustained: i.e. a long-term, planned process. The deliberate planner of such planned learning is the teacher or educator. We shall see later (Chapter 3) that these distinctions can be overdrawn, but many regard them as useful. For those who do, Christian religious education may be taken to be a term with a much narrower application than the term Christian learning. Certainly it is normally the case that in Christian religious education teaching facilitates learning, and this makes it more obvious and explicit. Examples will include the activities of adult Christian discussion and Bible study groups, of confirmation and church membership classes, and of Sunday schools and preachers. But we may also include other, less obviously educational activities such as worship, church outings, church council meetings and Christian giving/"stewardship" campaigns—provided that these are planned so as to develop Christian learning. More secular occasions that serve as examples of Christian learning, in that they lead to learning outcomes that we are willing to designate as "Christian", can also be deliberately planned so as to become examples of intentional Christian religious education. Thus, for example, I could open myself and others to experiencing the miracles of nature in the maternity hospital or on a country walk with the intention, among others, of moving our attitudes and ideas in a more Christian direction. Childbirth, like worship, is not entered into primarily as an educational experience, but it can fulfill that function—in addition to its main one!

Hence both Christian learning and Christian religious education may take place anywhere. Christians cannot do anything about the Christian learning that they can do nothing about (except rejoice in it). But Christian religious education, when it is construed as teacher-facilitated and intentional, is partly someone's responsibility; and Christians must be willing to recognize, and indeed to exercise, that responsibility wherever and whenever they can.

A criticism that often arises in the context of discussions such as this one is that Christian learning and Christian religious education so defined are concepts that have expanded out of all proportion. Just as some would say that liturgists try to make everything in the church into worship, and counselors make it all therapy, so it would seem that educationists want everything to be education. But everything is not education, the critics say, insisting (with the eighteenth-century Christian apologist and moral philosopher Joseph Butler) that everything is what it is, and not another thing.

I have some sympathy with this critique of the imperialistic, colonizing arrogance of certain disciplines, at least as far as the liturgists and counselors are concerned! Yet it has to be admitted that there are *some* categories of human activity that it is difficult not to see everywhere, and learning is one of them. Further, no one is saying that Christian learning covers everything in Christianity. There is praying and living the Christian life, as well as learning to be the sort of person who prays and lives it. Nor is Christian religious education the main driving force behind the planning of worship and pastoral ministry. Fundamentally such things are done for their own sake, or "for the sake of God", or "for others", and not for their educational results. But it remains patently the case that those who worship, and those who receive ministry, can and do learn to be more Christian through such activities. Worship and ministry thus have a function in facilitating Christian learning. Hence the intentional planning and practice of worship and ministry should include an acknowledgement of their learning effects and may therefore also count as (intentional) Christian religious education. We may agree that Christian learning/education is not everything in the church; but it is, or should be, an aspect of everything that happens in the church.[12]

OTHER ISSUES

Evangelism
It should be noted that I am using the phrase Christian religious education in a way that is broad enough to encompass evangelism as well as Christian nurture, that is, preaching the gospel with the aim of conversion as well as teaching the faith so as to "build up" the converts. Thus Christian religious education incorporates what in traditional Catholic language was separated as "evangelization" on the one hand and "catechesis" on the other. We may note how these terms are increasingly regarded as having overlapping references. Thus: "evangelization can precede or accompany the work of catechesis proper. In every case, however, one must keep in mind that the element of conversion is always present in the dynamism of Faith, and for that reason any form of catechesis must also perform the role of evangelization".[13] The traditional distinction between evangelization and catechesis, and the underlying New Testament distinction between *kerygma* and *didache*,[14] distinguishes the audience, content, methods and learning outcomes of these processes by differences that are only differences in degree and not differences

---

12. See John H. Westerhoff, III, "Towards a Definition of Christian Education", in Westerhoff, ed., *A Colloquy on Christian Education* (Philadelphia: Pilgrim, 1972), pp. 62-63; also his "The Liturgical Imperative of Religious Education", in James Michael Lee, ed., *The Religious Education We Need* (Birmingham, Ala.: Religious Education Press, 1977), p. 77.

13. Sacred Congregation for the Clergy, *General Catechetical Directory* (London: Catholic Truth Society, 1971), p. 27. See also Paul VI, *Evangelii Nuntiandi*, 1975, para. 44; Kevin Nichols, *Cornerstone* (Slough, England: St. Paul, 1978), pp. 14-16, 24. The traditional distinction between evangelization (and pre-evangelization) and catechesis (which is often seen as incorporating the ancient post-baptismal *didascalia*) is illustrated by various authors in Michael Warren, ed., *Sourcebook for Modern Catechetics* (Winona, Minn.: St. Mary's Press, 1983), Readings 3, 24 and 25. John Westerhoff's "catechesis" comprises both "evangelization" and "assimilation", the latter being nurture leading to "the adoption and internalization of Christian understanding and ways". See his "A Catechetical Way of Doing Theology", in Thompson, ed., *Religious Education and Theology*, pp. 220, 231 and "The Challenge: Understanding the Problem of Faithfulness", in John H. Westerhoff, III and O. C. Edwards, Jr., eds., *A Faithful Church* (Wilton, Connecticut: Morehouse-Barlow, 1981), p. 2.

14. See C. H. Dodd, *The Apostolic Preaching and its Developments* (London: Hodder & Stoughton, 1963; New York: Harper, 1940), pp. 7-8.

in kind.[15] On my view, Christian religious education is a term broad enough to cover both. Those who wish to draw a clear distinction between "educator" and "evangelist" often do so on the basis of the restricted, normative definition of education discussed in Chapter 3 below.

Teaching Religion versus Teaching about Religion

This is a popular distinction that has been used in countries like the United States where the public education system eschews religious observance and confessional religious education.[16] "Teaching religion" is taken to be a matter of teaching people to be religious, whereas "teaching about religion" denotes nonconfessional study of the beliefs, values and practices of one or another religion. Teaching religion thus defined is, in its Christian form, what this book calls Christian religious education. Teaching about religion is the sort of nonevangelistic and non-nurturing (nonconfessional) teaching

---

15. Thus: "there is no Christian education which does not involve evangelism". Randolph Crump Miller, *The Theory of Christian Education Practice* (Birmingham, Ala.: Religious Education Press, 1980), p. 159. Compare "there is no intrinsic difference between how one educates and how one evangelizes! The specific content of the message may differ, but the medium through which the transmission of the message is facilitated is the same." Lawrence O. Richards, *A Theology of Christian Education* (Grand Rapids, Mich.: Zondervan, 1975), pp. 55-56. See also William J. Abraham, *The Logic of Evangelism* (London: Hodder & Stoughton; Grand Rapids, Mich.: Eerdmans, 1989), pp. 95, 108-109.

16. It is worth recalling that it is only comparatively recently that the First Amendment to the U.S. Constitution was definitively interpreted as forbidding religious observance and religious instruction in the nation's schools; while permitting, and indeed encouraging, teaching about religion as part of a secular program of education. See Christopher J. Lucas, *Our Western Educational Heritage* (New York: Macmillan; London: Collier-Macmillan, 1972), pp. 520-522; N. Piediscalzi, "Public Education Religion Studies since the Schempp Decision (1963)", in Marvin J. Taylor, ed., *Foundations for Christian Education in an Era of Change* (Nashville, Tenn.: Abingdon, 1976). It has been argued that the nineteenth-century public day schools, although prevented from offering denominational teaching, taught a "common Christianity" (with a "prevailing Protestant content and character"). William Bean Kennedy, "Christian Education through History", in Marvin J. Taylor, ed., *An Introduction to Christian Education* (Nashville, Tenn.: Abingdon, 1966), p. 27. It was the continuing expression of this in Bible reading and prayer that was challenged in the courts in the early 1960s, leading to the Supreme Court decision (the 1963 Schempp decision) banning as unconstitutional schools' requiring teachers and students to engage in Bible reading and the recitation of the Lord's Prayer and other prayers. (Voluntary prayers conducted by people other than teachers may possibly be legal.) As one commentator put it at the time, "In the past America had a 'neutral' state—favorable to religion. We how have a state which is becoming truly neutral—favorable neither to belief nor unbelief." Daniel Callahan, "The New Pluralism: From Nostalgia to Reality", *The Commonweal* 78 (1963), p. 528. The debate has recently been reopened in the United States— see Stanley Hauerwas and John H. Westerhoff, III, eds., *Schooling Christians* (Grand Rapids, Mich.: Eerdmans, 1992). But it would be true to say that the received educational orthodoxy takes the view that it is the task of the churches to do (Christian) religious education, and to set up their own schools and colleges should they desire schooling that will promote this. A similar, completely secular, approach to public schooling that has forbidden any form of religious education (sometimes extending this ban to any nonevangelistic and non-nurturing teaching *about* religion) has, at least until very recently, been taken by France, New Zealand and many provinces in Canada.

that often bears the title "religious studies" in schools and colleges. It forms a large part of religious education in British schools, and is found in some public school systems in the United States as well. The distinction is useful, if only because some political commentators on education appear to be unable to distinguish (1) teaching someone to understand, and perhaps to evaluate, Christian or Muslim (or Marxist or occult) beliefs, from (2) teaching that is aimed at the formation, nurturing or inculcation of those beliefs. I shall use the phrase "teaching about religion", in distinction from Christian religious education, from time to time in this book.[17]

"Christian Education" Revisited

As indicated above, the phrase Christian religious education is used here to denote the educational process of learning the Christian religion. It is equivalent in meaning, if not in tone, to the American Protestant phrase Christian education. But in some contexts Christian education is a rather more slippery expression: for it is a term that may mean a number of different things. John Hull has claimed, at least for those countries where religion is taught in schools, that the use of the phrase usually conceals a confusion among: (a) "the processes and means whereby Christians bring up their children"; (b) "a Christian approach to, or philosophy of, general education"; and (c) "Christianity as curriculum content".[18]

It should be clear by now that I understand the phrase Christian education,

---

17. "Teaching religion" is best avoided because of its ambiguity. Thus it has been argued that, in addition to the meaning "teaching people to be religious", the phrase may also be understood as referring to an induction into the study of religion because the word *religion* "means two very different things: 1) a set of practices that particular communities engage in and 2) an object of scholarly and academic inquiry" (Moran, *Religious Education as a Second Language*, pp. 124, 136). Adopting sense (2) himself, Moran then objects to the phrase "teaching about religion" as introducing a second remove. See *ibid.*, p. 130; also Gabriel Moran, "Two Languages of Religious Education", *Living Light* 14: 1 (1977), p. 13 and *Interplay: A Theory of Religion and Education* (Winona, Minn.: St. Mary's Press, 1981), ch. 5. The distinction between teaching about religion and teaching religion has been criticized by others on the grounds that the terms are ambiguous. Writing in a British context, John Sealey prefers the nomenclature "religious education" (teaching those things "which will enable students to understand the religious life") and "teaching the religious life". John Sealey, "Teaching 'About' and Teaching 'What Is' in Religion", *British Journal of Religious Education* 2: 2 (1979), p. 58. Using Sealey's terminology, Christian religious education would be defined as "teaching the Christian religious life". For a further analysis of (a rather more limited understanding of) "teaching about" religion, which the author distinguishes from "teaching that", "educating in" and "teaching how", see R. M. Rummery, *Catechesis and Religious Education in a Pluralistic Society* (Sydney: Dwyer; Huntington, Ind.: Our Sunday Visitor, 1975), pp. 156-161.

18. Hull, *Studies in Religion and Education*, p. 39, also p. 206. See also his *School Worship: An Obituary* (London: SCM, 1975), pp. 73-74. Douglas Hubery seems to accept that the phrase "Christian education" can be applied to (his own understanding of) all three. See his *Christian Education in State and Church* (Redhill, England: Denholm House, 1972), p. 30 and *passim*. Compare also E. Orteza y Miranda, "Some Problems with the Expression 'Christian education'", *British Journal of Religious Education* 8: 2 (1986).

and therefore Christian religious education, in Hull's sense (a). I would, however, expand his definition to include (1) people over their lifespan (i.e. not just children); (2) the conversion to, as well as the nurture/formation of individuals and groups in, the Christian worldview, character and identity; and (at least for many Christians) (3) the development of critical, evaluative and analytic skills in the Christians so formed, so that they can evaluate for themselves the Christian culture and self-understanding into which they have been nurtured, from and within a Christian standpoint (what might be called "Christian self-criticism" brought about by "critical Christian religious education"—see below Chapter 5).

I shall not refer to Hull's category (c)—"Christianity as curriculum content"—as "Christian education" or "Christian religious education". In those countries where an entirely nonconfessional teaching about Christianity is permitted in publicly funded education[19] this is a very important category. It represents "education about Christianity" in the sense of a secular, scholarly elucidation and evaluation of the Christian religion. Here the objective is solely that of understanding the Christian tradition rather than, as with Christian religious education proper, conversion (with understanding) to the faith or growth (with understanding) in it. It may be argued that such education about Christianity is an important aim, and a proper aim, of any complete secular education. I shall not consider that debate here.

What of Hull's category (b): Christian education as an approach to, or (more generally) a perspective on, general education? This is what is often popularly referred to as a Christian "philosophy of" education. I shall not use the phrase Christian education (or Christian religious education) of these activities either, preferring to refer to them in two ways: as "a Christian critique of education" and "general education of a Christian kind".

A Christian critique of education: this phrase is meant to designate understandings of education that are developed with conscious and particular reference to the Christian viewpoint and which operate, positively or negatively, as critiques of other (for example more secular) accounts of education and educational activities.[20] Such critiques often operate with criteria that

---

19. This is the situation in principle in the United States, and in practice in many schools in a number of countries (where it is sometimes combined in different ways with confessional Christian religious education)—including Britain, Denmark, Sweden and (increasingly) Australia.

20. As examples of such an approach see Spencer Leeson, *Christian Education* (London: Longmans, Green, 1947), lecture V; M. V. C. Jeffreys, *The Aims of Education (Glaucon)* (London: Pitman, 1972), pp. 151-167; Patricia English, "A Christian Perspective on Classroom and School Discipline", *Journal of Christian Education* 60 (1977); Michael Hinton, "A Theology for the Classroom", in *Christianity in the Classroom* (London: Christian Education Movement, 1978); William K. Kay and Fred Hughes, "Christian Light on Education", *Religious Education* 80: 1 (1985); Michael L. Peterson, *Philosophy of Education: Issues and Options* (Downers Grove, Ill.: InterVarsity Press, 1986), chs. 4-7; Edward Hulmes, "Christian Education in a Multi-cultural Society", in V. Alan McClelland, ed., *Christian Education in a Pluralist Society* (London: Routledge, 1988), pp. 89, 91-92; Brian V. Hill, *That They May Learn: Towards a Christian View of Education* (Exeter, England: Paternoster, 1990).

are only characteristic of Christianity rather than distinctively Christian (i.e. specific to, and distinctive of, Christianity). Thus they may oppose indoctrinatory methods in education or espouse certain goals in moral education for reasons that are very similar to those given by other approaches to education. Occasionally, however, the Christian perspective will be a distinctive one that is not shared by other critiques of education.

The Christian critique of education outlined above may lead to a *general education of a Christian kind* or a "Christian scheme of education".[21] This phrase denotes general educational activity that is not directly focused on Christianity, but which is influenced by a Christian understanding of education. Again, in most cases, the Christian input will be in those areas that are characteristically, rather than distinctively, Christian—for instance concern for the value of the individual or concern for truth.[22] In these cases this "implicitly Christian education"—e.g. loving, caring education—will not necessarily differ in content or method, but only in motivation, from other loving or caring education that leads to personal growth. Some have argued, however, with Jacques Maritain, that the Christian educator's "mode or manner" of teaching will have a particular effect in conveying to the student a sense of the unity of knowledge and the "immortal value of truth": an effect that distinguishes such education from at least some other educational endeavors.[23] Others have reached the radical conclusion that, as "Christian presuppositions do provide an interpretative framework for all the forms of knowledge", "there must be a unique content to Christian education in all areas of study".[24] How this is worked out will vary from Christian to Christian, particularly from liberal Christian to conservative Christian.

In the hands of many conservative Christians this Christian comment on

---

21. John M. Sutcliffe and Philip Lee-Woolf, "Christian Education and RE", in Sutcliffe, ed., *A Dictionary of Religious Education*, p. 67. The works cited in note 20 above often make a contribution here as well. See also Edmund Fuller, ed., *The Christian Idea of Education* (New Haven: Yale University Press, 1957), p. viii and *passim*; Witold Tulasiewicz and Colin Brock, eds., *Christianity and Educational Provision in International Perspective* (London: Routledge, 1988), *passim*.

22. Thus Gabriel Moran writes of education as "the dealing critically and creatively with reality and the discovery of how to participate"; on this interpretation of (true) education "it has qualities and practices which deserve to be called religious". Gabriel Moran, "Of a Kind and To a Degree", in Mayr, ed., *Does the Church Really Want Religious Education?*, pp. 21-22. Similarly Leon McKenzie distinguishes religious education that is religious in the sense of teaching explicit religious subject-matter, religious education that is religious "by virtue of the intentionality of the teacher and learners", and religious education that is religious "by virtue of the context of education and the interpersonal processes that occur within that context". Leon McKenzie, "The Purposes and Scope of Adult Religious Education", in Nancy Foltz, ed., *Handbook of Adult Religious Education* (Birmingham, Ala.: Religious Education Press, 1986), p. 18. Many would be willing to write "Christian" in place of "religious" in the above quotations.

23. Jacques Maritain, "On Some Typical Aspects of Christian Education", in Fuller, ed., *The Christian Idea of Education*, p. 180.

24. Elmer J. Thiessen, "A Defense of a Distinctively Christian Curriculum", *Religious Education* 80: 1 (1985), p. 50.

and influence on general education may run very deep, taking a form that more liberal Christians would reject outright.[25] Others (Christians and non-Christians alike) will be suspicious of these categories as implying a sort of theological imperialism—an invasion and conquest of the autonomous practice of general education by alien principles. In my account above I have revealed my own rather liberal sympathies through my recognition of criteria that are characteristically, rather than distinctively, Christian. This emphasis will seem to some to render redundant these categories of a Christian critique and understanding of education. I would argue, however, that the Christian who is engaged in facilitating general learning, both in educational institutions such as schools and colleges and outside their walls, will want to work out her theory and practice of education in ways that connect to some extent with the *Christian* vision that motivates her whole life. (I prefer here to speak of an unspecified "connection", rather than any specific relationship.) Christianity does have implications for our approach to education in general, as it has for the rest of our life and work. But I would contend that very few of these implications will be distinctive of Christianity in the sense that they are not shared by any other religious or secular viewpoint. In a plural society this is a matter of practical comfort, for it means that Christian teachers can, for at least some of the time, work with and support approaches to public education that arise from non-Christian (although not "anti-Christian") sources.[26]

It is a mistake to refuse to designate anything "Christian" unless and until we are assured that it is a belief, attitude or viewpoint that is *only* to be found within Christianity. Much that is central to the teaching of Jesus and the contemporary self-understanding of the church simply is not distinctive in that way. Many traditional "Christian attitudes" like love, trust and hope are characteristic of Christianity, rather than distinctively peculiar to it; and the same goes for certain central "Christian beliefs" about God, creation and so on that are shared by other theistic religions. It may be argued that these attitudes and beliefs will always be found in what is truly Christian, but it cannot be argued that they are unique to Christianity.[27]

The above pages constitute, to some extent, an exercise in limiting the scope of the present work. I am concerned in this book with Christian reli-

---

25. For a taste of this emphasis see Mark Roques, *Curriculum Unmasked* (Eastbourne, England: Monarch, 1989). For a description of one extreme form of it see Alan Peshkin's fine study, *God's Choice: The Total World of a Fundamentalist Christian School* (Chicago: University of Chicago Press, 1986).

26. A valuable survey of the attitudes to education shown by a number of different religions and cultural perspectives is provided in Edward Hulmes, *Education and Cultural Diversity* (London: Longman, 1989).

27. We must guard against placing the Christian perspective "over against any given other one as if they were necessarily mutually exclusive", for "any modern Christian perspective will contain much that is not specifically Christian". Van Austin Harvey, *The Historian and the Believer: The Morality of Historical Knowledge and Christian Belief* (London: SCM, 1967), p. 242.

gious education understood very broadly as the process whereby people learn to be Christian (which includes learning to be more Christian). This work will not be much concerned with education about Christianity in a general educational context, nor with Christian approaches to general education, and I shall not use the phrases "Christian religious education" or "Christian education" for these educational activities. They are, of course, very important; and Christians with a concern for their faith and for education should be concerned with them. But they do not constitute, except for some passing comments, the subject matter of this study.

CHAPTER 2

The Philosophy of Christian Religious Education

THE NATURE OF PHILOSOPHY

Philosophy

Students who come new to a subject usually want to know what it is about. Their concern is very understandable, but it is sometimes difficult to give a proper answer at the outset. "Study it for a while and you will discover what it is" is often the only appropriate response. Philosophy (literally "the love of wisdom") is very much like that. Philosophers have often been tempted to follow the example of the British philosopher G. E. Moore, who when asked what his subject was would point at the books on his shelves and reply "It is what all these are about".

Antony Flew has distinguished between philosophy as (1) an "aphoristic overview" (i.e. one that is expressed in pithy maxims) embracing a person's value commitments and beliefs about the general nature of things, and (2) the academic discipline of philosophy which concerns itself primarily with an analysis of the meaning of certain key concepts and discussions about the validity of arguments employing them.[1] Such a distinction clears the ground a little and forbids our giving too wide a connotation to the word "philosophy", where "my philosophy" just means "my attitudes or views", or—slightly more restrictively—"the views that really matter to me and motivate my living". It also allows us to focus on the method of philosophy, which many consider more distinctive of the subject than its aims or subject-matter. Another scholar characterizes the *method* of philosophy along these lines:

(a) It is reflective. It proceeds by argument and criticism, not by experimental verification.
(b) It is general. It enquires into the general nature of things, or the mean-

---

1. Antony Flew, ed., *A Dictionary of Philosophy* (London: Pan/Macmillan, 1979), preface.

19

ing of certain general concepts; e.g. "What is knowledge?" or "What sorts of things are real?".

(c) It is definitional. It typically asks, "What is X?" requiring a verbal definition or exposition of its meaning.

(d) It is interpretative. By expounding the meaning and relations of various concepts, it presents a "way of seeing" the world; every philosophy has a distinctive approach, or insight.[2]

We can see from this that philosophy operates differently from the natural and human sciences, in that it proceeds by rational reflection alone without experiment and observation. Yet it cannot be overstressed that philosophy needs to be aware of, and must reflect on, the factual discoveries and theories provided by such empirical studies.

The account given above stresses the *analytic* role of philosophy, but much of the history of philosophy has been concerned with a more *synthetic* function of creating or revising general, systematic and coherent accounts of all reality. Such general views of the universe and humanity's place within it, particularly if they are seen as affecting practically-oriented as well as purely theoretical attitudes and beliefs, are often described as *Weltanschauungen* or "worldviews". This synthetic role,[3] into which analytic philosophy sometimes merges, tends to make philosophy distinguishable more by its subject-matter than by its methods.[4] The subject-matter of philosophy is sometimes taken to be "'ultimate things', either about the universe as a whole or about matters affecting human fate and conduct in the most basic way".[5]

It has to be acknowledged that much of philosophy, in its analytic as well as its synthetic role, has tended to select particular "philosophical problems" as its subject-matter, although often on a rather smaller scale than those outlined above. Certainly the different branches of philosophy tend to be distinguished by their subject-matter. For example epistemology (the theory of knowledge) asks questions about what knowledge is and how we can justify our knowledge claims; whereas metaphysics asks questions about the general nature of reality,[6] questions that may be as general as "What is the ulti-

---

2. Keith Ward, *Fifty Key Words in Philosophy* (London: Lutterworth, 1968), p. 57.

3. This synthetic role may be described as *producing philosophies* or philosophical systems (i.e. conclusions), whereas on the analytic model the philosopher is said to be involved in *doing philosophy*.

4. Thus: "Philosophy has sometimes been defined . . . as 'critical and reflective thinking'. But this definition is . . . unsatisfactory; for it does not indicate the distinctive character of the problems with which philosophic thinking is concerned. . . . For those whom we call 'scientists' certainly think reflectively, and yet we make a distinction between philosophy and the special sciences." John Herman Randall and Justus Buchler, *Philosophy: An Introduction* (New York: Barnes & Noble, 1942), p. 3.

5. A. R. Lacey, *A Dictionary of Philosophy* (London: Routledge & Kegan Paul, 1976), p. 159.

6. It should be noted that philosophy in the past was wide enough to include theories about essentially scientific matters, often of a rather "armchair" variety. Bertrand Russell

mate nature of things: mind, matter, or both?" or as specific as "Do human beings have free will?".

We must therefore recognize both a method element and a subject-matter element in any adequate definition of philosophy. Philosophy, then, is a *method of thinking*—of analysis and argument, clarification and criticism[7]— applied to a *particular range of issues and problems.*

Philosophy-of

In any encyclopedia of philosophy or series of volumes about the subject there will be several articles or books dealing with the traditional divisions of philosophy such as logic, ethics, metaphysics and the theory of knowledge. But we shall also find there a number of entries or titles of the "philosophy-*of*" variety: philosophy of language, philosophy of mathematics, philosophy of history, philosophy of natural science, and two areas that are of particular relevance to the present work—philosophy of education and philosophy of religion.

In these philosophy-of studies the authors will be attempting to apply the critical, reflective method of philosophical thinking to certain issues and problems from a particular phenomenon, area, field or discipline of study. This is often called "subject philosophy". Thus a philosopher of science reflects on the concepts and arguments used by scientists, picking up what is philosophically interesting in the work of science. She may or may not be a scientist herself, but it is important to recognize that when she is doing philosophy of science she is not doing science. She is analyzing and reflecting on science; she is not seeking to make scientific discoveries or create scientific theories. Rather, as a philosopher, her "philosophical antennae" are being used to pick up particular scientific ideas and reflections that have philosophical implications. Now it is not always easy to specify what sort of things a philosopher will find "philosophically interesting" or as "having philosophical implications" in the area being surveyed. Examples from the philosophy of science would include the understanding of causality and scientific law and how such laws might be justified in general, but not *particular* examples of cause-and-effect relationships or the evidence used to support

---

quips, "In every history of philosophy for students, the first thing mentioned is that philosophy began with Thales, who said that everything is made of water. This is discouraging to the beginner, who is struggling—perhaps not very hard—to feel that respect for philosophy which the curriculum seems to expect." Bertrand Russell, *History of Western Philosophy* (London: Allen & Unwin, 1961), p. 44.

7. The word "criticism" is of course being used here as a neutral term. It is not the task of philosophy to be negative and destructive, but to be critical in the sense of assessing and making judgments about the coherence of ideas and the validity of arguments (compare below Chapter 5). According to John Passmore, "the peculiarity of philosophy as a form of critical discussion lies in its being a critical discussion *of* critical discussion". This relates to philosophy's role as a "meta-inquiry"—an inquiry about inquiry. See his entry entitled "Philosophy", in Paul Edwards, ed., *The Encyclopedia of Philosophy*, Vol. 5 (New York: Macmillan and Free Press; London: Collier Macmillan, 1967), pp. 221-222.

particular laws. A philosopher of science might ask what it means to say that an electron exists or is real, especially when it is noted that electrons sometimes behave like particles and sometimes like waves. But he will leave it to the scientist to examine the evidence for the existence and nature of electrons. Similarly a philosopher of the social sciences will not do anthropology or social psychology. She will do philosophy—by reflecting philosophically on the work of social scientists, particularly their aims and methods. "Are the social sciences really sciences?", "Are social entities mere aggregates of individual entities?", "Can social science be value-free?" are questions of interest to the philosopher of the social sciences. These are questions that any particular social science, or even all of them together, cannot answer. They are not questions that can be settled *within* social science, as are questions about (for example) how people change their prejudices under different circumstances. The philosopher's questions are "at one remove" from social science: they are second-order questions.

PHILOSOPHY OF RELIGION AND PHILOSOPHY OF EDUCATION

Philosophy of Religion

This discussion of subject philosophy has so far treated it primarily in its analytic role. It should be noted, however, that "philosophies-of" also appear in other modes. Thus Keith Ward, writing of the philosophy of religion, describes philosophy as functioning there not only in its "Socratic mode" (as a "critical, analytic investigation"), but also in its "Platonic mode" (as an "independent attempt to fashion a world-view, founded upon rational speculation alone") and in its "Augustinian mode" ("understanding in the service of faith, defending and expanding the rational structure of a particular religion").[8] In our account of the discipline of philosophy of religion, however, we shall focus particularly on its analytic role.

In his introductory text on the philosophy of religion John Hick describes the subject along purely analytic lines, reserving the term for its proper meaning "namely, *philosophical thinking about religion*". He continues: "Philosophy of religion, then, is not an organ of religious teaching. Indeed, it need not be undertaken from a religious standpoint at all. . . . . . Philosophy of religion is, accordingly, not a branch of theology (meaning by 'theology' the systematic formulation of religious beliefs), but a branch of philosophy. It studies the concepts and belief systems of religion as well as the prior phenomena of religious experience and the activities of worship and meditation on which these belief systems rest and out of which they have arisen." Hick goes on to argue that philosophy of religion is thus a second-order activity, "standing apart from its subject matter" (the religious realm) but related to it as, for example, the philosophy of law is related to the realm of

---

8. Keith Ward, "Philosophy and the Philosophy of Religion in the *Encyclopedia of Religion*", *Religious Studies* 24: 1 (1988), p. 40.

legal phenomena, concepts and reasonings; the philosophy of art to artistic phenomena and to the categories and methods of aesthetic discussion; and the philosophy of science to the special sciences.[9]

The significance of the philosophy of religion for the topics covered in the present volume extends beyond its function as one example of subject philosophy. A great deal of what will be said about religious beliefs, religious understanding, religious attitudes and religious experience, and the interrelationships between these significant outcomes of Christian learning, will draw on the discipline of philosophy of religion. The role of philosophy in thinking about religion is fundamental, in some ways more fundamental than the role of theology. The methods of theological and philosophical reflection are somewhat similar, especially in their synthetic modes; but the theologian uses additional data and principles that the philosopher, *qua* philosopher, cannot acknowledge. Theology may well build on the insights of philosophy, but it does so in a way that incorporates various "theological givens" (such as revelation) or confessional criteria that relate to a specific religious tradition. These elements are not available to, and do not serve as restrictions on, philosophy *per se*. Philosophy may reflect on faith, but its criteria are not derived from any specific faith. If this account of the matter is accepted, and the relationship between philosophy and theology is admittedly a controversial one, then it would appear at first sight that philosophy may serve as a critical check on theology but that theology cannot repay the compliment. In the study of religion and of religious education, then, philosophy is important in its own right.

Yet the distinction outlined earlier between the activities of the philosopher and that of the religious person, particularly if that person is a *reflective* practitioner of the subject being studied, is often blurred. Once philosophy takes the step beyond pure analysis and clarification towards an analysis that includes making critical, reflective judgments about concepts and arguments, it no longer necessarily "leaves everything as it is".[10] Soon its methods may be used *within* the subject being studied to revise and reform concepts and arguments, and to synthesize a new set of beliefs, as well as to analyze those of other people. If this happens in the philosophy of religion the subject may become transformed into what is sometimes called *philosophical theology*. Christian theology has often made use of philosophy in this way: incorporating the ideas of philosophical systems and utilizing the judgments of philosophers in working out a system of Christian beliefs. Then

---

9. John H. Hick, *Philosophy of Religion* (Englewood Cliffs, N.J.: Prentice-Hall, 1990), pp. 1-2.

10. Ludwig Wittgenstein, the major influence on the development of analytic philosophy, suggested that philosophy should leave everything as it is. See his *Philosophical Investigations*, trans. G. E. M. Anscombe (Oxford: Blackwell, 1967), part I, para. 124. For a perceptive commentary on this text see Renford Bambrough, "Does Philosophy 'Leave Everything as it is'? Even Theology?", in Godfrey Vesey, ed., *The Philosophy in Christianity* (Cambridge: Cambridge University Press, 1989), especially pp. 235-236. See also John Wilson, *Preface to the Philosophy of Education* (London: Routledge & Kegan Paul, 1979), pp. 119-120.

philosophy is not just, as it were, observing religious belief. It is being employed in correcting and re-constructing (aspects of) religion.[11]

Philosophy of religion proper, however, unlike philosophical theology, is not an expression of religious commitment. It is not part of religion or theology. In that sense it is not necessarily "useful" — though it is always relevant—to the theologian or the religious believer. It is less involved, more of a disinterested spectator. So John Gaskin can define it as "the disinterested, rational discussion of the truth of religious claims, the meaningfulness of religious language, and the coherence of religious concepts".[12]

We may only adopt such a definition, however, if we frankly recognize that even philosophers need to stand somewhere in order to take a view of religion, or of any other subject or practice. They may strive to be "disinterested" but that does not imply that they have no standpoint, or any presuppositions, of their own.[13] Even a discussion that only attempts to clarify beliefs will do so by following some criteria of the nature of "clarification". Philosophical judgments about truth, meaningfulness and coherence will inevitably be determined by criteria of what are thought to constitute truth, meaningfulness and coherence. Similarly what purports to be a "rational discussion" will always be undergirded by beliefs about what constitutes rational discussion. In principle all these presuppositions of the philosopher may be called into question. Thus the bald statement made earlier about the relationship between philosophy and theology needs to be qualified, for in the philosophy of religion this calling-into-question may be done by religious believers and theologians as well as by other philosophers.

Philosophy of Education

In moving towards an account of what the philosophy of (Christian) religious education might be, it is important to turn our attention now to the work of the philosopher *of education*. Christian religious education is best seen as a species of education the substantive content of which is the Christian religion. Philosophy of religion is therefore an appropriate study for us, as we critically reflect on the nature of Christianity. But it is the philosophy of education that reflects philosophically on the activity, context, processes, approaches, methods and aims of education, and indeed on its substantive content in the form in which it exists in teaching and learning acts. Philosophy of

---

11. See M. J. Charlesworth, *Philosophy of Religion: The Historic Approaches* (London: Macmillan, 1972).

12. J. C. A. Gaskin, *The Quest for Eternity* (Harmondsworth, England; New York: Penguin, 1984), p. 190.

13. This is as true of the philosophy of education as it is of the philosophy of religion. Edel argues that "empirical, valuational and socio-historical components" play a role in philosophical analysis itself: "they determine in part the shape of analytic products". Abraham Edel, "Analytic Philosophy of Education at the Crossroads", in James F. Doyle, ed., *Educational Judgments: Papers in the Philosophy of Education* (London: Routledge & Kegan Paul, 1973), p. 252. See below Chapters 3 and 4, and Dennis Cato, "Getting Clearer about 'Getting Clearer'", *Journal of Philosophy of Education* 21: 1 (1987).

Christian religious education, in a broad sense, is thus a specialized aspect of this philosophy of education, distinguished by the specific phenomenon studied (Christian religious education). Similarly a philosophical study of moral education, physical education or education in the sciences could be appropriately designated as a philosophy of these educational activities.

Before proceeding further with this attempt to delineate the philosophy of Christian religious education, however, it might be appropriate to consider more generally the philosophy of education, and ask what that subject is a study *of*. Here I shall confine my comments to education involving teaching.[14] Such education may be properly designated a *practice*, either in the rather technical sense of a structured activity "specified by a system of rules which defines offices, roles, moves, penalties, defences, etc."[15] (like science, politics or religion), or in the rather broader sense of something that people do (i.e. teacher-learner interactions). Philosophers of education have been much exercised about what sort of practice counts as being education, but that is a discussion that we may leave until later. But that teacher-facilitated education is a practice, the aims, rules, principles, contents and processes of which may be subjected to philosophical scrutiny, may be taken as read. (It should be noted that education is here defined as a practice that properly incorporates *both* pedagogical procedures or ways of teaching *and* subject-matter content.)

A comment is required at this point about the distinction between a philosophy of education and a *theory of education*. The theory of a practice is usually taken to be an attempt to understand, explain and (at least in the case of most useful, "lower-level" theories) predict what is happening in the practice: "theory explains why, when, how, and under what circumstances a practice works".[16] Some philosophers have accepted that educational theory is only properly "theory" when it shares in the explanatory and predictive power of the observationally confirmed hypotheses and theories of the social sciences; a mere set of action-guiding rules or precepts does not constitute a theory.[17] Others, however, have characterized educational theory as

14. My preferred definition of education is broader than this (see below Chapter 3), but most philosophy of education has been directed to teacher-facilitated learning and indeed has often defined education so as to include a teaching dimension.

15. John Rawls, quoted by James E. McClellan, *Philosophy of Education* (Englewood Cliffs, N.J.: Prentice-Hall, 1976), p. 1. We may note that McClellan sees the philosophy of a practice essentially as an inquiry into the distinctive form taken by human reason in that practice and therefore defines the philosophy of education rather narrowly along those lines (see *ibid.*, p. 4).

16. James Michael Lee, *The Content of Religious Instruction* (Birmingham, Ala.: Religious Education Press, 1985), p. 388. See also his *The Shape of Religious Instruction* (Birmingham, Ala.: Religious Education Press, 1971), pp. 135-136, 145-148, 156-161, and "The Authentic Source of Religious Instruction", in Norma H. Thompson, ed., *Religious Education and Theology* (Birmingham, Ala.: Religious Education Press, 1982), pp. 117-123. See also Charles F. Melchert, "Theory in Religious Education", in Marvin J. Taylor, ed., *Foundations for Christian Education in an Era of Change* (Nashville, Tenn.: Abingdon, 1976).

17. D. J. O'Connor, *An Introduction to the Philosophy of Education* (London: Routledge & Kegan Paul, 1966; New York: Philosophical Library, 1957), chs. 4 and 5. See also his

a practical theory that seeks to formulate and justify principles of action in education (showing us what should be done, rather than just providing theoretical understanding), but which involves practical reasoning and reflection on values in formulating rational principles for educational practice.[18] In so far as the notion of "theory" may be broadened to include reflection on the "aims" of education (What should people learn? How ought they to be taught?), it is plausible to maintain that the philosopher should have his or her say there as well.[19] Such a "mixed economy" for educational theory will draw on the humanities, including philosophy, as well as on the social sciences.[20] It is only on this second understanding of the theory of education,

---

essay on "the nature and scope of educational theory" in Glenn Langford and D. J. O'Connor, eds., *New Essays in the Philosophy of Education* (London: Routledge & Kegan Paul, 1973). The "theorizing" of philosophers has been described by contrast as "no more than a sustained attempt to 'think things through' with particular regard for the meaning of words as the principal medium of thought". Robin Barrow and Ronald G. Woods, *An Introduction to Philosophy of Education* (London: Methuen, 1982), p. 183. Similarly Lee contrasts nonempirical reflection (*"speculation"*) and verifiable, predictive *theory* ("which flows from empirical data"). James Michael Lee, "The Blessings of Religious Pluralism", in Norma H. Thompson, ed., *Religious Pluralism and Religious Education* (Birmingham, Ala.: Religious Education Press, 1988), p. 99. It should be noted that Lee is not here identifying speculation with philosophy and has no quarrel with speculation that *does* have an empirical base and verifiable implications. He argues that in religious instruction a theological "macrotheory" (an overall, global theory incorporating theories with a narrower range) is useless because it fails to explain, predict and verify the pedagogical theories and practices falling under its domain in a comprehensive and systematic fashion. He claims that the social science approach to the teaching of religion is an (or, rather, the only) adequate and valid macrotheory. Both are theories, but only the latter is a valid and adequate theory for the practice of Christian religious education. See Lee, *The Content of Religious Instruction*, pp. 753-756; "The Authentic Source of Religious Instruction", pp. 121-144.

18. P. H. Hirst, "Educational Theory", in J. W. Tibble, ed., *The Study of Education* (London: Routledge & Kegan Paul; New York: Humanities Press, 1966) and "The Nature and Scope of Education Theory (2)" in Langford and O'Connor, eds., *New Essays in the Philosophy of Education*. See also R. F. Dearden, "Theory and Practice in Education", *Journal of Philosophy of Education* 14: 1 (1980). According to Thompson, theories "are statements regarding the justification of intended aims of the practice and the means to be adopted to further these". Keith Thompson, *Education and Philosophy: A Practical Approach* (Oxford: Blackwell, 1972), p. 87.

19. James Gribble, *Introduction to Philosophy of Education* (Boston: Allyn & Bacon, 1969), p. 184; Michael L. Peterson, *Philosophy of Education: Issues and Options* (Downers Grove, Ill.: InterVarsity Press, 1986), p. 17. The line between (1) the philosophy of education, and (2) this broader view of theory of education (what Langford calls "a philosophy of education"), is a thin one, but it is an important one. "The former is part of philosophy and is primarily concerned with understanding what education is rather than with how it should be carried on. The latter is part of educational practice and is primarily concerned with how education should be carried on, although its expression is bound to presuppose some view of what education is." The difference between them, he claims, is a difference of emphasis. Glenn Langford, *Education, Persons and Society: A Philosophical Enquiry* (Basingstoke: Macmillan, 1985), pp. 46-47, see also p. 50.

20. Paul H. Hirst, "Educational Theory", in Hirst, ed., *Educational Theory and its Foundation Disciplines* (London: Routledge & Kegan Paul, 1983), pp. 4-5.

which is often designated as a study of *principles of education*, that the philosophy of education provides it with any contribution. It may be argued, however, that the philosopher also has the right to reflect on the philosophical implications of the theories presented by the educational social sciences. These qualifications notwithstanding, the above discussion helps us to put philosophy of education in its place with regard to educational theory, which is as a philosophical commentator on—or, at the very most, a junior partner with—the other disciplines[21] that provide the major inputs to the theory of education.

Philosophy of education involves the analysis, clarification and assessment of the statements, inferences, concepts and arguments employed in education.[22] The delineation of the subject along these lines will seem a long way removed from what many people think the subject-matter of the philosophy of education should be.[23] Richard Peters has mapped a number of different approaches to the subject other than the one outlined here.[24] Peters distinguishes, for example, the approach traditionally adopted by many American Colleges of Education which treats the implications for education of philosophical schools of thought (Idealism, Realism, Pragmatism, etc.).[25] More typical of British courses on education has been an historical survey of educational ideas, what Peters describes as "the Great Educator's approach".[26] In the past others "did" their philosophy of education by means of a "Principles of

---

21. Philosophers of education frequently distinguish (1) subject-areas or "fields of knowledge" (more or less artificial units of interest studied through different disciplines, e.g. geography and religion), from (2) subject-disciplines or "forms of knowledge" which have their own distinctive canons and methods of reasoning (e.g. physics and history). Paul Hirst treats educational theory as a practical theory (using knowledge "to determine what should be done in educational practice") that draws on different forms of knowledge. Hirst in Tibble, ed., *The Study of Education*, p. 48. Some of his critics argue that educational theory exhibits characteristics both of a practical theory and of a field of knowledge—the focus of the field being the practice of education or "educational matters" (Gribble, *Introduction to Philosophy of Education*, pp. 187-189).

22. See George L. Newsome, "Analytical Philosophy and Theory of Education", in Joe Park, ed., *Selected Readings in the Philosophy of Education* (New York: Macmillan, 1963), pp. 570-576; John B. Magee, *Philosophical Analysis in Education* (New York: Harper & Row, 1971).

23. This is a problem peculiar to the justification of philosophical work. It does not seem to be shared to the same degree by any other discipline.

24. Richard S. Peters, "Philosophy of Education", in Hirst, ed., *Educational Theory and its Foundation Disciplines*, pp. 30-32.

25. See, for example, J. Donald Butler, *Four Philosophies and their Practice in Education and Religion* (New York: Harper & Row, 1968); Edward J. Power, *Philosophy of Education* (Englewood Cliffs, N.J.: Prentice-Hall, 1982) and Peterson, *Philosophy of Education*, chs. 2 and 3. For the British form of this approach, see A. V. Judges, ed., *Education and the Philosophic Mind* (London: Harrap, 1957). It is criticized, on the grounds that the supposed implications do *not* flow from the philosophical premises of some of these schools of thought, by Ludwig Wittgenstein, *Zettel*, ed. G. E. M. Anscombe and G. H. von Wright, trans. G. E. M. Anscombe (Oxford: Blackwell, 1967), paras. 412-414, and John Passmore, *The Philosophy of Teaching* (Cambridge, Mass.: Harvard University Press, 1980), ch. 1.

26. See, for example, S. J. Curtis and M. E. A. Boultwood, *A Short History of Educational Ideas* (London: University Tutorial Press, 1965).

Education" course, often dealing with the ethical and spiritual aspects of education—an approach that certainly exemplified a love of a certain sort of wisdom.[27] But the approach that focuses on the field or practice of education and its (philosophically interesting) problems by means of the lens of a philosophical method—thus *applying philosophy to education*[28]—has tended to dominate the philosophy of education in recent years.[29] It has placed a particular emphasis on analytic rather than synthetic philosophy. Even though some of its own practitioners have recently acknowledged that it can on occasions provide too narrow and piecemeal an approach, lacking in philosophical (and sometimes realistically human) depth and ignoring other disciplines and the context-dependence of the use of language,[30] it surely still provides the best model for a subject that is true to both philosophy and education.[31] For this reason it is the model that will be broadly followed in this book.

Analysis Analyzed

It should be made clear, however, that this approach does not commit the author—or the reader—to the view that philosophy is *merely* a matter of analysis, nor that such an analysis is necessarily a *reductive* conceptual analysis aimed at producing the one "essential" meaning of a concept. It is important to recognize three points. First, that philosophy is more than analysis, as it may properly include attempts at synthesizing worldviews and metaphysical systems.[32] Second, that in recent years many analytic philosophers have tended, quite properly, to adopt a rather more plural form of analysis that

---

27. Compare A. N. Whitehead, *The Aims of Education* (London: Benn, 1950; New York: Macmillan, 1929).

28. Thus: "Philosophy of education is concerned . . . with an examination of the nature and structure of educational arguments. It is uniquely concerned with those questions in education where we are unclear as to what constitutes an answer" (Thompson, *Education and Philosophy*, p. 16). This approach eschews, at least in principle, what has been described as the more "inspirational" and "prescriptive" purposes of other styles of philosophy of education, which present grand schemes of what education should be (see Power, *Philosophy of Education*, pp. 4-13).

29. Pioneering work was done by Israel Scheffler at Harvard, and in the United Kingdom by C. B. Hardie, D. J. O'Connor, and particularly Peters and Hirst (at the University of London Institute of Education). See articles by Paul H. Hirst and Ira S. Steinberg in Robin Barrow, ed., *Philosophy and Education (Educational Analysis 4:1)* (Lewes, England: Falmer, 1982).

30. Peters, "Philosophy of Education", pp. 33, 50-51, 53. See also P. H. Nidditch, "Philosophy of Education and the Place of Science in the Curriculum", in Langford and O'Connor, eds., *New Essays in the Philosophy of Education*, pp. 239-241.

31. It might be argued that John Dewey is one "Great Educator" who was at the same time properly a philosopher of education on this model, treating philosophy as a process of critical inquiry and applying it to the problems of education, as well as to human experience in general. See his *Democracy and Education* (New York: Macmillan, 1916), ch. XXIV.

32. Compare P. F. Strawson's "descriptive metaphysics" in *Individuals: An Essay in Descriptive Metaphysics* (London: Methuen, 1959), see p. 9. See also D. F. Pears, ed., *The Nature of Metaphysics* (London: Macmillan; New York: St. Martin's Press, 1966), Anthony Quinton, *The Nature of Things* (London: Routledge & Kegan Paul, 1973), pp. 235-251 and D. W. Hamlyn, *Metaphysics* (Cambridge: Cambridge University Press, 1984), ch. 1.

recognizes the variety of meanings of a concept, relating to the multiplicity of social contexts in which it is used.[33] Philosophers should not legislate *a priori* (i.e. without reference to experience) for a particular understanding of a concept without investigating the actual use of that concept, nor should they pretend to do their analysis from some general or universal, context-free "extrahistorical Archimedean point"[34] outside all social contexts, presuppositions and particular language users. Analysis is never presuppositionless, and it can never ignore the multiplicity of a plural world. Third, philosophy may be said also to have the innovative function of reflecting on possible conceptual forms in addition to the actual ones used in a practice. This "analysis of possibilities" involves an exercise of the imagination through "thought-experiments" which take us beyond a mere (conservative) analysis of the given towards the *reformation* of language and thought.[35]

Analysis is not enough in philosophy. But such analysis remains a very powerful tool in the philosopher's workshop. Some (albeit self-critical) use of it, in an "under-laboring" way,[36] is an essential part of the method of philosophy and therefore of the philosophy of education.

PHILOSOPHY OF CHRISTIAN RELIGIOUS EDUCATION

Philosophy of education, then, is understood here as a matter of applying the philosophical method of reflective, critical, argumentative, analytic (and, where appropriate and possible, innovative and synthetic) thinking to the practice of education. It focuses on philosophically interesting and philosophically tractable issues and problems that often relate to discussions in general philosophy, for example questions about the role of reason in education, or the meaning of concepts like "equality" and "neutrality".

Similarly, *a philosophy of Christian religious education* would be the application of this philosophical method to philosophically interesting and philosophically tractable issues and problems in the practice of Christian religious education, including the attempt to clarify the general nature of this practice,[37] and to comment philosophically on the various theories that are said to apply to it. It will take its lead from philosophy of education by pick-

33. See D. P. Gilroy, "The Revolutions in English Philosophy and Philosophy of Education", in Barrow, ed., *Philosophy and Education*; but compare John Wilson, "Concepts, Contestability and the Philosophy of Education" (and the reply by Philip Sneders), *Journal of Philosophy of Education* 15: 1 (1981).

34. Richard Rorty, "Pragmatism and Philosophy", in Kenneth Baynes *et al.*, eds., *After Philosophy: End or Transformation?* (Cambridge, Mass.: MIT Press, 1987), p. 58.

35. This is persuasively argued by Vincent Brümmer in his "Philosophical Theology as Conceptual Recollection", *Neue Zeitschrift für systematische Theologie und Religionsphilosophie* 32 (1990), pp. 53-73.

36. See John Locke, *An Essay Concerning Human Understanding* (1690), ed. A. D. Woozley (London: Collins, 1964), p. 58. Locke speaks of "clearing ground a little, and removing some of the rubbish that lies in the way to knowledge".

37. Compare Wilson, *Preface to the Philosophy of Education*, p. 6. Scheffler argues that other philosophies-of can make a contribution to education, as analyses of the forms of thought

ing up discussions within philosophy of education that are also relevant to the practice of Christian religious education. These will include a range of topics centered on the nature and use of reason (indoctrination, critical openness, autonomy etc.), as well as philosophically tractable issues about the nature of education that are also relevant to its concerns (e.g. the debate on freedom and belief, the nature of moral education and the balance between formative and critical education). Additionally, because of the specific nature of Christian religious education practice, the philosophy of Christian religious education—in dialogue with the philosophy of the Christian religion—will direct its attention to specific issues relating to the substantive content of the practice (e.g. the nature of religion and of Christian religious education; the role of the emotions in Christianity and in Christian religious education), as well as to particular problems peculiar to discussions about the nature of Christian religious education itself (e.g. the nature and education of religious commitment; relativism and the religious educator). In all such reflection the philosophy of Christian religious education will be applying a particular method to processes and contents that raise philosophically debatable issues. This analytic method is best seen as providing reflective comments on the broad practice of Christian religious education, rather than prescriptive, legislative norms of what it is or how it should be done. But analytic reflection often has practical implications, and I shall draw those implications wherever it seems pertinent in the chapters that follow.

I should explain that my particular philosophical approach to the issues of Christian religious education, although it will not systematically survey either the great "-isms" of philosophical systems and movements (classical or contemporary) or the work of major philosophers, will not ignore them. Wherever it seems relevant I shall endeavor to make reference to such philosophers and to the implications of their positions for the topic in hand. But in all these cases the discussion will start and finish with philosophical reflection on a topic within Christian religious education, rather than with the ideas of any particular philosophical thinker or school. The intention is to produce a philosophical reflection on themes in Christian religious education, rather than an account of philosophy or indeed of education.

One final word on the approach adopted in this book. As indicated in the Preface, when considering a particular issue or problem in Christian religious education I shall try at least to note different interpretations, analyses and arguments along with my own proposals. I hope in this way to make the book useful as a source for readers of a variety of theological, ecclesiastical, educational and philosophical standpoints, despite the fact that they will not all agree with my particular conclusions.

---

embodied in different subjects. This would justify our quarrying the philosophy of religion for contributions to the philosophy of Christian religious education. See Israel Scheffler, "Philosophies-of and the Curriculum", in Doyle, ed., *Educational Judgments*, pp. 214-217, and compare also Alan Montefiore, "The Philosophy of Education?", in Indira Mahalingam and Brian Carr, eds., *Logical Foundations* (Basingstoke: Macmillan; New York: St. Martin's Press, 1991), pp. 189-192.

Part II

Education
and
Christian Religious Education

CHAPTER 3

Defining Educational Terms

We should not proceed much further without some examination of the key terms "learning", "teaching" and "education", if only to attempt some justification for the rather broad way in which they are used in the present work in the phrases "Christian learning", "teacher facilitated Christian learning" and "Christian religious education".

LEARNING

Psychologists of education understand this word, as they do the cognate terms "teaching" and "education", in a wider sense than that recognized as proper by many philosophers of education. Despite the fact that this book deals specifically with philosophy of education, I shall be following the psychologists' usage in relation to these terms. I believe that the analysis of these terms usually offered by analytic philosophers gives an accurate account of a particular, restricted meaning that they have in a liberal,[1] critical educational

---

1. "Liberal education" was traditionally that form of education that befitted the free person, "liberal" being derived etymologically from the Latin *liber*, free. It was directed to a general cultivation and enlargement of the mind, rather than the particular vocational end envisaged by professional or technical training. As M. V. C. Jeffreys grandly expounds this view: "the nobility of the educational process ought not to be degraded, nor its full reach short-circuited, by the subordination of ultimate aims to immediate utilities". M. V. C. Jeffreys, *The Aims of Education (Glaucon)* (London: Pitman, 1972), p. 87. Liberal education, as a general rather than a specialized education, is defined more by outlook and method than by subject-content. It has been described as "open, self-regulating studies undertaken for their own sake and in the light of their own criteria of excellence". Anthony O'Hear, *Education, Society and Human Nature: An Introduction to the Philosophy of Education* (London: Routledge & Kegan Paul, 1981), p. 50; note also chs. 1 and 2. See also John L. Elias and Sharan Merriam, *Philosophical Foundations of Adult Education* (Malabar, Fla.: Krieger, 1980), ch. II. The phrase has come to designate a form of education that is intended to be "liberating" by focusing on the development of rationality, reflectiveness and "the critical attitude". John Henry Newman coupled a liberal education with the formation of a certain habit of mind "of which the attributes are,

---

tradition. The psychologists, however, offer us in their broader definitions a terminology that fits the more general usage better. To ask whether all such learning is *really* learning is to raise questions that the philosopher wants to raise about the criteria appropriate to his concept of "real learning". I do not want in any way to avoid these issues, indeed we shall be looking at some of them in considerable detail later. But nor do I want to preempt the discussion by adopting the philosopher's restrictive, normative connotation at the outset. In a sense, as we shall see, the contrast is essentially a semantic one.

Psychologists define learning as a lasting change in a person brought about by experience (rather than by growth and maturation, or by development through exercise). Thus Robert Gagné writes: "Learning is a change in human disposition or capability, which persists over a period of time, and which is not simply ascribable to processes of growth. . . . The change may be, and often is, an increased capability for some type of performance. It may also be an altered disposition of the sort called 'attitude' or 'interest' or 'value'."[2] The "change in human disposition or capability" referred to here is wide enough to cover the acquisition of knowledge and the learning of both intellectual and motor skills. The definition, therefore, is very broad. In the words of a psychologist of education: "what people learn is knowledge, skills and attitudes".[3]

Philosophers of education in recent years have often adopted a much narrower definition. They have tended to argue that the word "learning" implies a certain freedom, self-directedness, intention to learn, or "paying attention to relevant evidence", and (where appropriate) self-knowledge and a generalizable knowledge-with-understanding about the world. These are qualifications that would forbid its use of all "animal learning", or at least of the classical conditioning of reflexes.[4] Psychologists, on the other hand, include

freedom, equitableness, calmness, moderation and wisdom; or what . . . I have ventured to call a philosophical habit". John Henry Newman, *The Idea of a University*, Discourse V, in Vincent Ferrer Blehl, ed., *The Essential Newman* (New York: New American Library; London: New English Library, 1963), p. 180; see also Discourse VII. Newman's "intellectual excellence" thus contains both affective and cognitive dimensions—see F. Musgrove, "Curriculum Objectives", in Richard Hooper, ed., *The Curriculum: Context, Design and Development* (Edinburgh: Oliver & Boyd, 1971), p. 219. Arguments against the claim that rationality is the foundational principle of liberal education are comprehensively surveyed in Marie Schilling, "Knowledge and Liberal Education: A Critique of Paul Hirst", *Curriculum Studies* 18: 1 (1986). See below p. 73, n. 103.

2. Robert M. Gagné, *The Conditions of Learning* (New York: Holt, Rinehart and Winston, 1977), p. 3, italics removed from original.

3. H. S. N. McFarland, *Psychological Theory and Educational Practice* (London: Routledge and Kegan Paul, 1971), p. 169.

4. Michael Oakeshott, "Learning and Teaching", and G. Vesey, "Conditioning and Learning", in R. S. Peters, ed., *The Concept of Education* (London: Routledge & Kegan Paul, 1967); P. H. Hirst, "What is Teaching?", and D. W. Hamlyn, "Human Learning", in R. S. Peters, ed., *The Philosophy of Education* (London: Oxford University Press, 1973); John Wilson, *Preface to the Philosophy of Education* (London: Routledge & Kegan Paul, 1979), ch.

such phenomena within their broader definition of learning.[5] There is also a difference in the understanding of "experience" in these different definitions of learning. Philosophers usually wish to construe this as conscious experience; psychologists are more prepared to include subliminal "experiences" and other events of which the learner is not consciously aware, or even to drop the term "experience" altogether.[6]

I find the inclusiveness of the broader, psychological definition of learning useful. I must repeat, however, that in adopting it I allow for a secondary distinction between "learning-with-understanding" and other, doubtless less worthy, forms of learning. We shall come to this distinction in later chapters. I must also stress at the outset that my embracing of the psychologists' definition of learning does not mean that I embrace any particular theoretical account which may be associated with such a viewpoint. In particular this definition does not commit me to any theory of behaviorism that holds that mental entities and events do not exist.[7]

TEACHING

Psychologists concur with philosophers that learning does not imply teaching. People learn all the time, through a variety of "learning experiences"; but they are "taught" only when that learning is brought about or facilitated in some way by a teacher, who to some extent is influencing their learning experiences. Psychologists on the whole are more interested in giving accounts of learning than in defining either teaching or education, but we may take it that they would adopt a broad definition of teaching such as the following: "the arrangement of those situations and conditions which will most effectively facilitate desired learning outcomes in an individual".[8]

Many philosophers and psychologists agree that the concept of teaching

3; see also O'Hear, *Education, Society and Human Nature*, p. 87. An astute philosophical analysis that accepts a broader definition of learning is to be found in James E. McClellan, *Philosophy of Education* (Englewood Cliffs, N.J.: Prentice-Hall, 1976), pp. 54-69; see also D. W. Hamlyn, *Experience and the Growth of Understanding* (London: Routledge & Kegan Paul, 1978), pp. 147-148.

5. Thus, for example, Thomas L. Good and Jere E. Brophy, *Educational Psychology* (New York: Holt, Rinehart and Winston, 1977), ch. 5.

6. P. H. Hirst and R. S. Peters, *The Logic of Education* (London: Routledge & Kegan Paul, 1970; New York: Humanities Press, 1971), pp. 74-76.

7. Thoroughgoing behaviorists argue that "mental life and the world in which it is lived are inventions". B. F. Skinner, *About Behaviorism* (New York: Knopf; London: Cape, 1974), p. 104. See also his *Beyond Freedom and Dignity* (New York: Knopf, 1971; London: Cape, 1972), *passim*.

8. James Michael Lee, *The Shape of Religious Instruction* (Birmingham, Ala.: Religious Education Press, 1971), p. 8. Here, as elsewhere, Lee uses the term "instruction", which he specifically states is a synonym for teaching. See also his "The Authentic Source of Religious Instruction", in Norma H. Thompson, ed., *Religious Education and Theology* (Birmingham, Ala.: Religious Education Press, 1982), p.111. Lee uses the word instruction to highlight both the intentionality and the scientific base of the teaching act. See also Jerome S. Bruner, *Toward a Theory of Instruction* (Cambridge, Mass.: Harvard University Press, 1966), pp. 37, 40.

normally implies an intention on the part of the teacher (that the learner learns something).[9] Some argue that one cannot teach without intending to bring about learning, but that one can teach without succeeding in this intention. Learning is usually taken to be an "achievement", whereas teaching is normally understood as a "task";[10] and "the success of the teacher depends on the success of the learner".[11] Philosophers of education are more likely to restrict the notion of teaching to specific teaching activities, whereas the psychologist's broader view would include in teaching the general structuring of the learning environment, including such variables as its temperature and "affective climate"—i.e. the teacher as "stage manager" as well as the teacher as a "player" in the drama.[12]

There are other uses of the verb "to teach" that we may take to be parasitic on the meaning given above, for example when we speak (1) of a person *unintentionally* teaching something,[13] or (2) even of certain *events or expe-*

9. Hirst and Peters, *The Logic of Education*, pp. 78-79; Hirst, "What is Teaching?" and R. F. Dearden, "Instruction and Learning by Discovery", in Peters, ed., *The Concept of Education*, pp. 136-137. Others have argued that we *can* be taught specific things without any intention to do so, but that "teaching activities" are human encounters that only make sense in the context of an intention to promote learning. See McClellan, *Philosophy of Education*, p. 34, and compare Glenn Langford, *Education, Persons and Society* (London: Macmillan, 1985), p. 75. For a detailed critique of this criterion of intention compare the paper by Helen Freeman referred to in the following footnote.

10. Israel Scheffler, *The Language of Education* (Springfield, Ill.: Thomas, 1960), pp. 42, 60-61; Cornell M. Hamm, *Philosophical Issues in Education: An Introduction* (Philadelphia: Falmer, 1989), pp. 94-99. But contrast (on learning) McClellan, *Philosophy of Education*, pp. 69-77; and (on teaching) Helen Freeman, "The Concept of Teaching", *Proceedings of the Philosophy of Education Society of Great Britain* 7: 1 (1973), pp. 8-25 and John Passmore, *The Philosophy of Teaching* (Cambridge, Mass.: Harvard University Press, 1980), ch. 2. See below note 16.

11. Langford, *Education, Persons and Society*, p. 126; see also Hirst and Peters, *The Logic of Education*, p. 78.

12. Compare Hirst and Peters, *The Logic of Education*, p. 80 and James Michael Lee, *The Flow of Religious Instruction* (Birmingham, Ala.: Religious Education Press, 1973), ch. 9. D. W. Hamlyn criticizes the restrictive nature of Hirst's account of teaching, arguing that the category of teaching activities includes examples such as opening a window on the grounds that "an activity performed by a person will be a teaching activity provided that . . . it forms a necessary part of a set of activities that together are sufficient to bring about learning" (*Experience and the Growth of Understanding*, p. 133).

13. This is a phrase that is sometimes used of the hidden curriculum of a teacher's teaching (a set of tacit learning experiences whose role *as* learning experiences is hidden from the learners, and often from their teachers also). Compare Hirst, "What is Teaching?", p. 169; Freeman, "The Concept of Teaching", pp. 12-14, 22-23; John Kleinig, *Philosophical Issues in Education* (London: Croom Helm; New York: St. Martin's Press, 1982), ch. 3; Richard S. Peters, "Philosophy of Education", in Paul H. Hirst, ed., *Educational Theory and its Foundation Disciplines* (London: Routledge & Kegan Paul, 1983), pp. 43-44. For philosophical reflection on the hidden curriculum see D. C. Phillips, "Why the Hidden Curriculum is Hidden", and Nicholas C. Burbules, "Who Hides the Hidden Curriculum?", in C. J. B. Macmillan, ed., *Philosophy of Education 1980* (Normal, Ill.: Philosophy of Education Society, 1981); Jane R. Martin, "What should we do with a Hidden Curriculum when we find one?", *Curriculum Inquiry* 6: 2 (1976); David Gordon, "The Immorality of the Hidden Curriculum", *Journal of Moral Education* 10: 1 (1980).

riences "teaching us something".[14] Usage (1) frequently seems entirely natural, but on the whole it is preferable to regard this as an extension of the normal meaning of teaching. It is better to avoid case (2) altogether and retain the paradigmatic usage that refers only to *people* as teachers, instructors or facilitators of learning. People are agents who can be described as being responsible for a particular piece of learning, even on those occasions when they do not intend such learning.

I do not wish to adopt the highly restrictive account of teaching given by some philosophers of education. I am thinking here of definitions that limit teaching to activities "practised in such manner as to respect the student's intellectual integrity and capacity for independent judgment", definitions that distinguish teaching from conditioning and indoctrination.[15] My definition of teaching thus remains fairly broad: it is (normally speaking) the intentional facilitation of learning.[16]

EDUCATION

In many ways "education" is the most problematic of these terms.[17] The Christian religious educationist Charles Melchert has suggested six criteria

---

14. See Oakeshott, "Learning and Teaching", p. 157; Passmore, *The Philosophy of Teaching*, pp. 24-25.

15. Israel Sheffler, "Philosophical Models of Teaching", in Peters, ed., *The Concept of Education*, p. 120; contrast Hirst, "What is Teaching?", pp. 175-176 and see also B. Paul Komisar, "Teaching: Act and Enterprise", in C. J. B. Macmillan and Thomas W. Nelson, eds., *Concepts of Teaching: Philosophical Essays* (Chicago: Rand McNally, 1968), pp.72-74. I would also reject other restrictions on the notion of a teaching activity, e.g. that the teacher must indicate what is being learned and do so in a way that the pupil can learn what is being learned (Hirst, "What is Teaching", pp. 172-173). As Langford argues, these conditions apply to the social enterprise of (e.g. school) teaching, but do not represent "a logical truth about what teaching is" (*Education, Persons and Society*, p. 131). Teaching and education are broad terms that we should not confine within the walls of "educational institutions".

16. Those who argue against the intentionality-criterion may be interpreted as accepting an achievement-analysis rather than a task-analysis of the verb "to teach", in which "there is only one necessary condition which an activity must satisfy if it is to be correctly described as a case of 'teaching'—this is that the pupils *learn* something of what the teacher intends them to learn". James Gribble, *Introduction to Philosophy of Education* (Boston: Allyn & Bacon, 1969), p. 17. I am certainly conscious of a danger that resides both in the task-analysis and in focusing too closely on the intention-element of teaching: the danger of neglecting the only outcome that the teaching intention must intend, i.e. successful learning. I thus have some sympathy with Antony Flew who writes, "teaching has to be justified by reference not to the efforts or the intentions or the qualifications of the teachers, but rather to resulting educational achievement or non-achievement in the taught". Antony Flew, "Examination not Attempted", in Roger Straughan and John Wilson, eds., *Philosophers on Education* (Basingstoke: Macmillan, 1987), p. 26. On the whole, however, I prefer to retain the intentionality criterion for the normal use of the verb to teach, but see below Chapter 4 (on the consequences-criterion of indoctrination).

17. The English word originates either from the Latin *educere* ("to lead out", "draw out"—compare "educe") or from *educare* ("to bring up, rear, train"). Thus one may appeal to etymological support for very different understandings of the concept.

that an activity must meet in order to qualify as education. It must be (1) an intentional activity (2) of value that (3) involves knowledge and understanding in depth and breadth. It must also be a process that is (4) long lasting, involving (5) interpersonal interaction and (6) engaging the whole of a person and his/her relationships.[18] This definition is offered as an analysis of the "more specialized use" of the word education, as opposed to its more general sense of bringing up children and young people[19] or (even more generally) as "the broad process whereby a person learns something".[20] Philosophers of education often appeal to such a "normative or discriminatory concept of education"[21] as showing us what "real education" must be.

As we have already noted, however, there is no need for us to adopt such a definition at the outset, particularly if it is then to be used against us to show that what we would otherwise call "*Christian religious* education" is a contradiction in terms.[22] It would appear to be better to adopt the broadest definition of education that accords with ordinary usage (and fits the way the phrase "Christian religious education" and its synonyms are ordinarily used), and then tackle separately the question whether or not all the examples of education so defined come up to certain standards such as developing autonomy and rationality, and whether these standards are appropriate ones to apply in these (or indeed in any) cases.[23] Of course those who would then reject the processes that fail these standards as "noneducational" are entitled to do so, provided that they first define what *they* mean by "educational". These issues are substantial issues. At one level, however, it does not really matter what we mean by "education", as long as we say what we mean—and do not mean—by it.

Let us now take each of Melchert's criteria in turn:

(1) the *intentionality-criterion*. Philosophers often take education to be an intentional activity like teaching (and, some would add, learning), arguing that we cannot educate or be educated by accident.[24] But although intentionality is usually associated with education it does not seem to constitute an essen-

---

18. Charles F. Melchert, "Does the Church Really Want Religious Education?", *Religious Education* 69: 1 (1974), pp. 14-16.

19. John P. White, *The Aims of Education Restated* (London: Routledge & Kegan Paul, 1982), pp. 5-6, 131-132.

20. Lee, *The Shape of Religious Instruction*, p. 6. Contrast Hirst and Peters, *The Logic of Education*, pp. 23-26; R. S. Peters, "The Justification of Education", in Peters, ed., *The Philosophy of Education*, pp. 239-240 and his "Education and the Educated Man", in R. F. Dearden *et al.*, eds., *A Critique of Current Educational Aims* (London: Routledge & Kegan Paul, 1972), pp. 8-9.

21. Kleinig, *Philosophical Issues in Education*, p. 13. See below Chapter 4.

22. See below p. 41.

23. See Gribble, *Introduction to Philosophy of Education*, p. 17. We should note, as Aristotle puts it, that "men do not all prize most highly the same virtue, so naturally they differ also about the proper training for it". Aristotle, *The Politics*, Book VIII, ch. 2, trans. J. A. Sinclair (Harmondsworth, England: Penguin, 1962), p. 300.

24. R. S. Peters, "Education as Initiation", in Reginald D. Archambault, ed., *Philosophical Analysis and Education* (London: Routledge & Kegan Paul, 1965), pp. 91, 102.

tial element in the concept, which connotes more generally processes that lead to learning. "That was an educational experience" and "that was an education for me"—or, significantly, "a real education"—may properly be said without anybody having intending any learning.[25] Education that involves teaching is rightly taken to be deliberate if teaching is defined as an intentional activity, but "unintentional education" remains a proper use of words. Adopting the intentionality-criterion for education as well as teaching would certainly result in a drastic curtailment of the scope of Christian religious education. (Teacher facilitated Christian learning is, of course, intentional education if teaching is defined as intentional.)

(2) the *value-condition* and (3) *cognitive-condition*. It is a long-standing claim of Richard Peters and others that education proper involves the development, in "a morally unobjectionable manner", of desirable qualities in a person and (or "including") the development of that person's knowledge and understanding. To be educated is to learn certain sorts of (valuable) things with understanding.[26] In such discussions "education" is often distinguished from "training", the latter being simply a matter of inculcating in people a limited set of skills and beliefs; whereas educating a person involves developing a "wide cognitive perspective" in which one way of understanding or experiencing is related to other ways (i.e. is not just directed to specific ends). Peters contends that this concept of education "is almost indistinguishable from that of 'liberal education'".[27] R. S. Downie has similarly argued that being "independent-minded" (having an ability to understand and basing our beliefs on evidence and argument in a critical way) is a necessary part of the definition of being educated;[28] and Neil Cooper holds that only "understanding-knowledge" and not just any "bare knowledge" should be transmitted by "genuine education".[29]

To distinguish in this way true education from other activities, "education" from "training", or education-as-a-good-thing (of which we necessarily approve) from education-as-a-bad-thing, involves some sort of decision.[30]

---

25. See Hirst and Peters, *The Logic of Education*, pp. 76-77; Lee, "The Authentic Source of Religious Instruction", pp. 110-111. Wilson, who claims that education must fulfill the criteria of being both intended and successful, would regard the phrases quoted here as being "an extension or development of the central usage". Wilson, *Preface to the Philosophy of Education*, pp. 21-22.

26. See R. S. Peters, "Aims of Education", in Peters, ed., *The Philosophy of Education*; "What is an Educational Process?", in Peters, ed., *The Concept of Education*; "Education as Initiation"; and *Ethics and Education* (London: Allen & Unwin, 1966), ch. I. See also Hirst and Peters, *The Logic of Education*, pp. 19-20.

27. Peters, *Ethics and Education*, p. 43.

28. R. S. Downie, "On Having a Mind of One's Own", in Straughan and Wilson, eds., *Philosophers on Education*, pp. 82-85.

29. Neil Cooper, "The Transmission of Knowledge", in Straughan and Wilson, eds., *Philosophers on Education*, p. 72.

30. J. Wilson, "'Mental Health' as an aim of education", in Dearden *et al.*, eds., *A Critique of Current Educational Aims*, p. 89. According to McClellan, R. S. Peters's concept of education "both indicates and advances . . . a tendency to restrict the word 'education'" to socialization

Many would regard it as a contentious decision. Peters himself notes counter-examples to both the desirability-condition and the knowledge-condition: examples that arise when appeal is made to certain processes that are often described as education.[31] Indeed the conclusion of Hirst and Peters in *The Logic of Education* recognizes a spectrum of meanings for education, with the "Peters-concept" lying at one end, while at the other end of the continuum is "the older and undifferentiated concept which refers just to any process of bringing up or rearing in which the connection either with what is desirable or with knowledge is purely contingent" (i.e. it is not part of its meaning). Across this spectrum of uses of the word education there are some that link education solely with the development of desirable states without any emphasis on knowledge, while other uses pick out the development of knowledge without implying its desirability. At the far end of the spectrum lies "the more recent and more specific concept" which links such processes with "the development of states of a person that involve knowledge and understanding in depth and breadth, and also suggests that they are desirable".[32]

More recently Peters has been even more explicit in his recognition of the contestable nature of his own definition of education. He admits that the Peters-concept of education was "too specific" in concentrating on its connection with understanding and confesses that he was trying to extract too much from the concept of education, a concept which is more indeterminate than he was willing to acknowledge. He now contends that "the end or ends towards which processes of learning are seen as developing, e.g. the development of reason which we stressed so much, are aims of education, not part of the concept of 'education' itself and will depend on acceptance or rejection of the values of the society in which it takes place".[33]

It does seem, therefore, that there exists a less restrictive concept of education that we may beg leave to use in our study of what might constitute "Christian religious education". This practice does not need to fulfill the cognitive-condition in order to qualify as a species of education. The cog-

---

of the young that is "consciously, deliberately contrived to accord with fairly explicit standards of rationality and benevolence" (McClellan, *Philosophy of Education*, p. 19). Anthony O'Hear strenuously defends the liberal concept of education as the core of—but not all of—true education, but regards as highly questionable the arguments of Peters that education is necessarily a valuable process which develops rationality. See O'Hear, *Education, Society and Human Nature*, pp. 34-41.

31. See his "Education and the Educated Man"; and Hirst and Peters, *The Logic of Education*, pp. 20-25.

32. *The Logic of Education*, p. 25. R. J. Haack argues that Peters's conceptual analysis of education is defective in this area: R. J. Haack, "Philosophies of Education", *Philosophy* 51: 196 (1976), pp. 166-171.

33. Peters, "The Philosophy of Education", in Hirst, ed., *Educational Theory and its Foundation Disciplines*, p. 37. Compare also *ibid.*, pp. 41-43, Wilson, *Preface to the Philosophy of Education*, ch. 2 and Paul H. Hirst, "Richard Peters' Contribution to the Philosophy of Education", in David E. Cooper, ed., *Education, Values and Mind* (London: Routledge & Kegan Paul; New York: Routledge, 1986).

nitive-condition is undoubtedly one that would set too constraining a limit on our broad understanding of Christian religious education; but it might be argued that Christian religious education necessarily fulfills the value-condition, if that is understood in terms of those things that *Christians* value.

This is an appropriate point to note that the British philosopher of education Paul Hirst achieved some notoriety in the 1970s for his contention that Christian education is a contradiction in terms. His position appealed to a concept of education that appears to be even more restrictive, because it has more content, than the normative, restrictive concept of a liberal education to which the *highly formal* desirability and knowledge conditions attach.[34] Hirst distinguished between a "primitive concept" of education—"concerned with passing on to children what we believe, so that they in their turn come to believe it to be true"—and his preferred "sophisticated concept", on which "education should not be determined by what any group simply believes, but by what on publicly acknowledged rational grounds we can claim to know and understand".[35] According to Hirst, an "education based on a concern for objectivity and reason" cannot pursue commitment to any one set of religious claims but must teach "the radically controversial character of all such claims".[36] In a follow-up paper, he argued that this results not just in the position that Christian nurture in a "state run institution" would be "quite improper", but also in the broader claim that *any* form of religious nurture is not properly educational. The reason for this is that what "education in these terms would be aiming at in fact is clearly the basic development of children as autonomous rational beings", and built into this notion is the belief that "in matters of genuine controversy ... the presentation of particular commitments as if they were not radically disputable on rational grounds is seen as anti-educational".[37] Many critics have argued that Hirst went too far in these articles in denying the possibility of any relationship between nurture into the Christian faith and his notion of sophisticated (critical, open) education.[38]

---

34. Elsewhere Hirst recognizes that emotional, physical and moral development/formation belong to "a much wider, more generalized notion of education", rather than to the narrower conception of liberal education that "is concerned ... only with the development of the mind that results from the pursuit of knowledge". This broader concept of education cannot be justified by justifying the pursuit of knowledge, as can liberal education. See Hirst, "Liberal Education and the Nature of Knowledge", in Peters, ed., *The Philosophy of Education*, pp. 95, 99.

35. Paul H. Hirst, "Christian Education: A Contradiction in Terms?", *Learning for Living* 11: 4 (1972), pp. 7-8.

36. *Ibid.*, p. 9. Compare also: "In areas like religion where no such [appropriate, publicly agreed] canons exist for truth claims that are made, education cannot be concerned with pupils coming to know or believe the claims themselves." Paul H. Hirst, "Philosophy of Education", in John M. Sutcliffe, ed., *A Dictionary of Religious Education* (London: SCM, 1984), p. 260.

37. Paul H. Hirst, "Education, Catechesis and the Church School", *British Journal of Religious Education* 3: 3 (1981), p. 87.

38. See John M. Hull, *Studies in Religion and Education* (Lewes, England: Falmer, 1984), ch. 19; Leslie J. Francis, "The Logic of Education, Theology and the Church School", *Oxford Review of Education* 9: 2 (1983).

Later Hirst developed this distinction between primitive and sophisticated approaches to education so as to cover four "ideal types" or models of education.[39] *Education I* (the "traditionalist concept") is concerned with the transmission of specific beliefs, values, skills etc. within a particular tradition in a highly conservative fashion, without benefit of any "self-critical monitoring procedures". This is to be distinguished from *Education II* where a "progressivist", "open-ended" or "critical rational" approach is adopted, but only in areas such as the sciences—not in morals or religion. "Education II is thus split in two. At times it emphasizes observation, experiment, discovery, the testing of rival beliefs and theories, critical discussion. At times it stresses exposition, instruction, catechesis, indoctrination . . . ."

Education III tries to heal this internal split by allowing for autonomous belief claims, but only in a presupposition-based "tradition" that itself needs the traditional system of over-arching beliefs for its justification. Hirst rejects this view of education, along with its predecessors, as incoherent, proposing instead *Education IV* in which all areas of beliefs, values and attitudes are subject to rational critical appraisal. But Hirst now acknowledges that the form such criticism might appropriately take may vary from area to area, while concluding that "in all areas, beliefs, values, attitudes and so on [should be] held by individuals according to their rational status". Education may start (inevitably) within a tradition/culture, but "it is not itself aiming at the maintenance of that system". In Education IV people commit themselves to rationally justifiable beliefs and practices, while always being willing to revise such commitments. Christian religious education, Hirst continues, is only incompatible with *this* form of education if it is so conducted "as to prevent or undermine a rationally developing commitment". (But even then Education IV does not *include* evangelism or catechesis.) He claims that such an undermining is a danger that is likely to occur in church schools.

As Kevin Nichols argues in his reply to Hirst's paper, the debate must now continue with a discussion of the extent to which a tradition (any tradition) is radically revisable, and the extent to which the content of religious education (religious beliefs etc.) differs from other educational contents.[40] The place of reason in Christian (nurturing) religious education, an issue that is clearly relevant to Hirst's critique, is considered in detail in Chapters 4, 5 and 7 below. We need only note here that Hirst recommends a much more limited concept of education than the one with which we are operating in this book. This normative, critical-reflective concept of education is, I would argue, appropriate only to certain species of education. It is clearly too restrictive to cover all that has been recognized both as "education" and as "Christian religious education".

We may deal with Melchert's other criteria more briefly:

---

39. Paul H. Hirst, "Education and Diversity of Belief", in M. C. Felderhof, ed., *Religious Education in a Pluralistic Society* (London: Hodder & Stoughton, 1985); quotations are from pp. 7, 9, 13 and 14.

40. *Ibid.*, p. 19.

(4) the *time-criterion*. Education, it is often said, is a sustained activity, taking place over a period of years. This may be true when we speak of "receiving an education", but there seems to be no reason why we should not call particular processes "educational" however brief they may be. Of course we are always learning, and learning is a change or achievement that persists, but these factors do not mean that every learning process is long-lasting.

(5) the *interpersonal-interaction-criterion*. Education, claims Melchert, is an interaction of teaching interactions (between teacher, learner and subject-matter content) and learning interactions (between learner, what is learned and "whatever it was learned from"). This is a good way of defining the teaching-learning process. But if the set of educational occasions is larger than the set of teaching occasions, as I would argue, then there will be educational occasions that consist only of learning interactions.

(6) the *wholeness-criterion*. It does not seem to be true that "education necessarily involves the whole person", except on a very restrictive view of what constitutes education. Certainly the skills, beliefs, attitudes and other things that I have learned belong to me as a whole person, and they "interact"—or, better act together—precisely because I am a thinking-feeling-acting being rather than a set of discrete and separable faculties. Nevertheless, using the generalized concept of education, we *can* properly "speak of a person being educated *in*, or *for*, or *at* anything in particular".[41]

So although most or all of these restrictive criteria may be appropriate in a normative concept of what education ought to be in a certain context or for certain purposes, they need not restrict us in our descriptive general account of what education—and therefore Christian religious education—actually *is*.[42]

---

41. Despite Peters: see his "Aims of Education—A Conceptual Inquiry", in Peters, ed., *The Philosophy of Education*, p. 19. See also Wilson, *Preface to the Philosophy of Education*, p. 22.

42. Langford's criticism of the normative concept of teaching may be applied generally to discussions about the meaning of terms in education: "moves of this kind . . . can be compared to a conjuror taking a rabbit out of a hat; however baffled we may be by his skill, we are likely to insist that, even if we did not see him do it, he must have put the rabbit into the hat before taking it out. On the other hand, if this is admitted—if, in other words, the definition is admitted to be stipulative—then reasons must be given why it should be accepted." Langford, *Education, Persons and Society*, pp. 127-128.

CHAPTER 4

Indoctrination and Evidence

In this chapter I shall discuss the important notion of indoctrination, and explore its usefulness in discussions about what is proper in educational practice. I hope to show that the distinction between "indoctrination" and "rational education" is less clear-cut than is often supposed, and that we are dealing here with a spectrum of merging colors rather than a sharp border line of black and white. This being the case, those who employ the "indoctrination criticism", in their role as either critics or advocates of Christian religious education, may need to reconsider their position. (On the philosopher's use of the adjectives "rational" and "reasonable", as employed in this chapter, see Glossary.)

THE CRITERION OF INDOCTRINATION

In considering any concept we may distinguish between the definition of the term and its range of reference or application. In debates about the use of the term "indoctrination", especially with reference to the teaching of religion, disagreement is to be encountered in both areas. Naturally such disagreements about definition and application are not unrelated. In many contexts "indoctrination" has become a pejorative term,[1] and in giving an account of its meaning educationists are inevitably influenced by what they take to be paradigm cases of the application of what some regard as an educational insult. Definitions of indoctrination are often framed so as to exclude the definer's *bêtes noires*.

Much of the literature on indoctrination has focused on attempts to define the term by specifying the *criterion of indoctrination*: meaning here the necessary (and usually sufficient) condition for the correct application of the word. A number of different criteria have been suggested as definitive.

---

1. It was not always so. Until this century indoctrination had the quite neutral meaning of teaching or instruction. Richard H. Gatchel, "The Evolution of the Concept", in I. A. Snook, ed., *Concepts of Indoctrination* (London: Routledge & Kegan Paul, 1972), p. 9. It still has this connotation in some contexts (e.g. military ones).

44

The method-criterion

On this view what distinguishes indoctrination from other teaching is the methods that are used. Although "method" is the usual word used in the philosophical literature to refer to the instructional practice/ process, others who specialize in the dynamics of the teaching act reserve the term for a class of tactical instructional acts, less general than, for example, "style" and "strategy", but less specific than pedagogical "techniques" or "steps".[2] The philosopher's usage may be taken to cover quite generally a number of these elements in the practice of teaching.

The method-criterion (or "instruction"- or "practice"-criterion) is regarded by many as the predominant understanding of indoctrination in educational debate in the United States, where indoctrination is often understood as a controversial educational method, which may or may not be viewed as undesirable, for the uncritical implantation of beliefs.[3] For advocates of the method-criterion, indoctrination may be regarded as lying at one extreme (the authoritarian one) of a continuum of teaching methods ("liberal education" being the label often applied to the other extreme). Indoctrinatory methods can guarantee the acceptance of certain beliefs because they "induce beliefs in a way which bypasses the reasoning process of the person" or coerce that person's will,[4] so that the learner believes something without understanding the grounds for that belief. Such a method, it is usually accepted, is permissible and inevitable with young children.[5]

Method seems implausible as a criterion for indoctrination, however, because further analysis shows that indoctrinatory methods tend to be described as such on the grounds that they lead to indoctrinatory consequences such as a closed mind. Furthermore, many quite acceptable educa-

---

2. See James Michael Lee, *The Flow of Religious Instruction* (Birmingham, Ala.: Religious Education Press, 1973), pp. 33-35.

3. Willis Moore, "Indoctrination and Democratic Method", in Snook, ed., *Concepts of Indoctrination, passim*; Gatchel, *ibid.*, p. 15; Brian S. Crittenden, *ibid.*, p. 146. Hugo Meynell also adopts a method ("manner") criterion in his "Moral Education and Indoctrination", *Journal of Moral Education* 14: 1 (1974), pp. 18, 25. Barry Chazan, writing in a North American context, notes the use of the term indoctrination "as a term of disapproval": even those "who regard indoctrination as an indispensable and legitimate aspect of education, nevertheless consider it a 'necessary evil'". Barry Chazan, "'Indoctrination' and Religious Education", in Michael Warren, ed., *Sourcebook for Modern Catechetics* (Winona, Minn.: St. Mary's Press, 1983), p. 412.

4. P. J. Sheehan, "Education and Indoctrination: Some Notes", *Dialogue* 4: 1 (Melbourne, 1970), p. 66. It should be noted that Sheehan rejects the view that we have no direct control over our beliefs (p. 67); compare below Chapter 8. According to R. E. Young, teachers often adopt methods of communication that conceal the true aims of their teaching and which result in "students' accepting these claims on grounds other than reasons which seem valid to them in their own framework of relevance". He describes such a teaching structure as "formally indoctrinatory". R. E. Young, "Critical Teaching and Learning", *Educational Theory* 38: 1 (1988), pp. 54-59.

5. I. A. Snook, *Indoctrination and Education* (London: Routledge & Kegan Paul, 1972), pp. 24-25; John Wilson, "Emotion, Religion and Education: A Reply to Richard Allen", *Proceedings of the Philosophy of Education Society of Great Britain* 7: 2 (1973), p. 196.

tional processes "bypass"—because they are not aimed at—the development of a learner's cognitive powers.[6]

The content-criterion

This criterion has been more popular with philosophers of education,[7] who have noted the tendency to restrict the application of the term "indoctrination" to areas of political, moral and religious instruction. On this view indoctrination is focused on the passing on of beliefs, rather than attitudes or values;[8] and the beliefs singled out are often seen as either false or ideological (in a negative, irrational sense—contrast Chapter 5 below). A distinction is sometimes made between isolated beliefs and "doctrines": a doctrine being defined here as a belief system or "a set of beliefs", and indoctrination as "a systematic attempt to pass on as true a set of beliefs which are basically unfounded".[9]

Educationists often insist that (a) method and (b) content are not two distinct and separate realities. The two categories may be better described as (a) "structural content" (on the broad view of method adopted above, i.e. instruc-

---

6. Sheehan ("Education and Indoctrination", p. 66) contends that such methods are not to be deemed "indoctrinatory" in the case of young children, arguing that "because they do not come to believe *via* reasons and evidence it is hard to see what it means to say that they came to believe as a result of indoctrination rather than education". See also Chazan, "'Indoctrination' and Religious Education", pp. 415-417. According to David Cooper this criticism may be met "by insisting that manner and method are the criteria, but are relevant only in situations where different manners and methods were available" (which they are not in the case of the "nonrational" teaching of very young children). David E. Cooper, "Intentions and Indoctrination", *Educational Philosophy and Theory* 5: 1 (1973), p. 54.

7. John Passmore, "On Teaching to be Critical", in R. S. Peters, ed., *The Concept of Education* (London: Oxford University Press, 1973); Antony Flew, "Indoctrination and Doctrines" and "Indoctrination and Religion" in Snook, ed., *Concepts of Indoctrination*; John Wilson, "Education and Indoctrination", in T. H. B. Hollins, ed., *Aims in Education: The Philosophic Approach* (Manchester: Manchester University Press, 1964).

8. Snook, ed., *Concepts of Indoctrination*, p. 2. Many commentators speak of the "indoctrination" of beliefs but the "conditioning" of feelings and habits, see comments by the following authors in *Concepts of Indoctrination*: John Wilson, p. 17; Thomas F. Green, pp. 25-29; Antony Flew, pp. 82, 109, 112, but contrast p. 87. See also James Gribble, *Introduction to Philosophy of Education* (Boston: Allyn & Bacon, 1969), p. 29. But contrast John Kleinig, *Philosophical Issues in Education* (London: Croom Helm; New York: St. Martin's Press, 1982), pp. 62-68; Gatchel in Snook, ed., *Concepts of Indoctrination*, p. 15; R. F. Atkinson in Reginald D. Archambault, ed., *Philosophical Analysis and Education* (London: Routledge & Kegan Paul, 1965), pp. 177-181; and R. W. Hepburn, "The Arts and the Education of Feeling and Emotion", in R. F. Dearden *et al.*, eds., *Education and Reason* (London: Routledge & Kegan Paul, 1975), p. 106.

9. James Gribble, "Education or Indoctrination?", *Dialogue* 3: 2 (1969), p. 42. According to Ben Spiecker a "doctrine" is necessarily held without reference to its validity, for those who subscribe to doctrines screen them from criticism. Ben Spiecker, "Indoctrination, Intellectual Virtues and Rational Emotions", *Journal of Philosophy of Education* 21: 2 (1987), pp. 261-262. See also Tasos Kazepides, "Religious Indoctrination and Freedom" and Ben Spiecker, "Indoctrination: The Suppression of Critical Dispositions", in Ben Spiecker and Roger Straughan, eds., *Freedom and Indoctrination in Education* (London and New York: Cassell, 1991).

tional practice or procedure) and (b) "substantive content", and treated as two elements of the proper overall content of the teaching act (what the teaching teaches and the learner learns). The reason for this is that the way something is taught (i.e. the instructional practice) is itself a content of teaching, not least of religious teaching where the processes of instruction contribute considerably to a person's religious learning—especially their learning of values. This structural content is additional to what is more usually described as its "content"—i.e. its substantive, or "subject-matter", content. Thus: "the content which is taught is both what is taught and how the teaching occurs. [It] . . . is not only the substance which is taught but also the structure in and through which the substance flows and is changed."[10] In Christian religious teaching the substantive content is the Christian religion, and this is what in the indoctrination debate is described as its "content".

The root of the (substantive) content-criterion seems to be that indoctrinated beliefs are "not by any ordinary standards known to be true".[11] This introduces, however, an epistemological criterion that too easily slips into a sociological criterion, as we shall see later. Certainly it is hard to avoid language about "publicly acceptable tests" in any talk about "essentially controversial" statements, and thus to invite the question "acceptable to which public?". The liberal educator's views on democracy, human nature and ethics are certainly controversial, if not openly controverted to any great degree among educators in certain cultures.[12] The content-criterion of indoctrination looks suspiciously like a piece of special pleading on behalf of the restricted view taken by some philosophers about what constitutes *acceptable* beliefs.

The intention-criterion

This is perhaps the most popular criterion among those philosophers who comment on education. Richard Hare claims that indoctrination "begins when we are trying to stop the growth in our children of the capacity to think for themselves".[13] According to I. A. Snook a person is indoctrinat-

---

10. James Michael Lee, "Growth in Faith through Religious Instruction", in Lee, ed., *Handbook of Faith* (Birmingham, Ala.: Religious Education Press, 1990), p. 292, compare p. 266. See also his *The Flow of Religious Instruction*, pp. 28-31 and ch. 9 *passim*; *The Content of Religious Instruction* (Birmingham, Ala.: Religious Education Press, 1985), pp. 8, 13, 20-23, 106-107; and the "The Authentic Source of Religious Instruction", in Norma H. Thompson, ed., *Religious Education and Theology* (Birmingham, Ala.: Religious Education Press, 1982), pp. 170-174. For a general account of pedagogical process as a content, see J. Cecil Parker and Louis J. Rubin, *Process as Content: Curriculum Design and the Application of Knowledge* (Chicago: Rand McNally, 1966), ch. 1.

11. Flew, in Snook, ed., *Concepts of Indoctrination*, p. 75, see also p. 85.

12. See B. G. Mitchell, "Indoctrination", Appendix B to The Bishop of Durham's Commission on Religious Education in Schools, *The Fourth R* (London: National Society/SPCK, 1970), pp. 355-356 and papers by Edmund L. Pincoffs and Kurt Baier in James F. Doyle, ed., *Educational Judgments* (London: Routledge & Kegan Paul, 1973), chs. 4 and 5.

13. R. M. Hare, "Adolescents into Adults", in Hollins, ed., *Aims in Education*, p. 52 see also p. 69, and Spiecker, "Indoctrination: The Suppression of Critical Dispositions", pp. 21-22.

ing "if (i) in his teaching he is actively desiring that the pupils believe what he is teaching regardless of the evidence, or (ii) he foresees that as a result of his teaching such an outcome is likely or inevitable".[14] Snook widens "intention" in this way to include consequences that are not intended (in the usual sense) but are foreseen, so as to cover cases such as the influence of the hidden curriculum.[15] It is surely correct to recognize the broader responsibility of the teacher in this way, but should we still call this the teacher's "intention"?[16] In any case, this concentration on the aim of the educator allows no place for the (apparently acceptable) usage of "indoctrination" to cover *unrecognized* and nonintentional effects of teaching. It also appears to allow an educator to escape from the criticism of indoctrination by appealing to a fact about herself, rather than a fact about the learners in her charge.

The consequences-criterion

On this view indoctrination occurs when "the beliefs, attitudes, values, etc. taught are held in such a way that they are no longer open to full rational assessment": when the teacher/learner interaction results in the learners' "believing non-critically".[17] We would most naturally speak here of *persons* being indoctrinated, rather than content (e.g. beliefs); and distinguish indoctrination by reference to the learning outcomes of a piece of teaching rather than its aim or method. Indoctrination remains a species of teaching, however, and therefore a human activity for which someone must take responsibility,

---

14. Snook, *Indoctrination and Education*, p. 50; compare Snook, ed., *Concepts of Indoctrination*, ch. 12. See also J. P. White, "Indoctrination", in Peters, ed., *The Concept of Education* and William Heard Kilpatrick, "Indoctrination and Respect for Persons", in Snook, ed., *Concepts of Indoctrination*.

15. But only where the effects of the hidden curriculum are foreseen by the teacher. Compare Ian Lister, ed., *Deschooling: A Reader* (Cambridge: Cambridge University Press, 1974), and note 13 to Chapter 3 above.

16. Cooper argues that we should not ("Intentions and Indoctrination", pp. 46-53). John Hull distinguishes between a "naive indoctrinator (one who does not fully intend to indoctrinate)" and an "indoctrinator to the full sense". John M. Hull, "Indoctrination", in John M. Sutcliffe, ed., *A Dictionary of Religious Education* (London: SCM, 1984), p. 167. It has also been argued that indoctrinatory practices may be performed with a multiplicity of intentions, and therefore that indoctrination "cannot be reduced to any form of action . . . capable of being distinguished by a particular intention". Michael Leahy, "Indoctrination, Evangelization, Catechesis and Religious Education", *British Journal of Religious Education* 12: 3 (1990), p. 138.

17. Kleinig, *Philosophical Issues in Education*, p. 62; Harvey Siegel, "Indoctrination and Education", in Spiecker and Straughan, eds., *Freedom and Indoctrination in Education*, p. 31. See also P. H. Hirst, "What is Teaching?", in R. S. Peters, ed., *The Philosophy of Education* (London: Oxford University Press, 1973), pp. 175-176: "Indoctrination . . . would certainly seem to be picked out, at least in part, by the distinctive end state of mind of the learner, to which the teaching is directed. An indoctrinated person would seem to hold certain beliefs unshakeably." See also P. H. Hirst and R. S. Peters, *The Logic of Education* (London: Routledge & Kegan Paul, 1970), p. 85; Meriel Downey and A. V. Kelly, *Moral Education: Theory and Practice* (London; New York: Harper & Row, 1978), pp. 56-61; Anthony O'Hear, *Education, Society and Human Nature: An Introduction to the Philosophy of Education* (London: Routledge & Kegan Paul, 1981), p. 91.

but it no longer needs to be deliberate.[18] Teachers who intend indoctrination but fail to produce it may properly be described as "*unsuccessful* indoctrinators".

This last criterion seems the most plausible of the candidates that have been proposed as a necessary condition of indoctrination. It is possible sensibly to relate the content, methods and intentions of teachers to the indoctrinatory outcome of their teaching. John Dewey's definition of indoctrination—"the systematic use of every possible means to impress upon the minds of pupils a particular set of . . . views to the exclusion of every other"—may be analyzed along these lines. Indoctrinatory means or processes can be described as such because they result in indoctrinatory outcomes.[19] The consequences-criterion is also valuable in widening the debate to include the learning of attitudes, values and emotions, and impelling us to consider what is meant by the rationality of *these* learning outcomes.

The essence of indoctrination, then, is the production of fixed, unquestionable, closed learning outcomes. To put it in this way is to make the phrase "indoctrination is a bad thing" appear almost tautologous, at least for the post-Enlightenment liberal educator or the post-Freire liberation educator. This perhaps explains the apparent irregular conjugation of educational verbs: "*I* teach", "*you* are engaged in biased instruction", "*he* indoc-

---

18. By contrast, see J. P. White, in Snook, ed., *Concepts of Indoctrination*, p. 198. Adopting the usual definition of teaching as an intentional activity (see Chapter 3 above), we may say that a teacher intends some learning outcomes but not necessarily any indoctrinatory learning outcomes. On the consequences-criterion we may speak of indoctrination by omission: see Schools Council, *An Approach through Religious Education* (London: Evans/Methuen, 1969), p. 32. Note also the references in the literature to the "null curriculum" of "areas (content, themes, points of view) left out and procedures left unused (the arts, play, critical analysis)". Maria Harris, *Fashion Me a People: Curriculum in the Church* (Louisville, Ky.: Westminster/John Knox, 1989), p. 69.

19. John Dewey, *Education Today*, ed. Joseph Ratner (New York: Putnam's, 1940), p. 356. The claim by Gregory and Woods that "the components of content, method, and aim are necessary and conjointly sufficient conditions for indoctrination" is a different claim from the one I am making, but as Kleinig notes their paper contains many implicit references to the *outcome* of indoctrination as connecting the three. I. M. M. Gregory and R. G. Woods, "Indoctrination: inculcating doctrines", in Snook, ed., *Concepts of Indoctrination*, p. 171 and *passim*. See also Robin Barrow and Ronald Woods, *An Introduction to Philosophy of Education* (London: Routledge, 1988), ch. 5 and Chazan, "'Indoctrination' and Religious Education", pp. 421-423. Cooper agrees that "consequences must be relevant to identifying teaching as indoctrination", but argues that such teaching must have a *tendency* "to result in non-evidentially held beliefs"—this tendency being identified by the "manner and method of these activities". Otherwise, he claims, the situation would be equivalent to someone blaming me for "persuading" you to join the Foreign Legion, which would not be proper "unless what I said was the sort of thing likely to persuade people" (Cooper, "Intentions and Indoctrination", p. 53). But I would argue that it is quite proper to say that I "persuaded" (or "frightened" or "indoctrinated") someone, even though the acts I performed—in their "manner and method"—would not normally tend to produce these effects. Some verbs, like many trees, are best known by their unexpected fruits. For other criticisms of the consequences-criterion, and a spirited defense of it, see (for the former) Snook, *Indoctrination and Education*, pp. 40-41 and (for the latter) Kleinig, *Philosophical Issues in Education*, pp. 63-65.

trinates". But any detailed consideration of the issue will quickly lead us to the conclusion that we are not dealing here with a hard and fast distinction, but rather with a spectrum of learning outcomes that may be more or less "indoctrination",[20] and may be evaluated as more or less acceptable in different areas, by people of different standpoints.

INDOCTRINATION AND EVIDENCE

Definitions of indoctrination often make reference to the fact that indoctrinated beliefs lack openness to good counter evidence. Philosophers refer to such beliefs as being held "nonevidentially", "regardless of the evidence",[21] "even if presented with sufficient reasons" for believing a contradictory proposition,[22] or some such (perhaps less extreme) qualification. "Most teachers", it is argued, "subscribe to the belief that indoctrination . . . is anti-educational because it tends to fix beliefs and make them irrationally impregnable to any future reasoning."[23]

One of the problems here is that of the context dependence of notions of "good evidence", for it is by no means a neutral term. Who is to judge how good it is?[24] The difficulty is that what counts to a person as good evidence against (or for) her belief is dependent on the belief system that she holds. Indeed what is regarded as admissible as "evidence" at all by an individual is circumscribed by that person's worldview. This is clearly demonstrated by the refusal of the more positivist minded and naturalistically minded to consider the possibility of religious experience serving as evidence for religious beliefs, or anything at all as evidence for miracles.[25] To assert, with Donald Hudson, that a rational belief "must be supported by the relevant evidence", and that the person who holds it must be prepared to surrender it on finding what appears to that person to be a "good reason to do so",[26] is a remarkably context dependent—even knower dependent—claim.

20. See Green, in Snook, ed., *Concepts of Indoctrination*, pp. 26-27; also Moore, in *ibid.*, pp. 97-98.

21. Green, in *ibid.*, p. 33; Snook, *Indoctrination and Education*, p. 47, also p. 55; Siegel, "Indoctrination and Education", p. 34.

22. Mitchell, "Indoctrination", p. 356.

23. Charles Bailey, "Neutrality and Rationality in Teaching", in David Bridges and Peter Scrimshaw, eds., *Values and Authority in Schools* (London: Hodder & Stoughton, 1975), p. 122.

24. Compare: "Indoctrination attempts to give its content an authority and a normative value to which in fact the doctrines have no rightful social or intellectual claim" (Hull, "Indoctrination", p. 166); see also John Elliott, "Neutrality, Rationality and the Role of the Teacher", *Proceedings of the Philosophy of Education Society of Great Britain* 7: 1 (1973), pp. 49-50.

25. See, for example, Antony Flew, *God and Philosophy* (London: Hutchinson, 1966), chs. 6 and 7.

26. W. Donald Hudson, "The Rational System of Beliefs", in David Martin *et al.*, eds., *Sociology and Theology: Alliance and Conflict* (Brighton, England: Harvester Press, 1980), p. 80.

"Relevant evidence", "good evidence" and similar phrases are more problematic than they often appear. We cannot glibly speak of good evidence as that which is adjudged to be so by the "uncommitted", "neutral" judge, for there is no Olympian or Archimedean point outside all belief systems from which they can be evaluated in a nonpartisan manner. All evaluations take place from some standpoint: one cannot view anything without standing somewhere to do the viewing. Much rhetoric about "trusting to reason" seems to imply that such a presuppositionless and value-free position is possible, and that is surely a chimera.[27] This is a truism in epistemology which is accepted by philosophers of a wide variety of viewpoints. "Our judgements about what there is are always embedded in some theory. We can substitute one theory for another, but we cannot detach ourselves from theory altogether and see the world unclouded by any preconception of it."[28]

To assess the value of evidence for a particular belief is necessarily to become involved in highly controversial issues of epistemology, including the epistemology of religion (the theory of *religious* knowledge), in which our understanding of what is rational in religion will be tested to the uttermost.

The Problem of Metaphysics
One of the difficulties with religious belief systems, and other systems of beliefs, worldviews and ideologies, is that they often present themselves as metaphysical systems (i.e. as all-encompassing, fundamental interpretations of reality). This is a difficulty because metaphysical systems themselves decide what is to count as "real" or a "fact", and therefore as "evidence" either for or against themselves. As W. H. Walsh has put it: "there is no general agreement about what 'the facts' are". Facts obtain only from particular points of view, "and here points of view are in dispute". The consequence is that metaphysicians are necessarily judges in their own cases. They are obliged to take account of all the facts as they see them, but in the last resort they are the ones who take responsibility for saying what is fact and what not.[29] Thus metaphysical schemes do not just conceptually integrate "all that is", they also influence what those who adopt them believe there is—and could possibly be—in the first place. This is often forgotten both by advocates and by critics of Christian religious education.

---

27. The point is made well by Patricia Beattie Jung in Stanley Hauerwas and John H. Westerhoff, III, eds., *Schooling Christians* (Grand Rapids, Mich.: Eerdmans, 1992), pp. 116-125. There are very real problems in John Wilson's assertion that we should educate children "to adopt behaviour-patterns and have feelings which are seen by every sane and sensible person to be agreeable and necessary" in that "they derive from reality rather than from the values, fears, desires or prejudices of individual people". Who in fact is to judge this? See Wilson, "Education and Indoctrination", p. 34; and compare Hare, "Adolescents into Adults", p. 48, and below Chapter 9.

28. A. J. Ayer, "Wittgenstein on Certainty", in Godfrey Vesey, ed., *Understanding Wittgenstein* (London: Macmillan, 1974), p. 245.

29. W. H. Walsh, *Metaphysics* (London: Hutchinson, 1963), p. 178; see also Basil Mitchell, *The Justification of Religious Belief* (London: Macmillan, 1973), ch. 5 and pp. 114-115.

Metaphysical systems are not only systems of beliefs of considerable generality, they also frequently include beliefs about realities that transcend ("go beyond") ordinary sense experience. For both these reasons, metaphysical systems have a loose relationship even to the evidence that they recognize as such. A blanket that covers a single sleeper can easily be arranged to fit him snugly at most points, but a blanket spread out over a bedful of sleepers of assorted shapes and sizes will "touch down" only here and there. It is the same with the blanket of highly general beliefs (a "*world-view*" or metaphysical "cosmology") that attempts to make sense of, integrate, and cover all of reality; instead of restricting itself to a small part of it—as do scientific hypotheses concerned with specific areas. The high level explanations of metaphysical systems—more even than the intermediate level explanations offered by large scale scientific theories (e.g. evolution), paradigms or "research programs" (e.g. Newtonian physics)[30]—are notorious for their immunity to falsification by particular experiences. C. B. Daly argues: "No statement about reality as a whole could be empirically verifiable, in the sense of its 'being possible to describe in observational terms two different states of the Universe—one that takes place when the statement is true and another when it is not'." He contends that any statement about reality as a whole, and therefore every metaphysical statement, must be compatible with all states of the universe, or "neutral in respect of matters of fact".[31] Similarly Frederick Ferré writes: "a [metaphysical] model which is taken to include, in principle, all real or possible events, cannot be disproved by any real or possible events that come to pass. It has already, in germ, *accounted for* anything that might occur."[32]

Thus the metaphysical concept of God, which is part of the broad content of Christian religious education, has already been constructed so as to make sense of and hold together facts right across the universe. It contains within itself, for example, some more or less consistent explanations of the evil in the world. This is why it is not possible merely to point to the existence of any evil as evidence sufficient to falsify the supposition of God's existence. The metaphysical "God theory" explains all that it should explain because theologians have constructed it so that it will. A scientific hypothesis may fail (i.e. be falsified) when scientists are no longer able to adjust the hypothesis to cover apparently conflicting evidence.[33] But this is because the scientific

---

30. For a general survey see Ian G. Barbour, *Myths, Models and Paradigms* (London: SCM; New York: Harper & Row, 1974).

31. C. B. Daly, "Metaphysics and the Limits of Language", in Ian Ramsey, ed., *Prospect for Metaphysics* (London: Allen & Unwin, 1961), p. 202; also F. B. Dilley, *Metaphysics and Religious Language* (New York: Columbia University Press, 1964), pp. 121, 127-128, ch. 4.

32. F. W. Ferré, "Mapping the Logic of Models in Science and Theology", in Dallas M. High, ed., *New Essays in Religious Language* (New York: Oxford University Press, 1969), p. 81; see also Max Black, *Models and Metaphors* (Ithaca: Cornell University Press, 1962), p. 242.

33. Karl R. Popper, *The Logic of Scientific Discovery* (London: Hutchinson, 1968), ch. IV, and *Conjectures and Refutations* (London: Routledge & Kegan Paul, 1972), chs. 1 and 8.

hypothesis is less wide ranging, less remote from empirical facts, and less adaptable than in the theological case. Furthermore, it is often amenable to direct empirical test, and all scientific claims imply predictive promises; whereas God cannot be isolated experimentally for further investigation, we cannot compare the universe that God creates with a "control" cosmos that is not God's creation, and we cannot deduce verifiable predictions from theological assertions. For these reasons the justification of theology is likely to be very different from scientific confirmation. In these respects too, teaching about God and facilitating belief in God is likely to involve some differences that arise from the different nature of its content when compared with teaching about D.N.A. and facilitating the learning of genetics.

Such considerations may lead some theists to declare their belief system "unfalsifiable in principle". Others are less straightlaced and admit an in-principle falsifiability, but couple it with a high resistance to falsification in practice.[34] Yet even for these believers the criteria of justification of religious belief will be significantly different from those used in the testing of scientific or commonsense hypotheses. Ian Ramsey writes of the "empirical fit" of religious beliefs to empirical evidence, contrasting this with the experimental confirmation of the natural sciences:

> The theological model works more like the fitting of a boot or a shoe than like the "yes" or "no" of a roll call. In other words, we have a particular doctrine which, like a preferred and selected shoe, starts by appearing to meet our empirical needs. But on closer fitting to the phenomena the shoe may pinch. When tested against future slush and rain it may be proven to be not altogether water-tight or it may be comfortable—yet it must not be too comfortable. In this way, the test of a shoe is measured by its ability to match a wide range of phenomena, by its overall success in meeting a variety of needs. Here is what I might call the method of empirical fit which is displayed by theological theorizing.[35]

Empirical fit is by no means an "exact fit" to the evidence, but it is of considerable significance all the same. Ramsey claims that it is not only relevant to the justification of religious beliefs. It also serves as the criterion for justifying certain wide ranging assertions about people (e.g. "A loves B") and for many claims made in the social sciences (e.g. "he is a mild depressive"). It is crucial too in archeology and anthropology, where by the nature

---

34. See, for example, Basil Mitchell, "Theology and Falsification (C)" and John Hick, "Theology and Verification" in Basil Mitchell, ed., *The Philosophy of Religion* (London: Oxford University Press, 1971); also I. T. Ramsey, "History and the Gospels", *Studia Evangelica* III: 6 (1964), pp. 211-217. Quite the best book on the verifiability/falsifiability challenge to the meaningfulness of religious language (a topic which is not discussed here) is Raeburne Seeley Heimbeck, *Theology and Meaning: a Critique of Metatheological Scepticism* (London: Allen & Unwin, 1969). See also Basil Mitchell, "Faith and Reason: A False Antithesis?", *Religious Studies* 16 (1980).

35. Ian T. Ramsey, *Models and Mystery* (London: Oxford University Press, 1964), p. 17.

of the case conclusive verification is impossible.[36]

Now I would contend that the difference between "experimental verification" and "empirical fit" is simply a function of (a) the generality and wide-ranging nature of the assertion being tested (which in theology is often so general as to be "metaphysical"), and (b) the extent to which the object being modeled transcends the empirical world (i.e. the degree to which it is a "meta-empirical" entity). The wide- ranging nature of theological assertions constitutes one of their great strengths—but is also their greatest weakness. Of course a (mono)theistic metaphysics "fits" the whole world, for the whole world has been taken into account in the construction of such a metaphysical scheme. And it is a "constructed" (or "reconstructed") metaphysical scheme, and not simply a bare unqualified datum of religious experience, that is said to fit the facts of the universe. In a similar manner, an atheistic metaphysics may also be constructed so as to "fit" the cosmos; and the same may be said of polytheistic or naturalistic metaphysics, and so on. They all fit in different ways, but the empirical facts they fit do not bear their metaphysical interpretations on their sleeves. They are ambiguous enough (or neutral enough) to permit widely different metaphysical schemes to be constructed around them. How then are we to decide between all these different "fits"?

The answer to that question is likely to be a highly personal one, dependent on the answers to questions like: "Which facts do you think it is most important that a metaphysical scheme should fit well?". The answer here might be "the facts of evil", or "the facts of goodness", or "my personal life story", or "the history of Israel", or "the person of Jesus". But this is all a matter of personal choice, as is our choice of a "good" shoe. For we all have different feet (differently "shaped" worlds—at the very least different perceptions of what is significant in the world), and therefore the same shoe will fit different people to different extents. This aspect of the fit of a shoe or an explanatory theory is prior to its being tested more widely against the slush and rain of the world. A theory that fails this (personal) test is never "adopted" and therefore never tested further.[37]

I would argue that the empirical fit of a metaphysical theological assertion, like that of any other metaphysical claim, necessarily involves a considerable

---

36. *Ibid.*, pp. 38-40.

37. See Terrence W. Tilley, "Ian Ramsey and Empirical Fit", *Journal of the American Academy of Religion* 45 (1977) for his distinction between the initial "testing" of a shoe at the time of purchase, and the later testing that takes place outside the shoe shop. The first element of testing (mainly for comfort, "looks" etc.) may be regarded as equivalent to the more *a priori* testing of a theory for its likely adequacy in integrating those facts with which the individual is particularly concerned. Such a test is a very individual matter, as is one's choice of shoes. This is then followed by the more *a posteriori* testing (with reference to experience) of the shoe, mainly for waterproofness, durability, long term comfort, etc., which may be regarded as analogous to the empirical testing of a theory against the entire range of relevant empirical facts (i.e. not just those which the individual personally regards as more crucial). Compare also J. Astley, "Ian Ramsey and the Problem of Religious Knowledge", *Journal of Theological Studies* 35: 2 (1984) from which some of this discussion is drawn with permission.

personal and subjective element. All metaphysical schemes will appear to those who espouse them to fit the universe. If there are areas that they do not seem to fit well, the disciples of a particular metaphysic will adapt their scheme appropriately so as to explain the apparent exceptions. Even scientific *theories* are modified in this way so as to cover apparently conflicting evidence. Unlike small-scale *hypotheses*, they are not given up at the first hint of experimental failure.[38] But in the case of a metaphysical scheme—which is of an even higher order of abstraction and generality—this phenomenon is much more marked.

What price, then, a distinction between indoctrination and rational education (including Christian religious education) with regard to such beliefs? Such a distinction "presupposes that there are clear criteria of truth, cogency, correctness in any field to which it applies", and therefore "the more fugitive the criteria may be in a particular field, the harder will it be to distinguish instruction and indoctrination".[39] It is tempting for the hard-headed (or hard-hearted?) educator to dismiss as indoctrination all teaching of doctrines of "a wide-ranging generality that allow considerable freedom of manoeuvre in the sense that one can take up a distinctive position and not be easily dislodged".[40] The difficulty here is that this caveat would apply to *all* metaphysical claims, and metaphysics is not restricted to assertions about God. Propositions concerning the existence of a real world beyond our eyes and ears ("realism") are also metaphysical. The stipulation might even apply to wide-ranging claims about determining truth on the basis of evidence.[41] The indoctrination missile, if it is to be fired at all, will have to be directed to many targets and not just at the Christian religious educator.

THE RATIONAL SYSTEM OF BELIEFS

It is tempting to agree with Snook that teaching religious belief is inevitably indoctrinatory where such teaching seeks (I would say effects) the inculcation of doctrines "regardless of the evidence", right across the board of reli-

---

38. See Thomas S. Kuhn, *The Structure of Scientific Revolutions* (Chicago: University of Chicago Press, 1970), ch. VIII and his "Logic of Discovery or Psychology of Research?", in Imre Lakatos and Alan Musgrave, eds., *Criticism and the Growth of Knowledge* (Cambridge: Cambridge University Press, 1970), pp. 13-19 (also the article by Lakatos in the same collection). According to Quine, "any statement can be held to be true come what may, if we make drastic enough adjustments elsewhere in the system". Willard Van Orman Quine, *From a Logical Point of View* (New York: Harper & Row, 1961), p. 43. A sophisticated account of the similarities and contrasts between the epistemological status of scientific and theistic beliefs is to be found in Michael C. Banner, *The Justification of Science and the Rationality of Religious Belief* (Oxford: Oxford University Press, 1990).

39. Atkinson, "Instruction and Indoctrination", p. 173; see Patricia Smart, "The Concept of Indoctrination", in Glenn Langford and D. J. O'Connor, eds., *New Essays in the Philosophy of Education* (London: Routledge & Kegan Paul, 1973), p. 45.

40. Gregory and Woods, "Indoctrination: Inculcating Doctrines", p. 185.

41. *Ibid.*, p. 188.

gious beliefs and of the learner's intellectual development.[42] It is natural to wish to argue that such indoctrination can be avoided, even with the less mature, if "free and critical engagement is guaranteed" to the learner in considering the evidence.[43] Such language is highly abstract, however, and will not get us very far. What is needed are concrete examples of educational processes and their learning outcomes, particularly in Christian religious education, so that we may see what specific content can be given to this notion of "evidence", and of "free and critical engagement" with it. In any discussion of the limits of indoctrination, the problem of *evidence* remains.

It should be noted that authoritarian Christian religious educators are unlikely to accept the claim that they either intend or ensure that their learners hold their religious beliefs nonevidentially, despite their adoption of "authoritarian educational procedures".[44] On the contrary, such educators will say that they impress upon their learners the overwhelming significance of the "evidence" on which they must base those beliefs, for example the evidence of the inerrant propositions to be found in scripture or the evidence of self-authenticating religious experiences. They may well accuse others of being misled by their own incessant enquiry and criticism into ignoring such firm and convincing evidence. They might argue that other evidence which may seem to undermine the presuppositions that the Bible is inerrant and religious experience self-authenticating is not, in fact, *good* evidence. This may be shown, they might continue, by the very fact that it contradicts the clear word of, and experience of, the God of truth; and so on . . .

Criteria for the Rationality of Beliefs

To see if we can explore this problem further I shall now pick up Donald Hudson's criteria for the rationality of beliefs, two of which were quoted above (i.e. support by relevant evidence and liability to surrender in the face of good reasons). He offers us two others: the formal one that beliefs must not be self-contradictory and the material one that they should conform to "the rational system of beliefs".[45]

The first of these is fairly unobjectionable and is generally accepted, in principle if not always in practice. A self-contradictory belief asserts nothing

---

42. Snook, *Indoctrination and Education*, p. 84. Cooper argues that this is not a good description of the intentions of the "sincere" indoctrinators ("surely the normal type"), who cannot conceive of conclusive evidence against their doctrines but would want their learners to revise their beliefs should such evidence be forthcoming (Cooper, "Intentions and Indoctrination", p. 45). (This account is dependent on an intention-criterion, as the language of "sincerity" indicates.) See my comments in the next paragraph.

43. Edward Hulmes, *Commitment and Neutrality in Religious Education* (London: Chapman, 1979), p. 101.

44. Randolph Crump Miller, *The Theory of Christian Education Practice* (Birmingham, Ala.: Religious Education Press, 1980), p. 159.

45. Hudson, "The Rational System of Beliefs", pp. 80-81. A rational belief, Hudson argues, does not need to fulfill all these criteria. The adjective "rational" is being used here as a synonym for "reasonable" or "justified" (opposite irrational), and not as implying a derivation from reason alone (see Glossary).

and certainly disables any argument that uses it. There have been those who have claimed that certain theological statements may permissibly fail to fulfill such a criterion (e.g. "Christ is both human and divine", "God is both eternal and acts in time"), but further reflection will show that the tradition presents these as paradoxes—i.e. *apparent* contradictions.[46] This insight may well affect the nature of the educational programs in which they are taught. More radically, certain claims presented by religious mystics have been said properly to contravene the law of noncontradiction, as this logical law does not apply to mystical experience.[47] There are difficulties, however, with this position. It would be better in these cases to begin and end the discussion with the claim that both the experience and God are ineffable, rather than to continue to use descriptive language that is thoroughly self-contradictory. Self-contradictory language may be a useful device in evoking religious insight or expressing religious emotion, and therein may lie its usefulness to the religious educator, but it will not do as descriptive theology. Self-contradictions have no sense. Language about God may always be inadequate, but it simply cannot be used if it is *that* inadequate.

What of the criterion of "conformity to the rational system of beliefs"? For Hudson this is a system of propositions about what is the case, and principles about what people should do or choose, that are generally accepted in our society and "regulate what it makes sense to say or do". It should be noted at the outset that conformity to such a system constitutes a criterion of rationality, and the beliefs that comprise it are not themselves necessarily adjudged as rational on the other criteria. When the rational system changes this may be because of the application of these other criteria, but it can also happen simply because people "lose interest" or "stop caring" about some of the elements within it.[48] This system of "generally-held, regulative beliefs",[49] which people either profess or (more significantly)take for granted, is discoverable by the sociologist and must be conformed to by those theologians who wish their theology to "be intelligible or credible for those to whom it is addressed". The theologian's success in producing such conformity is itself something that is to be judged by the philosopher.[50]

According to Hudson, the contents of the rational system of beliefs include the criteria of self-consistency, relevant evidence and open-minded belief that we have already noted; but they go beyond these to cover:

---

46. See below pp. 169-170, 272.

47. This "Contradiction Theory" claims that the laws of logic are "the necessary rules for thinking of or dealing with a *multiplicity* of separate items", "but in the One there are no separate items to be kept distinct, and therefore logic has no meaning for it". Walter T. Stace, *Mysticism and Philosophy* (London: Macmillan, 1961), pp. 270-271. Compare Joseph Runzo, *Reason, Relativism and God* (New York: St. Martin's Press; London: Macmillan, 1986), pp. 105-107.

48. Hudson, "The Rational System of Beliefs", pp. 82, 86, 94.

49. They are "regulative" in that "they regulate what it makes sense to say or do", and "generally-held" in that "general assent is given to them in our society" (*ibid.*, p. 81).

50. *Ibid.*, pp. 92, 97.

(1) "Propositions which are so fundamental to our world-view that we cannot form a conception of what would count as evidence against—or even for—them." An example would be the statement that things do not disappear when no one is observing them.[51]

(2) "Propositions which are fundamental to certain specific disciplines" such as science and history: so fundamental indeed that they cannot be doubted within their respective disciplines of thought. An example would be the claim that nature is uniform.[52]

(3) "Propositions . . . which are very widely and consistently taken for granted in our society" (e.g. that no one has been to Mars, that dogs feel pain).

(4) "Generally-accepted principles of action"—i.e. "regulative beliefs about what it is appropriate to do (or to choose)".[53] This category comprises logical and practical principles, the latter including both moral principles (e.g. "we ought to help the weak") and nonmoral or expedient principles (e.g. "only make agreements with people who can be relied upon").

Now the existence of such a rational system of beliefs illustrates the complexity of the notion of rationality and its vulnerability to change. Hudson argues that this change may come both through the "normative" application of certain criteria of rationality to the other parts of the rational system of beliefs and by "fortuitous" changes within that system that are not provoked by such critical reflection. We may note that this account seems to confirm our stress on the role of sociological factors in defining rationality, for such a rational system of belief is patently a system that is socially definable. It is the system of "our society". Rational education may be understood, therefore, as an induction into this system.

Can Religious Education be Rational?
Presumably our society may include among propositions of Hudson's class (3), agnostic (as opposed to atheistic) beliefs and statements to the effect that there may be "something in" religion and it is worth studying to find out what.[54] In this way the rational system of beliefs may allow that Christianity ought to be studied (even in publicly funded educational establishments) or "taken seriously", but forbid such a status to astrology or Norse mythology.[55]

51. *Ibid.*, p. 83. Hudson develops these categories from the writings of the later Wittgenstein. Wittgenstein suggests this example of category (1): see Ludwig Wittgenstein, *On Certainty*, ed. G. E. M. Anscombe and G. H. von Wright, trans. Denis Paul and G. E. M. Anscombe (New York: Harper, 1969; Oxford: Blackwell, 1974), paras. 119-125, 314.

52. Wittgenstein's examples also include the claim that the earth existed long before we were born (*On Certainty*, paras. 80-92, 233-243, 311, 315-330). Such fundamental assumptions have been called "epistemic primitives": see Ronald S. Laura and Michael Leahy, "Religious Upbringing and Rational Autonomy", *Journal of Philosophy of Education* 23: 2 (1989).

53. "The Rational System of Beliefs", p. 84.

54. *Ibid.*, pp. 96-97.

55. See David Attfield, "Is Religious Education Possible?", *Journal of Philosophy of Education* 12 (1978), pp. 96-97. Keith Dixon notes that the criterion being applied here may be one of the "moral seriousness" or "worth" of a belief system. See his *The Sociology of*

It is a matter of empirical fact as to whether there is sufficient agreement (but what counts as "sufficient"?) in society in these areas: agreement that would allow the espousal of religion, or even just its serious examination ("teaching about religion"), to be a rational undertaking.

But Hudson's account would allow the critic of the authoritarian religious educator to argue that such a person is inculcating—doubtless by particular methods—a set of beliefs that are not open to "*full* rational assessment", in so far as they include beliefs that deny the relevance of rational assessment by *this* criterion of conformity to the rational system of beliefs. For example, they may cast doubts in general terms on the ability of a sinful world to perceive saving truths or, more specifically, reject one or more of society's generally accepted beliefs.[56]

However, this strategy of demanding openness to the criterion of conformity to the rational system of beliefs as a feature of all learning outcomes can be met. By way of response, the putative indoctrinatory religious educator could argue first that even Hudson will allow that this is only *one* criterion of rationality. A belief that fails this test may still be accepted as rational if it subscribes to one (or more, Hudson isn't clear on this) of the other criteria, e.g. self-consistency.[57] Second, it might be said that the rational system of beliefs is wrong and should be changed in some particulars (Hudson's elements (3) and (4) are especially vulnerable here). Such a change may be made on "rational" grounds, for example because some beliefs are "contrary to the relevant evidence",[58] and here we are back to the problem of "relevant evidence". Alternatively the change might result from other causes (Hudson's "fortuitous factors"), and here no justification for such changes is required.

Those religious educators who discuss the indoctrination criticism may also raise questions about the significance of Hudson's criterion of conformity to a system of generally accepted beliefs by asking embarrassing questions about its generality. Appeals to "our society" may cover over the great diversity even within Western societies with regard to beliefs and principles that are taken for granted. Does *this criterion* exclude those who believe in horoscopes, ghosts, UFOs and the efficacy of luck-tokens—beliefs that are perhaps more prevalent than beliefs about the *universal* uniformity of nature? As most people are not very good at holding beliefs systematically, should their beliefs be included as part of a rational *system* of beliefs anyway?[59] When their beliefs "are discovered to be self-contradictory, or contrary to the relevant evidence" do they in fact "lose their hold" eventually "upon the majority"?[60] Moreover, may the criterion be modified, as in practice it seems to be, by those

---

Belief (London: Routledge & Kegan Paul, 1989), pp. 57-58, 119.

56. An example of the latter might be the rejection of those moral principles that lead many people to regard the penal substitution theory of the atonement as immoral.

57. "The Rational System of Beliefs", pp. 80-81.

58. *Ibid.*, p. 85.

59. See David Martin, *The Religious and the Secular* (London: Routledge & Kegan Paul, 1969), pp. 18-19.

60. "The Rational System of Beliefs", p. 85.

who are willing to accept as a criterion of rationality conformity to what is generally accepted only in a smaller grouping of society—e.g. my social class, my church, my political "ginger group"? Cognitive claims to religious truth, for example, are usually tested for rationality against *believers'* beliefs rather than against the beliefs of a secular society. There was a time when most people in Western society accepted such truth claims, but this is no longer the case. To say that they are no longer rational because of this is to invoke an explicitly sociological criterion. And that is to arrive where we started, but hopefully with an increased clarity (perhaps equivalent to T. S. Eliot's knowing "the place for the first time").

The gains of this particular circular (spiral?) journey have included, for example, the recognition that the program of demanding reasons and testing evidence must stop somewhere. This is very important in epistemology in general and in religious epistemology, and therefore religious education, in particular. In the first two kinds of belief listed above (p. 58) we have examples of fundamental principles of knowing without which *either* we cannot get going in our thinking at all *or* (class (2) propositions) we cannot move forward to make discoveries in particular disciplines. The point about such beliefs is that we do not hold them on evidence, or justify them by evidence, in quite the way that some accounts of indoctrination seem to imply that we should be willing to treat all our beliefs. It is with regard to such principles that the later Wittgenstein claimed that we "have reached bedrock" and our "spade is turned",[61] and that we must recognize that we have to put a stop somewhere to the continual search for justifications for our beliefs. Here all we can say is: this is what we believe. "This language-game"—and this form of life with its rules of language and of practice—"is played".[62] It is pre-eminently the later writings of Wittgenstein (and *not*, of course, his earlier views which were taken up by Logical Positivists and which he himself came to modify greatly) that put this point most forcefully. To quote Wittgenstein further:

> All testing, all confirmation and disconfirmation of a hypothesis takes place already within a system. And this system is not a more or less arbitrary and doubtful point of departure for all our arguments: no, it belongs to the essence of what we call an argument. The system is not so much the point of departure, as the element in which arguments have their life.

> As if giving grounds did not come to an end sometime. But the end is not an ungrounded presupposition: it is an ungrounded way of acting.[63]

---

61. Ludwig Wittgenstein, *Philosophical Investigations*, trans. G. E. M. Anscombe (Oxford: Blackwell, 1968), I, para. 217.

62. *Ibid.*, I, para. 654 (compare para. 655). For further explication of this position see Chapter 7 below.

63. *On Certainty*, paras. 105, 110; see also paras. 160-171, 191-192, 246-250, and C. J. B. Macmillan, "*On Certainty* and Indoctrination", *Synthese* 56: 3 (1983). We may note here that Tasos Kazepides draws very different conclusions from Wittgenstein's analysis of "river-

Teaching Religion and Teaching Science

It is interesting that Hudson argues that to teach people how to think religiously cannot be indoctrination, even on a content-criterion, merely because the cognitive dimension of theistic religion is based on ultimate presuppositions such as the existence of God "which must be taken on trust" (class (2) propositions in the list above). For the same is true, Hudson claims, of other disciplines such as science and history.[64] He seems to suggest that there may be "reasons" for entering into some of these disciplines/forms of life and accepting their presuppositions, but that such reasons may not be the same in each case, and in no case are they *evidence* for the presuppositions. Thus science may be chosen because it extends our understanding and control over nature, religion (partly at least?) because it "enriches . . . the existence of those who embrace it". Both subjects "deliver the goods", but they deliver different goods.[65]

The critic of the teaching of religion will need to respond in one of three ways. One way would be to attack the view that the fundamental presupposition of religion (or of explanatory theology) is, because of this status, immune from rational criticism. The existence of God, he might say, *is* like a scientific existential hypothesis and thus we do know what counts for or against it.[66] It would be indoctrinatory, therefore, to teach this proposition so that it is held without regard to such evidence. Alternatively such a critic may claim that society "does science", i.e. it explains things in terms of the uniformity of nature, but it does not in general explain things in terms of God's existence. Hence the fundamental principle of theistic thinking is to be excluded from the (our) rational system of beliefs. (Not all the fundamental principles of all possible disciplines are to be included here, but only those that society actually approves of and follows. Alchemy also has its fundamental presuppositions, but modern Western society in general does not do alchemy.) A third, slightly different, reply could be that the group of propositions that are very widely and consistently taken for granted actually includes a *denial* of the existence of God, and that belief therefore cannot be included in our society's system of rational beliefs.[67]

---

bed propositions". Kazepides admits that they "enable us to think", but adds that this should be distinguished from religious doctrines which "act as *stoppers* that control, limit and channel free thought" ("Religious Indoctrination and Freedom", p. 13).

64. W. D. Hudson, "Trusting to Reason", *New Universities Quarterly* (Spring 1980), p. 252. See also W. D. Hudson, "Is Religious Education Possible?", in Langford and O'Connor, eds., *New Essays in the Philosophy of Education*, pp. 169-184 and "The Loneliness of the Religious Educator", in J. G. Priestley, ed., *Religion, Spirituality and Schools* (Exeter, England: University of Exeter, 1982), p. 29. This is clearly a rather restrictive account of religious thinking. It fits best the explanatory, systematic, disciplined reflection of theology. Hudson's argument is considered in more detail in Chapter 7 below. See also R. S. Laura, "To Educate or To Indoctrinate: That is Still the Question", in *Educational Philosophy and Theory* 15: 1 (1983), and Leahy, "Indoctrination, Evangelism, Catechesis and Religious Education", pp. 141-142.

65. Hudson, "The Loneliness of the Religious Educator", pp. 29-31.

66. Despite Hudson, *ibid.*, p. 28.

67. Compare references in note 55 above.

When it comes to defending the rationality of religious education, therefore, Hudson's general claims about the rationality of beliefs are more useful than his particular proposals in defense of the teaching of theistic thinking. Christian religious education must seek stronger arguments against the indoctrination criticism.

INDOCTRINATION AND THE THEORY OF KNOWLEDGE

The Search for Certainty

In the past epistemology was always turning up some beliefs that it claimed to be basic and foundational in the sense that they were regarded as the foundations of all other knowledge. These foundations were the self-evident truths of reason and the immediately-known incorrigible propositions that report sense experience. Philosophers who search for such certainties "think that once they have found this basis they can go on to justify at least some of their beliefs, but that without it there can be no defence against scepticism. Unless something is certain, we are told, nothing can be even probable."[68] For various reasons this position, which has been described as classical philosophical foundationalism, has had a bad press of late.[69] We may note, however, that it too—in a style rather different from the Wittgensteinian one espoused by Hudson and others—recognized that the demand for evidence, and therefore "openness to conflicting evidence", must stop somewhere. In classical foundationalism probable beliefs justified by inference are seen as needing (eventually) to be supported by noninferential beliefs that are certain. Some critics of foundationalism, on the other hand, hold that there are no such infallible beliefs, at least not any with any content.[70] A version of foundationalism may survive this criticism, however, if it maintains "that knowledge has foundations but it does not regard them as absolutely solid and incorrigible".[71]

The value of foundationalism in epistemology is the way that it draws attention to the proper limits of skepticism. For example Bertrand Russell's

---

68. A. J. Ayer, *Philosophical Essays* (London: Macmillan; New York: St. Martin's Press, 1954), p. 105.

69. See D. W. Hamlyn, *The Theory of Knowledge* (London: Macmillan, 1970), ch. 10; Jonathan Dancy, *An Introduction to Contemporary Epistemology* (Oxford: Blackwell, 1985), ch. 4; Nicholas Wolterstorff, "Introduction", and Alvin Plantinga, "Reason and Belief in God", in Alvin Plantinga and Nicholas Wolterstorff, eds., *Faith and Rationality* (Notre Dame, Ind.: University of Notre Dame Press, 1983); Richard Rorty, *Philosophy and the Mirror of Nature* (Princeton: Princeton University Press, 1979; Oxford: Blackwell, 1980), *passim*; D. Z. Phillips, *Faith after Foundationalism* (London and New York: Routledge, 1988), Part One.

70. Dancy, *An Introduction to Contemporary Epistemology*, p. 60. Arthur Danto writes, "There is knowledge only if, after having attained understanding, it is open whether what we understand is true or false. ... Quests for certainty ... forfeit, at once, the possibility of attaining knowledge. ... Truth does not lie *beyond* truth-and-falsity." Arthur C. Danto, *Analytical Philosophy of Knowledge* (Cambridge: Cambridge University Press, 1968), pp. 181-182.

71. Anthony Quinton, *The Nature of Things* (London: Routledge & Kegan Paul, 1973), p. 231.

"basic propositions"—which are "caused, as immediately as possible, by perceptive experiences"—are "such that, if questioned [they] will be defended by the argument 'why, I see it' or something similar".[72] In such cases, Russell licenses us to speak almost in the way that religious indoctrinators are said to speak: "No previous or subsequent occurrence, and no experience of others, can prove the falsehood of this proposition".[73] For Russell such a proposition *may* be false, but it cannot be proved to be false. Judgments that are made by commonsense on the basis of perception, because they go beyond it, may be shaken by conflicting evidence; but there cannot be a similar shaking of the "evidence of the senses". Here the foundationalist has a valuable insight, provided that it is not interpreted too rigidly.

It may be useful at this point to distinguish between the notions of incorrigibility and indubitability. If a statement is *incorrigible* then we cannot be in error in believing it. It is not "open to correction". Indubitability makes a lesser claim. A statement may be *indubitable*, in the sense that it cannot rationally be doubted or rejected, although the statement is itself corrigible. It is just that no one could ever have a reason to doubt it. Foundationalist philosophers have usually argued that basic propositions are incorrigible. These are statements that describe the present contents of one's experience, e.g. "I have a headache" or "I see a blue patch". But others more plausibly claim that all descriptive statements run some risk of being in error, of being misdescriptions or misidentifications, even those that describe the content of direct experiences.[74] Patently all experiences are certain in the sense that when we have them we are certain that we have them, but "the moment you try to *describe* the experience in words . . . you are going beyond the momentary sense-datum that you are attempting to report. A possibility of error thus arises in the very act of using language."[75] Hence no such statement can be incorrigible.

Yet even though there can be no "logical guarantee that our acceptance of a statement is not mistaken", it is not the case that nothing is therefore really *certain*. Careful philosophers note that "there are a great many statements the truth of which we rightly do not doubt; and it is perfectly correct to say that they are certain. We should not be bullied by the sceptic into renouncing an expression for which we have a legitimate use. . . . [The sceptic's] victory is empty. He robs us of certainty only by so defining it as to make it certain that it cannot be obtained."[76]

All of this, I think, is relevant to the question of evidence and therefore of

---

72. Bertrand Russell, *An Inquiry into Meaning and Truth* (Harmondsworth, England: Penguin, 1962), pp. 130-131.

73. *Ibid.*, p. 132.

74. A. J. Ayer, *The Problem of Knowledge* (Harmondsworth, England: Penguin, 1956), pp. 52-57.

75. John Hospers, *An Introduction to Philosophical Analysis* (London: Routledge & Kegan Paul, 1967), p. 542. See also Don Locke, *Perception and Our Knowledge of the External World* (London: Allen & Unwin, 1967), pp. 191-192.

76. Ayer, *The Problem of Knowledge*, p. 68.

indoctrination. Even our most secure beliefs about our own sense experiences run the risk of error; but this is, as it were, a technical error—a philosophical risk, rather than a practical one. Any philosopher who refused to swear in court that the traffic lights were "certainly" red, because no such knowledge claim could be "certain", would be guilty of confusing the court by misusing the word. For such a person it would be a technical term, for the rest of us it is a term of practical decision making. If pressed by a philosophical prosecuting attorney the philosophical witness would doubtless be willing to admit that there are many things that are "beyond reasonable doubt" which are in fact strictly corrigible. This is what the word "certain" means. "When we use the word 'certain' in ordinary speech we do not mean incorrigible; we mean beyond reasonable doubt. There is a normative element about the word, it asserts that the statements it is applied to do not *need* any further justification, that it is *right* to act on them with complete confidence, that it would be *irrational* to doubt them . . . . Even if it is logically possible that it is false and it is conceivable that it should turn out that it is false it does not follow that there is any reason to think that it actually is false."[77]

If we return now to those philosophers who are more influenced by the later Wittgenstein we find an even stronger presentation of this case. Norman Malcolm says of statements such as "here is an ink-bottle" and "5 x 5 = 25" that they lie beyond the reach of doubt:

> On both, my judgement and reasoning *rests*. If you could somehow undermine my confidence in either, you would not teach me *caution*. You would fill my mind with chaos! . . . If it is not a certainty that 5 x 5 = 25 and that here is an ink-bottle, then I do not understand what it is. You cannot make me doubt either of these statements or treat them as hypotheses. You cannot persuade me that future experience could refute them. With both of them it is perfectly unintelligible to me to speak of a "possibility" that they are false. This is to say that I know both of them to be true, in the strong sense of "know". . . . When *I* say that I know something to be so, using "know" in the strong sense, it is unintelligible *to me* (although perhaps not to others) to suppose that anything could prove that it is not so and, therefore, that I do not know it.[78]

This is perhaps to go too far.[79] But we have to take account of the fact that, although skepticism is always a theoretical possibility with every knowledge claim, some knowledge claims are practically immune from the attacks of future conflicting evidence.[80] In these cases it is just silly to teach them as

---

77. Quinton, *The Nature of Things*, p. 148; also p. 171.

78. Norman Malcolm, "Knowledge and Belief", in A. Phillips Griffiths, ed., *Knowledge and Belief* (Oxford: Oxford University Press, 1967), pp. 79, 81; see also p. 74.

79. See Danto, *Analytical Philosophy of Knowledge*, pp. 107-114.

80. It should be noted that the later Wittgenstein distinguishes between what we can doubt and what we cannot along these lines: "the *questions* that we raise and our *doubts* depend on the fact that some propositions are exempt from doubt, are as it were like hinges on which those

if they were not ("practically"?) certain. Is this improper education? Surely it is not.

Now this insight has a quite general applicability, which I wish to develop shortly. With regard to the concerns of the Christian religious educator, however, it is appropriate to point out here that questions of doubt and certainty have bedeviled the teaching of religion. Some insight into what is meant by the word "certain" in ordinary language might help the religious educator avoid many pitfalls when the word is used with regard to the cognitive content and cognitive outcomes of Christian religious education.

Education, Evidence and Religion

Epistemology is often concerned with limiting the pretensions of the skeptic, and this is important in any consideration of the limits of indoctrination. If a religious educator were to hold up (say) a New Testament or a chalice, would she or he be guilty of indoctrinating the learners by creating in them some firm—although rather trivial—beliefs about those objects, beliefs that would be highly resistant to erosion by contrary "evidence"? If the original evidence for a belief (e.g. "the New Testament is made up of 27 books" or "the wine in the chalice is red") is of a certain kind, e.g. examining a physical object closely in a good light, the resulting belief is normally, and quite properly, held so firmly that it is extremely unlikely that *any* future evidence would be able to change it. If this is indoctrination, is it not essential to learning?

The standard response to such a criticism is that it misinterprets the intentions of those who wish to distinguish between rational education and indoctrination. It may be argued that in the case of sense experience, with respect to purported basic statements that refer to immediate sensation (e.g. "this is a red patch") and perhaps even the commonsense statements erected on their basis (e.g. "this is red wine"), the charge of indoctrination finds no purchase since such beliefs *are* held according to the relevant evidence. These beliefs represent paradigm cases of beliefs open to full rational assessment, even if they are unshakable, because the positive evidence in their favor is always stronger than any possible future negative evidence against them. This is certainly so—at least from a particular epistemological perspective. But then we have to be very careful in plotting the limits of indoctrination to acknowledge our particular perspective. This is especially true for the Christian religious educator's acknowledgement of the particular perspective of religious understanding.

Limiting this exercise will surely not do. It can be claimed that certain beliefs do noncontroversially escape the indoctrination criticism. They include particular perceptual beliefs (which always involve interpretation

---

turn . . . it belongs to the logic of our scientific investigations that certain things are *indeed* not doubted . . . We just *can't* investigate everything, and . . . are forced to rest content with assumption. If I want the door to turn, the hinges must stay put." Wittgenstein, *On Certainty*, paras. 341-343.

that "goes beyond the [sense data] evidence"), together with more general "natural beliefs" or "framework propositions"[81] that we cannot help holding about the existence of the external world: beliefs which make metaphysical claims—e.g. about realism.[82] It may be that we should agree with Thomas Reid that we "may as soon, by reasoning, pull the moon out of her orbit, as destroy the belief of the objects of sense".[83] But does that mean that skepticism here is impossible, and therefore indoctrination irrelevant, whereas the case of *religious beliefs* is radically different?

Some theists have claimed that religious experience is similarly indubitable evidence for some religious believers, and that their religious belief is thus a sort of supernatural natural belief: that they are so constituted as not to be able to help themselves believing.[84] Alvin Plantinga's argument that belief in God is a "properly basic belief" presents a similar claim.[85] If this is the case then Christian religious education that resulted in the learning of that belief, either directly or via the evocation of religious experience, would similarly escape the indoctrination criticism. Dismissing such arguments gratuitously may reveal more about the critic than it does about the arguments.[86] The evidence for religion is not the same as the evidence for non-controversial perceptual beliefs, but that does not allow the critic of rational Christian religious education to rule it out of court as evidence (see Chapter 6 for some further reflections on religious experience).

---

81. See David Hume, *A Treatise of Human Nature* (1739), ed. L. A. Selby-Bigge (London: Oxford University Press, 1888), p. 187; compare Norman Kemp Smith, *The Philosophy of David Hume* (London: Macmillan; New York: St. Martin's Press, 1964), chs. XXI and XXII.

82. See also Kai Nielsen, "Religion and Groundless Believing", in Joseph Runzo and Craig K. Ihara, eds., *Religious Experience and Religious Belief: Essays in the Epistemology of Religion* (Lanham, MD: University Press of America, 1986), pp. 23-24.

83. Thomas Reid, Essay II, ch. XX: "Of the Evidence of Sense, and of Belief in General", in *Essays on the Intellectual Powers of Man* (1785), ed. A. D. Woozley (London: Macmillan, 1941), p. 181.

84. See John Hick, *Faith and Knowledge* (Ithaca, N.Y.: Cornell University Press, 1966; London: Collins, 1974), ch. 6 and *An Interpretation of Religion* (New Haven: Yale University Press; London: Macmillan, 1989), pp. 213-229.

85. Plantinga, "Reason and Belief in God". See also his "On Taking Belief in God as Basic", in Runzo and Ihara, eds., *Religious Experience and Religious Belief*. For critiques of Plantinga see R. W. Hepburn, "Attitudes to Evidence and Argument in the Field of Religion", in Roger Straughan and John Wilson, eds., *Philosophers on Education* (Basingstoke: Macmillan, 1987), pp. 135-139; Phillips, *Faith after Foundationalism*, Part One; and Caroline Franks Davis, *The Evidential Force of Religious Experience* (Oxford: Oxford University Press, 1989), pp. 86-92. See also Robert Audi, "Direct Justification, Evidential Dependence, and Theistic Belief", in Robert Audi and William J. Wainwright, eds., *Rationality, Religious Belief, and Moral Commitment* (Ithaca: Cornell University Press, 1986).

86. As our discussion of the "content-criterion" shows (see pp. 46-47), many philosophers wish to restrict the stigma of indoctrination to belief systems—ideologies or metaphysics—and do not regard it as applying to perceptual beliefs. It should be reiterated, however, that to interpret sense experience as experience of an externally existing object is already to commit oneself to a metaphysical system (realism).

Moral Education

Perhaps similar arguments may be developed with reference to some of the profounder elements of moral knowledge: those deep "intuitions" of value that are held in a firm and fixed way, and are often admired because they are so held. Such moral insights are often evoked by Christian religious educators. "It may seem", one might say—and be applauded for saying, "that *in this case* there are 'strong reasons' against my view that torturing children is wrong, but I shall stick to my principles". "Furthermore," a parent might continue, "because I cannot conceive of any evidence that *should* count decisively against this view" (or, for example, the view that discriminating against people because of the color of their skin is wrong), "I am entitled to believe that there can be no such evidence, and therefore entitled to 'indoctrinate' my children into these beliefs so that they will be firmly fixed in them."

The structure of the parent's argument is as follows. It appears that it is right for my children (and myself) to hold such moral beliefs firmly and unwaveringly whatever the apparent evidence against them, on the grounds that (I believe) there could never really be *any* evidence that counted, or counted decisively, against them. If that is the case, the implication seems to be that it is right for me to *ensure* that they hold these beliefs in this way. Indeed it would seem on this view that I have a moral duty to indoctrinate such beliefs, and this would override whatever (merely prudential?) duty I might also have to make my children more generally provisional, tentative or open in their beliefs. *That* would only be a good thing in certain circumstances, and those circumstances do not here obtain. This is certainly a more controversial claim than the one we have made for empirical beliefs, but again it would not be without its defenders.

It could still be argued, however, that this discussion is once more ignoring the heart of the criticism of indoctrination. A commentator may allow that sense experience beliefs and moral beliefs are not to be regarded as indoctrinated beliefs, despite their unshakableness and their peculiar relationship to future evidence, and yet continue to argue that there are other candidates which *do* deserve to fall victim to the criticism of indoctrination. The set of such suspect beliefs might still include the more explicitly religious claims that make up much of the cognitive content of Christian religious education.

Thinking about Religion

The criterion of indoctrination remains a formal one. To give it content we need to spell out what is meant by phrases like "full rational assessment" and "open to falsification by counter evidence". The content we give to these phrases will vary with the nature of the beliefs being considered. It is not clear that they would (could) have the same meaning in the case of religious beliefs that they have when applied to beliefs reporting sense experience, or beliefs incorporating scientific or historical theories, or even moral beliefs. Yet again we are forced back to considerations of the rational status of religious beliefs, and to detailed comparisons between such beliefs and other candidates for the indoctrination criticism, such as political beliefs, as well as apparently more acceptable educationally beliefs like those provided by history, the sciences and mathematics. This explains why the content-criterion for indoctrination has appealed to some philosophers, for it allows them to legislate in advance of learning outcomes as to the acceptability of teaching. This legislation is based on their own prior views of the logical status, and epistemological worthiness, of different beliefs. But such legislation inevitably remains highly controversial.

It might seem that one way to escape these problems would be to introduce into our discussion of indoctrination some explicit reflection on the *value of thinking* and, particularly, of people thinking-for-themselves and reflecting on their beliefs.[87] This may be regarded as an intrinsically valuable aspect of educated persons (valuable in and of itself), and/or as instrumentally valuable—in that it is likely to give rise to intrinsically valuable achievements like knowledge and understanding.[88] Adopting this view, the Christian religious educator may wonder how far critical reflection should form a part of Christian religious education. A number of points, however, may be raised in connection with this discussion

First, such values, if accepted, may need to be balanced against other intrinsic and instrumental goods that result from the educational enterprise in general, and the religious education enterprise in particular. Happiness, fulfillment, "peace of mind", close human relationships, or even particular religious attitudes, virtues or beliefs, will be esteemed by some more highly than autonomous, critical thinking. It may be the case (this is an empirical claim) that in certain situations the development of such attributes may be thwarted by this sort of thinking. Furthermore, although we feel that it is surely (in John Stuart Mill's words) "better to be Socrates dissatisfied than a fool satisfied",[89] this is only obviously true for those who are capable of being Socrates and are not by nature or nurture inevitably in the other category.[90] But are these the only two—rather extremely and emotively designated—end products of education? Most people are to be placed rather more in the middle of the spectrum. They are not fools. Yet many of them may not

---

87. See Wilson, in Snook, ed., *Concepts of Indoctrination*, p. 23; White, in *ibid.*, p. 200. Also Hare, "Adolescents into Adults", p. 52.

88. R. S. Peters, "The Justification of Education", in Peters, ed., *The Philosophy of Education*. See above Chapter 3.

89. As it is "better to be a human being dissatisfied than a pig satisfied": John Stuart Mill, *Utilitarianism* (1861), ch. II, ed. Mary Warnock (London: Collins, 1962), p. 260. I would agree with Hanfling that "it seems impossible to produce reasons . . . to prove that the human and Socratic lives really are superior to their alternatives. Our preference for the life of reason cannot itself be supported by reason." Oswald Hanfling, *The Quest for Meaning* (Oxford: Blackwell, 1987), pp. 144-145.

90. Mill assumes that Socrates *chooses* the Socratic life, but according to others "Socrates has no more choice in this matter than the pig" (see above note). Once his faculty of critical reflection has arisen Socrates is no longer capable of the "innocent piggishness of the pig". Robert C. Solomon, *The Passions* (Notre Dame, Ind.: University of Notre Dame Press, 1983), p. 22 footnote.

be, indeed patently are not, capable of the sort of valuable critical thinking that some liberal educationists recommend as universally possible and desirable. It is not unarguably the case that *for everyone* "the unexamined life is not worth living".[91] This may be particularly so in the case of the religious life.

Second, notions such as "thinking for yourself" remain highly context dependent, and therefore controversial. Indoctrinators *also* wish to produce people who will think-for-themselves, but only in the sense that they commit themselves to the transmitted doctrine X—i.e. "think-X-for-themselves". Whether or not we wish to regard this as "autonomy" in thinking is an open question (see below Chapter 8). What the critic of indoctrination is after here, however, is a *certain sort of thinking*: rational, critical, open thinking. This is thinking that is more risky, open-ended and uncommitted than the indoctrinator will allow. We shall have to accept that the difference between them is a matter of degree, and by no means a clear-cut distinction. We shall also need to acknowledge that "critical openness" means different things in different areas, to different people (see below Chapter 5).

Third, the broad definition of Christian religious education that I wish to adopt includes both "formative education" and "critical education" under its umbrella (see Chapter 1 and Chapter 5). Much discussion in education centers on the importance of critical education: the analysis and evaluation of knowledge claims. Yet education in general—and Christian religious education in particular—should recognize that, logically and psychologically, the formation of a person's identity and worldview must happen before such criticism can develop. Education first and foremost has a person-making function. Education makes persons, and Christian religious education makes Christian persons, and this necessitates that we learn to *be* someone. (Clearly we need to become someone-with-a-viewpoint before we can assess other people and their viewpoints; and certainly before we can be critical about, and rationally change, ourselves and our beliefs.)

WHAT IS WRONG WITH INDOCTRINATION?

Perhaps we should be willing to accept that indoctrination, according to the definition we have accepted, is not always and everywhere a "bad thing". Many would argue that on the liberal education to authoritarian education continuum described by Willis Moore, the wise educator will move to critical education from formative-indoctrinatory teaching in response to the increasing age and maturity of her learners.[92] Basil Mitchell justifies such a (movable) middle position on the grounds that "the liberal ideal of the wholly autonomous rational individual subjecting all his beliefs to criticism and

---

91. Despite Socrates (Plato, *Apology*, 38a) and Edward Hulmes ("Developing a Critical Faculty in Religious Education", *Occasional Papers* 9, Oxford: Farmington Institute, n.d., p. 1). See Peters, "The Justification of Education", p. 253.

92. Moore, in Snook, ed., *Concepts of Indoctrination*, p. 97. See also Gabriel Moran, *Religious Education as a Second Language* (Birmingham, Ala.: Religious Education Press, 1989), pp. 172-173.

retaining only those that survive the test cannot be realized. Every individual grows to maturity in a cultural tradition and cannot produce a rational 'philosophy' of his own from scratch."[93] Mitchell applauds the sensible educator as one who will not expect or intend to produce an educated adult who has no beliefs, values, or attitudes which that person cannot rationally defend against all comers, or who is "incapable of settled convictions, deep-seated virtues, or profound loyalties". But neither will the sensible educator produce adults "with closed minds and restricted sympathies". Mitchell writes:

> The process of being educated is like learning to build a house by actually building one and then having to live in the house one has built. It is a process in which the individual inevitably requires help. The extreme authoritarian helps by building the house himself according to what he believes to be the best plan and making the novice live in it. He designs it in such a way as to make it as difficult as possible for the novice to alter it. The extreme liberal leaves the novice to find his own materials and devise his own plan, for fear of exercising improper influence. The most he will do is provide strictly technical information if asked. The sensible educator helps the novice to build the best house he can (in the light of accumulated experience). He strikes a balance between the need to produce a good house and the desirability of letting the novice make his own choices; but he is careful that the house is designed in such a way that it can subsequently be altered and improved as the owner, no longer a novice, sees fit.

(We may note the evaluative judgments implied by "improved" and "sees fit".) Quoting Gilbert Murray's comment on Euripides, to the effect that learners with real vitality are the resultant of two forces—one forming them in a tradition and the other making them rebels against it, Mitchell concludes: "The liberal wants to make sure that we produce rebels; the authoritarian that we do not produce rebels. The sensible educator is concerned to produce good rebels."[94]

In the face of such a blurring of the education/indoctrination border, it may be desirable for critics of indoctrination to withdraw their troops back

---

93. *The Fourth R*, p. 357. In addition, Mitchell argues, (a) society depends on shared beliefs, values and attitudes and would suffer if the individual feels that they have no claim on him unless he can validate them for himself; and (b) the erosion of shared beliefs by "rational" criticism leaves an empty space in the individual or societal home that is likely to be filled by the devils of current fashion, rather than the good spirits of reason. In these remarks Mitchell shows himself to be far more realistic than the advocates of unrestricted rational criticism.

94. *Ibid.*, p. 358. See also Hare, "Adolescents into Adults", pp. 69-70. William Frankena puts it slightly differently: "education involves initiation in traditions of thought and action while aiming at creating individuals who can and will make new advances within those traditions". William K. Frankena, "The Concept of Education Today", in Doyle, ed., *Educational Judgments*, p. 31. See also R. T. Allen, "Rational Autonomy: the destruction of freedom", *Journal of Philosophy of Education* 16: 2 (1982), pp. 203-206.

to a lesser claim. This might be that a person has been indoctrinated *in a way that should be regarded as morally and educationally (and religiously?) wrong* if she has become (and has been taught to be) unable or unwilling, whether consciously or not, to think about her beliefs at all, or to relate them to other evidence, even when she accepts that to do so would be appropriate. We may regard such a person as lacking something that is a valuable attribute of human beings. That "something" may be described as intellectual autonomy, responsibility or accountability.[95] Her agency has been diminished by her beliefs, attitudes and values having been "corrupted by being cemented in".[96] They are not really hers, in the way that they would be if she were able and willing to reflect on them and subject them to her own rational appraisal (whatever that is, and however others may assess it). Indoctrination, it has been said, "in that it necessarily involves lack of respect for an individual's rationality is morally unacceptable", for indoctrinators essentially "treat their audience as means" and not as ends in themselves.[97]

Indoctrination understood along these lines remains the teaching of "fixed beliefs", and religious indoctrination the teaching of fixed religious beliefs. It may be argued, however, that such indoctrination is only to be regarded as regrettable when and where *the learner* wishes (or feels he ought) to modify or open up these beliefs to change.[98]

Two comments on this position may be made from one side of the discussion. First that it is possible to claim that it is not always "better", at least not in every way, to think for yourself. It is more important to think correctly: to hold *true* beliefs and morally (or at least prudentially) *right* attitudes and values. The religious educator is particularly likely to make such a claim. Autonomy may be an intrinsic good, but it is not always instrumentally a good thing in the educational enterprise, nor is it the only intrinsically good human quality. The second response is that we must be very cautious in ascribing too much freedom to human beings with regard to their holding of attitudes, beliefs and values. This is a very large issue, to be considered in Chapter 8 below. Suffice it to say at this point that freedom of belief is not on a par with freedom of choice or action, whether in terms of the philosophical analysis

95. We might say (adapting George Herbert Mead's distinction between an individual's active, asocial "I"-self and her fully socialized "me" part of the self) that such a person has been "oversocialized"—"the 'me' seems to have overwhelmed the 'I' so completely that to all intents and purposes its creative and impulsive energy has been eliminated". Krishan Kumar, in Dan Cohn-Sherbok and Michael Irwin, eds., *Exploring Reality* (London: Allen & Unwin, 1987), p. 55.

96. Kleinig, *Philosophical Issues in Education*, p. 65. This does not imply, however, that an indoctrinated person would not know that he had been indoctrinated—despite Alex R. Rodger, *Education and Faith in an Open Society* (Edinburgh: Handsel, 1982), p. 27.

97. Barrow and Woods, *An Introduction to Philosophy of Education*, p. 77.

98. Thus my concept of indoctrination does not *per se* have pejorative or morally unacceptable connotations. It is only wrong under certain circumstances. Contrast Elmer J. Thiessen, "Indoctrination and Religious Education", *Interchange* 15: 3 (1984), pp. 27-43 and his *Teaching for Commitment: Liberal Education, Indoctrination and Christian Nurture* (Montreal: McGill-Queen's University Press; Leominster, England: Fowler Wright, 1993).

we can give of it, the evidence for it, or its value.

A counter-response to these comments from the opposite side of the debate may include the following claims. One is that autonomy is not the only human good, but it is one of them. It may have to be balanced against others such as happiness, knowledge, and personal and moral virtues, but it must always be brought into the equation. "All other things being equal" it will bulk large in that equation, at least where the learners both are "capable of it" and also recognize its importance—i.e. where their own natures lead them to reflect on their beliefs.[99] If indoctrination restricts such autonomy—and it does seem that, sometimes at least, those who intend indoctrination aim at preventing the development of this autonomy—that is a serious fault, although it is not the only sin that education can commit.[100]

The second counter-argument might begin by recognizing that "free" may be the wrong word to describe the educated man and woman's relationship to their beliefs, let alone their attitudes and values. It may admit that freedom only belongs to actions, and only very indirectly to cognitive and affective states. But it will continue by claiming that we should still be willing to speak of our "outer freedom" in these areas: that is our being externally unconstrained and thus able to express and fulfill our beliefs and desires (whatever their internal source). Here the parallel with freedom of choice and action is with talk about smiling bridegrooms being "free" to marry—because not restricted or compelled by fathers with shotguns; or released prisoners having gained their "freedom" from locked cells. This is language that we can quite properly engage in without overplaying the freedom card and certainly without reference to metaphysical subtleties about free will and determinism.[101] In this context, it provides us with an "output-", rather than an "input-", notion of freedom of belief and attitude. This freedom, at least, is a possible reality; and one that should be valued.

Taking up particularly this second response, one may comment that perhaps a learned inability or unwillingness to consult evidence or question my own beliefs, *even when (in my better moments) I admit to the relevance of such evidence or the propriety of such questioning*, is rather like a constraint put on me from outside myself that affects my ability to express my own

---

99. And, perhaps, where the *nature* of the beliefs (in the case of religious, moral or political belief systems) is such that they may be regarded as *personal* beliefs which properly should "ultimately rest on an individual's acceptance or rejection". Chazan, "'Indoctrination' and Religious Education", pp. 420-422.

100. Miller, The *Theory of Christian Education Practice*, pp. 174-175. Many deny that indoctrination is properly "education", adopting a normative view of education—see *ibid.*, pp. 180, 279-280, but contrast above Chapter 3. See also Moran, *Religious Education as a Second Language*, p. 218.

101. See Antony Flew, "Divine Omnipotence and Human Freedom", in Antony Flew and Alasdair MacIntyre, eds., *New Essays in Philosophical Theology* (London: SCM, 1955), pp. 149-150; Anthony Kenny, *Freewill and Responsibility* (London: Routledge & Kegan Paul, 1978), pp. 31-34. Such a view of freedom was held by Thomas Hobbes, David Hume and John Stuart Mill. It has been labeled "soft-determinism" or "decisionism".

personality and agency *in ways that I really feel are proper to me*. If we retain such references to the learner's sense of what his own rationality requires of him (compare Hudson's "what he believes to be good evidence for his belief") and what it would be for him to hold a belief *fully* as his own, then many of the proper criticisms of the notion of indoctrination are met. The result is an account that licenses the Christian religious educator, along with the secular educator, to allow instances of indoctrination ("acceptable indoctrination"), but also to limit—quite strictly—the application of indoctrinatory methods so as to to avoid "unacceptable indoctrination". *But the focus is now on a person's sense of responsibility for his/her own beliefs and reasoning, rather than on some impersonal, universal canons of rationality.*

One criticism that can be made of this position is that it implies that the (earlier and) more thorough the indoctrination, and the earlier it occurs in the learner's life, the less offensive it is.[102] It might be said that, according to my account, if we catch them early enough and indoctrinate them thoroughly enough they will never feel the need to think: self-critical reflection will never develop as an element of their mental nature. Surely, it will be said, everyone needs to develop the capacity to be self-critical, although not everybody needs very often to be self-critical. My response can only be that each person is to be judged on his/her own merits and that there must be no *a priori* assumptions, particularly in Christian religious education, as to which capacities and abilities an individual is capable of, or which will become for that individual a real part of their individuality, their personhood or their sense of self-responsibility.

Formative initiation into the ways of a culture or tradition is inevitably the major element in the education of young children. I am happy to describe much of this as (laudatory?) indoctrination. Others would argue that a charge of indoctrination (construed perjoratively) is inapplicable under these circumstances, in what Elmer Thiessen calls the "initial initiation phase of liberal education".[103] After that initial period it is proper for all learners to experience some critical education which seeks to develop their capacity for critical reflection, in Christian religious education as elsewhere. But educators need carefully to monitor and assess the learners' potential for and

---

102. This objection and the next one were presented sharply to me by Richard Smith. I fear that he may not judge that I have adequately met them.

103. Thiessen argues that our notion of liberal education should be reconstructed so as to recognize both a transmissionist initiation and a rational/critical phase. Elmer John Thiessen, "Two Concepts or Two Phases of Liberal Education?", *Journal of Philosophy of Education* 21: 2 (1987), pp. 223-234; and "Christian Nurture, Indoctrination and Liberal Education", in Jeff Astley and David Day, eds., *The Contours of Christian Education* (Great Wakering, England: McCrimmon, 1992). See also Marie Schilling, "Knowledge and Liberal Education: A Critique of Paul Hirst", *Curriculum Studies* 18: 1 (1986) and T. H. McLaughlin, "Parental Rights and the Religious Upbringing of Children", *Journal of Philosophy of Education* 18: 1 (1984). I prefer to speak of formative and critical education, rather than of initiation and rational criticism (see below Chapter 5).

readiness for such rational reflection. Some people have an enormous capacity for it and (therefore?) it is an essential element of their personhood. For many others, however, the development of critical reflection will never be more than a small component—a minor outcome among the effects of their education. A substantial proportion of the population may not be capable of it at all.

In principle, many would argue, we should all be taught to think critically, in so far as we are capable of thought at all; as we should all be taught to write, draw, do arithmetic, develop our motor skills and muscles, play music, read, care, empathize, appreciate beauty, and so on. Sensitive educators will use their experience and perceptiveness in assessing a learner's potential in each of these areas, and in many others. No doubt every person should be educated so as to develop *as fully as is possible and proper* all her or his potentialities that we value. But that does not mean that each of them will be developed to the same degree. The degree of "possible and proper" development of each potentiality should depend *both* on the learner's in-built structure of capacities (some learners are not capable of much self-critical thought) *and*, I would suggest, on the learner's developing felt "investment in", "ownership of" and "valuing of" these capacities. "The fascinating thing here is not just the capacity, but the interest which goes with it. Our faculties demand use; we need to do what we are fitted for."[104] But not always. I repeat: for some, critical reasoning is essential to their sense of being who they are. But it is not so for many others. The same arguments apply to the development of dramatic skills, mathematical skills, geographical or scriptural knowledge, skills of artistic expression, etc. They may also apply to the development of attitudes, religious and otherwise. Critical reflection is but one among many learning outcomes. For many people it is not among the most valued.

A further criticism of the position argued here is that my analysis of being self-critical and thinking about one's beliefs might appear to be an "all-or-nothing" account. Yet within the range of human beliefs there are some that *everyone* should think about, in particular beliefs that relate to our attitudes to others. To do this is not to scrutinize one's entire belief system, but it is a reflection that is not likely to be restricted to isolated beliefs (because of the interrelationship between beliefs). I accept this point: it fits in with the argument about the rational system of beliefs used earlier. Critical reflection is more appropriate at some times, when focused on some beliefs, than at other times and with regard to other beliefs. It may be that being critically reflective of the beliefs that relate to our attitudes to and relationship with others is one capacity that we ought to try to develop in most people—in so far as their potentialities and interests allow. This is relevant to the way we answer such questions as: "Did that man intend to insult me?", "Can I trust her if she behaves like that?", "Does this church leader tell the truth?" Critical reflec-

---

104. Mary Midgley, *Heart and Mind: The Varieties of Moral Experience* (New York: St. Martin's Press, 1981; London: Methuen, 1983), p. 41, see also p. 35.

tion has an immediate practical purpose, as well as an academic role that may not be immediately relevant to everyday life. In holding out against the sweeping generalizations of the indoctrination criticism and the proponents of a fully critical education, I should not be seen as presenting an equally all-or-nothing response. The answers to these problems are best given in the qualified language of degree, extent and range.

What Is Wrong with Indoctrinatory Christian Religious Education?

The question remains whether the qualified critique of the notion of indoctrination outlined above is worth having, and examples of this sort of unacceptable indoctrination worth expunging from Christian religious education practice. I think that such a distinction between proper and improper education *is* worth retaining. Certainly I have met people who seem to have been subjected to what I regard as unacceptable indoctrination according to my definition, often particularly through some form of Christian religious education. Their personhood or sense of self-responsibility has been violated because they were capable of—and would have valued—thinking for themselves. I do not, however, feel the same about those who have been taught to hold beliefs unshakably but who do *not* themselves think it appropriate, proper or worthwhile to reflect on their beliefs, or consider their evidential status. Some people can be fully themselves and fully value themselves without self-evaluation or critical reflection, as others can be fully themselves and value themselves without expressing themselves artistically or through close personal relationships. But there are people who need some or all of these elements in their lives in order to be fully realized. For those who need to *think* in order to be themselves, and to think about their religion in particular, indoctrination puts chains on their self-realization and their religious self-realization. Their beliefs are not truly theirs unless they think about them critically. In such cases—and there are very many of them in schools and churches, but "very many" is not the same as "everybody"—indoctrination is unacceptable.

Of course the pursuit of truth is a social activity and not just an individual one. Society in general, and the social entity of the church in particular, needs people who are self-critical and forever searching for evidence for and against their beliefs, in order that further knowledge may be gained. Advances are only to be made, in the areas of knowledge where it is appropriate to think of such progress, through "conjectures and refutations": inspired imaginative leaps to bold new insights that must be rigorously tested and need to be held with a passionate tentativeness while the hunt is mounted for falsifying evidence.[105] Our society and church need to do this, but not *everyone* in our society and church has to do it. For many people such

---

105. Popper, *Conjectures and Refutations, passim.* I shall be arguing in later chapters, however, that much "religious knowing" is *not* of this kind. It does not make "progress" in this fashion.

endeavors represent the fulfillment of their very being, but it is not so for all. Those who can think like this *must* think like this, for they need to and their society needs them to. However, there are others—let us be realistic, and I make no attempt to quantify the proportion in the population—who cannot, will not, and/or do not want to think like this. They will make their own contributions, often much greater ones, elsewhere. They will be fulfilled in different ways. We must avoid intellectual snobbery in our evaluations of nonintellectuals, particularly in the church. "What", after all, "is supposed to be *that* good about cleverness?".[106] Thinking about beliefs is actually much more of a marginalizing activity than some educational rhetoric allows. It is not just the sociologist who finds herself at the edge of a society looking in on activities and beliefs that she cannot perform or hold in the same way as the participants.[107] All critical thinking runs that risk, and it is a *risk*.[108] It can be a serious risk for the Christian learner and the Christian religious educator.

I would strenuously combat the accusation that my position here is paternalistic, or that it underestimates the reasoning abilities of "ordinary people". I do believe that very many people are capable of a fairly high degree of reflective critical thought; but I would contend that much fewer of them really want, or need, to engage in it in order to fulfill themselves *in their own eyes*. The real height of paternalism, surely, is seeking to develop people's potential in ways that they themselves do not recognize (even after such development) as being valuably self-fulfilling. I fear that many philosophers of education are guilty of this vice. It would be a pity to incorporate it

---

106. For example, is it so much more important "than being kind, brave, friendly, patient, and generous"?. Mary Midgley, *Beast and Man: The Roots of Human Nature* (Ithaca, N.Y.: Cornell University Press, 1978; London: Methuen, 1980), pp. 255-256. Midgley argues for a notion of rationality that is wider than cleverness and includes "integration"—i.e. "having a character, acting as a whole, having a firm and effective priority system" ("based on feeling") (pp. 262, 256). Such integration on its own is "something of enormous value" and worthy of respect. See also Stanley Hauerwas's critique of over-intellectualist accounts of moral growth, with their assumption that "the more 'self-conscious' we are of our values and principles, the better chance we have for *moral* growth". He writes, "while I suspect any significant moral tradition must develop some who are self-conscious, it is by no means clear that all need to be such. We must remember that the Gospel does not require us to be self-conscious as our first order of business. Rather it requires us to be faithful." Stanley Hauerwas, "Character, Narrative, and Growth in the Christian Life", in James Fowler and Antoine Vergote, eds., *Toward Moral and Religious Maturity* (Morristown, N.J.: Silver Burdett, 1980), p. 483.

107. See Gwen Kennedy Neville and John H. Westerhoff, III, *Learning through Liturgy* (New York: Seabury, 1978), pp. 76-80.

108. See Patrick Burke, *The Fragile Universe* (London: Macmillan, 1975), p. 92. Isolation is not the only risk run by those who adopt critical thought. There is also a sense in which "reflection can destroy knowledge". This is particularly the case in areas like ethical knowledge, where it "disturbs, unseats, or replaces" traditional concepts. Bernard Williams, *Ethics and the Limits of Philosophy* (London: Collins, 1985), pp. 148, 167-168. Such considerations should not, however, lead us to suppress reflection; but rather to expect rather less of reflection than we often do, and to recognize that a tradition that incorporates reflection has been (often radically) modified in that process. See Chapter 5 below.

unthinkingly into policies of Christian religious education.

The hyperintellectualism of some rhetoric about Christian religious education is greatly to be regretted, even when it originates from a philosophical source (whether analytic or neo-Marxist). Christian religious education, as I shall argue in subsequent chapters, is not solely—or even primarily—an intellectual matter. Nor should Christian learners be reduced to, or judged in terms of, their cognitive abilities alone. There is much more to Christianity and to Christian religious education than that.

CHAPTER 5

Formative Education and Critical Education

INTRODUCTION

A useful distinction has been adopted by some secular and religious educators between formative education and critical education. According to Leon McKenzie, formative education aims "principally at the formation of the learners", whereas critical education is organized so as to "maximize evaluative thinking on the part of the learners".[1] He distinguishes critical education, as "ordinated toward the examination of educational 'givens'", from formative education which is "ordinated toward the reception of educational 'givens'". Formation is conceived here as a process by which a learner is shaped by an educator according to some *a priori* ideal or model. In critical education, on the other hand, the learner is engaged with the teacher in "a systematic inquiry relating to the issue at hand".[2]

McKenzie notes that the distinction needs some qualification. All critical education involves some formation in values (including, presumably, the value of critical thinking); and most formative education in our culture goes along with at least some elements of critical education. Further, formative and critical education really occupy two points on a continuum along which

---

1. Leon McKenzie, *The Religious Education of Adults* (Birmingham, Ala.: Religious Education Press, 1982), p. 36. In a personal communication, McKenzie writes of the influence on him both of discussions about "whether education should serve as conservator or challenger of prevailing cultural values" and the view of Hans-Georg Gadamer and others that "it is quite impossible to interpret the world and one's place in the world without the leverage of a tradition" (Letter from McKenzie, 1987). See Hans-Georg Gadamer, *Truth and Method*, trans. Garrett Barden and John Cumming (New York: Crossroad, 1982), pp. 245-253, and note Gadamer's opposition to Jürgen Habermas's stress on emancipation from tradition as expressed, for example, in the latter's *Philosophical Hermeneutics* (Berkeley: University of California Press, 1976), pp. 26-42.

2. McKenzie, *The Religious Education of Adults*, pp. 37, 64.

actual education programs may be plotted (we might prefer to think of them as abstractive elements of concrete educational practices). McKenzie describes formative education as systematized, instructional enculturation (the learning of the culture into which one is born) or acculturation (learning aspects of a "new" culture), where the stress is on the learner's acquiescence in, and acceptance of, society's ways. Critical education, on the other hand, fosters individual insight whereby this "cultural 'furniture' is taken apart and reassembled in new ways". He adds that "formative education that excludes critical education is little more than indoctrination".[3]

The formative education/critical education distinction is to be found wearing various clothes from the wardrobe of educational and theological debate, particularly when it is applied to religious cognition. Thus Karl-Ernst Nipkow draws on Hans Urs von Balthasar's distinction between "kneeling theology" (praying faith) and "sitting theology" (systematic knowledge about faith), so as to discriminate between a type of theology characterized by "positional identity" (confessional, proclaiming, identifying) and one characterized by "critical dissociation" (rational, reflective, open).[4] Nipkow argues that the two need to be combined, as the learner both expects and needs the strengths of the two approaches: "the openness and reflection of the self-critical type of theology and the living authenticity and positionality of the other type."[5] He identifies this as "a liberal approach": rational, open-minded and consonant with the methods of free enquiry; yet not neglecting the nonrational, affective values of the heart of religion.[6]

In a later work McKenzie, drawing on John Dewey and Jacques Derrida, distinguishes the "reconstruction" of experience, which "points to ideas of formation, growth and the development of social capacity",[7] from its "deconstruction" or critical evaluation and the analysis and "destruction of selected meanings".[8] The balance between the two processes might be said to underlie some of the distinctions McKenzie makes in the same book between different types of worldview ("comprehensive interpretive understanding"):

---

3. *Ibid.*, pp. 65-66.

4. Karl-Ernst Nipkow, "Can Theology have an Educational Role?", in M. C. Felderhof, ed., *Religious Education in a Pluralistic Society* (London: Hodder & Stoughton, 1985), p. 31. In the same collection Stewart Sutherland extends the metaphor: "much of what goes on in theology and in education involves holding at arm's length what is most naturally and appropriately held in embrace ... beliefs and values ... [that] are ... matters of deep-seated conviction which involve emotion as well as intellect, soul as well as mind" (*ibid.*, p. 140). This arm's-length, critical appraisal, some have argued, is essential to the nature of "an educational institution". See Michael Leahy, "Indoctrination, Evangelization, Catechesis and Religious Education", *British Journal of Religious Education* 12: 3 (1990), p. 142.

5. Nipkow, "Can Theology have an Educational Role?", p. 32.

6. *Ibid.*, pp. 33-34.

7. Leon McKenzie, *Adult Education and Worldview Construction* (Malabar, Fla.: Krieger, 1991), p. 31. See also John Dewey, *Democracy and Education* (New York: Macmillan, 1916), pp. 89-92.

8. McKenzie, *Adult Education and Worldview Construction*, pp. 29-32. For deconstruction, see Jacques Derrida, *La Dissemination* (Paris: Editions du Seuil, 1972).

including those between provisional and fixed worldviews, active and passive worldviews, and (especially) critical and uncritical worldviews.[9]

The Case Against a Purely Critical Education

As our discussion of indoctrination indicated (Chapter 4 above), it is possible to have instruction and Christian religious education that is almost purely formative. But it would appear that no educational policy or practice, whether religious or secular, could consist simply of critical education— for reasons that may be variously categorized as logical, psychological or moral.

The *logical difficulty* is (at least) fourfold. In the first place only statements that are explicitly derived from identifiable premises can be critically tested by examining those premises and the inferential processes that led from them. But according to Michael Polanyi we know more than we can tell, for much of our knowledge is inarticulate, acritical tacit knowing, and this undergirds our explicit knowledge. Since "we cannot reflect on our tacit awareness of an experience", as we can on something explicitly stated, the idea of knowledge based on wholly identifiable grounds collapses; and Polyani concludes that the transmission of knowledge between the generations must be predominantly tacit.[10] We cannot learn everything by the critical examination of explicit grounds, premises and first principles and the construction of a new edifice of knowledge for ourselves on the basis of such raw materials; nor can we engage in this criticism at all where the grounds of our knowledge are hidden.

This leads to the criticism of what Neil Cooper calls the "private-enterprise" theory of knowledge, for which "what is or is not knowledge is dependent on the route the individual follows in arriving at a certain conclusion".[11] On this account you only know what I know if you can follow my cognitive route. But this is "unduly restrictive on what we can count as knowledge", excluding truths based on testimony or trust (i.e. authority), and putting too much reliance on the "lone cognitive entrepreneur" and her ability to verify

---

9. McKenzie, *Adult Education and Worldview Construction*, pp. 65-69; but compare also pp. 112-116.

10. Michael Polanyi, *The Study of Man* (Chicago: University of Chicago Press; London: Routledge & Kegan Paul, 1959), p. 14 and *passim*. On "tacit knowledge" see also Polanyi's *The Tacit Dimension* (Garden City, N.Y.: Doubleday, 1967); "The Logic of Tacit Inference", *Philosophy* 41: 155 (1966); "Faith and Reason", *Journal of Religion* 41: 4 (1961); "Knowing and Being", *Mind* 70: 280 (1961) and *Personal Knowledge* (Chicago: University of Chicago Press, 1958; London: Routledge & Kegan Paul, 1962). See also R. T. Allen, "Rational Autonomy: The Destruction of Freedom", *Journal of Philosophy of Education* 16: 2 (1982), pp. 201-202. John Stuart Mill, we may note, objected to language about "foundations" (first principles) of a science on the grounds that "their relation to the science is not that of foundations to an edifice, but of roots to a tree, which may perform their office equally well though they be never dug down to and exposed to light". John Stuart Mill, *Utilitarianism*, ch. I, ed. Mary Warnock (London: Collins, 1962), p. 252.

11. Neil Cooper, "The Transmission of Knowledge", in Roger Straughan and John Wilson, eds., *Philosophers on Education* (Basingstoke: Macmillan, 1987), pp. 73-74.

truths for herself. The notion of knowledge as a social product is considerably more plausible, and that notion implies *social* formation.

To make a different point we may appeal to Richard Peters's criticism of those "for whom being critical is a substitute for being well informed about anything". Peters quips: "content without criticism is blind, but criticism without content is empty".[12] Criticism needs something to work on; you cannot rearrange the furniture—let alone rebuild it—before it has been delivered.

A further logical difficulty with the idea of a critical education innocent of any formative element is that it is a prior condition of the evaluative task that people possess (are formed in) the skills, criteria and beliefs with which to conduct such an assessment. As Anthony Quinton puts it, "external authority is the original source not only of items of information, singular and general, but also of language, logic and method, the indispensable means for the formulation and critical assessment of our beliefs".[13] Critical thinkers need to be formed in critical thinking before they can exercise the skill. In the words of a religious educationist: "by learning a culture we acquire the knowledge, attitudes, values, skills and sensibilities that enable us to develop critical and intelligent responses to social reality".[14]

It is possible that the difficulties outlined above might be met, in which case it is important to recognize that these logical considerations shade into a *psychological point* about what is practically possible for the learner, a point that we have raised before (Chapter 4 above). Without long-term and long-lasting processes of formation, a person's identity and belief system will not be established strongly enough for him to have sufficient confidence in himself to embark on critical education. We must recognize that "having a world-view is not only cognitively essential; it is also deeply reassuring. Therefore people will hold to their world-views very firmly indeed as orientating items of the utmost importance to their well-being."[15] For psycho-

---

12. R. S. Peters, "Education as Initiation", in Reginald D. Archambault, ed., *Philosophical Analysis and Education* (London: Routledge & Kegan Paul, 1965), p. 104. See also Basil Mitchell, "Faith and Reason: A False Antithesis?", *Religious Studies* 16: 2 (1980), pp. 142-144 and above p. 70.

13. A. M. Quinton, "Authority and Autonomy in Knowledge", *Proceedings of the Philosophy of Education Society of Great Britain* V: 2 (1971), p. 208. Quinton argues that cognitive autonomy is still genuine since "these instruments do not owe their acceptability to the very authorities to which they are applied" (p. 215).

14. Kenneth Barker, *Religious Education, Catechesis and Freedom* (Birmingham, Ala.: Religious Education Press, 1981), p. 183.

15. Martin Prozesky, *Religion and Ultimate Well-Being: An Explanatory Theory* (London: Macmillan; New York: St. Martin's Press, 1984), p. 129. Therefore even secular educational institutions have nurturing functions. "The school is not the Church nor is it the home. It is a sort of city—an area both of protection and of prudent exposure." John Courtney Murray, "The Christian Idea of Education", in Edmund Fuller, ed., *The Christian Idea of Education* (New Haven: Yale University Press, 1957), p. 161. It may be argued, however, that we should apply this description to the church and the home as well, in so far as they attempt *critical* Christian religious education. Many liberal educationists would claim that any institution that is entirely nurturing-protective is not fully "educational".

logical as well as logical reasons we learn to be someone-with-a-viewpoint before we can shift our point of view through a critical (and piecemeal) self-examination of our cognitive and evaluative "platform". Such a change *is* possible (John Hull calls it "inner-ideological" self-criticism[16]), and is encouraged by critical education. What is *not* possible, however, is for us to "jump out of our skins" of beliefs, attitudes and values and move to some purely "objective" or "neutral" viewpoint. (That would result, in any case, in our ending up with no viewpoint at all.) To become a person, even a critical person, is to have been *formed* within that "skin". We may utilize here the language, if not all of the views, of Glenn Langford who persuasively argues that "to become educated is to learn to be a person" (as a member of a society), and that this framework account may be given a particular content by Christians in terms of "a Christian ideal of what a person ought to be".[17]

Even if we could set aside these logical and psychological considerations a *moral issue* would remain. The moral difficulty with purely critical education is that any culture justifies its passing on of its own attitudes, values, beliefs and practices on moral grounds.[18] This cultural formation, based as it is on a common cultural consensus, is necessarily compatible with only a limited amount of cultural critique.[19] The critical approach or attitude is therefore rare in the history of ideas, with the exception of scientific thought. It is particularly problematic in the area of religion.[20] There are of course important cultural reasons, relating to the *stability* of interpretations, why "the social world intends, as far as possible, to be taken for granted". "Socialization achieves success to the degree that this taken-for-granted quality is internalized. It is not enough that the individual look upon the key meanings of the social order as useful, desirable or right. It is much better (better, that is, in terms of social stability) if he looks upon

---

16. John M. Hull, *What Prevents Christian Adults from Learning?*, (London: SCM, 1985), pp. 78-85. It has been argued that the deep, subjective, personal intellectual element in human reasoning cannot be fully exchanged for another's standpoint, nor can we stand outside its structure to criticize it. Our nature is there to be used, not analyzed: "Our being, with its faculties, mind and body, is a fact not admitting of question, all things being of necessity referred to it, not it to other things". John Henry Newman, *A Grammar of Assent* (London: Green, 1913), p. 346. Such a view must put a question mark against some of the more extreme accounts of critical reason.

17. Glenn Langford, *Education, Persons and Society: A Philosophical Enquiry* (Basingstoke: Macmillan, 1985), pp. 181 and 187. See also Michael Warren, "Religious Formation in the Context of Social Formation", *Religious Education* 82: 4 (1987) and Adrian Thatcher, "Learning to Become Persons: A Theological Approach to Educational Aims", *Scottish Journal of Theology* 36 (1983).

18. Basil Mitchell, "Religious Education", *Oxford Review of Education* 6: 2 (1980), p. 135. See also Don S. Browning, "Practical Theology and Religious Education", in Lewis S. Mudge and James N. Poling, eds., *Formation and Reflection: The Promise of Practical Theology* (Philadelphia: Fortress, 1987), p. 82.

19. John McIntyre, "Multi-Culture and Multi-Faith Societies: some Examinable Assumptions", *Occasional Papers* 3 (Oxford: Farmington Institute, n.d.).

20. Anthony O'Hear, *Experience, Explanation and Faith* (London: Routledge & Kegan Paul, 1984), pp. 244-249.

them as inevitable, as part and parcel of the universal 'nature of things'."[21]

The implications of such a position for schooling and education generally, as well as for Christian religious education, are clear. One may almost go so far as to say that "education does not hand on tradition; education *is* tradition, the process of handing on, and within the process the asking of critical questions about the past".[22] (The notion of the Christian tradition that I would want to defend would be one which had a central place for attitudes, emotions, values and practices, as well as cognition.) There is a proper place for critical education, but it can only function properly within the context of formative education.

The Qualified Critical Approach

Donald Hudson has written of the "composite nature" of rationality itself along lines that run parallel with our discussion of formative and critical education. The rational enterprise, he claims, involves two essential elements: *conformity* and *criticism*. (See Glossary for the understanding of "rational" in use here, as synonymous with "reasonable".) "Being rational is a process of concurring in, and operating with, standards which determine in their respective fields what counts as a reason and what does not." But criticism "subjects accepted standards of explanation or decision to ever more exacting tests of their effectiveness and where they fail, rejects them in favour of more effective ones." Rationality requires both. If rationality is exclusively conformity, Hudson claims, the end result is bigotry ("the refusal to allow the rational enterprise to fail"). But if it is solely a matter of criticism, the result is licence ("the refusal to let it succeed"). Education also requires both: "What is taught will necessarily conform to some sort of received opinion; but it will also be perpetually exposed to every relevant kind of critical opinion".[23] (Let us note the use of the word "relevant".)

The philosopher and humanist Ronald Hepburn argues similarly for a *qualified* critical approach, contending that adopting "a policy of constant, sustained and intense critical onslaught" against a person's own fundamental beliefs would prevent that person from "participating at all effectively in the way of life appropriate to those beliefs, and in consort with others who share them". Practical educational wisdom, he insists, "requires finding a mean, between on the one side such a relentless self-critical campaign, and on the other a complacent, or an over-anxious, refusal ever to reappraise".[24] This is certainly the case in the area of Christian religious education.

---

21. Peter L. Berger, *The Social Reality of Religion* (= *The Sacred Canopy*, Garden City, N.Y.: Doubleday, 1967) (Harmondsworth, England: Penguin, 1973), p. 33.

22. Gabriel Moran, *Religious Education as a Second Language* (Birmingham, Ala.: Religious Education Press, 1989), p. 49, compare also pp. 51, 78, 155-161.

23. W. D. Hudson, "Learning to be Rational", *Proceedings of the Philosophy of Education Society of Great Britain* 11 (1977), pp. 41, 42-43, 51.

24. R. W. Hepburn, "Attitudes to Evidence and Argument in the Field of Religion", in Straughan and Wilson, eds., *Philosophers on Education*, p. 145. Hepburn's position is very similar to that of the Christian philosopher Basil Mitchell—see above pp. 69-70.

It is not surprising that when philosophers are seen or see themselves as critical educators *par excellence*, they should find themselves "almost unemployable". Nor is it surprising that "overcritical" critical educators are sometimes regarded as having an effect on their learners that is "unkind . . . unnecessary and counter-productive". Furthermore, there is certainly some truth in Albert Camus's aphorism: "Beginning to think is beginning to be undermined".[25] A critical outlook is a two-edged sword: in hacking away at error it may wound the one who wields it. There is an inevitable risk of destruction in critical (= judging, evaluating) reason and no amount of stress on its concomitant constructive role should hide this from us. Those who rhapsodize over critical education in religion, because they themselves have found it illuminating, releasing, or just plain exciting, often reveal a considerable naïvety. Thus some liberal theologians rather naïvely assume that their re-interpretations of Christian doctrines (such as the doctrine of the Fall) do not imply radical repercussions throughout the entire system of Christian theology. Others tend to be dismissive of the extent to which biblical criticism can (and often, I would argue, should) undermine their own assumptions about revelation and salvation history. There may be no alternative to having electricity in the house, and it is certain that it has made our lives immeasurably easier, but let us not pretend that its power is thereby tamed and that it can no longer harm us—or others.

Formative and Critical Learning Outcomes

McKenzie concentrates on cognitive learning outcomes and distinguishes within that category between those that result from formative education and those that are the products of critical education. Using Benjamin Bloom's taxonomy of cognitive educational objectives,[26] he places *knowledge* (as measured by recall of material taught), *comprehension* (understanding what is being communicated) and *application* (of learning to other areas) in the category of formative learning outcomes. Critical education, on the other hand, McKenzie claims, results in *analysis* and *synthesis* of what has been taught, and its *evaluation* using internal evidence (e.g. consistency) and external criteria (Bloom's "judging by external standards"). It appears that critical education primarily fosters in the learner certain intellectual abilities and skills of the cognitive domain ("*think*ing critically"). This is an example of what educationists often call a "process content" ("think*ing* critically"), although it inevitably entails the employment of these processes to produce

25. Don Cupitt, "Religion and Critical Thinking—I", *Theology* 86: 712 (1983), p. 244; Brenda Watson, *Education and Belief* (Oxford: Blackwell, 1987), p. 58; Albert Camus, *The Myth of Sisyphus and Other Essays*, trans. Justin O'Brien (New York: Knopf; London: Hamilton, 1955), p. 12. Critical thinking has been defined as the appropriate use of "reflective scepticism" by J. E. McPeck in his *Critical Thinking and Education* (Oxford: Robertson, 1981), p. 7.

26. See Benjamin S. Bloom *et al.*, *Taxonomy of Educational Objectives: the Classification of Educational Goals. Handbook I: Cognitive Domain* (New York: McKay; London: Longmans, 1956), pp. 201-207 and *passim*; McKenzie, *The Religious Education of Adults*, pp. 36-37.

other learning outcomes ("critical *thought(s)*", e.g. specific evaluations of religion) that may be described as "product contents".

These processes and products of critical education are essentially centered on the learner, who "critically assesses that which is taught in the light of his own experiences".[27] The focus here is on the learner rather than on the content learned (the tradition). Formative education, however, shapes or "forms" the learner in religion, rather than enabling her to analyze and evaluate it. In the cognitive field formation "passes on" received religious knowledge/beliefs (product content) together with cognitive skills (processes of understanding). These skills—although they are skills of the learner—are so taught and learned that they result in a comprehension of the knowledge received in which that knowledge is spelled out in *its own terms*. Formative education produces no reconstruction or critique of the tradition *in the learner's own terms*.[28]

The distinction between the two types of education becomes even clearer when we focus on two other major areas, namely affective states and overt behavior, as we must if we are to give a complete account of education and particularly of Christian religious education. Formative education is (or should be, and at least can be) whole person education, whereas critical education often apparently bypasses affect and lifestyle and focuses on the cognitive dimension alone. Formative education forms not only cognitions in the learner, but also attitudes, dispositions, values, emotions and lifestyle as both products and processes. It does this in a receptive, uncritical way. In Christian religious education these learning outcomes include the formed affections and dispositions to overt behavior of the Christian, which many would regard as the most important Christian learning outcomes. It would be the task of critical education with regard to these sorts of learning outcome to engender *cognitive skills* that allow the learner to *think*-for-herself about, and *critically evaluate*, her behavior and feelings on the basis of various criteria.[29]

But is this solely a matter of cognition? It need not be an "objective reflection which minimizes personal experience in favor of its anonymous content and abstracts from *self*-consciousness as much as possible". It could be a "subjective" reflection which is self-involved, but "*perspicaciously* self-involved and aware of its self-involvement" in reflecting on our personal

27. McKenzie, *The Religious Education of Adults*, p. 37.

28. Formative education seems close in this regard to what Paul Tillich calls "inducting education". "Its aim is not development of the potentialities of the individual, but induction into the actuality of a group, the life and spirit of community, family, tribe, town, nation, church." Paul Tillich, *Theology of Culture* (London: Oxford University Press, 1959), p. 147. I would say that Tillich's "technical education"—the transmission of knowledge and skills—is also a part of formative education in a broad sense, whereas his "humanistic education" is close to the understanding offered here of critical education. But contrast John Westerhoff, III, "Formation, Education, Instruction", *Religious Education* 82: 4 (1987), p. 581.

29. See R. S. Peters, "Education and Human Development", in R. F. Dearden *et al.*, eds., *Education and Reason* (London: Routledge & Kegan Paul, 1972), pp. 123-124.

investments.[30] In order for a learner fully to learn to become critical, critical education must develop in that person what many would call (perhaps rather sloppily) a "critical attitude". Is this purely a cognitive state, which might be better described as a "critical mentality", or are there affective dimensions to this phenomenon that are appropriately captured by the term "attitude"? The same issue is raised by phrases such as "critical stance", "critical orientation", "critical outlook" and "critical disposition". Interestingly, the Krathwohl taxonomy recognizes "faith in the power of reason and in the methods of experiment and discussion" (as an example of commitment to a value which amounts to "conviction") as part of the affective domain.[31]

John Passmore suggests that "'being critical' is ... more like the sort of thing we call a 'character trait' than it is like a skill", and Joel Feinberg notes that there can be no "*ex nihilo* creation of the habit of rational reflection" since "the commitment to reasonableness itself" must be implanted in a person's character.[32] As McKenzie has indicated, critical education is formative of certain values. Similarly Alasdair MacIntyre lists among the virtues not only those dispositions that sustain practices and societies by and in which we can seek for the good together, but also "the virtues necessary for philosophical enquiry about the character of the good"; and Mark Schwehn argues persuasively for the cultivation in the academy of higher learning of the spiritual virtues of humility, faith and self-denial.[33] It would appear therefore that there are certain attitudes, virtues, values and dispositions that are formed by critical education. Critical education is thus neither purely cognitive nor purely critical (in the sense of nonformative). This is a necessary, although perhaps only a minor, qualification of any description of the predominantly cognitive nature of the outcomes of critical education.

CRITICAL CHRISTIAN RELIGIOUS EDUCATION

A Rational Critical Christian Religious Education

Let us now pursue the discussion more explicitly in the context of Christian religious education. To affirm that formative and critical educational processes are "complementary", and that both are needed in a proper program

30. Robert C. Solomon, *The Passions* (Notre Dame, Ind.: University of Notre Dame Press, 1983), p. 79. See below Chapter 9.

31. David R. Krathwohl *et al.*, *Taxonomy of Educational Objectives: the Classification of Educational Goals. Handbook II: Affective Domain* (New York: McKay; London: Longmans, 1964), pp. 149-150.

32. John Passmore, "On Teaching to be Critical", in R. S. Peters, ed., *The Concept of Education* (London: Routledge & Kegan Paul, 1967), p. 195 and Joel Feinberg, in James F. Doyle, ed., *Educational Judgments* (London: Routledge & Kegan Paul, 1973), p. 166. See also John Passmore, *The Philosophy of Teaching* (Cambridge, Mass.: Harvard University Press, 1980), ch. 9.

33. Alasdair MacIntyre, *After Virtue* (London: Duckworth, 1981), p. 204; Mark Schwehn, "Knowledge, Character, and Community", in Stanley Hauerwas and John H. Westerhoff, III, eds., *Schooling Christians* (Grand Rapids, Mich.: Eerdmans, 1992), pp. 43, 48-53.

of Christian religious education,[34] is to make an implicit judgment about the value of critical education outcomes. My broad definition of what constitutes both Christian learning and Christian religious education does not prevent— indeed it demands—the developing of some normative criteria so that we may distinguish between "good" and "bad", "proper" and "improper" educational processes in this context. My discussion of indoctrination has led me to make some minimal claims about the importance, even in Christian religious education, of developing those critical skills and attitudes that are perceived by the learners as an essential part of their personhood. For many learners a formative Christian religious education without any critical element whatever would be a stunting of their proper development. Hence it would be negatively "indoctrinatory", in that it would frustrate their personal realization. Many Christians, perhaps most adult Christians, do need to develop in these ways to some extent.[35] If this is the case, then they should experience critical Christian religious education along with the formative kind.[36] But I do not believe that this is necessarily true of *all* Christians. Education needs to be tailored to the learners. Learners differ in their interests, their potential and (most of all) in what fulfills them. For *some*, it must be said, formative education is what—and all—they both want *and need*.

The church as a whole, however, desperately needs more critical education. If Christianity is to survive and develop as a lifestyle and as a belief system into the twenty-first century it must undergo continual re-formation spurred on by continual critical evaluation from within the household of faith. This is not the same, however, as saying that every six-year-old, ninety-year-old, or even thirty-year-old in the church must be engaged in this critical task. Thinking critically about religion is always only part of what Christian religious education is about.

Therefore in making room for—and indeed in welcoming—critical Christian religious education, our earlier caveats from Chapter 4 must still be borne in mind. Critical learning produces a critical stance from which critical skills are exercised, but this viewpoint is no neutral, nonpartisan platform. Evaluation can only be on the basis of certain principles and presupposi-

---

34. McKenzie, *The Religious Education of Adults*, p. 64. See also Randolph Crump Miller, *The Theory of Christian Education Practice* (Birmingham, Ala.: Religious Education Press, 1980), pp. 174-175.

35. McKenzie writes: "the critical appraisal of meaning structures is a process that is an integral part of many adult lives. We cannot effectively forbid adults to be critical. . . . Further, it is better to help adults appraise religious tradition from within the confines of church than to fail by default and allow them to critique religious teachings outside the context of church." Leon McKenzie, "The Purposes and Scope of Adult Religious Education", in Nancy Foltz, ed., *Handbook of Adult Religious Education* (Birmingham, Ala.: Religious Education Press, 1986), p. 12.

36. If Christian religious education is regarded as corresponding both with the etymology that relates "education" to *educare* (to train, mold) and with that which tracks it back to *educere* (to lead out), it might be argued that the former specifies the substantive content-centered approach of formative education while the latter fits better with the learner-centered approach expressed most clearly in a critical education that realizes the learner's critical skills.

tions, and these are usually highly controversial ones. If the critical stance to be adopted is that of "trusting to reason", in the sense of adopting Hudson's criteria of rationality,[37] then critical education must confess to this and recognize its implications. There is nothing *less* critical and rational than developing in oneself and others evaluative skills and attitudes while allowing or ensuring that such evaluators remain ignorant of, or willingly unreflective about, the implicit criteria of their evaluations. Many forms of Christian religious education are frequently open to this criticism, and should be as objectionable as fundamentalist indoctrination to those who seek a *properly* self-critical critical education. Certainly philosophers of education are now beginning to recognize the extent to which certain forms of education that are closely allied to—and often presented as entirely made up of—critical educational elements also incorporate particular values such as tolerance, individualism and a particular pluralistic vision.[38]

It should be noted at this point that critical Christian religious education comes in various guises, depending on the critical standpoint and evaluative principles and procedures that it advocates. The way it has been described thus far suggests a stress on a *rational* critique, informed by a liberal educational tradition and Western philosophical method. Many Christian religious educators would construe Christian critical religious education along these lines. Charles Melchert is an eloquent proponent of this position, arguing against those who assume that an educational ministry has the same purposes as the church, especially those of nurturing faith and evangelizing. Melchert agrees that the church must be concerned with faith, but contends that "the specific responsibility of an educational ministry is not so much for the presence or intensity of that faith, but with the how and the why of faith. For example, the educator will not be satisfied with an intense and real faith which is primarily a defense against or withdrawal from a world perceived as hostile or 'dirty'." The focal concern of this sort of educational ministry is "neither the intensity nor the object of that faith, but rather the structure, style and grounds for exercising Christian being".[39] This type of critical Christian religious educator will thus, among other things: (1) "increase openness" in her learners (to the Christian heritage, to non-Christians, to "affirmation and criticism of the church and Christianity"); (2) help them connect life, faith and the gospel, and resist a fragmented mentality; and (3) be sensitive to doubt and criticism.

It would not be proper for us to move on from this type of critical Christian religious education without acknowledging its attractiveness and power.

---

37. See pp. p. 56 above.

38. Brenda Cohen, "Return to the Cave: New Directions for Philosophy of Education", *Educational Analysis* 4: 1 (1982), p. 99. See also John McIntyre, "Multi-Culture and Multi-Faith Societies"; and David Day, "Agreeing to Differ: The Logic of Pluralism", in Frank Coffield and Richard Goodings, eds., *Sacred Cows in Education* (Edinburgh: Edinburgh University Press, 1983).

39. Charles F. Melchert, "What is the Educational Ministry of the Church?", *Religious Education* 73: 4 (1978), pp. 435-436.

Although—as we have seen—it needs some qualification, the notion of education as a process that orients us to "a fundamental openness and receptivity to truth"[40] cannot be ignored in any attempt to construct aims and objectives for a fully adequate Christian religious education.

A Political Critical Christian Religious Education

The account summarized above, however, does not represent the only style of critical religious education. Some religious educators, while wishing to promote Christian learning outcomes that include the learner's criticism of the tradition (i.e. are not just formative), adopt a rather different account of what that critical stance should be. I am thinking here in particular of those educators who are influenced by liberation theology and "liberation education", for whom all stances are political. In their understanding critical evaluation is not an apolitical rational evaluation, but a moral sociopolitical critique resulting from the "hermeneutics of suspicion" and incorporating critical moral reflection on received understandings and the learner's own practice.[41] Relevant to such accounts is the educationist's rejection of the "banking" model of education, described by Paulo Freire as a transfer of capital in which the teacher "'makes deposits' which the students patiently receive, memorize and repeat" and where "the scope of action allowed to the students extends only as far as receiving, filing and storing the deposits"[42]—a particularly conservative type of formative education. Freire rejects this in favor of the educational goal of "the posing of the problem of men in their relations with the world": i.e. "problem-posing" or "liberating education". This strives for "the *emergence* of consciousness and *critical intervention* in reality". Education for "critical consciousness" or "conscientization" (*concientizacion*) involves promoting reflection on the learner's own historical experience, and the learner's "demythologizing" or "decoding" of the myths that conceal the true facts that explain how people exist in the world, in a way that leads to the "unmasking" of oppressive societies and structures in a revolutionary fashion.

---

40. *Ibid.*, p. 438. See also J. Gordon Chamberlin, *Freedom and Faith: New Approaches to Christian Education* (Philadelphia: Westminster, 1965), p. 126.

41. Barker, *Religious Education, Catechesis and Freedom*, p. 152 and ch. 4 *passim*.

42. Paulo Freire, *Pedagogy of the Oppressed*, trans. Myra Bergman Ramos (New York: Herder and Herder; Harmondsworth, England: Penguin, 1972), p. 46. Quotations from Freire in the paragraph following are from pp. 52-58 and 77-78 of this book. Kevin Nichols argues that Freire's view and the Western liberal education tradition show striking similarities, despite the different philosophical categories. "Both are concerned with standing on your own feet, with being critically conscious of the world, with taking your destiny in your own hands." Both see education as a liberating force, rejecting unreflective acceptance of the *status quo* in favor of a critical autonomy. "The liberal 'critical openness' and Freire's 'critical self-consciousness' look-alike, blossom on the same hedgerow." But the latter is more concerned with the inner self and its outer constraints, and with thought "translated into and tested by action"; whereas the former represents an attempt at a cooler, "purer" and more detached analysis. Kevin Nichols, "Education as Liberation", in Dermot A. Lane, ed., *Religious Education and the Future* (Dublin: Columba, 1986), pp. 143-144.

This form of education, according to Freire, is not to be seen as a neutral technique. In his view education always has political consequences. Freire believes that problem-posing education is "humanist" and "liberating", for it "posits as fundamental" that people subjected to domination "must fight for their emancipation". Thus Freire's translator can write that "'conscientization' refers to learning to perceive social, political and economic contradictions, and to take action against the oppressive elements of reality".[43] And Freire himself insists that conscientization, as "a critical attempt to reveal reality", "must ... be related to political involvement".[44]

Those who follow such insights interpret critical education, which is for them an essential element in Christian religious education (often together with formative socialization),[45] as promoting both a critical reflection on present activity and experience and a dialectical critique between the received Christian tradition and the learner's understanding. According to Thomas Groome, by asking critical questions such as the following our Christian religious education inevitably becomes political: "What does the community's Story mean for (affirm, call in question, invite beyond) our stories, and how do our stories respond to (affirm, recognize limits of, push beyond) the community Story?".[46] Groome writes: "By what we reclaim from our past heritage or propose for our future, by what we ignore from our past and refuse for our future, Christian religious educators are being political". He insists that we have no choice about whether or not Christian religious education will have political implications, only about "the direction in which we should shape the future of society by our present engagement as Christians within it".[47]

It should be noted that this emphasis on the political nature of a proper Christian religious education is not *necessarily* wedded to a politically reformist, liberal, left wing or revolutionary outcome. The claim that Christian religious education is "inevitably political" needs to be glossed by a broad definition of political activity as "any deliberate and structured intervention in people's lives which attempts to influence how they live their lives in society".[48]

In such accounts the adjective "critical" could be understood solely in terms of a reflective, judging form of reason that is used to evaluate the present and uncover the past (through "a reflection upon one's reflection").[49]

---

43. Ramos in Freire, *Pedagogy of the Oppressed*, p. 15, n. 1.

44. Paulo Freire, "Education, Liberation and the Church", *Religious Education* 79: 4 (1984), p. 528. See also Daniel S. Schipani, *Religious Education Encounters Liberation Theology* (Birmingham, Ala.: Religious Education Press, 1988), especially chs. 2 and 4. Schipani argues that in liberation theology "critical reflection" consists of an analysis of concrete situations so as to understand the nature and causes of oppression. This analysis inevitably leads to "political and ideological critiques", the concern being not so much for the (Kantian) liberation of reason as for the (Marxian) transformation of the situation (*ibid.*, pp. 159-160).

45. Thomas H. Groome, *Christian Religious Education* (San Francisco: Harper & Row, 1980), pp. 121-127.

46. *Ibid.*, p. 217.

47. *Ibid.*, p. 26.

48. *Ibid.*, p. 15.

49. *Ibid.*, p. 186.

In this sense of the term we cannot predict the outcome even of a political critical Christian religious education. But Groome and others stand in a tradition which has a certain view of the *particular* political criteria that are to be employed in evaluating the past and present, and envisioning the future. This tradition is for Groome consciously grounded on what has been described as "critical theory": i.e. the emancipatory, transformative thinking of the neo-Marxist Frankfurt School.[50] Its most potent theological expression is "critical theology", a broad movement incorporating so-called theologies of hope, political theologies, feminist theology and other liberation theologies: theologies that make particular claims about the political and social implications of the Christian gospel.[51]

For Groome the ultimate purpose of Christian religious education is "to lead people out to the Kingdom of God" with its personal, spiritual, and sociopolitical values, and one of its immediate purposes is the promotion of human freedom which includes "freedom within our social and political contexts".[52] It is clear that Groome regards the formative educational processes of religious socialization as insufficient to produce the "creating, liberating, and transforming activity" of a freedom-oriented Christian religious education.[53] Critical education is necessary for that goal. This stress on human social freedom as a product content of education, rather than just as a formal requirement for critical thinking, reveals the sort of meaning given by liberation educators to notions of critical education.

Richard Shaull expresses the political *motif* of critical education in a quite general way in this well-known passage:

> There is no such thing as a *neutral* education process. Education either functions as an instrument which is used to facilitate the integration of the younger generation into the logic of the present system and bring about conformity to it, *or* it becomes "the practice of freedom", the means by which men and women deal critically and creatively with reality and discover how to participate in the transformation of their world.[54]

---

50. *Ibid.*, pp. 169-175. Compare, e.g., Rex Gibson, *Critical Theory and Education* (London: Hodder & Stoughton, 1986); Tom Bottomore, *The Frankfurt School* (London: Tavistock, 1984); Jürgen Habermas, *Communication and the Evolution of Society*, trans. Thomas McCarthy (London: Heinemann, 1976; Boston: Beacon Press, 1979), *passim* and *The Philosophical Discourse of Modernity*, trans. Frederick Lawrence (Cambridge: Polity, 1985; Cambridge, Mass.: MIT Press, 1987), pp. 116-130.

51. Groome, *Christian Religious Education*, pp. 43-49. See, e.g., Alistair Kee, ed., *The Scope of Political Theology* (London: SCM, 1978); Christopher Rowland, *Radical Christianity: A Reading of Recovery* (Cambridge: Polity; Maryknoll, N.Y.: Orbis Books, 1988); Ann Loades, ed., *Feminist Theology: A Reader* (London: SPCK, 1990).

52. Groome, *Christian Religious Education*, pp. 35, 47, 96; compare ch. 5 *passim* and his essay "Christian Education for Freedom: A 'Shared-Praxis' Approach", in Padraic O'Hare, ed., *Foundations of Religious Education* (New York: Paulist, 1978), pp. 16-19.

53. Groome, *Christian Religious Education*, p. 125.

54. Richard Shaull, "Foreword" to Freire, *Pedagogy of the Oppressed*, pp. 13-14.

Further Considerations

Groome's position thus stands in opposition to the claims of those who think that Christian enculturation itself is a transforming and liberating thing.[55] By contrast, John Westerhoff has sometimes argued that the Christian tradition can be a transforming tradition if the gospel it contains is properly internalized[56] and acted upon, so that the faith community becomes "a community of cultural change acting on behalf of the Gospel".[57] Thus for Westerhoff—for whom Christian religious education is primarily intentional enculturation— socialization and liberation are compatible activities *within* the Christian "counterculture". In learning the church's ways, he appears to suggest, we learn to liberate and re-form the world—and the church.

This is somewhat paradoxical.[58] It is a claim that can be saved from outright rejection, however, by a little analysis. The position may be regarded as a recognition that formative Christian religious education can pass on knowledge and understanding of the Christian story that itself sets up a "chain (educational) reaction" in learners that leads them to new, transforming and liberating insights. Hence the Christian learner may be formed by the church's tradition into someone who takes the Christian gospel very seriously, and *that* may involve the learner in a critical (and often negatively critical) reassessment of that tradition—particularly on social issues—as well as of the world's (and the learner's own) practice.[59] In this way, perhaps, "catechesis implies more than conserving", and transformation becomes a part of formation.[60]

This combination of conserving-formation and reforming/ liberating-transformation is now usually presented by Westerhoff as a function of Christian religious education's being made up of the "two interrelated processes" of formative education ("formation") in the tradition and critical

---

55. Groome, *Christian Religious Education*, pp. 121-127.

56. John H. Westerhoff, III, "Christian Education: Kerygma v. Didache", in John Ferguson, ed., *Christianity, Society and Education* (London: SPCK, 1981), pp. 192-195.

57. John H. Westerhoff, III, *Will Our Children Have Faith?* (New York: Seabury, 1976), p. 66. See also his "Reshaping Adults", in John H. Westerhoff, III and Gwen Kennedy Neville, *Generation to Generation* (New York: Pilgrim, 1979), pp. 152-159, and *Living the Faith Community* (San Francisco: Harper & Row, 1985), p. 74. See further David R. Hunter, *Christian Education as Engagement* (New York: Seabury, 1963), p. 18.

58. James Michael Lee, *The Content of Religious Instruction* (Birmingham, Ala.: Religious Education Press, 1985), p. 731; P. A. White, "Socialization and Education", in R. F. Dearden *et al.*, eds., *A Critique of Current Educational Aims* (London: Routledge & Kegan Paul, 1975), pp. 120-124; John M. Sutcliffe, *Learning and Teaching Together* (Nutfield, England: NCEC, 1980), pp. 44, 52.

59. John H. Westerhoff, III, "The Liturgical Imperative of Religious Education", in James Michael Lee, ed., *The Religious Education We Need* (Birmingham, Ala.: Religious Education Press, 1977), pp. 81-82 and "A Catechetical Way of Doing Theology", in Norma H. Thompson, ed., *Religious Education and Theology* (Birmingham, Ala.: Religious Education Press, 1982), pp. 222-223.

60. Westerhoff, "Religious Education and Catechesis", in Felderhof, ed., *Religious Education in a Pluralistic Society*, pp. 62-63; see also John H. Westerhoff, III and O. C. Edwards, Jr., eds., *A Faithful Church* (Wilton, Conn.: Morehouse-Barlow, 1981), ch. 1 *passim*; Westerhoff and Neville, *Generation to Generation*, p. 8.

education ("education"—which takes seriously prophetic "critical reflection" on the Christian tradition and the learner's experience).[61] But my point is that formative education *itself* can also function as a sort of theological/ethical critical education, by forming people in a particular position (with a particular set of attitudes, beliefs and valuations) which is the base for their critical thinking not only about other cultures, but also about the received Christian tradition and their own (Christian) position. It is this that gives support to the claim that enculturation can be radical, transformative and liberating. This sounds paradoxical partly because we tend to speak of a tradition as a single entity, forgetting that every tradition is always really a complex of traditions, i.e. of different, though interrelated, elements in a culture that are being passed on. It would be a contradiction to claim that people could be socialized into a reformist attitude to the *whole* of the tradition they have received, for to be critical of the whole tradition is not to have been *formed* in it at all. Some elements within the tradition in which people are formed are in practice necessarily "not open to criticism": including the beliefs etc. that form the platform of the viewpoint from which other parts of the tradition (and other traditions) are critiqued. It is *these* parts of the tradition which, when passed on, can result in a changing of the tradition as they give rise to the critical reflection that liberates people from other parts of the tradition.[62]

A "self-critical tradition" is not, therefore, a contradiction in terms, not even in Christian religious education. Viewed in this way, we may claim that the Christian tradition is itself creative (re-creative), reconstructive and self-transforming.[63] I take it that this is consonant with the suggestion that the "transforming impulse within the faith-community that generates new insights and opens new worlds" may be "the symbol of the kingdom coming in Jesus Christ".[64] Unless *that* is passed on, and left untrameled in its power ("not evacuated of meaning through disuse and neglect"), there is indeed a real danger that tradition-formation will be simply an instrument for domestication. But if that *is* passed on, then there is a "built-in provision for creative dissent".[65] The true message of the gospel, passed on with the rest of the Christian tradition, thus provokes and catalyzes our critical reformation of that tradition.

---

61. Westerhoff, *Living the Faith Community*, pp. 85-87; "Religious Education and Catechesis", pp. 66-67; "Fashioning Christians in Our Day", in Hauerwas and Westerhoff, eds., *Schooling Christians*, p. 267. In recent writings Westerhoff endorses Groome's notion of a dialogue in Christian religious education between scripture/tradition and reason/experience, "but always within the context of a faith community". John H. Westerhoff, III, *Building God's People in a Materialistic Society* (New York: Seabury, 1983), p. 43; also pp. 50, 56-57.

62. This point is taken up in the discussion of critical openness below. Compare Wittgenstein's remarks quoted on pp. 64-65 above (Ch. 4, note 80).

63. See Mary C. Boys, "Access to Traditions and Transformation", in Padraic O'Hare, ed., *Tradition and Transformation in Religious Education* (Birmingham, Ala.: Religious Education Press, 1979).

64. Barker, *Religious Education, Catechesis and Freedom*, p. 233.

65. *Ibid.*, p. 230.

Here again we find a form of critical education that specifies a particular platform (primarily *theological*, and only by implication political/moral—i.e. liberation theology) from which the critique is to be mounted. All critiques are in fact mounted from somewhere, as all perspectives imply a "standpoint" occupied by the artist. The firm base of this sort of critique is to be found within the beliefs and values of the Christian tradition. This is self-critical Christianity. The criteria for the evaluation of the tradition on this account are therefore internal to that tradition,[66] albeit as a (pure) part of a larger (sinful) whole. They thus look rather different from the criteria that constitute the starting point for the "rational" critical enquiry that is advocated by some philosophers,[67] or for any secular "political" critique. *Critical Christian religious education* may therefore not be identical in all respects with secular education's critical education, which itself cannot be presuppositionless and nonpartisan because criticism is never launched from mid-air. Although we should normally welcome the inclusion of critical education within the wider set of Christian religious education activities, we must recognize that the precise nature of such a Christian critical education needs to be specified, debated and defended. *Many would argue that that discussion must involve reference to religious and moral, as well as "rational", criteria.* There are Christians who will reject such a distinction between the criteria of critical Christian religious education and those of secular critical education, arguing that in any critical wrestling no holds may be barred. I would contend, on the other hand, that if Christian religious education is to be justified in retaining the qualification "Christian" it needs to admit that the *outcomes* of such a process must be more restricted in scope. Thus, for example, if the conclusions of critical education were to result in a denial of some fundamental elements of Christianity, then we should have no real reason for calling it "Christian" (except in the minimal sense that its criticisms have been applied to Christianity).

Critical Openness in Christian Religious Education

The phrase "critical openness" is common currency in British thinking and writing about religious education and is highly relevant to our theme of critical education. It is used to denote a feature both of Christian nurture and of secular education about religion that is claimed to make them immune to the charge of indoctrination. John Hull has made much use of the phrase and, presumably as a result, it has found its way into the British Council of Churches' publications *The Child in the Church* and *Understanding Christian Nurture.*[68] I shall concentrate here on the application of the concept to reli-

---

66. David Heywood, "Christian Education as Enculturation", *British Journal of Religious Education* 10: 2 (1988), pp. 70-71.

67. For example: "critical activity involves the testing of any claim to knowledge or understanding at the bar of some impersonal, rational criterion". A. C. MacIntyre, "Against Utilitarianism", in T. H. B. Hollins, ed., *Aims in Education: The Philosophic Approach* (Manchester: Manchester University Press, 1964), p. 19.

68. *The Child in the Church* (London: British Council of Churches, 1976), *Understanding Christian Nurture* (London: British Council of Churches, 1981).

gious nurture/Christian religious education.

Hull poses the liberal educator's rhetorical question and offers his own response: "Are Christians to be conformist, passive acceptors of authority, unable to adapt to crises, too set in the received ways to think creatively? Only a Christian nurtured in critical openness can have characteristics other than these."[69] Critical openness is a "value" which the Christian may possess and is variously described by Hull as a "critical, testing attitude", a "humble attitude", and a "discipline" that "suggests listening, respecting, being inter-dependent, being in relation".[70] It is not so much a basic Christian concept as "a derived or consequential attribute of Christian living".[71] Hull sees critical openness as a type of "thinking for yourself", a popular phrase that also covers autonomy. But "autonomy" seems to connote self-enclosed inde-pendence, whereas critical openness "conveys a meaning which is closer to Christian faith" and includes interdependence.[72] What in this chapter has been called "critical education" is a set of processes that have as their out-comes the development of such attitudes, which in turn allow the exercise of the (learned) critical skills of evaluation and assessment. Thus "critical edu-cation" is education for and towards "critical openness".

According to Hull there are in some senses "definite limits to this criticism" in Christian nurture, although in another sense there are "no limits to the spirit of criticism" for it is "a critical testing of all things". The acceptable lim-its to criticism are presumably partially defined by the firm ground on which the Christian is to stand while critically testing and assessing more doubtful terrain. Criticism is therefore "directed towards the uncertainties but it (springs) from the certainties".[73] Hull claims to be describing here an attitude that is reflected in New Testament logia about enquiring into spiritual insights or the scriptures, judging for yourself, testing the spirits, self-examination etc.[74] It may be described, then, as "the product of Christian faith",[75] and is claimed to be compatible with the Christian doctrines of both humanity and divini-ty. Thus a Christian anthropology that views human beings as unfinished

---

69. John M. Hull, *Studies in Religion and Education* (Lewes, England: Falmer, 1984), p. 211.

70. *Ibid.*, pp. 190, 193, 205, 220, 209. *Understanding Christian Nurture* says that the phrase suggests "interdependence, receptivity, and a loving, listening attitude" (p. 8). Such quo-tations indicate that critical openness is primarily conceived of as a learning outcome. Not surprisingly, however, the phrase has come to be applied to educational processes; thus crit-ical openness is "a method of approaching religious education", promoting a certain sort of study of religion. Brenda Watson *et al.*, *Critical Openness* (Oxford: Farmington Institute, n.d.), pp. 8 and 5.

71. Hull, *Studies in Religion and Education*, p. 219.

72. *Ibid.*, p. 209; compare *Understanding Christian Nurture*, p. 6 and below Chapter 8.

73. Hull, *Studies in Religion and Education*, p. 193; also p. 220.

74. *Ibid.*, pp. 191-193; p. 201; see also *Understanding Christian Nurture*, pp. 9-10.

75. Hull, *Studies*, p. 199. See also Alex R. Rodger, *Education and Faith in an Open Society* (Edinburgh: Handsel, 1982), p. 17.

and needing to make themselves to some extent allows for openness; as does a theology that regards God as no dictator, but one who seeks with us a fellowship of minds—"Come let us reason together". God too, it appears, is "critical and open".[76]

Hull's assertion of the importance of not restraining criticism[77] suggests that, although critical openness springs from "the certainties", the Christian may (and sometimes must) shift her ground from time to time, adopting another position and testing her original one from there. This is a more radical criticalness than we have so far allowed. Here *everything* does seem to be open to test, but not all at the same time.[78] The analogy that springs to mind is that of Theseus's ship being repaired at sea: each plank is subject to removal and replacement, but only while the repairer is standing on the safe support of wood that is not *at the same time* being removed. Such an activity is perhaps logically possible but, as the analogy indicates, it would be risky!

This concept of openness includes openness to the future of the learner, but the *intention* of the nurturer is to target her teaching so as to produce an *outcome* that can be plotted within the definition "Christian".[79] At this point we surely uncover another proper limitation on openness, and meet again a proper qualification of critical Christian religious education. There are logical restrictions on the openness—in the sense of the open-endedness—of what may properly be described as a *Christian* nurturing or *Christian* religious education process. Hence there are limits to the openness of the Christian learner, although these limits are simply a function of where we draw the boundaries around what we are willing to regard as Christian learning outcomes. It is clear that so-called "liberal" Christian religious educators draw these limits more widely than do "conservatives", and are much less willing than the latter group to describe as a "Christian future for our children" a situation in which the children's "own distinctive contribution to it" was distinctly curtailed.[80] It should be clear, therefore, that a "wide" critical openness is a *liberal* Christian religious education virtue: using the adjective here—as many do—to indicate an indebtedness to the educational tradition of "liberal education" (see pp. 33-34 above). It most easily accommodates a *theologically* liberal understanding of human nature, God, revelation, spirituality, finality and authority.[81] Hull's views on these theological topics will only be acceptable to Christians of a liberal theology. The more theologically conservative would not find themselves in agreement with this interpretation

---

76. Hull, *Studies*, pp. 202-204, 211, 216-217; see *Understanding Christian Nurture*, pp. 18-22.

77. Hull, *Studies*, p. 220.

78. See Arthur J. Rowe, "Critical Openness and Religious Education", *British Journal of Religious Education* 8: 2 (1986), p. 63.

79. *The Child in the Church*, pp. 23-24; *Understanding Christian Nurture* p. 6; Hull, *Studies*, p. 221.

80. *The Child in the Church*, p. 24; *Understanding Christian Nurture*, pp. 12, 15-19.

81. Hull, *Studies in Religion and Education*, ch. 18; John L. Elias, *Studies in Theology and Education* (Malabar, Fla.: Krieger, 1986), pp. 40-41.

of the proposition that "Christian faith is constantly critical of itself"; nor would many conservatives be happy with the claim that "there is no fixed and final form of Christian faith, and this is why there can be no fixed and final form of nurture into it".[82]

Here we face again the problem of the openness of openness. And we may remind ourselves that this is not merely a theological problem. The tradionalists's jibe that a window stuck open is worse than a window stuck closed has some merit. In Mary Midgley's words: "opening windows is a healthy habit, but it is not much use when you are lost in a snowstorm".[83] Some limits need to be, *and implicitly always are*, built-in to the attitudes and skills that constitute critical openness. We ought indeed to be open to "fresh evidence", the "experience of others" and their "real needs and situations". We ought particularly to be open "to critical assessment of the ease with which people, including oneself, can be self-deluded".[84] But we still need to ask what the constraints are on such openness, for constraints there must be. It is neither possible nor desirable to educate someone into a completely open openness.

We may bring to mind those students who are always convinced by the last book they have read, skeptics who purport to believe nothing because the evidence is never all in and deception is always a logical possibility, or individuals who fit the description of "children, tossed to and fro and carried about by every wind of doctrine".[85] Individuals such as these are rarely presented to us as models of fully educated persons. Unqualified "openness" is not, therefore, an educational virtue. It is rather a *"critical* openness" that is being commended here, and that involves the necessary limitations of *judgment*. I would agree that the qualifier "critical" is intended to signal that this openness is not "openness to every influence, idea or whim but . . . openness informed by analysis and rational judgement".[86] Theological considerations apart, openness can only be commended in a qualified form.

It should also be noted that the rhetoric of openness can be dangerous if it is used as an intentional, or more often an unintentional, cloak for a certain sort of intolerance. We should not be brow-beaten into accepting another person's position for the sake of a content-free "openness to change". Surprisingly, many open-minded "liberals" are more intolerant of opposing views than their more conservative critics.

It has been claimed that the adjective "critical" has been misunderstood by some to mean negative, destructive criticism, and even "hijacked by the secularist to remove some of the crucial areas" in school-based education about

---

82. *The Child in the Church*, p. 23.

83. Mary Midgley, *Heart and Mind: The Varieties of Moral Experience* (London: Methuen, 1983), p. 13.

84. Brenda Watson, "Openness and Commitment", *Occasional Papers* 20 (Oxford: Farmington Institute, 1985) and *Education and Belief*, p. 44.

85. Ephesians 4:14. The verse adds significantly: "dupes of crafty rogues and their deceitful schemes" (N.E.B.).

86. Watson, *Education and Belief*, p. 40.

religion (e.g. the area of commitment). Brenda Watson therefore prefers to speak of *critical affirmation*. This, she claims, involves more than "openness", is "warmer" and more positive, and may be combined with "commitment" and "certainty". It includes a search for insights, understanding and commitment which shows rigorous criticism "but not for the sake of destruction", together with "the desire to make other people's insights one's own". "Such an attitude goes beyond the advocacy of reason *per se*."[87] Certainly there are practical educational problems associated with the way that "critical openness" is understood by some educators in the field of religion.

As far as Christian religious education is concerned, many Christians would expect some "openness" to be the mark of any adult Christian religious education. To affirm this is like being in favor of virtue. The question still remains as to the nature—and limits—of such openness in any given Christian religious education experience.

It is possible to hold that the limits of critical openness are as much psychological as they are logical, epistemological or theological. As I argued earlier in this chapter, the most anyone can manage is a clearer view of the foundations on which he or she stands. Critical reason cannot help us to lay, or re-lay, such foundations. Some, at least, would claim that the foundations of *religion* are essentially psychological foundations with epistemological implications, rather than vice versa (see Chapter 6 below). At any rate there are profound psychological as well as theological issues involved in any discussion as to whether, and how far, Christian religious education should be an "open-ended", "tentative" and exploratory searching for meaning within the Christian tradition,[88] and how far it might include a more radical "testing to destruction" of Christian affirmations.[89] The psychological issues, as we have seen, include considerations about the nature of persons—and of Christian persons—and their attitudes, values, virtues, emotions and overt behavior. Arguments about the extent of any critical openness that is appropriate to the Christian learner cannot ignore these elements of personhood: elements that

---

87. Watson *et al.*, *Critical Openness*, pp. 3, 6-7; and *Education and Belief*, pp. 54-55, 78. Watson is mainly writing of teaching about religion in the passages quoted here, but her comments have a wider relevance. Compare also Passmore, *The Philosophy of Teaching*, pp. 173-174, and his distinction between criticism and "cavilling".

88. Kevin Nichols, "Commitment, Search and Dialogue" in his *Voice of the Hidden Waterfall* (London: St. Paul, 1980).

89. This activity is regarded by Donald Mackinnon, writing in a British context, as essential to the task of theology in a secular university. His essay in Teodor Shanin, ed., *The Rules of the Game* (London: Tavistock, 1972) describes this as "a place where Christian belief is tested to destruction, where individual *credenda* are submitted to the most meticulous scrutiny . . . . where nothing is taken for granted in respect of the historically observable future of Christian institutions". MacKinnon writes of a Christian teacher of theology in such a situation as someone who is at once committed and uncommitted, committed to "a grave fundamental seriousness about the problems of Christian belief" yet at the same time prepared to find the outcome of this work totally other than his or her hopes and anticipations. Such a person "will learn, in a hard school, something of the cost of following the argument whithersoever it leads, something of the price of seeking the truth" (p. 168).

are classified as belonging to the affective and lifestyle, rather than the cognitive, domains. We shall encounter some of them in later discussion.

But even if we restrict ourselves to the cognitive area, we still meet the question as to whether any particular *learning outcome* is Christian or not. Such a judgment will depend on our notion of what it is for a belief (or emotion or action etc.), and a believer (feeler, actor), to be Christian. We must draw the line somewhere. Many Christian religious educators will be reluctant to judge pure critical openness, in and of itself, as a Christian attribute or an element in a proper Christian religious education. They would rather judge it by its fruits, including among them—but not restricting them to—its cognitive fruits. A completely open openness is not only suspect educationally and as a character trait, it also lets in too many beliefs (emotions, actions, etc.) that would be regarded as non-Christian even on the widest definition. Many would therefore argue that a more restricted, *Christianly-biased openness* is more commendable in the Christian learner, when his learning is judged by Christian standards. They will be willing to talk of a *Christian* critical education which leads to such *Christian* critical openness. Clearly this debate will involve us in normative theological judgments (see Chapter 6 below). Certainly there is no neutral *educational* criterion that will decide such matters noncontroversially. "Critical openness" cannot serve us as a shibboleth for proper Christian religious education; not until we are told what it really means.[90]

Ideology and Christian Religious Education

The attitude of "critical openness" outlined above is appealed to in some discussions of Christianity as an *ideology*. Before proceeding to analyze such an account, it would be useful to explicate the precise way in which the word ideology is being used here.[91] The term is not intended to denote a rigid, closed set of cognitive beliefs—propounded often in the face of conflicting empirical evidence and rejecting self-critical intellectual analysis—that

90. Note that any Christian formation worthy of the name, however "critically open", needs to result in *some* nontentative claims—if only that Jesus is "a good thing".

91. Many writers on ideology, while recognizing a pejorative usage designating a closed set of assumptions serving to support particular power structures (see the "interest theory" described below), also argue for a valid neutral sense of the term that is worth preserving. Thus Juan Luis Segundo writes of a non-pejorative use of the term ideology to denote a "system of goals and means" and "a system of interconnected values". Juan Luis Segundo, *The Liberation of Theology*, trans. John Drury (New York: Gill & Macmillan, 1977), pp. 102, 104, contrast chapter I; see also Karl Mannheim, *Ideology and Utopia: An Introduction to the Sociology of Knowledge*, trans. Louis Wirth and Edward Shils (London: Routledge & Kegan Paul, 1936; New York: Harcourt, Brace, 1956), p. 239. For an extended discussion of some of the issues involved see Patrick Corbett, *Ideologies* (London: Hutchinson, 1965). The deprecatory use of the word, as designating a false consciousness (of social and economic realities) or a collective illusion shared by a particular social class and serving their interests, derives from Karl Marx. See Karl Marx and Friedrich Engels, *The German Ideology* (completed 1846, published 1932), excerpts in English translation in Lewis S. Feuer, ed., *Marx and Engels: Basic Writings on Politics and Philosophy* (New York: Doubleday, 1959), pp. 287-288;

expounds some Grand Scheme about the world and history. Nor does it carry the implications of falsehood, distortion and the serving of class interests. Here the word is used far more neutrally, simply to mark *a system of ideas and norms that underlie, and serve to justify, promote and defend, a particular culture or practice*. An ideology is therefore a system of ideas and values espoused in a particular way and for a particular purpose—i.e. in an interested, committed, justificatory and apologetic way, so as to motivate and direct action. Examples include the cognitive dimension of worldviews and religions. On this definition, then, we may say that religions, like cultures, are broader than ideologies, but incorporate them. Thus ideology has been defined as "that part of culture which is actively concerned with the establishment and defence of patterns of belief and value",[92] and religion as "a system of symbols which acts to establish ... moods and motivations ... by formulating conceptions of a general order of existence ... ".[93] Religions therefore contain ideologies of a certain type. Such religious ideologies are often metaphysical in form, but we must add that their content is related to (affect-loaded) questions of salvation. As Patrick Burke puts it, "a religion is a culture acting in a certain way, namely, attending to salvation". It is "a way of life focused on salvation".[94]

John Hull appears to claim that it is critical openness that allows the development of a "self-critical" rather than a dangerously "self-inflated" ideology. The main way of achieving this is through "ideological self-criti-

---

David McLellan, *The Thought of Karl Marx* (London: Macmillan, 1980), pp. 135-136. Yet "'ideology' did not begin as a term of abuse, and in current usage it often so far escapes any implications of exposé or denunciation that it embraces any subjectively coherent set of political beliefs" or "any system of ideas and norms directing political and social action .... [or] all ideas of every sort ... [including] the most disinterested and objective science". David Braybrooke, "Ideology", in Paul Edwards, ed., *The Encyclopedia of Philosophy*, Vol. 4 (New York: Macmillan and Free Press; London: Collier Macmillan, 1967), p. 124, and the entry "Ideology" in Antony Flew, ed., *A Dictionary of Philosophy* (London: Pan, 1979), p. 150. See also Elias, *Studies in Theology and Education*, ch. 11. The above definition is even more neutral than the one used in the body of this text. We may compare Charles Glock's description of the "ideological dimension" of a religion, as comprising the scope, content, salience, strength and style of religious beliefs. See his "On the Study of Religious Commitment", reprinted in Charles Y. Glock and Rodney Stark, *Religion and Society in Tension* (Chicago: Rand McNally, 1965), pp. 2, 23-27.

92. Clifford Geertz (quoting Lloyd A. Fallers) in Robert Bocock and Kenneth Thompson, eds., *Religion and Ideology* (Manchester: Manchester University Press, 1985), p. 83. Geertz himself defines culture as "an historically transmitted pattern of meanings embodied in symbols, a system of inherited conceptions expressed in symbolic forms by means of which men communicate, perpetuate, and develop their knowledge about and attitudes toward life" (*ibid.*, p. 66).

93. *Ibid.*, p. 67. Both ideology and religion are therefore cultural *systems*.

94. Patrick Burke, *The Fragile Universe* (London: Macmillan; New York: Barnes & Noble, 1979), pp. 40-41, 53. On religions of salvation and liberation see John Hick, *An Interpretation of Religion* (New Haven: Yale University Press; London: Macmillan, 1989), ch. 3 and passim.

95. Hull, *What Prevents Christian Adults from Learning?*, pp. 74, 78.

cism".[95] Hull recognizes that no one can escape completely from his or her ideology without abandoning it. Hence *extra*-ideological criticism "from outside" is only possible, for those who wish to retain their ideological identity, through "partial and occasional suspension of belief". "*Inter*-ideological criticism" is a more viable notion in Christian religious education, as the Christian learner engages in dialogue with other worldviews from within his or her Christian perspective. The most important critical element in (adult) Christian education, however, is *inner*-ideological criticism. This involves re-ideologizing, rather than de-ideologizing, faith: a process in which Christianity has continually been engaged down the ages.[96]

Hull argues that a Christian learning "which involves Christian criticism"[97] is the necessary therapy for the pathological condition of the "unlearning religious person"—the Christian adult who is resistant to the change of learning.[98] Here again we meet the claim that proper Christian religious education needs elements of critical education to complement its formative educational processes. Many adults, Hull contends, are hindered in their Christian learning by a fear of it. He draws on various accounts in the psychology of belief of a human being's "need to be right" and of "the pain of learning".[99] He then goes on to describe usefully various tactics that people can employ to reduce this discomfort of new learning. I attempt to enumerate them below, as they represent an interesting contribution to the phenomenology (pathology?) of the Christian who is resistant to learning.

The first group is regarded by Hull as most characteristic of religious sects and represents extreme reactions. (It is appropriate to add the qualification that they may be more widely represented than Hull suggests.) They include:

(1) *Separation* from the world and its beliefs, either socially or psychologically (an "inner migration"). This often produces a religious form of tunnel vision: "The Jehovah's Witness sees the pages of the Bible but he sees nothing else".[100]

(2) *Thought-stopping* techniques. Certain Christians abandon or suppress all reflection (whether critical or otherwise) about their beliefs, surrendering themselves to a sense of relief by not engaging these particular intellectual gears. G. K. Chesterton's memorable aphorism may be applied to this situation and its dangers: "There is a thought that stops thought. That is the only thought that ought to be stopped."[101]

---

96. *Ibid.*, pp. 75, 79.

97. *Ibid.*, p. 134.

98. *Ibid.*, p. 123; also pp. 7-10, 113.

99. *Ibid.*, ch. 3. Particular reference is made to Leon Festinger's theory of cognitive dissonance and George Kelly's personal construct theory. See Leon Festinger, *A Theory of Cognitive Dissonance* (Stanford, Calif.: Stanford University Press, 1962) and George A. Kelly, *A Theory of Personality: the Psychology of Personal Constructs* (New York: Norton, 1963).

100. Hull, *What Prevents Christian Adults from Learning?*, p. 118.

101. Gilbert K. Chesterton, *Orthodoxy* (London: Bodley Head, 1911), p. 56.

(3) *Ideological hardening*. Here passive learning, based on authoritarian teaching, is allowed, but no active exploration of the faith. "Ideological compensation" is often engendered, whereby the belief system explains away uncomfortable truths (e.g. Why do so few believe?).

(4) *Mission and Evangelism*. These activities can flow from wholly proper motives of course, but they also result in an emotional "high" for the sufferer from religious learning sickness, who is "proved" right by converts joining his or her church. One of the more worrying insights thrown up by cognitive dissonance theory is that evangelism may sometimes be entered into as a compensatory technique when people's hopes have been "proved" false.[102]

(5) A *distraction* of attention away from Christian beliefs and towards "Christian" fellowship, drama or table tennis.

The second group of tactics are described as more characteristic of Christians in mainstream religious traditions (although the distinction is somewhat arbitrary, and there is considerable overlap). They constitute "a wide range of milder but often less stable forms of accommodation".[103] Hull includes here:

(6) *Vagueness*: a retreat from specific belief, accompanied by a lack of clarity, and often also by . . .

(7) *Piety*: "we leave these things to the Lord" (and therefore suspend our critical faculties).

(8) A *respect for authority* is found here, as it also is within the sects, but in mainstream churches in an appropriately mitigated form. The minister (or the Bible) knows the answers, but we don't trouble them with our questions. This can also take the form of a fervent but uncritical enthusiasm for a particular Christian author.

(9) The development of a *"one-dimensional" belief structure*[104] in which religious belief becomes unreal, remote, superficial and emaciated, losing its complexity and its "guts".

(10) The *objectification of belief*, as when the Bible or theology is studied at arm's length (perhaps historically) and not in any personal, internalized, what-it-means-to-me way. (One might suggest that critical education can itself contribute to this defense mechanism, as observer-study is less painful than participant-reflection.)[105]

(11) A spirituality of *passivity*, in which responsibility is passed over to others; and active, personal enquiry abandoned. Hull inveighs against the passive voice of the language used by many churchgoers about being "led" in prayer, being given a blessing, and "recharging the batteries" through wor-

---

102. Leon Festinger *et al.*, *When Prophecy Fails: A Social and Psychological Study of a Modern Group that Predicted the Destruction of the World* (New York: Harper & Row, 1956). But these findings have been challenged: see Robin Gill, *Competing Convictions* (London: SCM, 1989), ch. 3.

103. Hull, *What Prevents Christian Adults from Learning?*, p. 132.

104. *Ibid.*, p. 140.

105. See the use of the "arm's length" metaphor for critical education cited in note 4 above.

ship; arguing that many people prefer the passivity of a service because it offers possibilities for dreamy inward migration, "whereas to be exposed with others, especially with children and young people, is always to bring one to the point of contact with the dreaded belief system".[106]

This is a perceptive analysis of the games people play in order to escape the pain of new learning in Christianity. We should note that Hull regards the unlearning condition as pathological not just because Christianity must be continually reinterpreted (re-ideologized), but also because the unlearning state is sometimes actually recognized by those who exist in it to be unsatisfactory. I think that this latter factor is the key one, but that it is rarer than Hull seems to imply. I contend that it is not the task of *every Christian* to reinterpret the faith for each generation, or even for themselves. To begin with, many people are simply incapable of that. And in any case knowledge is not advancing so quickly that major re-ideologizing is needed for each new generation. The points "where the shoe pinches" for Christian belief today have not really been created by space travel, information technology or the ethics of nuclear war; but rather by scientific, philosophical, technological and historical developments of the nineteenth, eighteenth and even the seventeenth centuries. Further, it is not the case that every Christian needs his or her own reinterpretation. People are not as different from one another as that, and it is my *personal appropriation* of the tradition as it is re-ideologized by others that is the process that allows me to "own" this new faith for myself. I do not need to have created it (rethought) it myself.

Rather, the problem comes when people feel the inadequacy of their own belief systems, often because they recognize the puerile and incoherent nature of their own beliefs.[107] This painful condition, in which adults can be chronically disabled in their thinking by their fear that Christianity is not really rationally defensible, their fear of being wrong, and their fear of the pain of unlearning and of new learning, is certainly a pathological—and often guilt-ridden—state. For a person in such a state, critical education is surely the necessary therapy. But the number of people for whom their lack of (appropriate) cognitive learning is a felt need is probably much smaller than is often assumed. Critical Christian religious education is essential for the church as a whole, to the extent that the faith needs to be continually reinterpreted as it faces new challenges. But not every Christian needs to do this. Furthermore, it must always be recognized that a discussion of cognitive learning and relearning relates only to one dimension of Christian religious education, a dimension that I will argue is not the most significant one. There is perhaps a greater, although different, danger in neglecting the appropriate affective and lifestyle aspects of Christian religious education. A concern for the cognitive is important, but it should not turn us into cognitive imperialists about religious education.

Critical education thus has the limited—but significant—task of helping

---

106. *Ibid.*, p. 143.
107. *Ibid.*, pp. 116-117; also pp. 9, 124.

some learners by creating in them the ability to think critically (in an evaluative fashion) about their religion. But before they can get that far, adult
Christian learners will need, like all adult learners, to become more fully
conscious of the beliefs that "operate not only in front of our eyes but from
behind our backs", thus "increasing the responsibility and integrity of the
self".[108] In this way the learner can be set free to re-ideologize her or his
faith. As I have indicated already, however, this is not possible for all beliefs.
Furthermore, developmental psychologists claim that it is only possible at all
when the learner has reached a certain cognitive developmental stage. Critical
education is not as universal a panacea as it may sometimes appear.

We may at this point profitably consider further the notion of religion as an
ideology. Students of ideology have tended to adopt either (a) an *interest theory* or (b) a *strain theory*. These involve interpreting ideologies either (a) as
deriving from the interests of a dominant group and constituting a "mask" or
"weapon" working to the advantage of that group by encouraging ideas for
(their) pursuit of power; or (b) as deriving from a sense of tension, dislocation
or unease, and constituting a remedy for such ills: i.e. as a system of ideas for
escaping anxiety.[109] Although there is often some truth in interpretation (a), it
has always seemed to me rather artificial when applied generally to religious
traditions. I believe that it is analysis (b) that is most illuminating of religion.
A religious belief system is not to be seen, as it is by proponents of any con-
spiracy theory, simply or wholly as an ideology created by the powerful for
their advantage. Rather it is primarily a set of beliefs that are oriented towards
healing, release and wholeness—in a word towards salvation.

Because of this salvific orientation, we should note, religious belief is
never just theoretical metaphysics. It is practical, spiritually-forming and
action-directing. Thus Christian faith is not a *speculative* ideology, but "a form
of life, a passionate commitment to the quest for deliverance from the world,
for salvation and spiritual perfection". It is a "commitment to live by certain
values and subject to a particular standard".[110] Salvation and ethics, not theological reflection, are the driving forces of Christianity.[111] To quote two
other writers, the first a classical Protestant theologian and the second a contemporary Catholic student of religion: "To know Christ means to know his

---

108. *Ibid.*, pp. 67, 55.

109. Geertz, in Bocock and Thompson, eds., *Religion and Ideology,* pp. 76-78. See also
Prozesky, *Religion and Ultimate Well-Being,* p. 150: "As the creators of culture we exter-
nalise our needful selfhood so that we may internalize our euonic support. Thus human beings
are physicians to their own infirmity." For a survey of various theories of religious behavior
relevant to such claims, see Michael Argyle and Benjamin Beit-Hallahmi, *The Social
Psychology of Religion* (London: Routledge & Kegan Paul, 1975), ch. 11.

110. Don Cupitt, *The Sea of Faith* (London: British Broadcasting Corporation, 1986), p.
258 (see also p. 221), and Don Cupitt, *Taking Leave of God* (London: SCM, 1980), p. 113 (see
also pp. 124-125).

111. See O'Hear, *Experience, Explanation and Faith,* p. 249.

112. Philip Melanchthon, *Loci Communes Theologici,* Dedicatory Letter, ed. Wilhelm
Pauck, trans. Lowell J. Satre and Pauck, *Melanchthon and Bucer* (Philadelphia: Westminster
Press; London: SCM, 1969), pp. 21-22.

benefits, and not . . . to reflect upon his natures and the modes of his incarnation . . . . Christ was given us as a remedy and . . . . a saving remedy."[112] "Christian believers who attempt to direct their life-aims according to the ideal set before them by their religion would protest that no merely academic study can ever discover what the Christian Way really is . . . . Rather, they would say, Jesus Christ himself *is* the Way who leads his followers to their God-given end."[113]

It is in spirituality and morality that religious truth finds its proper home, rather than as a contribution to some transcending, metaphysical cosmology. This, of course, is a normative judgment about religion. I would claim that religious truth is *essentially* practical, saving truth. In the Bible to know God is to do—and reflect—the will of God.[114] It is only really in this sense that religion can allow itself to be described as a system of ideas: only if the ideas are thoroughly practical and salvific. In the case of religious beliefs it must be said that "by contrast with science or philosophy the cognitive interest is no longer primary", but gives way to the moral-valuative interest. Talcott Parsons argues that acceptance of a religious belief is a commitment to its implementation in life in a way that acceptance of a philosophical belief is not. Thus "a philosophical belief becomes religious in so far as it is made the basis of a commitment in action".[115]

Such a "socially constructed" meaningful order ("nomos") or world has been described as "a shield against terror"—the terror of "the danger of meaninglessness".[116] Students of religion often claim that even a religion's theodicy (its attempt to understand and cope with the problem of evil) is to be seen not so much as providing happiness as providing meaning. The "redemption" that religions offer is often no more—but no less—than "the redeeming assurance of meaning itself". And this meaning is always a *human* meaning: "religion is the audacious attempt to conceive the entire universe as being humanly significant".[117]

These claims will be taken up in Chapter 6. I introduce them here only to support the view that, while on the more neutral definition that I have given of ideology (see p. 100) Christianity is certainly in part an ideology. That

113. Francis Clarke, *The Christian Way* (Milton Keynes, England: Open University Press, 1978), p. 69.

114. See Brian Haymes, *The Concept of the Knowledge of God* (Basingstoke: Macmillan, 1988), pp. 89-93, 116-119.

115. Talcott Parsons, *The Social System* (New York: Free Press; London: Collier-Macmillan, 1951), p. 367.

116. Berger, *The Social Reality of Religion*, pp. 31-32.

117. *Ibid.*, pp. 37, 66; see also p. 87. On the meaning of "meaning" here, see below Chapter 6.

118. Hence: "religion on one side anchors the power of our symbolic resources for formulating analytic ideas in an authoritative conception of the overall shape of reality, . . . on another side it anchors the power of our, also symbolic, resources for expressing emotions". Thus religious symbols provide a cosmic guarantee for our ability not only to comprehend the world, but also to give precision to our emotions so that we may endure it. Clifford Geertz, in Bocock and Thompson, eds., *Religion and Ideology*, pp. 71-72, see also p. 7. See also Chapters 6 and 9 of the present book.

term can only be taken on its own as an adequate description of the Christian religion if the affective,[118] volitional and lifestyle components of Christianity are seen as included with, implied by, arising from, or as sources of, the ideas of this ideology. In religion it is certainly never a matter of "ideas alone" or "pure ideas".

We must now return to John Hull's argument. Hull takes a positive view of ideologies, as essential for effective social action, but he also recognizes their dark side. It is this more negative dimension of some well-known ideologies (particularly political ones)—ideologies that have substituted rigid conformity of belief for critical thinking—that has led many to claim that Christianity is not an ideology.[119] Hull recognizes that all ideologies tend towards such a "falsifying" and "absolutizing" character. They are "inspirational not educational", mobilizing and justifying the group's action in a way that *can* lead to the sloganizing, simplification and stereotyping of thinking; and also to an absolutizing of its truth and authority as the only possible point of view. Such tendencies may result in "ideological closure", in which the ideology selects one orthodox interpretation from the many that are possible, closing the ideological mind to novel insights. It can also lead to "ideological lag": a phrase that labels the gap in time between "external" events and their impact on the ideological community which is in the grip of its traditional stereotypes.[120]

It is these restrictions on new thinking and new learning that lead Hull to appeal for "self-critical ideologies not self-inflated ideologies". He argues that any full Christian religious education must avoid trapping people in yesterday's ideology, whether their own or the church's "official" one. The only alternative is *ideological self-criticism*, which fractures the received ideology by educating people into a recognition of the relative relativeness (if I may be allowed the phrase) of the ideology. Thus a proper historical sense, which is the basis of much of critical thinking, must be developed in the learner. By means of this she will be able to spot the difference between the first century Jesus tradition and its twentieth-century counterpart—and the difference between each of these and thirteenth century and eighteenth century interpretations. This enables the learner to think for herself about Jesus.

In a striking passage Hull describes what is going on here as a fracturing of the ideological medium so that the primordial saving realities of Christianity can become contemporarily present to the learner, and thus create a Christian-ideology-for-today. He defines the task of the Christian religious educator of adults as that of facilitating those kinds of learning experiences which, while keeping the Christian learner within the Christian ideology, set her free from naïve and absolute ideological enclosure. To this end the Christian adult religious educator will mainly use inner-ideological techniques, for he or she will be educating from faith to faith. This educator will seek in this way

    119. See Karl Rahner, "Ideology and Christianity", *Theological Investigations*, Vol. VI (London: Darton, Longman & Todd, 1969), pp. 43-57.
    120. Hull, *What Prevents Christian Adults from Learning?*, pp. 63, 64, 68.

to discriminate between the various layers of the ideology so as to create

> that hermeneutical distance which exposes those cracks in the ideology
> through which the power of the saving events may still break through. It
> is true that the ideology itself is intended to prolong those savings events
> and to make the community dynamic in its response to them, but the dan-
> gers of falsification, time-lag and absolutization can only be avoided by
> educational procedures which relativize the ideology, not destroying it, but
> breaking it so that it becomes a more supple and more faithful channel for
> the saving realities.[121]

Hull describes this as the re-ideologizing of the faith of faithful adults.

These are powerful words. Many will accept that they are applicable to the
church as a whole, as well as to those Christians who feel restricted or
trapped by an absolutizing religious ideology. But what of other Christian
learners? Can we say that they too are trapped (objectively), even though
they do not recognize it (subjectively)? Can this educational therapy help
them? And what of those who, on any assessment, will never have the cognitive skills—or inclination—to re-ideologize their faith along these lines?
I have indicated my own reservations on these points in this chapter and the
previous one. Those whose theological understanding of the nature of
Christian truth and of the Christian tradition is different from that espoused
by Hull will have other reservations. Such reservations notwithstanding,
there is a great deal in Hull's account that is of signal importance for the
contemporary task of the serious Christian religious educator.

---

121. *Ibid.*, p. 85. A "hermeneutical distance" is a recognition of the gap (which creates a
tension) between the interpreter's horizon of understanding and the tradition (or text's) self-
understanding. See Gadamer, *Truth and Method*, p. 273; Anthony C. Thiselton, *The Two
Horizons: New Testament Hermeneutics and Philosophical Description* (Exeter, England:
Paternoster, 1980), pp. 51-84, 314-319. On the notion of "relativizing" the Christian ideology, see below Chapter 10.

Part III

Christianity
and
Christian Religious Education

CHAPTER 6

The Nature of Christianity

LISTING THE CHRISTIAN ATTRIBUTES

What is Christianity? If the Christian religion represents the substantive content of Christian religious education, and if Christian religious education's primary aim is that of teaching people to be Christian (which includes becoming "more Christian"), then the question of the nature of Christianity can hardly be avoided. Of course anyone who faces this question must do so in the face of the powerful theological lobby that distinguishes the gospel of God's act and revelation from that most human, fallible and mundane of phenomena—religion.[1] Yet such a prophetic critique will not in the end get us very far, for if God is to reveal himself there must be a human pole for such a revelation, and if God is to act in the world there must be some worldly effects of such divine action. Human religion is the mundane locus of those putative divine events. Religion is usually the soil for the gospel. Eventually it is also the fruit, albeit a somewhat bruised fruit, that grows from the gospel. Christianity—unfortunately perhaps, but inevitably—is a religion.

The material that follows in this chapter surveys some of the main dimensions of the Christian religion and of Christian religious education, with particular reference to those that I regard as being of prime importance. This will serve as an opportunity for some philosophical discussion about certain of these dimensions.

It would be useful at this stage to attempt to list a number of attributes of a person that may be designated "Christian" attributes, the development of

---

1. Karl Barth's account of "The Revelation of God as the Abolition of Religion" is often appealed to for support here—see Karl Barth, *Church Dogmatics*, Vol. I, Part 2, trans. G. T. Thomson and Harold Knight (Edinburgh: Clark, 1956), especially pp. 303, 314, 325-361. But we should note that Barth distinguishes "religion as unbelief" from "true religion": the latter being the Christian religion justified, sanctified and exalted by God's revelation and grace. See Herbert Hartwell, *The Theology of Karl Barth* (London: Duckworth, 1964), pp. 87-91. See also Chapter 7 below.

which might be regarded as appropriate learning outcomes for Christian religious education. As we shall see, this is inevitably a normative task. Some of these attributes are *characteristic* of Christianity, but not peculiar to Christians; others (especially some of the Christian beliefs-that) are *distinctively Christian* attributes. But there is no suggestion here that, for example, Christian trust, Christian love or Christian good works are *essentially* different from similar attitudes, emotions and overt behavior in non-Christians. They may differ from them, however, in their depth and range, the objects to which they are directed, and their accompanying motivations or cognitions.

Despite the nouns used in my list, I intend the categories outlined below to be inclusive of both product and process contents. This is a distinction between (a) an achieved consequence or completed end result of a process ("product"), and (b) the process-task or performance itself ("process").[2] It enables us to distinguish (a) faith, trust, beliefs, understandings, experiences, meanings, feelings and attitudes as *achieved states, orientations or dispositions* ("products"), from (b) "faith-ing", trusting, believing, thinking, valuing, "meaning-making", experiencing, feeling, loving, evaluating and analyzing as *acts, performances and operations* ("processes"). Although this can be a useful distinction, those who use it recognize that product content and process content always exist together, the distinction between them arising from conceptual abstraction.[3]

My list of (overlapping) categories of Christian attributes would read as follows:[4]

(1) *Christian beliefs-that, understanding and knowledge*: including beliefs about God, Jesus, the church, human nature and the world;

---

2. Compare Jerome S. Bruner, *Toward a Theory of Instruction* (Cambridge, Mass.: Harvard University Press, 1978), p. 72; N. L. Gage, *The Scientific Basis of the Art of Teaching* (New York: Teachers College Press, 1978), p. 23; James Michael Lee, *The Content of Religious Instruction* (Birmingham, Ala.: Religious Education Press, 1985), pp. 78, 84, chapters 2 and 3 *passim*.

3. Lee, *The Content of Religious Instruction*, p. 36.

4. The list seems to me to cover the range of "objectives of Christian religious education" to be found in the literature. See Randolph Crump Miller, "The Objective of Christian Education", in Marvin J. Taylor, ed., *An Introduction to Christian Education* (Nashville, Tenn.: Abingdon, 1966); John H. Westerhoff, III, "Religious Education and Catechesis: Appendix II", in M. C. Felderhof, ed., *Religious Education in a Pluralistic Society* (London: Hodder & Stoughton, 1985), pp. 71-74; D. S. Amalorpavadass, "Catechesis as a Pastoral Task of the Church", in Michael Warren, ed., *A Sourcebook for Modern Catechetics* (Winona, Minn.: St. Mary's Press, 1983), pp. 342-343, 353-355; D. C. Wykoff, "Goals", in Iris V. Cully and Kendig Brubaker Cully, eds., *Harper's Encyclopedia of Religious Education* (San Francisco: Harper & Row, 1990). Compare also Lee, *The Content of Religious Instruction, passim*. Lee makes the additional point that many elements of the content of religious education, e.g. "faith" and indeed "religion", are intellectual abstractions or constructs, rather than observable entities and activities. Such concepts need to be "operationalized into demonstrable behaviors which are observable both to the learner and to the religious educator." Lee, *Content*, p. 615; see also James Michael Lee, *The Shape of Religious Instruction* (Birmingham, Ala.: Religious Education Press, 1972), pp. 72-74 and his essay in Lee, ed., *Handbook of Faith* (Birmingham: Ala.: Religious Education Press, 1990), pp. 271-275.

(2) *Christian beliefs-in*: including faith and trust in God, or in salvation, baptism etc.;

(3) *Christian attitudes and values*: covering Christian spirituality and moral virtues; the valuing of Jesus, mercy etc.;

(4) *Christian emotions and feelings*: including awe, thankfulness, pity, joy etc. (this category may be entitled "subjective religious experiences");

(5) *Christian experiences*, in the sense of "objective religious experiences" of God, Christ, the Spirit etc. and their activity;

(6) *Christian moral actions*: e.g. active love, forgiveness, trust, obedience;

(7) *Christian religious actions*: e.g. prayer, profession of faith, evangelism, worship, church membership/involvement;

(8) *Christian or theological reflection and criticism*: including those interpretative and evaluative cognitive skills and processes—with their related attitudes, unless these are placed in category (3)—that lead to active "Christian reflection" and/or "doing theology".

As I shall argue below, these categories should not be too rigidly distinguished. The above account must be recognized as an analysis that separates elements that are always found together in human beings. It is not an attempt to recreate a faculty psychology, with distinct and unrelated "parts" or "activities" of a fissile person. If human experiences, attitudes, beliefs and overt behaviors are in this way to be distinguished as component states and activities of human beings, it can only be in a qualified manner. They are to be understood either as *interrelated* and *interacting* components, or treated merely as *conceptual abstractions* from the concrete whole that is a thinking-feeling-experiencing-acting person.

All the above Christian attributes can be learned, and indeed the majority will have been learned. Most are learned directly as lasting changes in beliefs, attitudes, skills, emotions, dispositions to act, and so forth. It might be argued that others are only learned indirectly, as we learn the continuing states or dispositions that (for example) tend to give rise to, or predispose us to, experiences of God or overt moral and religious behavior.[5]

At first sight it might seem that Christian criticism has a less stable position within the complex of Christian attributes than the others included in this list. I have argued in Chapters 4 and 5 above, however, that for some it is an essential ingredient in their Christian being and Christian learning, but that this is not the case for all. Thus some may be "Christianly educated" to the limit of their potential without developing Christian criticism because there is no significant critical element in their natures to be developed. They will

---

5. The evocation of religious experience through prayer, worship and more secular experiences may be regarded as a proper part of Christian religious education in so far as the experiences so evoked themselves generate learning. See David Hay, "Religious experience and its induction", in L. B. Brown, ed., *Advances in the Psychology of Religion* (Oxford: Pergamon, 1985). On a possible role for the learning of the Christian concept of God in the evocation of experiences of God see Jeff Astley, "The Idea of God, the Reality of God, and Religious Education", *Theology* 84: 698 (1981).

never be "critical thinkers"; but feelers, and doers, or believers. Others may learn to be critical, but never value this attribute or feel fulfilled in exercising it. Nevertheless, those educational practices that strive to prevent *anyone* from developing Christian criticism will inevitably stunt the human potential and fulfillment of some Christian learners. That is a greater fault, and it is, in any case, usually counterproductive.

The claim just made with regard to Christian criticism may also be offered for a number of the other categories in this list. Thus the mentally or physically handicapped are limited in their beliefs and actions, but it seems perverse to judge them as falling outside the category of Christian on those counts. Many people would also argue that emotionally or experientially limited people can still be Christian, although the position adopted in this chapter might challenge this to some extent. The present list represents a "complete account" of the "fully" Christian/Christianly-educated individual, that is the person who has (has learned) the full range of Christian attributes. But in any given case the reality may be less than our ideal. It cannot, however, fall so far short of that ideal as to miss the mark entirely.

In this chapter I shall be taking a particular normative position about what constitutes the core of the Christian religion. This is to stray somewhat into the domain of the theologian, but it is unavoidable. I can comment only very briefly here on the more substantive theological question as to whether listing Christian attributes is or is not the same as defining what it is to be Christian.

Although Ellis Nelson's claim that "there is one major objective in Christian education: helping a person become a Christian" seems noncontroversial,[6] yet the account given so far of what that involves will seem deeply unsatisfactory to many. Some readers may feel uneasy with my analysis of the Christian because it is an interpretation that is worked out in terms of believing, feeling, and doing "Christianly". They will ask: Is this what it is to *be* a Christian? Surely we have missed something out? They will argue that the Christian attributes are themselves only contingent expressions of, or "helpful steps along the way" to, or even conditions of, something else. It will be claimed that this "something" is far more fundamental: it might be a human act (such as baptism), or a divine act (such as the gift of the Spirit), or a divine-human relationship (such as justification).

I would argue, however, that we need to recognize that education is a practical activity. Learning is defined as a change in a person brought about by experience. This definition, framed within the context of the *practical* concerns of education, presupposes that such changes are in principle, and in large part, "observable" (either publicly to other people or by the introspective activity of the learner—who might then tell other people about them). There may be other changes: necessarily mysterious, metaphysical, "super-

---

6. C. Ellis Nelson, "Our Oldest Problem", in Padraic O'Hare, ed., *Tradition and Transformation in Religious Education* (Birmingham, Ala.: Religious Education Press, 1979), p. 66.

natural", or ontological changes of essence, status or relationship. But surely Christian religious educators cannot take them into account in the practice—and therefore the theory—of Christian religious education? Philosophical and theological debate notwithstanding, *educational practice needs a definition of being Christian that is of some use to it*. Epistemology takes precedence over ontology in education, and *the* useful epistemology is a version of empiricism. The argument here is not that "only the observable is real". My point is that it is only realities that are either observable (I would include introspectively observable), inferrable from observables, or transcendental conditions of observation and knowledge as such, that can be *known* to be real. Christian religious education needs to be empirical. It needs to be guided by evidence in order to get anywhere.

The ontological theologian may, of course, stick to her guns. Let her describe her account as an account of what it is *to be* in the right relationship with God, "in Christ", redeemed, reconciled, re-created, etc. Let her interpretation stand, at least as an account of what it is *to have* the Spirit, God's grace, God's hand upon one's heart, etc. To be "Christianly-educated", to have "learned Christianity", is a good thing, she will readily admit. It is not, however, what she means by "being a Christian". Christian religious education is not necessarily the same activity as creating citizens of heaven, saving people from hell, or producing redeemed saints for God. This must be allowed. But any Christian religious educator who takes this line must also accept two conditions. The first is a recognition on his part that he also needs an account of being Christian that can be *used* by evangelists, nurturers and educators in planning their work—an account that will enable us to *know* when someone is (more) Christian. If we do not have that, we shall not know when we have done our work successfully, or indeed what it would be "to have succeeded" in evangelizing, nurturing or educating someone into Christianity, and therefore what it would be like to have partially succeeded. The second condition is that definitions of what it is to be a *religious adherent—to be* Christian or Muslim, *to have* Buddhism or Christianity—cannot be worked out solely in terms of metaphysical changes within people. Religions are phenomena that appear in the world. Religious behavior is in large part observable. Religious beliefs, attitudes, values etc. are introspectible, or at least they can be inferred from observable overt behavior. This is what allows them to be assessed by human beings. Religion is a human affair, and the criteria for being "religious" are derived from human decisions based on human knowledge. Hence religiousness cannot be *simply* a matter of mysterious changes unobservable by human beings.

Perhaps the most straightforward resolution of the argument outlined above is to affirm that "to be Christian" is to have the Christian attributes, but that "to be Christ/Spirit/God-related" is (may be?) something different; although, we may hope, it is something that is affected by and expressed in the Christian attributes. Theology may focus solely on hidden states such as God-relatedness if it wishes. But it will inevitably find itself with little to say that is of much practical use. The practical subject of Christian religious education, however, can only function with a definition of being a Christian similar to the one outlined above.

THE MULTIDIMENSIONAL APPROACH

The Dimensions of Religion

It would appear from the previous section that Christianity is many-sided. Students of the sociology and psychology of religion have long recognized this fact.[7] Thus Robert H. Thouless listed a range of factors in the development of a "religious attitude"—*viz* intellectual, social, the experiential in various forms, and personal.[8] Charles Y. Glock and Rodney Stark designated five core dimensions of religiousness: belief, ritual and devotional religious practice, religious experience, intellectual knowledge, and consequential effects on general conduct.[9] The more empirically-based factor analytic studies of Morton B. King and Richard A. Hunt found various religious dimensions, including credal assent, personal devotion, church attendance, talking and reading about religion, and financial support for it.[10]

More recent empirical work has identified similar dimensions of religion relating to an individual's attitudes, beliefs, values and reported behavior. Thus the European Value Systems Study Group discerned, among other dimensions, church attendance, attitudes towards the church, religious beliefs, subjective religious disposition (measuring the importance of religion in one's life etc.), spiritual experience and (respect for) moral beliefs.[11] The psychologist of religion Laurence Brown lists knowledge, beliefs, attitudes, experiences, belonging and practice as individual factors of religiousness; together with truth, doctrines, consequences and rituals under the heading of "social contexts".[12]

---

7. It should be noted, particularly in this area, that social scientists are here necessarily engaging in conceptual analysis as well as empirical study.

8. Robert H. Thouless, *An Introduction to the Psychology of Religion* (Cambridge: Cambridge University Press, 1971), pp. 18-19.

9. Rodney Stark and Charles Y. Glock, *American Piety: The Nature of Religious Commitment* (Berkeley: University of California Press, 1968), pp. 11-17. See also their *Religion and Society in Tension* (Chicago, Ill.: Rand McNally, 1965), ch. 2; and compare Robert Towler, *Homo Religiosus: Sociological Problems in the Study of Religion* (London: Constable, 1974), ch. 7.

10. Morton King, "Measuring the Religious Variable: nine proposed dimensions", *Journal for the Scientific Study of Religion* 6 (1967); Morton B. King and Richard A. Hunt, "Measuring the Religious Variable: amended findings", *Journal for the Scientific Study of Religion* 8 (1969) and "Measuring the Religious Variable: national replication", *Journal for the Scientific Study of Religion* 14 (1975).

11. Stephen Harding *et al.*, *Contrasting Values in Western Europe: Unity, Diversity and Change* (Basingstoke: Macmillan, 1986), ch. 2.

12. L. B. Brown, *The Psychology of Religion: An Introduction* (London: SPCK, 1988), p. 132, see also pp. 15-16; L. B. Brown, *The Psychology of Religious Belief* (San Diego, Calif.: Academic Press, 1987), pp. 6-7, 87-90, 100-106. See also Marie Cornwall and Stan L. Albrecht, "The Dimensions of Religiosity: A Conceptual Model with an Empirical Test", *Review of Religious Research* 27: 3 (1986).

Such research[13] has encouraged students of religion to move away from thinking of religion "as a coherent 'thing' with rather sharp boundaries, rather than as a somewhat imprecise bundle of rites, beliefs, knowledge, and experiences".[14] "Bundle" has the wrong connotations, perhaps, but this recognition of the multiplicity of religious dimensions is surely to be welcomed.

A similar multidimensional account of religion is to be found in the work of certain theologians and philosophers of religion. John Henry Newman recognized that religion has three aspects: the dogmatical or philosophical, the devotional or properly religious, and the practical or political.[15] Ninian Smart's more developed conceptual analysis of religion distinguishes the six dimensions of doctrines, myths, ethical teachings, rituals, social institutions and practices, and religious experiences.[16] The phenomenological study of religion has taken up this analysis and stressed the importance of studying the whole complex of these dimensions in the observable phenomena of religious expression. Organizing Smart's six dimensions into the initially most obvious broad categories of ideas/concepts, feelings/experiences and actions, the authors of *A Groundplan for the Study of Religion* argue that these are like the three dimensions of a solid object. Any study of a cube that attempts to portray it only in two dimensions, or even worse one-dimensionally, will inevitably be inadequate and misleading. We need all three dimensions for a full account ("in depth") of the reality of a religion.[17]

As a preliminary to later discussion we may note two qualifications to this model. First, Smart himself offers his account as an interpretation of the notion of *a religion*. He adds that "when it comes to considering *religion* (as distinct, at least in conception, from the religions) we are here dealing with 'ultimate' value questions related to the meaning of human life. And to

13. For related accounts of the "dimensions of religion" or "religious variables" from social scientists and other students of religion, see also Melford E. Spiro, "Religion: Problems of Definition and Explanation", in Michael Banton, ed., *Anthropological Approaches to the Study of Religion* (London: Tavistock, 1966), pp. 96-98; Michael Argyle and Benjamin Beit-Hallahmi, *The Social Psychology of Religion* (London: Routledge & Kegan Paul, 1975), pp. 2-6; Geoffrey E. W. Scobie, *Psychology of Religion* (London: Batsford, 1975), ch. 5; Roland Robertson, *The Sociological Interpretation of Religion* (Oxford: Blackwell, 1972), ch. 3; Mary Jo Meadow and Richard D. Kahoe, *Psychology of Religion: Religion in Individual Lives* (New York: Harper & Row, 1984), ch. 21; Bernard Spilka, Ralph W. Hood, Jr., and Richard L. Gorsuch, *The Psychology of Religion: An Empirical Approach* (Englewood Cliffs, N.J., Prentice-Hall, 1985), ch. 2.

14. J. Milton Yinger, *The Scientific Study of Religion* (New York: Macmillan, 1970), p. 27.

15. For example John Henry Newman, *The Via Media of the Anglican Church I* (1877), p. i, reprinted in Erich Przywara, ed., *A Newman Synthesis* (London: Sheed & Ward, 1930), p. 164.

16. Ninian Smart, *The Phenomenon of Religion* (New York: Herder and Herder; London: Macmillan, 1973), pp. 42-43; Ninian Smart, *The Religious Experience of Mankind* (New York: Scribner's, 1969; London: Collins, 1971), pp. 15-25.

17. Schools Council Religious Education Committee Working Party on Aims and Objectives, *A Groundplan for the Study of Religion* (London: Schools Council, 1977), p. 19. Unfortunately the cube metaphor rather implies that each dimension is to be regarded as equally significant.

understand a religion we need to have some grasp of its relationship to these values and meanings."[18] One might say that what makes the dimensions of a religion "religious" is their relationship to religious questions about meaning and the conservation and enhancement of values. We will be taking up this point later in arguing for a key role for meaning and valuation in the religious life.

Second, we may note that Stephen Sykes has argued that experience is importantly different from the other five of Smart's six dimensions, both in that it cannot be directly inspected and because "religious experiences are themselves an essential aspect of each of the other dimensions".[19] Thus each of the religious dimensions has both an external and an internal aspect, the latter being the accompanying intentions and sentiments that give it meaning. We may wish to correct this claim slightly in that the external, public aspect (or expression) of each dimension may be contrasted with an internal aspect that is broader in scope than Smart's dimension of religious experience and his category of valuation taken together. Doctrinal, moral, social and mythic beliefs can all be held in the "mind" as much as in the "heart" without being expressed. It is mainly religious action (including verbal behavior and other overt expressions of beliefs, attitudes and feelings) that can be observed.[20]

---

18. Ninian Smart, "What is Religion?", in Ninian Smart and Donald Horder, eds., *New Movements in Religious Education* (London: Temple Smith, 1975), p. 20. Thus teaching about religion needs to have a concern for "implicit religion" and human experience issues, as well as with explicit religious phenomena. See above Chapter 1.

19. Stephen Sykes, *The Identity of Christianity* (Philadelphia: Fortress; London: SPCK, 1984), p. 31. Ursula King seems to make a similar point about the related category of spirituality in her essay in Felderhof, ed., *Religious Education in a Pluralistic Society*, p. 94.

20. Many psychologists use the term "behavior" to refer not just to overt behavior but to any activity of an organism, including "inner" cognitive or affective activities. Philosophers, however, are keen to distinguish between actions on the one hand and happenings, states, feelings, processes etc. on the other: the former category being restricted to the "active" exercise of a power to make something happen. Thus: Alan R. White, ed., *The Philosophy of Action* (London: Oxford University Press, 1968), Editor's "Introduction". See also A. I. Melden, "Action", in Donald F. Gustafson, ed., *Essays in Philosophical Psychology* (Garden City, N.Y.: Anchor Books; London: Macmillan, 1964). The standard case of action, some philosophers argue, involves overt behavior in a way that excludes merely "mental doings". See D. G. Brown, *Action* (London: Allen & Unwin, 1968), pp. 28-32. It is pertinent to note that Wittgenstein famously argued that "an 'inner process' stands in need of outward criteria" in the sense of overt behavior patterns etc. that are *necessarily* evidence for the inner process (e.g. it is part of the meaning of the condition of being in pain that it is necessarily identifiable through "pain behavior"). See Ludwig Wittgenstein, *Philosophical Investigations*, trans. G. E. M. Anscombe (Oxford: Blackwell, 1968), part I, para. 580; Rogers Albritton, "On Wittgenstein's Use of the Term 'Criterion'", in George Pitcher, ed., *Wittgenstein* (London: Macmillan, 1966); P. M. S. Hacker, *Insight and Illusion* (London: Oxford University Press, 1972), ch. X. This analysis is very different from *identifying* inner processes with overt behavior, which is "the behaviorist's reduction of inner thoughts and feelings to their natural expression in behavior". Stuart Hampshire, *Thought and Action* (London, Chatto & Windus, 1959), p. 143. Contrast John B. Watson, "Psychology as the Behaviorist Views It", *Psychological Review* 20 (1913) and B. F. Skinner, "Behaviorism at Fifty", *Science* 140: 3570 (1963).

Nevertheless, Sykes's widening of the scope of the dimension of religious experience is significant, and the stress on experience that is to be found in both Smart and Sykes is one that I wish to take up later in reflecting on the motive power of religion.

Multidimensional Religious Education

Taking up this multidimensional analysis of religion, we may argue that formative religious education must also ensure that it is developing the whole range of learning outcomes appropriate to being religious. Thus Christian religious education cannot just be a matter of teaching Christian beliefs or knowledge claims, for this would be to develop only what some have called "belief-commitments". Such a concentration on the cognitive ("thinking") element of Christianity, to the neglect of the affective ("feeling")/attitudinal and conative/volitional/lifestyle elements (or "attitude-commitments" and "action-commitments"),[21] is not uncommon in Christian religious education. But it results in teaching only one element of the Christian religion.

James Michael Lee has strenuously argued the thesis that the content of religious instruction (teaching) is the whole of religion and not just its cognitive dimension, and certainly not just theology.[22] He describes religion as a form of lifestyle, a way of life, and an activity of the whole person that expresses and enfleshes that person's relationship with the transcendent through her or his knowledge, belief, feeling, experience and practice.[23] Theology is only part of religion, whether it is understood as one kind of theory about—or rational cognitive appraisal of—the way of life that is religion, or as a system of religious beliefs that are descriptive of God and God's activity (reflective "God-talk").[24] In either case it is primarily, and therefore restrictively, a cognitive affair. Lee writes: "Theological instruction properly

---

21. Shivesh Chandra Thakur, *Religion and Rational Choice* (London: Macmillan; Totawa, N.J.: Barnes & Noble, 1981), pp. 29-31. See below p. 209.

22. James Michael Lee, "Key Issues in the Development of a Workable Foundation for Religious Instruction", in Padraic O'Hare, ed., *Foundations of Religious Education* (New York: Paulist, 1978), p. 53.

23. James Michael Lee, "The Authentic Source of Religious Instruction", in Norma H. Thompson, ed., *Religious Education and Theology* (Birmingham Ala.: Religious Education Press, 1982), p. 100 and *The Content of Religious Instruction*, pp. 39-49 and ch. 9. See also Thakur, *Religion and Rational Choice*, p. 31 and Leszek Kolakowski, *Religion* (Glasgow: Collins, 1982), p. 218. Similarly: "The religious vision of the world . . . is a matter of perception, commitment and evaluation indissolubly bound together in the response of the whole person. . . . It is a total reaction to the world." Keith Ward, *Holding Fast to God* (London: SPCK, 1982), p. 91.

24. Or, even more restrictively, as "the theory of God" (Lee, "The Authentic Source . . .", pp. 109, 154). Theology is defined by most theologians as a systematic, comprehensive and reflective intellectual endeavor involving the critical clarification and revision of, and speculation about, religion (and/or revelation)—particularly of religious beliefs and "talk about God". See, e.g., Dietrich Ritschl, *The Logic of Theology: A Brief Account of the Relationship between Basic Concepts in Theology*, trans. John Bowden (London: SCM, 1986; Philadelphia: Fortress, 1987), p. xxii and *passim*; David R. Mason, "Faith, Religion, and Theology", *Journal of Religious Studies* 15: 1-2 (1989), p. 10.

and legitimately has cognitive content as its primary proximate goal. However, religious instruction has all the contents involved in Christian living as its primary proximate goal." Lee espouses a position he calls "holistic functionalism" which recognizes human cognitive and affective activities as contrasting, but interrelated and interdependent, functions of the same person: "there is no intellectual activity without some sort of concomitant affect, and there are no affective functions taking place without cognitions being somehow involved". "Cognitive activity is never un-affected . . . every human behavior has its cognitive component, its affective component, its psychomotor component, and so forth."[25] In speaking of Christian learning outcomes, then, we are speaking of the beliefs, attitudes, emotions, experiences and overt actions of *people*. But people do not come in compartments—or departments—with each part being completely and independently responsible for its own activities. The human being is *one*. And it is this one person who thinks, believes, feels, trusts and acts. Such an holistic understanding of human beings fits well with an holistic, "integrated" or "confluent" Christian religious education in which the different elements (cognitive, affective, lifestyle behavior) are all present in dynamic integration, so that the whole person is addressed. This form of religious education is advocated by a number of recent writers.[26]

There is a long-standing debate about how far Christian religious education is concerned with ideas, thoughts and beliefs and how far it is concerned with emotions. Most dichotomies are misleading and this distinction, if treated as a sharply defined division, is more misleading than most. If all human activity has both a cognitive and an affective dimension, each of which is prominent to a greater or lesser degree, then anything that abstracts out the affective dimension leaves us with only a partial description. Far too much of Christian religious education satisfies itself with cognitive learning alone.[27] Certainly this is of fundamental importance as a content of Christian religious education; but it is not the only content, and not the only important one. Nor can it be properly learned in a sanitized fashion, by stripping it of its affective and lifestyle concomitants. Lest the pendulum swing too far in the other direction, however, it is important not to underrate the significance of the cognitive element in Christianity and in Christian religious education.[28] As is often the case in religion and edu-

---

25. Lee, *The Content of Religious Instruction*, pp. 141, 131; see also pp. 199-202, 487-488.

26. The position is summarized in James Michael Lee, "The Blessings of Religious Pluralism", in Norman H. Thompson, ed., *Religious Pluralism and Religious Education* (Birmingham, Ala.: Religious Education Press, 1988), p. 76, n. 54; Suzanne M. De Benedittis, *Teaching Faith and Morals* (Minneapolis: Winston, 1981), pp. 4, 7-18, 58; Timothy Arthur Lines, *Systemic Religious Education* (Birmingham, Ala.: Religious Education Press, 1987), pp. 191, 201-202, 230.

27. See John H. Westerhoff, III, *Will Our Children Have Faith?* (New York: Seabury, 1976), p. 9.

28. Gabriel Moran, "Where Now, What Next", in O'Hare, ed., *Foundations of Religious Education*, pp. 105-106, 109 and *Interplay* (Winona, Minn.: St. Mary's Press, 1981), ch. 5. Compare Jim Wilhoit, *Christian Education and the Search for Meaning* (Grand Rapids, Mich.: Baker, 1986), pp. 32-35, and above Chapter 5.

cation, Both-And is better than Either-Or.

Christian religious education has been described by John Bernsten as primarily a matter of "the shaping of religious emotions and affections in the context of teaching doctrine".[29] Drawing on contemporary writing in philosophy, some of which will be reviewed later in this book, Bernsten contends that we cannot drive a wedge between emotion/experience and belief/doctrine. He reminds us that all human acts are cognitive-affective, and that merely affective or merely cognitive acts do not exist. Since emotions have a "logic", that is a grammar, form and determinacy that derives from, and must be understood in conjunction with, the accompanying thoughts, beliefs and objects of the emotion, it is possible for religious teachings to "be held in the mode of the emotions".[30] Bernsten goes on to argue that it was this way of teaching doctrine that was central to the pedagogy of the catechists of the fourth century. He writes:

> The early catechists showed in their pastoral activity that the Christian teachings demanded the life of the affections. Their concern for the latter, however, did not represent the commitment to an experiential catechesis *as against*, say, an instructional one. The disposition of the heart was of such importance not as a surrogate for the Church's teachings but precisely in virtue of the place those teachings must find in the life of the newly baptized. The fear, remorse, zeal and joy of the paschal season were marks of religious understanding.[31]

Even the more explicit and "academic" educational processes that may form a proper and appropriate part of Christian religious education must therefore go along with the more implicit shapings of religious emotions and attitudes that often best take place through more "experiential" learning occasions. Adopting the distinction taught us by split-brain research, we may claim that the former are verbal, cognitive, often analytic and critical— i.e. philosophical—"left lobe" ("Western lobe") activities. The latter, however, are intuitive, aesthetic, imaginative, and nonverbal "right lobe" ("Eastern lobe") activities.[32] The point is that the good health of Christian religious education is dependent upon the operation of both lobes of the brain: Christianity is best learned both affectively and cognitively. It is when rea-

---

29. John A. Bernsten, "Christian Affections and the Catechumenate", *Worship* 52 (1978), p. 194. This is actually Bernsten's definition of "catechesis", but others would use that word differently—see above Chapter 1.

30. *Ibid.*, p. 200.

31. *Ibid.*, p. 208; compare also Paul L. Holmer, *Making Christian Sense* (Philadelphia: Westminster, 1984), pp. 55-60.

32. See, for example, Spilka, Hood and Gorsuch, *The Psychology of Religion*, pp. 166-169 and Gloria Durka and Joanmarie Smith, eds., *Aesthetic Dimensions of Religious Education* (New York: Paulist, 1979), *passim*. The above paragraphs are reprinted with permission from my article "The Role of Worship in Christian Learning", in *Religious Education* 79: 2 (1984). I have corrected the designation of the two lobes of the brain from the original printing.

son and emotion are divorced that religion most rapidly loses its sense and its power for people. Religion is intrinsically a cognitive-affective activity.

Because of the implications of a holistic view of the Christian learner, and the intrinsic difficulties of the philosophical analysis of categories like emotion, attitude, belief and overt behavior, a satisfactory systematic taxonomy of Christian religious education outcomes is hard to come by. No sooner have we agreed on the headings of cognitive/affective/conative or thinking/feeling/acting than the arguments start about where to place "valuing", and "What is a 'feeling' anyway?" I cannot ignore all such questions, but I am not satisfied that I can convincingly answer many of them. Reading among the philosophers and psychologists suggests, however, that whatever the detailed analyses of learning outcomes they offer us, there are two elements that are of fundamental importance—because implied by or related to, and often powerfully influential on, many of the others. These are *valuations* and *experiences* (including *emotions*). In offering my account of the significant features of religious learning, therefore, I shall keep coming back to these two categories. Significantly they are both particularly relevant to, and indeed perhaps components of, what many would still wish to demarcate as the affective domain—the domain of "feeling".

I have another reason, however, for focusing on these elements. I take the view that religion in general and Christianity in particular are phenomena in which these things not only are (descriptively) central, but ought to be (normatively) central. If slogans were not dangerous, I should adopt two as the conclusion I intend to work towards here: "religion is primarily a matter of experience, attitudes and valuation", and "religious learning is primarily a matter of learning feelings".[33] But slogans, lacking the benefit of qualification, *are* dangerous.

I regard such normative claims as, in broad terms, *theological* claims. Theology is here exercising its quite proper normative function of defining and articulating the nature of the Christian religion.[34] Christian theology will want—and should have—its evaluative say in defining the authentic and valuable Christian attributes that Christian religious education should promote, as it has its own account (related to other accounts) of what constitutes human fulfillment. Theological evaluation is intrinsically involved in any account of what it is to be religious. And different theological positions will produce different accounts. A Christian religion innocent of theology cannot of itself provide a valid norm to evaluate whether it is itself *Christian*. That

33. Compare Irene S. Caldwell, "Communicating the Gospel", *Religious Education* 60: 5 (1965), p. 350. Others regard lifestyle or activity (way of life) as the most important element in religion and in religious education, and as a category that integrates affective and cognitive elements. For reasons that I hope will become clear later in this chapter, however, I regard experience and affect as the more significant categories. In any case, philosophical analysis has little to say about overt behavior.

34. See J. Astley, "Essay Review", *Religious Education* 81: 1 (1986), p. 144; but compare Lee, *The Shape of Religious Instruction*, pp. 245-246 and "The Authentic Source of Religious Instruction", pp. 181-182.

is a normative theological judgment and certainly not, for example, an educational judgment or one based on the (descriptive) social sciences.

RELIGIOUS EXPERIENCE: THE CORE OF CHRISTIANITY?

Religious experience has been the subject of an enormous amount of research and reflection. In what follows I shall concentrate mainly on the analysis of religious experience given by philosophers and philosophers of religion.

Varieties of Religious Experience

Sykes's development of Smart's dimensional account of religion, which we considered above, suggests a certain primacy for the experiential dimension of Christianity and indeed of any religion. Now the phrase "religious experience", like the word "experience" (something lived through or undergone), is ambiguous. It may refer to "subjective" feeling states of acceptance, worth, justification, election, guidance, etc. (analogous to "I feel elated/depressed", "I experience elation/depression"). On the other hand the phrase may denote an "objective" experience of a religious reality: in the Christian case, a supposed experience of (the activity of) God/the risen Christ/the Holy Spirit (analogously "I feel the table", "I experience the light").[35] There are many surveys of religious experience, a number of which cover both "subjective" and "objective" experiences as they are defined here.[36] Philosophers frequently refer to this latter group as "cognitive religious experiences" because they are regarded as experiences that give rise to a cognitive claim about the factuality or existence of their object. (Here "cognitive" is to be understood as "factual" or "truth claiming", see Glossary.) Philosophers with an interest in the epistemology of religion are naturally most concerned with these types of religious experience. These veridical "experiences *of*" a supernatural entity lead to feeling states, of course. God is not just experienced neutrally, but in awe and joy. Thus in both cases we shall eventually be brought back to a concern for feelings.[37]

---

35. Compare, e.g., Anthony Kenny, *Action, Emotion and Will* (London: Routledge & Kegan Paul, 1963), pp. 52-53; Antony Flew, *God and Philosophy* (London: Hutchinson, 1966), pp. 125-126.

36. Or an even broader compass: see William James, *The Varieties of Religious Experience* (Cambridge, Mass.: Harvard University Press, 1985; London: Collins, 1960); Glock and Stark, *Religion and Society in Tension*, ch. 3; André Godin, *The Psychological Dynamics of Religious Experience*, trans. Mary Turton (Birmingham: Ala.: Religious Education Press, 1985); Alister Hardy, *The Spiritual Nature of Man: A Study of Contemporary Religious Experience* (Oxford: Clarendon, 1979); Andrew M. Greeley, *The Sociology of the Paranormal: A Reconnaissance* (Beverly Hills, Calif.: Sage Publications, 1975); David Hay: *Religious Experience Today: Studying the Facts* (London: Mowbray, 1990). For an overview of much of the empirical research see Spilka, Hood and Gorsuch, *The Psychology of Religion*, chs. 7 and 8, and Kenneth E. Hyde, *Religion in Childhood and Adolescence* (Birmingham, Ala.: Religious Education Press, 1990), ch. 9.

37. One of William Alston's "religion-making characteristics" is "characteristically religious feelings (awe, sense of mystery, sense of guilt, adoration), which tend to be aroused in

A related type of, or understanding of, religious experience has been argued for by John Hick. Hick describes religious faith as the interpretative element within religious experience, which is thus not just an experience but an "experience-as".[38] The unbeliever sees and hears the world, people and human history just as world, people, history. But religious men and women experience the same things *as* God's gift, his children and the theatre of his will. We should note that this recognition- or interpretation-experience also gives rise to religious feelings, in the same way as does its secular analogue of seeing an object as a snake, or recognizing marks on paper as a love letter.

Objective Religious Experiences: Their Role in the Epistemology of Religion

Many theologians and philosophers of religion have claimed that religious experience has a crucial part to play in the genesis and justification of religious beliefs, attitudes and activities. A number of them have construed religious experience on the model of sense experience (often including experience-as). On this understanding, religious experience is a sort of "knowledge by acquaintance" or "cognition in presence". We know God intuitively— in the sense of noninferentially—through our experience, as we know the objects of the senses.

Richard Swinburne's "exclusive and exhaustive" classification of religious experiences with evidential value ("cognitive significance"), particularly as pointing to the existence of God, distinguishes two main categories. There are, first, religious experiences that are not mediated by sensations: e.g. mystical experience of God through "nothingness" and experience of a divine call that arises without auditory or other sensations (see note 40).

---

the presence of sacred objects and during the practice of ritual, and which are connected in idea with the gods". William P. Alston, "Religion", in Paul Edwards, ed., *The Encyclopedia of Philosophy*, Vol. 7 (New York: Macmillan and Free Press; London: Collier Macmillan, 1967), p. 141. Sutherland notes that such feelings are not "peculiar to the religious emotions" but are also associated with aesthetic contemplation, and moral and personal depth experiences. Stewart R. Sutherland, *Atheism and the Rejection of God* (Oxford: Blackwell, 1977), p. 54. Note also Michael Paffard's account of the feelings (particularly awe, joy, and fear) that tend to be associated with a variety of what he calls "transcendental experiences": Michael Paffard, *Inglorious Wordsworths* (London: Hodder & Stoughton, 1973), p. 35, compare Michael Paffard, *The Unattended Moment* (London: SCM, 1976), *passim*. In André Godin's survey of subjective and objective religious experiences he significantly remarks that collective charismatic experience is "interpreted as the immediate presence of the spirit. In fact what is immediate is a certain jubilation" (*The Psychological Dynamics of Religious Experience*, p. 107). See also Fraser Watts and Mark Williams, *The Psychology of Religious Knowing* (Cambridge: Cambridge University Press, 1988).

38. John Hick, *God and the Universe of Faiths* (New York: St. Martin's Press; London: Macmillan, 1973), ch. 3; for further details see below Chapter 8. For an analysis of Christian learning in terms of "learning to see various things . . . as manifestations of God", see William P. Alston, "The Christian Language-Game"; in F. J. Crosson, ed., *The Autonomy of Religious Belief* (Notre Dame, Ind.: University of Notre Dame Press, 1981), p. 143, see also pp. 137, 146-147.

Second, there is the category of religious experiences that are mediated by sensations. This second class subdivides further into:

(1) Religious experiences that are mediated by public objects/events (i.e. by "public perceptions" which any rightly positioned observer with the same sense organs, concepts etc. could have). This subclass comprises:

(a) experiences in which the supernatural object is perceived in perceiving an ordinary nonreligious object; and

(b) those in which the religious experience is mediated through perceiving "very unusual public objects"—e.g. Jesus's miracles or resurrection appearances.

(2) Religious experiences that are mediated by private sensory perceptions. This subclass comprises:

(a) those in which the experience may be described in normal sense experience language—e.g. visual and auditory sensations in dreams of angels; and

(b) those in which the sensations are only analogous to sense experiences.[39]

This classification of objective religious experiences would thus include—in the Second Class, Section (2)(b)—so-called numinous experiences in which God is known in an "outer" experience as an holy presence: a transcendent, "Wholly Other" reality over against the experiencer. It also embraces (in the same category and in Class One) mystical experiences: "inner" experiences of the soul's union or identity with the immanent God.[40] Category 1(a) of this Second Class may also be said to encompass some at least of the

---

39. Richard Swinburne, *The Existence of God* (Oxford: Clarendon, 1979), pp. 249-252, somewhat amended in form. For a wider classification by a philosopher of religion, see Caroline Franks Davis, *The Evidential Force of Religious Experience* (Oxford: Oxford University Press, 1989), chs. 1 and 2, and p. 177.

40. The terminology of the "numinous" experience of the holy, a form of cognition that he claims "does not rely on the evidence of the senses", is from Rudolf Otto, *The Idea of the Holy*, trans. J. W. Harvey (London: Oxford University Press, 1925); compare also his *Religious Essays: A Supplement to "The Idea of Holy"*, trans. B. Lunn (London: Oxford University Press, 1931). His phenomenological account of the nature of the experience, as combining dread and fascination, has been very widely praised; but Otto's "Kantian" analysis of the holy as an *a priori* category, and his account of the process of "schematization" whereby the experience is represented in language by appeal to analogous human experiences, has been criticized by many philosophers. See H. J. Paton, *The Modern Predicament: A Study in the Philosophy of Religion* (London: Allen & Unwin, 1955), pp. 129-145; G. Dawes Hicks, *The Philosophical Bases of Theism* (London: Allen & Unwin, 1937), pp. 135-140. With regard to mysticism, we may note that "introvertive" mystics deliberately shut off their senses, plunging into the depths of their own selves to be united with God, unlike the "extrovertive" nature mystics of Swinburne's Class Two who utilize their physical senses. Introvertive mystics are to be placed in Swinburne's Class One. See Walter T. Stace, *Mysticism and Philosophy* (Philadelphia: Lippincott; London: Macmillan, 1960), p. 61. Christian mystics tend to speak of direct contact with God, rather than of identification with him or absorption in him—which is much more common in Eastern religions (and much less easy to justify philosophically). See H. D. Lewis, *Our Experience of God* (London: Collins, 1970), p. 270. This latter, "monistic", form of mysticism can only cautiously be described as an "objective" experience of God (or Brahman), since

examples of experiencing-as religious experiences considered above (these may be occurrent, particular experiences or dispositions so to interpret ordinary sense experience and moral experience).

A great deal of traditional religious education in many faith traditions is devoted to the learning of dispositions and states that are preconditions of some of these forms of religious experience (through which God may be said to be *revealed*—see below Chapter 7). Religious education may also result in the direct evocation of such experiences. It is not surprising, therefore, that some have claimed that religious education's primary task is "to teach insight, to evoke disclosures".[41]

In religious epistemology the claim is often made that religious experience is an "external experience", i.e. an "experience of an externally existing object", and/or that experience of God is evidence for the independent existence of God.[42] William P. Alston has produced the fullest defense of the claim that experience of God is a form of *perception*. He argues for the justification of the socially-rooted "doxastic practice" (i.e. way of forming beliefs and evaluating them) that is religious experience (he calls it "mystical perception").[43] This, religious educators should note, is described as "socially established by socially monitored learning". Richard Swinburne offers a much briefer, but in many ways closely allied, defense of the rationality of *individual* beliefs based on religious experience. I shall give some account of Swinburne's arguments here.

Swinburne defines a religious experience as "an experience which seems (epistemically) to the subject to be an experience of God". (This is the epistemic sense of "seems" connoting what the subject is inclined to believe on the basis of his or her present sensory experience.) According to Swinburne, such an experience is really an experience of God if and only if its seeming to the experiencer that God is present is in fact caused by God's being present.[44]

---

the duality of the subject-object distinction that underlies most veridical experiences is here claimed to be transcended. Stace, *Mysticism and Philosophy*, pp. 218, 231-232. R. C. Zaehner claims that Christian mysticism is essentially theistic, and therefore dualistic. Even though "the soul feels itself to be united with God by love" the mystic's individual ego is not annihilated nor identified with God, only "transformed and 'deified'". The appropriate analogy is that of close sexual union. R. C. Zaehner, *Mysticism, Sacred and Profane* (London: Oxford University Press, 1957), pp. 29, 151-152. For philosophical evaluations of mystical claims see Richard Woods, ed., *Understanding Mysticism* (Garden City, N.Y.: Image Books, 1980; London: Athlone, 1981), Part IV, and Steven T. Katz, ed., *Mysticism and Philosophical Analysis* (New York: Oxford University Press; London: Sheldon, 1978).

41. Ian T. Ramsey, "Christian Education in the Light of Contemporary Empiricism", *Religious Education* 57: 2 (1962), p. 95; see also his "Discernment, Commitment and Cosmic Disclosure", *Religious Education* 60: 1 (1965) and Randolph Crump Miller, *The Language Gap and God* (Philadelphia: Pilgrim, 1970), ch. V.

42. J. C. A. Gaskin, *The Quest for Eternity* (Harmondsworth, England: Penguin, 1984), p. 80. (Note, however, that Gaskin then defines the experience in terms of an intersubjectivity that is only available for sense experience!)

43. William P. Alston, *Perceiving God: the Epistemology of Religious Experience* (Ithaca and London: Cornell University Press, 1991). The quotation that follows is from p. 163.

44. Swinburne, *The Existence of God*, pp. 245-249.

The usual criticism of this claim to objectivity or veridicality for religious experience is that, unlike sense experience, the criteria of testing for objectivity/veridicality are absent. In the case of sense experience we utilize such tests as the following: checks against other senses, checks under different 'lighting conditions', the fulfillment of empirical predictions arising from the experience, consistency with other experiences, and agreement with other perceivers.[45] But defenders of the veridicality claim about religious experience could argue that there are three factors that may make such tests inapplicable in the case of religious experience. First, there is the nature of the experience as a unitary and distinctive religious "sense" (unlike the five different senses of sense experience), the "faculty" of which may not be possessed by everyone. Second, we must take into account the nature of God as a meta-empirical entity of whom it can be said both that his general activity relates to the whole universe (and therefore may not imply particular, falsifiable empirical claims—see Chapter 4 above), and that God is free to give or to withhold particular self-disclosures in a way that most objects of sense experience are not. The third factor relates to the nature of human beings as fallible and sinful subjects and interpreters of religious experience: experiencing subjects who may need to be in some particular spiritual condition before they are able to experience God.

Swinburne argues for two fundamental principles as essential to any defense of the objectivity of religious experience. The first is the Principle of Credulity which he claims as a basic principle of rationality—"what one seems to perceive is probably so" (in the sense of *more probable than not*). This principle should normally be followed in the absence of special conditions such as the following: (a) that the conditions or subject of the experience have been found in the past to be unreliable; (b) that similar perceptual claims have been found to be unreliable; (c) that on background evidence the object of the experience was probably not present; and (d) that the putative object of the experience was probably not its cause.[46] With reference to condition (d), Swinburne notes that a *creator* God will always be among the causes of my experience, so that even "naturalistic" or "psychological" explanations of religious experience need not defeat the claim to objectivity.[47] (The difficulty then arises, however, that there cannot be perceptions

45. See C. B. Martin, *Religious Belief* (Ithaca, N.Y.: Cornell University Press, 1959), ch. 5; Kai Neilsen, "'Christian Positivism' and the Appeal to Religious Experience", *Journal of Religion* 42 (1962); George I. Mavrodes, *Belief in God* (New York: Random House, 1970), ch. III; T. R. Miles, *Religious Experience* (London: Macmillan; New York: St. Martin's Press, 1972), ch. 4; Anthony O'Hear, *Experience, Explanation and Faith* (London: Routledge & Kegan Paul, 1984), pp. 45-49; Richard M. Gale, *On the Nature and Existence of God* (Cambridge: Cambridge University Press, 1991), pp. 302-308. Contrast Alston, *Perceiving God*, pp. 209-225.

46. Swinburne, *The Existence of God*, pp. 254-271. For a more detailed study of such challenges see Davis, *The Evidential Force of Religious Experience*, chs. 4 and 5. See also Michael A. Slote, *Reason and Scepticism* (London: Allen & Unwin; New York: Humanities Press, 1970), ch. 6.

47. Compare Ronald W. Hepburn, *Christianity and Paradox* (London: Watts, 1958), chs.

of the absence of God.) Swinburne concludes that "a religious experience apparently of God ought to be taken as veridical unless it can be shown on other grounds significantly more probable than not that God does not exist".[48] We shall return to the significance of this qualification later.

Swinburne's second principle, the Principle of Testimony, complements the Principle of Credulity by claiming that "(in the absence of special considerations) the experiences of others are (probably) as they report them". The special considerations here would include evidence of these others lying, exaggerating or misremembering. If these considerations do not apply, Swinburne claims that we may rationally trust other people's religious experiences. He would thus reject the view of John Hick and others who, while arguing that religious experiencers may properly trust their *own* experiences, deny that others may have this confidence at second-hand.[49] If Swinburne's position is accepted, Christian religious education may not need to result in the learner having his or her *own* religious experiences, but can restrict itself to passing on the claims to religious experience of others. If Hick is right, Christian religious education must somehow result in individual learners experiencing God for themselves, if their claims about God's existence are to be justifiable (by means of religious experience).

In the debate over religious experience those who take it to be veridical or cognitive are divided between those (such as Swinburne and Alston) who make what has been called the "strong claim" to know the reality of God by direct experience, and those who adopt the "weaker position" that the God-assumption is merely the best explanation for religious experience.[50] It is often said that religious believers, like believers in trees and people, speak of *directly experiencing* the object of their belief.[51] John Cook Wilson is often quoted here. "If we think of the existence of our friends; it is the 'direct knowledge' which we want: merely inferential knowledge seems a poor

3 and 4; J. L. Mackie, *The Miracle of Theism* (Oxford: Oxford University Press, 1982), ch. 10; Davis, *The Evidential Force of Religious Experience*, ch. 8.

48. Swinburne, *The Existence of God*, p. 270.

49. *Ibid.*, pp. 271-274; Hick, "Our Experience of God", in Michael Goulder and John Hick, *Why Believe in God?* (London: SCM, 1983). Alston is to be placed on the Swinburnian side in this debate, with qualifications: see *Perceiving God*, pp. 279-284.

50. Gaskin, *The Quest for Eternity*, p. 83.

51. A line is sometimes drawn between (a) having a "real experience" of *x* and (b) concluding that *x* is present as an "interpretation of" or "inference from" your experience. It is said that the claim that *x* is present stands in need of justification in case (b), but not in case (a). According to some philosophers, (a) only applies to situations in which we take something to have a sensible characteristic/relation (being red, round, similar to another object, smooth, making a similar noise etc.). If we take something to have a non-sensible characteristic/relation, however, that is not itself regarded as adequate evidence to suppose that it does. But Swinburne and Alston argue that no such line can be drawn, for "clearly we are justified in holding many perceptual beliefs about objects having non-sensible characteristics which cannot be backed up in terms of beliefs about objects having 'sensible' characteristics". Thus we recognize our friends and taste our tea, we do not infer their existence and nature from sense perceptions of their faces or more primitive experiences of "the taste of tea". Swinburne, *The Existence of God*, pp. 257-259. See also Alston, *Perceiving God*, pp. 35-48, 186.

affair." To most people, he argues, it would be "as surprising as unwelcome to hear it could not be directly known whether there were such existences as their friends, and that it was only a matter of (probable) empirical argument and inference from facts which are directly known". He continues by claiming that our actions prove that we have a confidence in the existence of our friends which could not be derived from any empirical argument ("which can never be certain"); and concludes, "we don't want merely inferred friends. Could we possibly be satisfied with an inferred God?"[52]

On the other hand, the existence of God may be treated as the *best explanation* for the phenomenon of religious experience, in the way that the "real" existence of a tree may be proposed as the best explanation of my sense data (my sensings of the tree, my "seeming to see, feel, smell" the tree). This seems plausible when we recall that theism is essentially a metaphysical scheme as is realism (the view that material objects exist external to, and independent of, our sense experiences). Both can be tested for coherence, consistency, simplicity and their general "fit" to our experiences; but neither can be directly verified by observation.[53] And yet the only real "evidence" for the truth of these metaphysical systems—in the sense of grounds for, *and* originating source of, the beliefs they contain—remains a form of experience, i.e. religious experience or sense experience. It may be logically possible to deny the existence of the tree, despite your "experience" of it, for tree-claims go beyond what is incorrigibly given in sense experience; yet such claims carry conviction despite this theoretical doubt.

Peter Donovan has criticized all perceptual models of religious experience, contending that religious experience is something (a phenomenon) that has to be interpreted and explained—involving inferential reasoning—by the general explanatory structure of the theistic belief system. He outlines the structure of such an argument to the existence of God along these lines:

(a) If God (as described in belief-system S) exists, then experiences open to interpretation under S will be likely to occur. (For example, if S is Christianity, there are likely to be experiences of prophetic revelation, a holy or numinous presence, answered prayers, the sense of forgiveness after confession of sins, renewed lives following acts of faith, and so on.)
(b) Experiences interpreted under S do occur.
(c) No better ways of explaining the occurrence of those particular experiences are known.
(d) Therefore it is reasonable to conclude that God exists.

Here "the truth or falsity of an interpretation is not to be found by looking merely at the experience involved. It is necessary as well to examine the

---

52. J. Cook Wilson, *Statement and Inference*, Vol. II (Oxford: Oxford University Press, 1926), p. 853; compare John Hick, *Arguments for the Existence of God* (London: Macmillan, 1970; New York: Herder and Herder, 1971), ch. 7.
53. See above Chapter 4.

whole theological system in terms of which the interpretation of that experience is made." Thus our estimate of the value of any particular experience should depend on how we evaluate "the total belief system in terms of which that experience is thought to be significant".[54]

But Basil Mitchell has argued that the "forced choice" that is often offered to us by philosophers of religion, between viewing the God-claim as an uncertain, inferred, explanatory hypothesis and treating God as an experienced reality of which we can be certain, is not an exclusive one. He offers an instructive analogy. A sailor's claim to see a lighthouse through the storm can only be judged in terms of "some overall appraisal of the situation": using other reports, comparing other "sightings", referring to calculations of map positions, etc. But that does not make the lighthouse "merely an inferred entity and not an experienced reality". The point is rather that direct experience often needs the support of indirect reasoning in order to justify our claim to *knowledge* by observation. In the words of Caroline Franks Davis: "a perceptual claim in need of verification may form part of the evidence in its own favour . . . and . . . an experience may be 'interpreted' in terms of the very doctrines . . . for which it constitutes part of the evidence".[55] Mitchell writes:

> It is assumed that claims to direct awareness of God must be either self-authenticating or disguised inferences. Since they are clearly not self-authenticating they must be disguised inferences. I suggest a third possibility: that they are what they purport to be, cases of direct awareness, but that the claim that this is what they are relies upon there being a theory or conceptual scheme in terms of which the claim can be adequately defended.[56]

This position should confirm us in the view that any language about "self-authenticating" religious experiences or "incorrigible" religious intuitions should be avoided. Although one may well be psychologically certain that one has an experience, any description of the object of that experience is inevitably open to correction. If this is true of sense experience, it must also be true of religious experience. In both cases, although the primary basis for a knowledge claim may be the experience itself, the claim may need further support, including support from inductive-type reasoning—whether inductive causal explanatory reasoning or metaphysical explanatory reasoning.[57] In

54. Peter Donovan, *Interpreting Religious Experience* (New York: Seabury; London: Sheldon, 1979), pp. 91, 35, 72.

55. Davis, *The Evidential Force of Religious Experience*, p. 144, and chapter 6 *passim*. See also p. 249.

56. Basil Mitchell, *The Justification of Religious Belief* (London: Macmillan, 1973; New York: Seabury, 1974), pp. 112-113, 115.

57. See Donald D. Evans, "The Problem of Knowledge and Christian Theism", *Sophia* I: 2 (1962). Defenses of self-authentication in religious experience are offered by H. J. N. Horsburgh, "The Claims of Religious Experience", *The Australasian Journal of Philosophy* 35: 3 (1957) and Robert Oakes, "Mysticism, Veridicality and Modality", *Faith and Philosophy* 2 (1985), pp. 217-218. They are countered by Alston, *Perceiving God*, pp. 80, 210-211.

the case of religious experience, whether seeming to experience God is sufficient grounds for supposing that one does will depend in part on just how probable or improbable is the existence of God, on background evidence. And this is a judgment that may well depend on the overall coherence, consistency, comprehensiveness, simplicity and "satisfactoriness" of the theistic position.[58]

This discussion is highly relevant to the task of the Christian religious educator. If religious experience has the primacy often proposed—as the originating source of and only real justification for religious feelings, beliefs and other "religious attributes"—then Christian religious education needs to be oriented, in a large part, towards the development of (the preconditions of) these experiences. But if, as has also been argued, religious experience cannot stand alone epistemologically, but needs the support of a coherent theistic framework if it is to be plausibly treated as an experience of God, then Christian religious education that is oriented towards *justifiable* religious beliefs *also* needs to teach the Christian belief system. Evoking religious experience, or facilitating a disposition for religious experience, is not sufficient on its own. The conceptual scheme of Christianity must also be passed on, and this (many would claim) must be rationally defensible. If this does not happen, the Christian learner may be left in the position of the sailor peering through the rain, thinking that he sees "something" but without a framework of defensible beliefs into which this apparent sighting can fit. Such a person will not know what he sees. Thus although religious experience is very important in religion and in religious education, it does not—and cannot—stand alone. (A similar point may be made in terms of an experiencing-as analysis: see p. 124 above and note 38.)

Subjective Religious Experiences: A Normative Claim

The inductive, "best explanation" argument to God from religious experiences can be extended to cover subjective religious feeling states as well. A creative, judging and saving God may thus be invoked as the best explanation of my subjective experiences of dependence, guilt and acceptance. However, such an argument is much less plausible than in the case of the category of objective religious experience, since many feeling states "just happen" to us without our needing to postulate any particular external cause,[59] and many clearly originate within the experiencing subject.

In any case, I would wish to argue that the primary significance of religious affect lies elsewhere, and is independent of any epistemological implications it may have. On my analysis of what it is to be Christian, affect is an essential learning outcome in any "full" or "real" Christian religious education. One reason for adopting this, admittedly normative, view is that without any evi-

58. See Chapter 4, and recall Swinburne's qualifying clause (p. 128 above). Alston's account of our reliance on the background system of Christian belief in our perception of God is also relevant here. See Alston, *Perceiving God*, pp. 93-99, 206, 292-302.

59. But note Swinburne's criticism of naturalistic explanations of religious experience above (p. 127).

dence of a person's *felt* sense of dependence, guilt or acceptance, most people would be unwilling to say that that person really had the relevant Christian beliefs. "God is genuinely known only when God's identity is established in a manner that includes one's passions."[60] We may perhaps have minimal beliefs-that (as intellectual convictions) about creation, sin or salvation without feeling anything; but would such beliefs count as *religious* beliefs in anything other than an etiolated sense?[61]

Certainly, to "believe in" these religious doctrines, or rather these religious realities, is to give your heart to them and to be moved by them—as we shall see in more detail later. And to *act* on such beliefs, or in ways appropriate to them, is normally to be motivated by their accompanying feeling states. Further, we may act without passion on the basis of passionless beliefs; but not only are we less likely too, but also such actions are far less likely to be adjudged *religious* actions—or even *moral* actions. Normally speaking, religious feeling is a constitutive element in religious being, and thus a crucially important religious learning outcome. I would claim that the person who is without religious feeling is not (fully) religious. Feeling is normative in religion and hence it must be a prime focus of Christian religious education.

The classic defense of this claim is to be found in Jonathan Edwards's treatise of 1746 on *The Religious Affections*. (I do not, however, subscribe to every aspect of Edwards's position.) "True religion," Edwards writes, "is evermore a powerful thing; and the power of it appears, in the first place in inward exercise of it in the heart, where is the principal and original seat of it." He draws his conclusion that "true religion lies much in the affections" from his claims (a) that true religion "is of a practical nature" and God has so constituted human nature that the affects are "very much the spring" of human action, and (b) that the things of religion take hold of human souls "no further than they affect them". These claims are supported by the place given in the Bible to affects "such as fear, hope, love, hatred, desire, joy, sorrow, gratitude, compassion and zeal".[62]

---

60. Dean M. Martin, "Learning to Become a Christian", *Religious Education* 82: 1 (1987), p. 103.

61. *Something* of this is captured in Newman's famous distinction between notional assent (to the truth of abstract "notions" or concepts), and the more personal, real assent (to the concrete reality itself, grasped in an image that appeals to our passions and our will). John Henry Newman, *A Grammar of Assent* (London: Longmans, Green, 1913), ch. IV. We find it more explicitly in Kierkegaard's insistence that "subjectivity" and "the entire passion of the infinite"—the "how" of religion rather than its "what"—is central to faith. Even an idol worshiper can have true faith on this account. See Søren Kierkegaard, *Concluding Unscientific Postscript*, trans. David F. Swenson and Walter Lowrie (Princeton, N.J.: Princeton University Press, 1941), pp. 177-183, 540.

62. Jonathan Edwards, *Select Works, Volume III: Treatise Concerning the Religious Affections* (London: Banner of Truth, 1961), pp. 27-53. Psychologists have produced a considerable fund of evidence showing that there are often only weak, unreliable relations between *particular* attitudes (affect) and beliefs on the one hand, and *specific* overt behaviors on the other. See, for example, Hugh Hartshorne and Mark A. May, *Studies in Deceit* (*Studies in the Nature of Character*, Vol. 1) (New York: Macmillan, 1928); Martin Fishbein, "Attitude and

Of course, definitions of what it is to be religious and what it is to be Christian are, in the end, decided on by us—even if we adopt them on the basis of revelation. We are those who decide who is to be called "religious" ("Christian"), because we are the ones who use this language. The distinction between descriptive claims and normative ("evaluative", "prescriptive") claims is important here. Some of those who are engaged in *teaching about* Christianity and other religions proceed as though they are merely giving a "neutral", "objective" description of the phenomena of the religion with which they are concerned. But they are not. All such accounts logically imply a prior *selection* of the phenomena that are to count as "Christian", "Buddhist", "Muslim" etc. The use of criteria for this selective process inevitably introduces a normative element. Giving an account of what it is to be a Christian—and thus specifying the substantive content of Christian religious education—is a matter of saying what an individual or group need to believe, feel and practice in order for them to be designated "Christian" by whoever is selecting the sample of Christians. Thus it is to say what (in the selector's view) Christianity "really is", which is at least very close to saying what "real Christianity is", or what Christianity "ought to be".

Discussions within Christianity about the nature of Christianity tend to lay stress on one dimension of the Christian faith at the expense of the others, arguing that therein lies its "essence" or "originating impulse". This favored dimension (e.g. doctrine or religious experience in general) or component of a dimension (e.g. a particular doctrine or experience) is selected on the basis of the theological presuppositions of the selector. As Stephen Sykes puts it:

> There is *no* perspective on Christianity which relativizes all other perspectives. So long as it is grasped that any platform which we may construct from which to survey the material before us is constructed out of substances which themselves have been fashioned from a survey of the material, the interesting questions turn out to be not purely methodolog-

---

the Prediction of Behavior", in Martin Fishbein, ed., *Readings in Attitude Theory and Measurement* (New York: Wiley, 1967), pp. 477-492; Allan W. Wicker, "Attitudes versus Actions: The Relationship of Verbal and Overt Behavioral Responses to Attitude Objects", *Journal of Social Issues* 25: 4 (1969), pp. 41-78. But it must be stressed that behavior often depends on factors of the situation other than beliefs and attitudes, and a person's *real* beliefs and attitudes are not easy to assess. Our attitudes and beliefs only influence our behavior indirectly (perhaps through our intentions), and when attitudes and beliefs are tested many of those selected are so action-unspecific that correlations are never likely to be great. It is clear, however, that at least certain beliefs, emotions and attitudes, including religious ones, are often powerful contributory causes of behavior when they are fully integrated into the cognitive-affective-lifestyle reality that is a human being. See C. Daniel Batson *et al.*, "Brotherly love or self-concern?: behavioral consequences of religion", in Brown, ed., *Advances in the Psychology of Religion*, ch. 13. For a thorough account of the recent literature, see J. Richard Eiser, *Social Psychology: Attitudes, Cognition and Social Behaviour* (Cambridge: Cambridge University Press, 1986), ch. 3 and Allen E. Liska, "A Critical Examination of the Causal Structure of the Fishbein/Ajzen Attitude-Behavior Model", *Social Psychology Quarterly* 47 (1984).

ical, but substantial. If one perpetually asks what the criteria are for theological positions, one does not arrive at a bedrock method, but an infinite
(and infinitely boring) methodological regression.[63]

Sykes's words are pertinent both for Christian religious educators and for those
who (only) "teach about" Christianity. In *selecting* this aspect of Christianity
to teach (or teach about), and passing over that aspect—a process that is an
inevitable prerequisite of any teaching activity—they are painting a picture
of Christianity. Pictures can only be painted from particular perspectives or
"viewpoints". Part of what is involved in an artist having a viewpoint is that
it is a selective viewpoint. The painter sets up his easel here, rather than
there; or she invites these models to sit for her, rather than any others. To
adopt, in Sykes's phrase, "a viewpoint upon Christianity . . . a platform from
which it may be surveyed" is the task of the secular teacher of Christian
studies,[64] just as much as it is of the Christian theologian seeking to articulate the essence or identity of Christianity. It is certainly the task of the
Christian religious educator. The construction of such a platform at this particular point, out of these particular materials, is the result of a decision.
That decision—if it is not entirely arbitrary—is based on grounds ("this is
the best place from which to view Christianity, *because* . . ."). It is just not possible that normative judgments about what is of importance and interest
(including theological importance and interest), and therefore probably also
about what is true and of value, in Christianity should not be included among
those grounds. These judgments will arise along with, and will inevitably
influence, descriptive judgments about what it is that particular Christians
claim to be true and of value. "What *is* Christianity?" remains, at least in
part, a persistently normative question. The responsibility for answering it is
not one that the Christian religious educator can slough off.

Some readers may think that the position adopted above about the importance of affect in Christianity is too extreme. I should repeat here that in
order to pass the "test" of being a Christian the learner does not need "to
attempt all the questions". The fully Christianly educated person—that is
the person who possesses a full range of beliefs, attitudes, emotions and
actions—is the ideal candidate we are looking for, but as reasonable exam-
iners we should be willing to pass a number of those who lack some of these
qualities. Yet if I had to point out a Christian in an identity parade/line-up, it
would be the one with the Christian affects whom I would most readily recognize. This is an unashamedly *normative* position, in the sense of "tending
to establish a standard by prescription". All interesting accounts of Christianity
involve some such normative prescription of what Christianity really is, or
ought to be.

---

63. Sykes, *The Identity of Christianity*, pp. 241-242.
64. See Alex R. Rodger, *Education and Faith in an Open Society* (Edinburgh: Handsel,
1982), p. 114 and Jeff Astley, "Theology and Curriculum Selection", *British Journal of
Religious Education* 10: 2 (1988). Some of the discussion here has been drawn from this latter source.

In this chapter and in Chapter 9 I argue for the centrality of affect in the religious life. Affect comprises or leads from religious experience (which itself often results in belief). It is entailed by or forms part of religious believing, especially of belief-in (see pp. 152-153). It provides an essential element in the motivation of overt religious behavior. On this (admittedly more extreme, and certainly partisan) view, Christian religious education should have as a primary objective the evoking and development of religious experience, broadly conceived, and in particular of religious feeling states. No one can be fully and properly Christian who does not feel appropriately. This claim undergirds all that I have to say in the rest of this chapter. None of this, however, should be taken to imply that a person without religious feeling is not "saved" (or created, come to that), or in "a relationship with God". These states of affairs may obtain without their being felt, or believed, or even acted upon—by infants, for example, or handicapped adults. I claim only that the person who is without religious feeling is not (or not fully) religious; not that he or she is not (or even not fully) loved and accepted by God.

RELIGIOUS AFFECT

Feelings, Emotions and Attitudes

In giving an account of these phenomena, which are so central to Christianity and therefore to Christian religious education, one is immediately immersed in the problems of definition and classification. Affect or affection is characterized by feeling, rather than cognition (here "thinking") or volition ("willing", "acting"). But the category of *feelings* is seen by philosophers either as a rather narrow one[65] or as a very wide one.[66]

Although in everyday parlance feelings are often equated with *emotions*, the latter is a more complex category.[67] According to William Lyons we may analyze an occurrent emotion into the following aspects, components or accompaniments:

(1) *a cognitive belief*; which is the basis for
(2) *an evaluation of, or view about, the object of the emotion in relation to oneself*; which normally leads to
(3) *an appetitive ("conative") reaction of want or desire*; which, together with element (2), gives rise to
(4) *a feeling state*; and frequently predisposes the subject to
(5) *reactive behavior and physiological upset.*[68]

---

65. Gilbert Ryle, *The Concept of Mind* (Harmondsworth, England: Penguin, 1963), ch. IV.

66. William P. Alston, "Emotion and Feeling", in Edwards, ed., *The Encyclopedia of Philosophy*, Vol. 2.

67. And often a very broad one. It has been defined as "an umbrella term for any of a number of subjectively experienced, affect-laden states . . .". Arthur S. Reber, *Dictionary of Psychology* (London: Penguin, 1985), p. 235.

68. William Lyons, *Emotion* (Cambridge: Cambridge University Press, 1980), pp. 70, 179 and *passim*. Components (1), (2) and (3) together constitute "the core part of an occurrent emotional state" (p. 128). For more on emotions, see below Chapter 9.

We may be willing to speak of the Christian's love, awe, fear, sense of peace etc. as emotions that can be analyzed along these lines. We should note that the belief component of an emotion is best understood as a disposition that a person has, but of which she is not necessarily conscious, which gives rise to her feeling states and is implied by them. "Untargeted" emotions, without belief components that relate them to *particular* objects, are best described as "moods".[69]

Attitudes are, if anything, even more difficult to analyze than emotions, but are usually taken to be internal states that influence a person's action responses.[70] Many writers regard attitudes as having (1) cognitive, (2) affective and (3) behavioral components, in so far as they relate to, give rise to, or "include" (1) beliefs, appraisals and ideas, (2) emotions (as positive or negative affect) and (3) predisposition to action.[71] But attitudes appear *predominantly* to be affective orientations.[72] Most philosophers tend to regard an attitude as having cognitive implications, but as itself consisting of a "*disposition* to act in a certain manner" and/or "to show a certain emotive reaction to someone or something". We may note that attitudes are usually treated as dispositions, (most) emotions as occurrences (see Glossary).[73]

All attitudes are either pro- or con-attitudes, approvals or disapprovals:[74] that is dispositions to feel and/or to act either for or against the "intentional objects" to which they are directed. They have been described as "predominantly a matter of affective evaluation", representing a positive or nega-

---

69. Donald D. Evans, *Faith, Authenticity and Morality* (Toronto: University of Toronto Press; Edinburgh: Handsel, 1980), p. 254. Solomon writes of joy and despair as moods (although he denies any sharp distinction between moods and emotions), on account of their being omnidirectional—see Robert C. Solomon, *The Passions* (Notre Dame, Ind.: University of Notre Dame Press, 1983), p. 172. Interestingly he claims that religious passion more usually takes the form of a mood than an emotion, and argues that "the universal nature of religious objects is due to the fact that they are objects of a metaphysical mood. A particular emotion would inevitably shrink . . . the object of worship to particular size" (p. 133). Compare also Holmer, *Making Christian Sense*, pp. 40-42.

70. Gordon W. Allport, "Attitudes", in Carl Murchison, ed., *A Handbook of Social Psychology* (Worcester, Mass.: Clark University Press, 1935), p. 810. On the concept of attitude see further the excerpts from Gordon Allport, Theodore M. Newcomb and Solomon E. Asch, in Marie Jahoda and Neil Warren, eds., *Attitudes* (Harmondsworth, England: Penguin, 1966).

71. Harry C. Triandis, *Attitude and Attitude Change* (New York: Wiley, 1971), pp. 2-3.

72. Martin Fishbein and Icek Ajzen, *Belief, Attitude, Intention and Behavior: An Introduction to Theory and Research* (Reading, Mass.: Addison-Wesley, 1975), pp. 1-16.

73. Vincent Brümmer, *Theology and Philosophical Inquiry* (London: Macmillan, 1981; Philadelphia: Westminster, 1982), p. 104. Compare "Attitude" in Horace B. English and Ava Champney English, *A Comprehensive Dictionary of Psychological and Psychoanalytical Terms* (New York: Longmans, Green 1958), p. 50. Richard Brandt calls attitudes "conative-emotional dispositions". Richard B. Brandt, "Emotive Theory of Ethics", in Edwards, ed., *The Encyclopedia of Philosophy*, Vol. 2, p. 494.

74. See S. Stansfeld Sargent and Robert C. Williamson, *Social Psychology* (New York: Ronald, 1966), p. 244-245; Eiser, *Social Psychology*, pp. 11-12.

tive—favorable or unfavorable—orientation towards some reality.[75] Although attitudes are fundamentally affective, on the one hand there may be some attitudes that do not give rise to emotions (e.g. carefulness or neutrality), while on the other hand certain emotions may be held in a dispositional way as attitudes without being occurrently "active" as felt emotions at any given time (e.g. love, hate or fear). In many ways attitudes are more than simply dispositions or the occurrent expressions of such dispositions, being (introspectible?) *states* of a person.

Evans's Attitude-Virtues

Certain basic attitudes have been surveyed by the Canadian philosopher Donald Evans. He claims that they give rise both to beliefs and worship in religion and to beliefs and conduct in ethics, and designates them *attitude-virtues*. He describes them as pervasive stances for living, or "modes of being in the world". These attitude-virtues are existential categories as well as dispositions to act in certain ways. They constitute, accounting to Evans, the "style" or "timbre" of a person's personality.[76] His account, as we shall see, can be of signal value in an analysis of the aim and content of Christian religious education.

On Evans's view human fulfillment occurs when the attitude-virtues in their mature forms predominate steadily over the opposing attitude-vices. The attitudes are "pervasive", both internally and externally, in that they influence all of a person and all of that person's situations. They are "unifying" in that they unify all a person's being and all of his or her experiences and environments. Evans indicates the important part they play in our emotional life, and the difficulty of describing them as simply "giving rise" to emotions. Emotional/feeling tone seems to be part and parcel of the very nature of many of them.

Evans boldly claims that the attitude-virtues that he has recognized represent what "ought to be", and that they are therefore intrinsically valuable states of the personality. These eight normative attitude-virtues discerned by Evans are: basic trust, humility, self-acceptance, responsibility, self-commitment, friendliness, concern and contemplation. I cannot do justice here to his perceptive and sensitive account of these attitudes, and will simply list them below with the briefest of descriptions. Their relevance to any account of the substantive content of Christian religious education will be clear.[77]

---

75. Melvin Manis, "Attitudes", in Adam and Jessica Kuper, eds., *The Social Science Encyclopaedia* (London: Routledge & Kegan Paul, 1985), p. 51. The phrase "affective valuation" may seem to be problematic for reasons discussed below.

76. Donald Evans, *Struggle and Fulfillment* (Cleveland: Collins, 1979), pp. 15, 186-187 and *passim*. See also his *Faith, Authenticity and Morality*, ch. 7.

77. Evans describes attitude (1)—basic trust—as the most fundamental and foundational, and notes that the others form a hierarchy, the development of each being dependent on the prior development of the attitudes listed before it. He notes briefly that his order corresponds with Erikson's eight life stages. On this view the development of attitude (5) is the work of ado-

(1) *Basic trust* [opposite: basic distrust]
This is an attitude of cosmic trust-readiness or confidence that reality has meaning, can be accepted and appreciated, and will satisfy our deepest needs. It incorporates "assurance", "receptivity", "fidelity", "hope" and "passion". Evans writes that basic trust is an inner stance "which one brings *to* each situation . . . It is an initial openness to whatever is life-affirming in nature and other people and oneself."[78]

(2) *Humility* [opposites: pride or self-humiliation]
This is the realistic acceptance and exercise of our own powers and freedom.

(3) *Self-acceptance* [opposite: self-rejection]
This is the acceptance of oneself and the rejection of pervasive guilt about oneself.

(4) *Responsibility* [opposite: irresponsibility]
This is the conscientiousness and competence of a trustworthy person.

(5) *Self-commitment* [opposite: alienated dissipation of self]
This is the integration of personality and the attitude of "being true to oneself".

(6) *Friendliness* [opposite: self-isolation]
This is the willingness of a person to enter an I-Thou relationship of love.

(7) *Concern* [opposite: self-indulgence]
This represents a person's willingness to help others pastorally or prophetically.

(8) *Contemplation* [opposite: self-preoccupation and self-consciousness]
Evans describes this in terms of the stance of a person "who profoundly appreciates the reality and uniqueness of each particular in the universe", including himself or herself, and is "liberated from the self-preoccupation and self-consciousness which distort and subjectivize our usual perception of reality", and "participates in a reality which is ultimate". It is fostered by various forms of meditation that discipline the attention, cleanse the vision, and open the heart.[79] This last attitude-virtue incorporates "detachment", "attention", "celebration" and "peace".

Interestingly enough, from an epistemological point of view, Evans

---

lescence, and attitude (6) is laid down mainly during young adulthood. Evans, *Struggle and Fulfillment*, p.157; compare Erik Erikson, *Childhood and Society* (New York: Norton, 1964; London: Granada, 1977), ch. 7 and James W. Fowler, *Stages of Faith: The Psychology of Human Development and the Quest for Meaning* (San Francisco: Harper & Row, 1981), ch. 14. We should note further that attitudes (6), (7) and (8) are described by Evans as together constituting "love", the supreme goal of human life, for which attitudes (1) through (5) are prerequisites.

78. Evans, *Struggle and Fulfillment*, p. 2.

79. *Ibid.*, p. 7. It is presumably also therefore nurtured by some aspects of Christian worship. See Gwen Kennedy Neville and John H. Westerhoff, III, *Learning Through Liturgy* (New York: Seabury, 1978); Daniel W. Hardy and David F. Ford, *Jubilate: Theology in Praise* (London: Darton, Longman & Todd, 1984), *Praising and Knowing God* (Philadelphia: Westminster, 1985).

believes that these eight attitude-virtues are necessary conditions for the discernment of the divine in religious experience, our trust in God enabling us to discern God.[80] The formation of such attitudes, therefore, might properly be regarded as an educational precondition of the religious learner's having an experience of God. In addition to this claim, Evans offers a "neo-Kantian" argument for belief in the existence of God as "a presupposition or implication of an attitude which ought to be cultivated because it is necessary for human fulfillment".[81] As human beings we need to adopt these attitudes, he argues, and these attitudes seem to imply certain cosmic beliefs. Thus we need to engage in basic trust, and basic trust implies the existence of one who is cosmically trustworthy. We shall return to this argument later.

Following Evans, we might focus on attitudes and argue that to be religious is to have certain religious attitudes and to engage in certain patterns of behavior that are expressive of such attitudes, the attitude predisposing the person to behave in that way. Clearly religious people have such attitudes at least partly because they have learned them. They have developed them as a result of certain experiences, including their experiences of other people. Very often these experiences have been placed in their way by Christian religious education. Austin Farrer's claim for the belief aspect of religion— "How did religion get into our heads? It was taught to us, was it not?"[82]—may thus be extended to its attitude component, and to our hearts. And that extension must be made if learning a religion is regarded as largely a matter of learning values, attitudes and dispositions to act, such as Evans describes. Many would claim, indeed, that religious learning is only secondarily a matter of learning the religious beliefs (or stories or metaphors) that are components of such attitudes, or support them psychologically and logically.[83]

---

80. Evans, *Struggle and Fulfillment*, p. 171; compare H. H. Price, *Belief* (London: Allen & Unwin; New York: Humanities Press, 1969), pp. 455-488.

81. Evans, *Struggle and Fulfillment*, p. 173. According to Kant's "moral argument" the complete or perfect good consists in holy wills (moral goodness) rewarded by happiness, and this situation can only be achieved on the assumption (a) that we are immortal and (b) that a good, all powerful God exists who will reward virtue in heaven. As morality bids us achieve this "highest good", moral obligation presupposes both immortality and God. Immanuel Kant, *Critique of Practical Reason*, Part I, Book II, Ch. II, trans. Lewis White Beck (Indianapolis: Bobbs-Merrill, 1956). Evans's argument has a similar structure. For further explorations of the phenomenon of human trust that seem to lead to an affirmation of God, see Francis Dunlop, *The Education of Feeling and Emotion* (London: Allen & Unwin, 1984), pp. 118-119 and Hans Küng, *Does God Exist?*, trans. Edward Quinn (New York: Random House, 1981), parts E and F.

82. Austin Farrer, *Faith and Speculation* (London: Black; New York: New York University Press, 1967), p. 3.

83. The most radical version of this claim is to be found in Richard Braithwaite's classic paper, "An Empiricist's View of the Nature of Religious Belief", in which he argues that Christianity is essentially a matter of commitment to a way of life, supported by stories. His position has been developed by Richard Hare: see R. M. Hare, *Essays on Religion and Education* (Oxford: Oxford University Press, 1992), ch. 1 (see also ch. 2). For Braithwaite's essay and some critical discussion, see Ian T. Ramsey, ed., *Christian Ethics and Contemporary Philosophy* (New York: Macmillan; London: SCM, 1966), chs. 3 and 4; Renford Bambrough,

Christian Spirituality

Many philosophers of education seem to take a very different line, however, assuming that Christianity is fundamentally a type of metaphysical worldview and that religion in general is simply (metaphysical) theology. This is perverse. Religions are surely not primarily high level explanations of reality, although they may contain and/or imply such high level explanations. I would side with those who contend that religions are essentially ways of coping with and triumphing over our experience. They are not so much explanations of the world as ways of salvation within—or "out of"—the world. Religions are essentially pragmatic and practical. It is after all when they cease to be of any *use* that they are given up.[84]

Whatever else it is and does, Christianity is a religion that offers to people a set of symbols and stories that affect them. It introduces them to, and "imposes" on them, certain spiritual values. Those who learn Christianity adopt some elements of Christian spirituality that lead to their (this worldly and/or other worldly) "release" and "healing". Christians may disagree as to the nature of this Christian spirituality and the precise mechanisms—psychological and/or metaphysical—of this Christian salvation. I only wish to argue here that it is some such form of Christian spirituality, experienced as salvific, that constitutes the heart of the Christian religion. It is in commitment to the values of Christian spirituality that a new life is engendered which is seen by the believer both as intrinsically valuable and (therefore?) as salvation. To be Christian is to have this life. Thus if Christianity is to be learned in any sense, this is what there is to be learned.

I am clearly using the word "spirituality" in a very broad sense here. I use it to describe "those attitudes, beliefs, and practices which animate people's lives and help them to reach out towards super-sensible realities" (with the emphasis on attitudes).[85] On this view, Evans's attitude-virtues could be

Reason, Truth and God, (London: Methuen, 1971), ch. II; William H. Austin, *The Relevance of Natural Science to Theology* (London: Macmillan; New York: Barnes & Noble, 1976), ch. 3; D. Z. Phillips, *Religion without Explanation* (Oxford: Blackwell, 1976), ch. 9. It should be noted that the claim made in the text does not necessarily lead to such a noncognitive (nonfactual) view of religious language.

84. See James, *The Varieties of Religious Experience*, p. 484; Martin Prozesky, *Religion and Ultimate Well-Being* (London: Macmillan; New York: St. Martin's Press, 1984), pp. 9, 18 and *passim*; Dean M. Martin, "Learning to Become a Christian", pp. 112-113. See also Chapter 5 above, especially pp. 104-105.

85. Gordon Wakefield, "Spirituality", in Alan Richardson and John Bowden, eds., *A New Dictionary of Christian Theology* (London: SCM, 1983), p. 549. Spiritual attitudes may be described as "virtues" in that a virtue is "a settled attitude, which conduces to habitually good action in some respect". John Macquarrie, ed., *A Dictionary of Christian Ethics* (Philadelphia: Westminster; London: SCM, 1967), p. 354. See also Keith Ward, *Ethics and Christianity* (London: Allen & Unwin; New York: Humanities Press, 1970), ch. V. These attitude-values or attitude-virtues have received a considerable emphasis in the Christian tradition. The Pauline list of the "fruit of the spirit" in Galatians 5:22-23 refers to love, joy, peace, longsuffering, kindness, goodness, faithfulness, meekness, and self-control. The traditional seven virtues of mediaeval moral theology comprised the "theological virtues" of faith, hope and love, together with the "cardinal virtues" (prudence, justice, temperance and fortitude) needed to

seen as components of an essentially human (salvific) spirituality. But is it a *Christian* spirituality? According to the theologian Hans Küng, being Christian "is not an addition to being human" but "an elevation or—better—a transfiguration of the human, at once preserving, canceling, surpassing the human". He agrees that "*Christian* does not mean everything that is true, good, beautiful, human", arguing rather that "everything can be called Christian which in theory and practice has an explicit, positive reference to Jesus Christ".[86] But what does this Christological reference amount to? For Küng, its effect is on a person's attitudes, and the life that flows from such attitudes. "In the light of Jesus Christ . . . the basic attitude and basic orientation of a person"—that is the person's form of life, lifestyle and way of life—"can be described both comprehensively and concretely". Küng argues that the whole Christian message does not merely aim at certain decisions, enterprises, motivations or dispositions, "but at a wholly new approach to life: at an awareness transformed from the roots upward, a new basic attitude, a different scale of values". This is a radical rethinking and conversion of the whole person, for which a historical figure is convincing in a way that would be impossible for any impersonal idea, ideal, abstract principle or universal norm. "Jesus of Nazareth is himself the *personification* of this new way of life."[87] Thus Christian spirituality may be described, in Gordon Wakefield's words, as a "praying and living in Jesus Christ"; and we may argue that the formation of this spirituality focused on the person of Christ can be seen as an important aspect of the celebration of Christ in worship, and of the stress on the imitation of Christ (conformity to Christ) in much Christian moral education.[88]

What is it then to learn Christianity? As we have seen, any answer to the central question of the content of Christian religious education must be a normative answer, and not merely a descriptive one. My own normative response would be that to learn Christianity *implicitly* is primarily to learn the affective attitude-virtues that comprise salvific human spirituality, and those

---

express them. See R. C. Mortimer, *The Elements of Moral Theology* (London: Black, 1953). Holley distinguishes certain attitudes that are of intrinsic value as *ontic values* "because they are the very structure of the spiritual subject: they are the actual constituents of a person's spiritual nature". Raymond Holley, *Religious Education and Religious Understanding: An Introduction to the Philosophy of Religious Education* (London: Routledge & Kegan Paul, 1978), p. 108.

86. Hans Küng, *On Being a Christian*, trans. Edward Quinn (Garden City, N.Y.: Doubleday, 1976; London: Collins, 1977), p. 601-602 and 125. Ninian Smart similarly writes: "It is not possible to define an essence of Christianity, beyond saying that the faith relates to Christ, either in historical continuity or through religious experience or both." Smart, *The Phenomenon of Christianity* (London: Collins, 1979), p. 128.

87. Küng, *On Being a Christian*, p. 546.

88. Gordon Wakefield, "Christian Spirituality", in Mircea Eliade, ed., *Encyclopedia of Religion*, Vol. 3 (New York: Macmillan; London: Collier Macmillan, 1987), p. 452. See also Astley, "The Role of Worship in Christian Learning"; Susanne Johnson, "Education in the Image of God", in Jack L. Seymour and Donald E. Miller, eds., *Theological Approaches to Christian Education* (Nashville, Tenn,: Abingdon, 1990).

beliefs and practices with which they are integrally related. These outcomes are *characteristic* of Christianity. To learn Christianity *explicitly*, however, involves more than this. It is to learn these attitudes in their Christian form, with an explicit positive reference to Jesus Christ and in dialogue with the Christian tradition that speaks of him.[89] And that, I would contend, is the essence of "formative Christian learning", in the sense of formation in the learning outcomes that are *distinctive* of Christianity.

The Role of Value Judgments

Frederick Ferré has defined religion as "an institutionalized way of valuing most comprehensively and intensively".[90] He significantly comments that "valuing is relevant to all aspects of a person. . . . We value . . . as whole persons. No aspect of ourselves is left untouched."[91] John Haught has argued that we commonly ask three questions about religions. The prior question is the *validity* question (Do they have any grounds? Are they true?), but the other two questions are more intimately related to attitudes and valuations. The first of these is the question of *congruity*: Do they "fit" and "consolidate" my experience? Are they "meaningful" for me? Do they animate me? The second is the *value* question: Do they have any value for me, or others? Do they seem worthwhile, wholesome?[92]

Alston distinguishes between emotions, attitudes, dispositions and character traits, but argues that "what binds these all together is that they all, in various ways, involve *evaluations* of objects".[93] We have seen the important part played by such evaluations as components of emotions and attitudes: these are largely cognitive appraisals, although the term "evaluation" has a wider connotation also (see next section). However, the language of "*valuing*", "valuation", "value judgments" and "values" is usually seen as having a rather different status. Admittedly, some social scientists regard values essentially as beliefs (albeit with an affective component) and attitudes as organizations of beliefs,[94] and some philosophers refer to value appraisals as cognitions (being beliefs or judgments).[95] But others stress the importance of distinguishing the essentially noncognitive nature of valuing, in the philosophical sense of noncognitive (i.e. non fact asserting). They thus retain the

---

89. See also Jeff Astley, "Will the Real Christianity Please Stand Up?", *British Journal of Religious Education* 15: 1 (1992).

90. Frederick Ferré, *Basic Modern Philosophy of Religion* (New York: Scribner's; London: Allen & Unwin, 1967), p. 73. Religion is a *comprehensive* way of valuing in that what is valued is relevant to the whole of life; it is *intensive* in that this is valued above all things.

91. *Ibid.*, p. 61.

92. John F. Haught, *Religion and Self Acceptance* (Washington, D.C.: University Press of America, 1980), p. 7.

93. Alston, "Emotions and Feelings", p. 485.

94. See Milton Rokeach, *The Nature of Human Values* (New York: Free Press; London: Collier Macmillan, 1973), ch. 1.

95. Solomon, *The Passions, passim* (see below Chapter 9).

distinction between factual and value judgments.[96] I would agree with those who describe valuing itself, and therefore religious valuing, as basically affective: value being a matter of feeling for something, having a positive orientation towards it, being "for" it, believing "in" it.[97]

In valuation we ascribe value to something and thus give it meaning, for "we . . . know the meaning of something when we know what attitude we ought to have towards it", and we find meaning in something when we love it for its own sake.[98] This explains the important part played in our language by expressive and prescriptive speech acts. These are words and phrases that declare, evoke and "convey" meaning, by expressing and prescribing the attitudes deemed appropriate to the object in question. Through language we declare, persuade others of, and prescribe the proper "*on-looks*": that is the ways in which we "look on" something, and feel that others should look on it.[99] The educational implication of this position is illustrated well in some words of D. W. Hamlyn: "the issues over learning to have a certain attitude or emotion towards something turn on analogous issues over learning to see things in certain ways".[100] Christian religious education is clearly a significant influence on the way Christians view themselves, others, the world and God.

In religion and religious education the proper attitudes towards God are of major significance. One may argue that the *fundamental* attitudes of religion are those valuational attitudes that undergird religious emotions and

---

96. A gap emphasized by David Hume—see his *A Treatise of Human Nature*, Book III, Part I, Sect. I. Compare J. L. Mackie, *Hume's Moral Theory* (London: Routledge & Kegan Paul, 1980), pp. 61-63. It is possible to make too much of this gap, forgetting that all descriptive language (in which beliefs are framed) is already subtly valuational or presupposes institutionalized obligations—see, e.g., J. R. Seale, "How to Derive 'Ought' from 'Is'", *Philosophical Review* 73 (1964) and Don Cupitt, *The Long-Legged Fly* (London: SCM, 1987), chs. 3-6. On the is/ought debate more generally see W. D. Hudson, ed., *The Is-Ought Question* (London: Macmillan, 1969; New York: St. Martin's Press, 1973); Alan H. Goldman, *Moral Knowledge* (London: Routledge, 1988), ch. II; and Philip Hefner, "Is/Ought: a risky relationship between theology and science", in A. R. Peacocke, ed., *The Sciences and Theology in the Twentieth Century* (Stocksfield, England: Oriel, 1981).

97. Price, *Belief*, p. 452; Alan Montefiore, *A Modern Introduction to Moral Philosophy* (London: Routledge & Kegan Paul, 1958; New York: Praeger, 1959), p. 147; Lee, *The Content of Religious Instruction*, p. 227.

98. Brümmer, *Theology and Philosophical Inquiry*, p. 121 and ch. 9 *passim*; John Wilson, *A Preface to Morality* (London: Macmillan; Totowa, N.J.: Barnes & Noble, 1987), pp. 81, 85. These authors are writing of the "meaning" of things, events or actions, not of the meaning of words (linguistic meaning). See the section on "Religious Meaning" below.

99. Donald D. Evans, *The Logic of Self-Involvement* (London: SCM, 1963; New York: Herder and Herder, 1969), pp. 124-141. The primary source for the idea of language "doing things" through its "performative", or "illocutionary" and "perlocutionary", power is J. L. Austin. See his *Philosophical Papers*, ed. J. O. Urmson and G. J. Warnock (Oxford: Oxford University Press, 1970), pp. 98-103 and 233-252, and *How To Do Things with Words* (Oxford: Oxford University Press, 1962).

100. D. W. Hamlyn, *Experience and the Growth of Understanding* (London: Routledge & Kegan Paul, 1978), p. 124. See Chapter 9 below.

dispositions, that is our value judgments about the worthiness and goodness of God which form part of, or predispose us to, our love for God and worship of God.[101] Our pro-attitude towards God, which is our disposition to praise and appreciate, honor and serve God—i.e. to feel and to act "for God"—is essentially the same attitude that runs through all our religious emotions. We are pro-God when we view God as good, holy, just, perfect, worthy of worship and trustworthy—as the supreme good, the summation of all these intrinsic goods that we are also "for".[102] I should be willing to assert that a religious belief without this accompanying valuation is not truly a *religious* belief (or, at least, not truly a religious *belief-in*[103]). Without it the emotions and attitudes that are at the heart of religious being cannot be engaged. Attitude-commitments of this nature, in which we commit ourselves to the adoption of a pro-attitude to an object, may be called *value-commitments*. It is a large part of the task of Christian religious education to evoke such commitments.

Valuation and Evaluation

Educationists often describe evaluation as part of the cognitive domain of educational objectives. Bloom's "evaluation" is defined as "the making of judgments about the value, for some purpose, of ideas, works, solutions, methods, material etc.", involving the use of certain criteria or standards of appraisal.[104] (We can of course evaluate—assess, grade, judge, appraise—something favorably or unfavorably.[105]) Evaluation is routinely distinguished by educationists from "valuing", which is classified in the *Taxonomy of Educational Objectives* as an element of the affective domain. There valuing is described as a matter of holding a value, or recognizing that "a thing, phenomenon, or behavior has worth". This is expressed in affective language such as "desire" for, emotional acceptance of, "deep involvement" with, "devotion" to, or "preference for" a value.[106]

---

101. Brümmer, *Theology and Philosophical Inquiry*, p. 259.

102. Fundamentally, then, Christians are "for" certain values and "for" God, Jesus and the church. These religious objects are approved of and sought out. We recognize their worth or value, or (others would say) ascribe worth to them. We esteem them. These processes are all fundamental elements in an object's being thought of as "good", for "the basic reference of good . . . is to that which we like, welcome, desire, seek to gain or to preserve, whilst bad refers to that which we dislike, fear, resist, shun and to which we are accordingly averse". John Hick, *Evil and the God of Love* (New York: Harper & Row, 1966; London: Collins, 1968), p. 12. Technically a *logical* gap does exist between liking, wanting or choosing something and regarding it as "good", but Hick surely captures the thrust of the normal linkage between these notions. See Chapter 9 below.

103. See below pp. 152-153 and Chapter 8. The point is made with great beauty of language by Jonathan Edwards (*The Religious Affections*, pp. 192-217).

104. Benjamin S. Bloom *et al., Taxonomy of Educational Objectives: the Classification of Educational Goals. Handbook I: Cognitive Domain* (New York: McKay; London: Longmans, 1956), pp. 185-195.

105. See J. R. Searle, "Meaning and Speech Acts", *The Philosophical Review* 72 (1962).

106. David R. Krathwohl *et al., Taxonomy of Educational Objectives. Handbook II: Affective Domain* (New York: McKay; London: Longmans, 1964), pp. 180-182.

The interchangeability of the language of value and worth here should be noted. The adoption of a value such as justice, democracy, equality, impartiality, rationality, creativity or truthfulness *both* (a) is the basis of subsequent appraisals of (say) political or educational behavior, when this behavior is judged against the adopted scale, *and* (b) is itself a (positive) appraisal of the worth of the phenomenon or ideal. Bloom's cognitive "evaluation", on the other hand, appears to be a sort of reflective and comparative, "extrinsic" or "utilitarian" evaluation of something for certain purposes, assessing it according to specific nonideal criteria of value or worth: "standards of excellence", other viewpoints, the criterion of logical consistency etc. The affective attachment to ("valuing of") a particular idea, ideal, activity, person, group, object or cause is presented in the *Taxonomy* more in terms of its perceived "intrinsic" value or worth in and of itself—i.e. on a thoroughly normative ("ideal") scale of worth, of what is worthwhile for its own sake. Thus *valuing* involves a particular kind of appraisal, assessment or *evaluation*. The difference between the two lies partly in the type of scale or criterion used in the appraisal, but also in the fact that valuing is normally seen to be (or include) the *adoption* of the intrinsic worth scale itself with an emotional acceptance of its ratings, such that positive ratings are cherished or desired, whereas in other evaluations the scale may be used without being itself adopted. Presumably by extension, the adoption of other scales of evaluation may be regarded as a species of valuing (if "consistency", for example, is seen as having intrinsic worth). (Dictionaries often give "appraise" or "assess" as synonyms for both evaluation *and* valuing, and at least one dictionary of psychology offers almost identical definitions of "to value" and "evaluation", in terms of determining/assessing the value or worth of something.[107] Philosophers often use the term "evaluation" of moral and aesthetic "valuation".)

The orientation aspect of an attitude or disposition, i.e. the pro- or con-element of being positive or negative (or neutral) about something, is absolutely central to its nature. In its occurrent form it is manifested in *feeling* favorably or unfavorably (or neutrally) towards something, i.e. it is an affect. But the evaluation of the point occupied by that thing on a person's rating scale, which underlies this pro- or con-attitude, may be described as a cognitive (in the sense of "thinking") process. The nature of the original adoption of the scale, however, is not so easy to determine. Is the adoption of such a scale or criterion simply a cognitive matter? There is something to be said for the view that adoption of many scales of ideals, values, excellences etc. may be a fundamentally affective process. On the psychological cognitive theory of the emotions the appraisal component ("cognitive evaluation") is often described in terms of the "desirability", "praiseworthiness" and "appealingness" of the emotion-inclusive situation.[108] The adoption of any

---

107. Reber, *Dictionary of Psychology*, pp. 253, 810.

108. See Andrew Ortony *et al.*, *The Cognitive Structure of Emotions* (Cambridge: Cambridge University Press, 1988), ch. 3; Klaus R. Scherer and Paul Ekman, eds., *Approaches to Emotion* (Hillside, N.J.: Erlbaum, 1984), pp. 208-210, 213, 222, 242-248, 261, 404-409.

scale may be described largely as an affective process if it is agreed that (a) this adoption is a consequence of the recognition of the intrinsic worth of that scale—i.e. its "value", together with the basic (unavoidable?) adoption of the scale of intrinsic worth, and (b) the subsequent rating of other things *and norms* against it is primarily a matter of feeling. (Thus we "esteem", "cherish", "desire", "like", or "hold dear" that which we "value".) The difficulty is compounded in that the recognition of the worth of something is rarely a direct process, but includes the rating of that thing against various ideals or norms each of which is regarded as itself of worth or value. Thus the worth of a political act may be appraised in terms of how far it shows (i.e. where it ranks on a scale of) justice, truthfulness, prudence, distributive good, promise keeping, etc. Some or all of these norms may be regarded as intrinsically worthy or valuable (an affective process?), but perhaps to different degrees. But the worthiness of the act itself is somehow assessed *through* these other reflective and comparative assessments.[109]

Religious Meaning

In discussions about the meaning of life, or of particular experiences and situations, "meaning" is not being used in its semantic or linguistic sense: i.e. in terms of what a word, phrase or sentence refers to or represents, or its semantic entailments or denials. This aspect of what users "mean" (imply, understand, signify) by a word can best be understood as a *conceptual* skill: the mental skill that they exercise when they use that word. But the meaning of the meaning of life, and of things, events, actions, experiences and situations, relates rather to much wider issue of "the value, significance or purpose" of these things.[110] These are issues that cannot be answered by logicians or by looking at dictionaries. They are closely associated with the affective and valuational lives of individuals. Hence "meaning" here often connects with, and on occasions may be replaced by, the word "purpose"; and is readily inserted into phrases about "meaning-giving", "meaning-making", "meaning-finding", "meaning-framework", etc. Meaning, in this usage, is thus to be distinguished from mere linguistic knowing or understanding.[111]

Those who have written on the notion of the meaning or meaningfulness of life in a religious context often refer to "value maintenance": for example,

---

109. For a helpful philosophical discussion see William K. Frankena, "Value and Valuation", in Paul Edwards, ed., *The Encyclopedia of Philosophy*, Vol. 7, pp. 229-230.

110. See Brümmer, *Theology and Philosophical Inquiry*, p. 69, see also pp. 46-55, and chs. 9 and 10 *passim*.

111. See Susanne K. Langer, *Philosophy in a New Key* (Cambridge, Mass.: Harvard University Press, 1957), ch. X; John Wisdom, "The Meanings of the Questions of Life", in his *Paradox and Discovery* (Oxford: Blackwell; New York: Philosophical Library, 1965), ch. IV; Oswald Hanfling, *The Quest for Meaning* (Oxford: Blackwell, 1987), pp. ix-xi and *passim*; Daniel W. Hardy, "Religious Education—Truth-claims or Meaning-giving?", in M. C. Felderhof, ed., *Religious Education in a Pluralistic Society* (London: Hodder & Stoughton, 1985); James W. Fowler, "Faith and the Structuring of Meaning", in James W. Fowler and Antoine Vergote, eds., *Toward Moral and Religious Maturity* (Morriston, N.J.: Silver Burdett, 1980), p. 53; Fowler, *Stages of Faith*, pp. 24-25, 292.

"religious and metaphysical systems do provide a kind of meaning, because they maintain and enhance values".[112] Sociologists often also write of "reality maintenance", and of religions as maintaining socially defined reality by grounding such constructed worlds in ultimate realities.[113] To function in this way, valuational affect often goes hand in hand with these more metaphysical and cosmological aspects of religion. Thus religious valuations are to be seen as central in the whole "meaning-making" project of religion.

The significance of this function in human life can hardly be overstated. From the human world perspective, it may be said, "things only exist insofar as they have meaning—interest, value, purpose, function—for us . . . . the only way we recognize things in the world is by conferring meaning or value on them".[114] Religious educators who facilitate the valuing and meaning-making activities of their learners can truly be said to be helping them create, find and live in a "religious world". *Christian* religious educators who engage in such educational endeavors are co-workers in the new creation of a "Christian world" of Christian meaning and Christian values. Their task is as important as that.

The Centrality of Affect
By way of reinforcing some of the main conclusions of the present chapter, we may note Robert Solomon's contention that any true religious faith worthy of the name is not concerned "with Reality and objectivity but with values and the passions". Solomon presses his claim using extreme language: "The usual retreat of religion to objectivity and metaphysics is symptomatic of the loss of religious faith, the drying out of passion to yield merely dubious if not incomprehensible 'knowledge'."[115] Such a view connects with normative claims about the relative significance of the doctrines of salvation and creation, and of accounts of "God-as-God-is-towards-us" and "God-as-God-is-in-himself" in Christian theology. It also reinforces the position of those who stress the experiential, especially the salvific-experiential, component of Christian being.[116] The centrality of affect in religion is not surprising if we accept the argument that affect is both more distinctively human, and stronger, than cognition.[117] These are all claims with profound implications

---

112. Ninian Smart, *The Science of Religion and the Sociology of Knowledge* (Princeton, N.J.: Princeton University Press, 1973), p. 87; see also Ninian Smart, *The Philosophy of Religion* (New York: Random House, 1970; London: Sheldon, 1979), ch. 3.

113. Peter L. Berger, *The Social Reality of Religion* (*The Sacred Canopy*, Garden City, N.Y.: Doubleday, 1967) (Harmondsworth, England: Penguin, 1973), chs. 1 and 2.

114. Krishan Kumar, in Dan Cohn-Sherbok and Michael Irwin, eds., *Exploring Reality* (London: Allen & Unwin, 1987), p. 42; see also Ferré, *Basic Modern Philosophy of Religion*, pp. 353-361. We may prefer, with Ronald Hepburn, to speak of "both creating or projecting and discovering" meaning. R. W. Hepburn, *"Wonder" and Other Essays* (Edinburgh: Edinburgh University Press, 1984), p. 174.

115. Solomon, *The Passions*, p. 73.

116. John Hick, *An Interpretation of Religion* (New Haven: Yale University Press; London: Macmillan, 1989), chs. 2, 3, 4 and 17. See also pp. 100, 104-105.

117. See Lee, *The Content of Religious Instruction*, pp. 199, 205-206.

for the content of Christian religious education.

Certain secular educationists, representing something of a minority report over against their colleagues' more usual position, argue for the centrality of affect in their field also. Thus Francis Dunlop recognizes that feeling rather than thought "is our ultimate or foundational guide to reality, because it is only in direct feeling-experience that we actually *encounter* reality".[118] This is an important insight. Educational theory and practice, following intellectual reflection in general and philosophy in particular, has too often allowed human emotion too small a place in its account of what it is to become an (educated) person. Dunlop's position finds support in the writings of philosophers such as Robert Solomon and John Macmurray and the central place they give to the emotions. "Our passions constitute our lives," Solomon writes. "It is our passions, and our passions alone, that provide our lives with meaning."[119] Macmurray claims that: "The emotional life is not simply a part or an aspect of human life, . . . subordinate, or subsidiary to the mind. It is the core and essence of human life. . . . . . . the emotional life is our life . . ."[120] We shall be returning to this important theme in more detail in Chapter 9.

Ninian Smart offers as his "tentative definition of religion" a definiens that places the expression and evocation of religious affect (coupled with the activity of worship) in a central position. "A religion," he writes, "is a set of institutionalized rituals identified with a tradition and expressing and/or evoking sacral sentiments directed at a divine or trans-divine focus seen in the context of the human phenomenological environment and at least partially described by myths or by myths and doctrines."[121] These "sacral sentiments" are, I believe, the key to religion, and therefore they should be of central concern in religious education.

Robert Coburn, drawing on Stephen Toulmin, has spoken of "religious limiting questions" as the sort for which religion uniquely provides an answer (or, better, a "response"). These are not literal or theoretical questions, but "Why" or "What" questions that express "some 'inner' passion or action", such as grief or despair, or worshiping, marveling or blaspheming. They include questions of this nature: "Why did he die?"; "Why does anything exist?"; "What is the ultimate significance of life?"; "Why is life often so hard and cruel?".[122] Such "questions from the emotions" are different from theoretical, metaphysical questions because of their affective nature. They—and therefore their answers in terms of "God"—involve our deepest concerns and emotions, and direct our behavior. Religious claims, as responses to these limiting questions, express and evoke attitudes. Hence to know God is

---

118. Francis Dunlop, "Feeling as Guide to Reality", in Rex Gibson, ed., *The Education of Feeling* (Cambridge: Cambridge Institute of Education, 1983), p. 7.

119. Solomon, *The Passions*, p. xvi.

120. John Macmurray, *Reason and Emotion* (London: Faber & Faber, 1962), p. 75, compare p. 49.

121. Smart, *The Science of Religion and the Sociology of Knowledge*, p. 15.

122. Robert C. Coburn, "A Neglected Use of Theological Language", *Mind* 72 (1963), pp. 371-375, 384-385.

to love him, fear him or hate him; to believe in God is to respond to him in worship, praise, thankfulness and contrition. Kai Nielsen comments: "to recognise that religious statements are answers to limiting questions is to recognise why it is they could—logically could—not fail to be inextricably linked with the passions."[123] Other commentators have similarly stressed the extent to which religion is an expression of, or grounded in, the emotions. They are often criticized for being anti-intellectual or "irrational". Such criticism is misplaced. It would be better to acknowledge that religion is often, in its origins, "nonrational" or *arational* (see Glossary, p. 294). Even if and when it is an expression of—and constructed from and by—reason (see Chapter 7), that reason must in the end be seen in some sense as "emotional reason"[124] (see Chapter 9). In the light of all these arguments, I conclude that formative Christian religious education can only be effective when it is affective.

THE ROLE OF BELIEFS

Christian Beliefs-that, Understanding and Knowledge

This category of Christian learning outcomes is regarded as of signal importance by most philosophical commentators on religion and religious education. Unlike many psychologists of religion, philosophers take care to distinguish beliefs-that from beliefs-in.[125] The category of beliefs-that covers

---

123. Kai Nielsen, *An Introduction to the Philosophy of Religion* (London: Macmillan, 1982; New York: St. Martin's Press, 1983), p. 75.

124. Macmurray, *Reason and Emotion*, p. 63.

125. Psychologists often define belief affectively, as "an emotional acceptance of a proposition or doctrine". English and English, *A Comprehensive Dictionary of Psychological and Psychoanalytical Terms*, p. 64. Milton Rokeach treats a belief as composed of three principal processes: cognition, affect and motivation to action. Rokeach, *The Nature of Human Values*, p. 7. Lee understands it as a psychological construct, which he treats in his chapter on affective content because of its largely attitudinal (and hence affective) base. He writes that "belief is a kind of attitude which contains a great deal of cognitive structuring" (Lee, *Content*, p. 219). (An opinion is described as a more cognitive and less affective sort of belief.) Many of these authors seem to conflate two categories that are separated in my classificatory scheme: beliefs-about and beliefs-in. For most philosophers *belief-in* is, or includes, a valuational attitude and, very often, an attitude of trust (an "emotional acceptance"?). They regard *belief-that* ("mere belief", beliefs "about") as more firmly in the cognitive domain, being in principle a component of—or a second-best to—knowledge. The failure to distinguish beliefs-in and beliefs-that might cast doubt on many survey results, as "Do you believe in God?" is not logically the same question as "Do you believe that God exists?" (although most respondents may not make the distinction, and the phrases can be interpreted differently - see Chapter 8, note 3 below). Support for the account given here of the nature of beliefs-that is also to be found in the work of some psychologists of religion. See Brown, *The Psychology of Religious Belief*, pp. 29, 165, 183 and H. Newton Malony, in Brown, ed., *Advances in the Psychology of Religion*, pp. 119-120. In my more detailed comments on belief in the present chapter and in Chapter 8 the attitudinal/affective element is given a proper place. In Chapter 7 the affective component of religious understanding itself is also stressed. But these accounts serve only to offer qualifications of an overly cognitive account of belief-that and understanding. They should not blind us to the very real distinction that remains between religious belief-that and religious belief-in.

beliefs about such objects of belief as the world, human beings, the church, the last things, Christian ethical norms, and the nature and activity of God and Christ. Philosophers regard these beliefs as including both continuing dispositions and states, and the occurrent "mental acts" of a person who entertains a belief and assents to it. This assent combines an all-or-nothing element ("I believe this, not that") with a degree element ("I believe this strongly/weakly"; "I am more/less sure of this").[126]

I shall argue in Chapter 7 that *"Christian understanding"*, in the sense of an understanding (process and product) of Christian concepts, is a matter of degree. It forms a necessary part of Christian belief-that, in that someone must have some minimal understanding of any proposition before it can be said that he or she believes that proposition. A Christian belief-that about God, however, is more than an understanding of the Christian concept of God, precisely in that it includes assent to (adoption of) that belief. In teaching *about* religion, of course, the primary aim is the development of understanding. In such a context the element of assent is not an objective of the teaching. It should also be noted that Christian religious education, in addition to having religious assent among its outcomes, is often directed to the growth of this understanding beyond the minimum required for assent.

"Belief-that" as intellectual assent is usually taken to be weaker than *knowledge*. It has been called "mere belief".[127] The contemporary philosopher's standard analysis of knowledge describes it as well-grounded, true belief. In other words, "I know that x is true" (or "I know that x") is equivalent to: (a) I believe (or I am sure) that x; (b) I have good grounds (evidence) for x; and (c) x is true.[128] This analysis implies that we can never know, although we may think that we know, anything that is not actually true. Thus ancient peoples did not "know" that the earth was flat, they only believed it. Similarly no one of them could have "known" that the earth went around the sun, even though it does, because they did not have good evidence for that belief.

One difficulty with the analysis is as follows.[129] As we can only know

---

126. See below Chapter 8, and Glossary (for dispositions, occurrences).

127. See Richard Swinburne, *Faith and Reason* (Oxford: Oxford University Press, 1981), pp. 106-107, 122. We only "believe", but do not "know", that the doorbell is being rung by our friend. When we open the door and see him standing there our belief is upgraded to the status of knowledge (or, better, of a claim to knowledge). This analysis fits such language as "I do not know. . . ., but I believe that. . . .". Admittedly there is a different usage, which seems to make belief firmer than knowledge. This is exemplified by such claims as "I don't just know (that he is the best candidate, or that God is in charge of the world), I *believe* it". But this is best interpreted as a *belief-in* which is "more than" the knowledge claim only in its possession of additional attitudinal components.

128. Compare, for example, A. J. Ayer, *The Problem of Knowledge* (Harmondsworth, England: Penguin, 1956; New York: St. Martin's Press, 1965), p. 35. Ayer and others take the three clauses to be individually necessary and jointly sufficient. See also D. M. Armstrong, *Belief, Truth and Knowledge* (Cambridge: Cambridge University Press, 1973), ch. 10.

129. There are other, rather technical, criticisms. For a criticism mainly directed at the claim that the three criteria of knowledge are together sufficient to give us knowledge, see

that x if x is true, then we can only *know that we know that* x when we know that x is true. But we can never know something is true without knowing it! In other words condition (c) of the analysis is in a sense redundant, for we can never apply it. This means that there is not really a great deal of difference between this sort of belief (belief-that) and knowledge. *Knowledge claims* are all we have. We can never be certain that we have true knowledge, and a knowledge claim is simply a belief for which (we claim that) there is good evidence. To say "I know x" is to register my commitment to the highest possible cognitive claim and to commend it to others as something to rely on.[130] Hence "I know that God exists" is just another way of saying "I believe that God exists, and I believe that I have—or that there are—good grounds for that belief". On this interpretation, no amount of pounding the table by religious educators or evangelists will make it mean more than that.

It should be clear, however, that there is a further problem with the analysis of knowledge given above. It cannot apply to cases of immediate or direct knowledge through sense experience or introspection. Rather, the analysis is of *inferential knowledge-that*: knowledge that is based on reasons and argument. Those who accept that God's existence, and some aspects of his nature, can be proved through inferential argument might be happy to understand the phrase "knowledge of God" along these lines.[131] For many others, however, God can only be known noninferentially, through "acquaintance" with God in religious experience or via some other species of direct awareness.[132] We have seen that such *knowledge by acquaintance* of God is often said to be "immediate" (nonmediated) in the sense that it is not based on inferential reasoning. But it is also said that this knowledge is "mediated" in the sense that the awareness "comes through" a medium—an empirical situation in nature, history etc. through which God is disclosed.[133] Such "objective" religious experiences have been discussed above. Many religious edu-

Edmund L. Gettier, "Is Justified True Belief Knowledge?", in A. Phillips Griffiths, ed., *Knowledge and Belief* (London: Oxford University Press, 1967). For amended analyses see Roderick M. Chisholm, *Theory of Knowledge* (Englewood Cliffs, N.J.: Prentice-Hall, 1966), p. 23 n. 22; Robert J. Ackermann, *Belief and Knowledge* (Garden City, N.Y.: Doubleday, 1972), ch. 5; Jonathan Dancy, *An Introduction to Contemporary Epistemology* (Oxford: Blackwell, 1985), ch. 2. For the criticism that the "evidence condition" (b) leads to an infinite regress—knowing that x involving knowing some other proposition as evidence for x—see Armstrong, *Belief, Truth and Knowledge*, ch. 11.

130. J. L. Austin, "Other Minds", *Proceedings of the Aristotelian Society* Supp. Vol. XX (1946).

131. See below Chapter 7.

132. For an analysis of the various senses in which the phrase "knowing God" is used, see Brian Haymes, *The Concept of the Knowledge of God* (London: Macmillan; New York: St. Martin's Press, 1988).

133. For accounts of such mediated religious intuition see Ian T. Ramsey, *Religious Language* (London: SCM, 1957; New York: Macmillan, 1963), ch. I; John E. Smith, *Experience and God* (New York: Oxford University Press, 1968), ch. III; H. P. Owen, *The Christian Knowledge of God* (London: Athlone, 1969), ch. 6; A. C. Ewing, *Value and Reality: The Philosophical Case for Theism* (London: Allen & Unwin; New York: Humanities Press, 1973), ch. 6.

cators—like many theologians—regard them as the prime means by which people come to know God.

Some philosophers argue, however, that noninferential awareness of God, or of any other entity, is not itself a form of knowledge, but merely a causal condition for knowledge. It is not knowledge because it is essentially contentless, nonpropositional and nonjudgmental.[134] Intuitive discernments or experiences of God would then have to be spelled out in terms of propositional truths ("beliefs-that") in order for us to speak of "religious knowledge". The same point may be made of the accounts of nonpropositional revelation that are often espoused by religious believers. They argue that it is God himself who is revealed in revelation, rather than a set of propositions about God. God is thus known as an encountered reality. It is (fallible) human beings who later describe this God in propositional language, or in other language (e.g. imperatives) that implies propositions.[135] Such a position is common in certain types of Christian religious education. But whatever form this primordial revelation may take, in order for there to be knowledge (or belief) about it the revelatory experience needs to be transcribed into truths. Only then can it count as a revelatory experience of God. For: "even if one holds that it is God who is revealed, and not propositions about God, this cannot be rendered intelligible in a form which does not entail that the person to whom God is revealed is thereby made aware of some critical truths about God."[136] We should therefore resist loose talk about nonpropositional religious knowing from religious educators who emphasize religious experience and revelation.

Christian religious educators who take account of these philosophical points might bring more clarity to their discussions of the cognitive element of religious education.

Christian Beliefs-in

To believe *in* God, Jesus or the church (or baptism, marriage, Christian morality etc.) is more than to believe that they exist and have a certain nature. Belief in God, in the sense of the phrase used here, embraces *both* beliefs-that *and* certain attitudes, in particular trust in God and other pro-attitudes towards

---

134. See H. L. A. Hart, "Is There Knowledge by Acquaintance?", *Proceedings of the Aristotelian Society* Supp. Vol. XXIII (1949); Albert Hofstadter, "Does Intuitive Knowledge Exist?", *Philosophical Studies* VI (1955), pp. 81-82; D. W. Hamlyn, *The Theory of Knowledge* (London: Macmillan, 1970), p. 106.

135. For a general survey see John Baillie, *The Idea of Revelation in Recent Thought* (New York: Columbia University Press, 1964); Avery Dulles, *Revelation Theology: A History* (New York: Herder and Herder, 1969; London: Burns & Oates, 1970), ch. 6 and *Models of Revelation* (Garden City, N.Y.: Doubleday; Dublin: Gill & Macmillan, 1983), Part One; John Hick, *Faith and Knowledge* (Glasgow: Collins, 1974; Ithaca, N.Y.: Cornell University Press, 1957, 1966), pp. 27-31. Hick's *Philosophy of Religion* (Englewood Cliffs, N.J.: Prentice-Hall, third edition, 1983), pp. 68-75 provides the clearest presentation of this position.

136. Terence Penelhum, *Problems of Religious Knowledge* (London: Macmillan, 1971; New York: Herder and Herder, 1972), p. 92. See also Jeff Astley, "Revelation Revisited", *Theology* 83: 695 (1980) and Paul Helm, *Divine Revelation: The Basic Issues* (London: Marshall, Morgan & Scott, 1982), ch. 2.

God that are expressed in praise and worship of God as good, holy, "Lord" etc.[137] Because of the affective element that is a component of, or a natural consequence of, valuations and attitudes we must recognize that *religious "believing", in the sense of possessing religious beliefs-in*, is essentially affective.[138]

The human phenomenon of *faith* has been variously interpreted by theologians and religious educators. Among the latter group, those who adopt predominantly cognitive approaches understand faith as a way of interpreting reality and "faith-knowing".[139] Others give a more central place to an affective dimension in faith as a "favorable . . attitude toward God", shown particularly in trust.[140] Yet others write of faith as having three "essential and constitutive dimensions": a belief conviction, a trusting relationship, and a lived life of agapé.[141] I treat faith as involving both beliefs-that and, even more fundamentally, affective pro-attitudes such as trust (which are often expressed in actions)—i.e. as a belief-in. I would therefore argue that religious educators who seek to promote it are engaged in affective education as well as promoting assent to religious knowledge claims.

---

137. Price, *Belief*, Series II, Lecture 9. See below Chapter 8. To cover the case of "protest atheism" (rebellion against God by one who believes that God exists), some have claimed that belief-in requires some affective response but that this can be hate or rebellion rather than love. See D. Z. Phillips, *Faith and Philosophical Inquiry* (London: Routledge & Kegan Paul, 1970), pp. 29-33. I disagree (see Chapter 8 note 3).

138. It is often pointed out that the original usage of the verb "believe", like that of the noun "faith", was associated with trust and fidelity. "It signified to love, . . . to give allegiance, to be loyal to; to value highly", i.e. to set one's heart. Wilfred Cantwell Smith, *Belief and History* (Charlottesville, Va.: University Press of Virginia, 1977), pp. 41-45. However "belief" is *now* usually understood as a propositional and cognitive enterprise connoting intellectual assent— i.e. as "belief-that". See also Wilfred Cantwell Smith, *Faith and Belief* (Princeton, N.J.: Princeton University Press, 1979), ch. 6.

139. James Fowler has described faith as faith-knowing, but he argues for a "logic of conviction" that is broader and more holistic than the narrower, specialized "logic of rational certainty". See Fowler's essays in Craig Dykstra and Sharon Parks, eds., *Faith Development and Fowler* (Birmingham, Ala.: Religious Education Press, 1986), pp. 23, 33, 286-287 and his *Stages of Faith*, p. 103. For criticisms of Fowler's position on this, see the essays by David Heywood and Romney M. Moseley in Jeff Astley and Leslie J. Francis, eds., *Christian Perspectives on Faith Development* (Grand Rapids, Mich.: Eerdmans, 1992), chs. 4.1 and 4.2. Fowler certainly attempts to make room for an element of affect in his concepts of faith and meaning-making. See Jeff Astley *et al., How Faith Grows: Faith Development and Christian Education* (London: National Society, 1991), pp. 3-4, 48-49, 81 n. 12.

140. Lee, *The Content of Religious Instruction*, p. 57. Lee is here writing of those religious educators for whom faith involves an affective dimension. Among those who treat faith primarily as affective he lists Morton Kelsey—see his *Can Christians Be Educated? A Proposal for Effective Communication of our Christian Religion* (Birmingham, Ala.: Religious Education Press, 1977), chs. 5, 6, and 7. Lee himself prefers to view faith more actively as "primarily lifestyle", being "lived through holistic lifestyle activity". See his essay in Lee, ed., *Handbook of Faith*, pp. 294-302. For Lee faith is essentially a construct describing a lifestyle that blends specific cognitive, affective and overt behavior areas.

141. Thomas H. Groome, *Christian Religious Education* (San Francisco: Harper & Row, 1980), pp. 57-66, 73-77. However, Lee argues that Groome "regards the essence of faith as cognitive". Lee, *Content*, p. 73.

From Beliefs-in to Beliefs-that

Many religious valuations and attitudes seem to imply factual beliefs (beliefs-that) about the existence and nature of God. This, it is often said, is part and parcel of the logic of attitudes and valuations. Thus Vincent Brümmer argues that we can *describe someone else's* thanksgiving to and trust in God, by using the word "God", without ourselves believing that such a God exists; but we cannot *express our own trust* in God and our own thanksgiving to God, "without presupposing that this God exists in fact".[142] Such beliefs may be said, in David Pailin's words, to "express the components of faith which make claims about what is the case".[143]

Donald Evans opines that trust is a stance directed towards some reality, usually a person. He recognizes that this does not mean that the focus of this trust must actually exist, since the one who trusts may be mistaken. But the trusting person "must believe that the reality exists". This is a logical implicate of the word "trust" being correctly used. If this is not the case, Evans writes, then the person has "a mood rather than a stance" which "should perhaps be described as 'serenity' or 'calmness'".[144]

Evans argues that an attitude like basic trust is externally pervasive and uni-fying and therefore has a *cosmic* focus, i.e. God. As we have seen, he further claims that as basic trust is an attitude that is necessary for human fulfillment, and therefore ought to be cultivated and adopted, the theistic belief that it implies is rational. But he adds the disturbing caveat that the argument "leaves wide open the possibility that the true cosmic beliefs are those which are implied by attitudes which are in conflict with human fulfillment. Maybe we have to believe what is false in order to be fulfilled. Maybe reality is not in tune with human fulfillment."[145]

Beliefless Religion?

In any case, it should be recognized that not all religious attitudes and valu-ations carry similar belief implications. The attitude of universal, unqualified love (*agapé*), for example, does not imply any explicitly religious belief-that about God. (Indeed the suggestion has been voiced that *disinterested* love is actually psychologically less likely when supported by religious

---

142. Brümmer, *Theology and Philosophical Inquiry*, p. 268; see also Terrence W. Tilley, *Talking of God* (New York: Paulist, 1978), p. 109.

143. David A. Pailin, *Groundwork of Philosophy of Religion* (London; Epworth, 1986), p. 34; see also Roger Trigg, "Reason and Faith—II", in Martin Warner, ed., *Religion and Philosophy* (Cambridge: Cambridge University Press, 1992).

144. Evans, *Struggle and Fulfillment*, p. 174. See also p. 212 n.28. Of course the psycho-logical attitude may develop (in infancy) well before we can give conscious consent to its logical implicate. On "moods" see above note 69.

145. *Ibid.* p. 179. An attitude or emotion may be real enough, although its object is illu-sory (does not in fact exist): see Lyons, *Emotion*, pp. 109-112. Nietzsche similarly argued that a belief may be a condition of life and nevertheless be false. Friedrich Nietzsche, *The Will to Power*, trans. Walter Kaufmann and R. J. Hollingdale (New York: Vintage Books, 1968), para. 483.

beliefs-that.[146] "My God I love thee not because I hope for heaven thereby" is a hymn that is more than a little difficult for the believer to sing seriously.) A list of other religious attitudes that do not imply beliefs about God might include our willingness to forgive, although (like love) this may be *psychologically generated* by our belief in God's forgiveness of us. Other interpersonal attitudes may come into the same category, together with certain attitudes of wonder or contemplation directed to the natural world. Therefore not all religious attitudes and valuations imply beliefs about *God*.

An atheist might be willing to grasp Evans's nettle and to argue that in the case of attitudes like trust the attitude must be developed for the sake of human fulfillment, but its apparent belief-implicates denied. The atheist might argue that trust is good—both for individuals and for society—but theism is false. On Evans's view this would seem to imply that trust is a good but irrational attitude, a position that might also be adopted for other attitude-virtues. The values held by such an atheist might have a paradoxical quality; but he could argue that they are the best to be had, despite the fact that they seem to imply implausible beliefs. Could this atheist consistently fulfill many of the aspects of the role of a Christian religious educator in the terms in which we have defined that role?

Let us widen the question. Can we have religious attitudes and values without religious beliefs (beliefs-that)? Can we think of God as good, certain actions as right, or certain situations as evil, without also believing that these realities (God, actions, situations) exist? Clearly we can, but only in a conceptual sense. We may describe the *idea* of God as good, and a *hypothetical* action or situation as right/wrong or good/evil. In the case of radical religious noncognitivists, for whom religious language implies no factual knowledge claims, God just is the concept of God: there is no reality that instantiates the concept. For them the worship of God involves—or, better, "is"—the ascription of supreme worth to the notion of unconditional love. The *valuation* in such a case is in fact the same valuation as that of the "theological realist" who believes that there is a reality "God", such that "God is unconditionally loving" is true. To say that God is good is fundamentally to say that God is admirable, worthy of praise, to be sought and emulated. Indeed to say that God is good may be thought of as tautologous, if "God" is a description rather than a proper name and *means* (linguistically) "our object of worship" or "what we aim for".[147] The theological realist and the theological noncognitivist have much the same *moral* concept of God. For one it is an ideal—admirable, but nowhere completely realized. For the other it is both

---

146. Don Cupitt, *Taking Leave of God* (London: SCM, 1980; New York: Crossroad, 1981), pp. 9-10, 96, 126 and *Only Human* (London: SCM, 1985), p. 200.

147. Don Cupitt, *The Sea of Faith* (London: BBC, 1984), p. 246. The view that the word "God" is a description rather than a proper name is persuasively argued in Peter Geach, *God and the Soul* (London: Routledge & Kegan Paul, 1969), chs. 4 and 8; but contrast Michael Durrant, *The Logical Status of God* (London: Macmillan; New York: St. Martin's Press, 1973), preface and ch. 1 and Durrant, *Theology and Intelligibility* (London: Routledge & Kegan Paul, 1973), pp. 75-86.

an ideal and a reality. *But the valuation is the same in each case.*

We may take as analogies the cases of a full-scale global nuclear war, the ending of all human disease, or the achievement of immortality on earth. People can and do argue about whether these events would be good or bad (in given circumstances). But the events are hypothetical; they do not exist. Yet we can still be "for" or "against" them in our attitudes and valuations. My attitude to the concept of a global nuclear war should not be different from my attitude to a real nuclear war, just because it does not exist. Existence does not add anything to a concept. To claim that x exists is merely to claim that the concept of x is instantiated (has an instance).[148]

It is thus possible to have some religious valuations without having the "concomitant" religious beliefs. When considering attitudes and values, and the educational processes that lead to them, the concept of beliefless religion (and therefore of beliefless religious education) is not absurd. It is certainly not orthodox, for in Christian orthodoxy "believing in God is not like believing in a principle" but more like trusting a person.[149] But that is a different issue.

Of course it is also possible in religion to have beliefs without valuations; but whether we should call them *religious* beliefs is a moot point, as we have seen. Some people believe that God exists while not showing the religious attitudes towards God of worship, thankfulness, trust or love, and some even without evaluating God as good—without being "for" God. It is arguable that a person with some of the right religious attitudes and valuations, who nevertheless did not believe that God exists, might properly be regarded as "more religious" than a "believer" who thought God evil and possessed none of the normal religious attitudes towards God. In which case, the answer to the question "What sort of God do you *believe in?*" may be more important than the answer to the question, "Do you *believe that* such a God exists?"[150]

It seems strange to assert that there may not be any great discernible difference between the activities of some atheistic and some "believing" Christian religious educators (at least in some areas). It sounds even stranger to claim that one might on occasions prefer the atheist! But this is the conclusion to which this argument about belief and valuation leads.

---

148. See Kant's critique of the ontological argument and his denial that existence is a logical predicate—Immanuel Kant, *Critique of Pure Reason*, trans. Norman Kemp Smith (London: Macmillan, 1933), pp. 500-501. See also Bertrand Russell's analysis of the logic of "exists" in his *Logic and Knowledge* (London: Allen & Unwin; New York: Macmillan, 1956), pp. 232-234.

149. J. Kellenberger, *The Cognitivity of Religion: Three Perspectives* (Berkeley: University of California Press; Basingstoke: Macmillan, 1985), p. 35; see also Kai Nielsen, *Scepticism* (London: Macmillan; New York: St. Martin's Press, 1973), ch. 2.

150. Don Cupitt, *Creation out of Nothing* (London: SCM; Philadelphia: Trinity Press, 1990), p. 117.

CHAPTER 7

Reason, Understanding and Religion

REASON IN RELIGION

Formative Factors in Belief

John Macquarrie's checklist of "formative factors in Christian theology",[1] which we may construe more widely as factors giving rise to and modifying Christian beliefs, reads as follows (in a summarized form):

(1) *Experience*: "of the life of faith", including both specifically religious experience and the "religious dimensions" of everyday experience.

(2) *Revelation*: which takes place through nature, history, persons and Jesus Christ. Communities of faith trace their origins back to a primordial/classic revelation, but often acknowledge continuing supplementary revelations.

(3) *Scripture*: which Macquarrie describes as "a kind of memory". It is "not itself revelation, but it is one important way ... by which the community of faith keeps open its access to that primordial revelation on which the community of faith has been founded".

(4) *Tradition*: that which the church "hands on" (rituals, ways of reading scripture, theological pronouncements of Councils etc.). Like scripture it is a bulwark against individualism. According to Macquarrie it is "no rival to scripture but ... its necessary complement". It has often been treated as a complementary source of revelation.

(5) *Culture*: "if theology is to be intelligible, it has to use the language of the culture within which it is undertaken".

(6) *Reason*: according to Macquarrie, theology may or may not acknowledge the power of "speculative reason" (e.g. the arguments for the existence of God, which give rise to a "rational religion" based on reason); but theology always needs "architectonic" (constructive, systematizing), elucidatory, and corrective reason so as to develop and defend a "reasonable religion". He

---

1. J. Macquarrie, *Principles of Christian Theology* (New York: Scribner's; London: SCM, 1966), pp. 4-17. (It should perhaps be noted that neither Macquarrie's list, nor my widening of its application, is based on controlled empirical research.)

157

includes these last two species in the general category of "critical reason".[2]

I am primarily concerned at the moment with "formative factors" in the sense of factors that may serve as the sources for religious belief (fundamentally belief-that), and in particular with the claim that reason is, or can be, or should be a source of religion. Although philosophers should never ignore the findings of social scientists, it is true to say that psychologists of religion (and historians) are on the whole more concerned with sources of and reasons for religious belief in the sense of *motives for* or *causes of* belief, whereas philosophers are more interested in reasons and sources as *grounds for the justification of* belief. The philosopher of religion is particularly concerned with those arguments, experiences and disclosures that lend support to, and can thus justify, beliefs about God, whatever the original psychological or autobiographical origins of those beliefs might be.

There are three main ways by which people have claimed to know that God exists: by proving it by inference from other facts—i.e. by arguments for the existence of God (this is Macquarrie's "speculative reason"); by knowing it noninferentially through some experience of God—i.e. by religious experience; and by having it disclosed by God himself—i.e. by revelation. (We shall see that the second and third ways are very closely related.)

Decisions about the substantive content of Christian religious education are frequently profoundly affected by the religious educator's views about such claims within the epistemology of religion ("theory of religious knowledge"). As theological debate has frequently revolved around such epistemological issues it is necessary to explore briefly here some influential theological positions on the place of reason in the Christian religion.

"Natural Religion"

Those who defend the role of speculative reason as a basis for religious belief speak of being able to know that God exists, and certain things about God, by the use of their "unaided reason": that is by using their normal mental gifts without any additional supernatural aid from God. They are thus following the path that results in what is often described as *natural theology* or *natural religion*, defined as knowledge of God through human reason alone. This is to be contrasted in particular with the supernatural knowledge

---

2. Thomas Aquinas distinguished three different functions of philosophy—the foundations of which are "the principles of reason"—in religion. They are the demonstrative (speculative), the analogical (elucidatory) and the defensive-apologetic. He writes, "Christian theology may call on philosophy to perform three offices. First, to demonstrate the groundwork of faith, for the truths of natural religion—for instance, that God exists, that there is one God, and so forth—can be proved by philosophy and are pre-supposed to religious belief and are necessary elements in the science of faith, or Christian theology. Second, to declare analogies common to nature and grace . . . Third, to resist attacks on faith, by showing that they are either wrongly conceived or at least unsupported and cannot be pressed." Thomas Aquinas, Exposition, *de Trinitate*, ii, 3, trans. Thomas Gilby, *St. Thomas Aquinas: Theological Texts* (London: Oxford University Press, 1955), pp. 7-8. See also M. J. Charlesworth, *Philosophy of Religion: The Historic Approaches* (London: Macmillan; New York: Herder and Herder, 1972), pp. 62, 72-78.

of God claimed by those who appeal to revelation (*revealed theology/religion*). The implication of the former position is that Christian religious education might have among its objectives, at least for some learners, the development of their cognitive skills and knowledge in order that they may understand, and be convinced by, the arguments for God's existence and nature.

Many argue that God may be known both through natural theology *and* revealed theology. They often allow that there is an overlap between the two types of theology: some truths (e.g. that God exists) being both revealed by God and discoverable by human reason, whereas other truths can only be known by revelation (e.g. the doctrines of the Trinity and of the person of Christ). This view was held by Thomas Aquinas, and a similar position was espoused by the seventeenth-century English philosopher John Locke (although he thought that the doctrine of the Trinity was to be rejected as "contrary to reason"). The overlapping of revelation and reason may be illustrated by the diagram below.[3] Such a position might suggest a "belt-and-braces" approach to Christian religious education, in which both the truths of revelation and the skills of natural theology are taught to the learners.

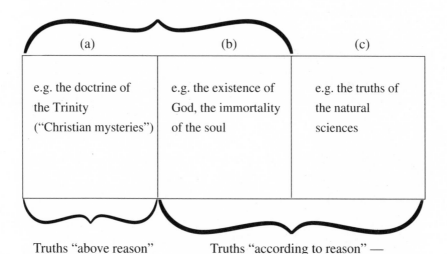

Truths
revealed by God

	(a)	(b)	(c)
	e.g. the doctrine of the Trinity ("Christian mysteries")	e.g. the existence of God, the immortality of the soul	e.g. the truths of the natural sciences

Truths "above reason"   Truths "according to reason" —
i.e. truths that are naturally
knowable (provable by human reason)

In this analysis, category (B) represents "natural theology". The overlap of the brackets indicates that its truths are not only provable by human rea-

3. Amended from Knut Tranøy, "Thomas Aquinas", in D. J. O'Connor, ed., *A Critical History of Western Philosophy* (New York: Free Press, 1964), p. 103.

son but are also revealed by God for the benefit of nonphilosophers.[4] According to Locke, however, reason itself determines what is to be regarded as a revelation; in Locke's view by applying the tests of whether or not it fulfills prophecy or is accompanied by miracles. Locke insists:

> If they say they know it to be true, because it is a revelation from God, the reason is good; but then it will be demanded how they know it to be a revelation from God. . . . .
> If [God] would have us assent to the truth of any proposition, he either evidences that truth by the usual methods of natural reason, or else makes it known to be a truth which he would have us assent to by his authority, and convinces us that it is from him, by some marks which reason cannot be mistaken in. *Reason must be our last judge and guide in everything.*[5]

Revelation, then, must itself be reasonable, not least in conforming to reason's independent criteria of truth and reliability. On this view one might argue that Christian religious education has a further responsibility for developing critical reasoning powers in (at least some?) Christian learners to complement the formative education through which they learn the putative Christian revelation. For unless they—or at least some of them—have the critical skills to assess revelation, how will they be able to accept the true revelation as true and reject false claimants as false? Such a view would find a ready hearing among the more cognitively-inclined religious educators.

There are many today who still regard natural theology as possible, either accepting the validity of the theistic arguments (arguments for the existence of God) treated deductively,[6] or affirming that these inferences give a positive probability to the existence of God if we treat them inductively.[7] A substantial body of philosophers of religion, however, now reject these argu-

---

4. For Mediaeval and even Enlightenment thinkers this group included children, idiots—and women! As Aquinas put it, without revelation "the rational truth about God would have appeared only to few, and even so after a long time and mixed with many mistakes". Thomas Aquinas, *Summa Theologiae*, Ia, I, q. I, art. 1, trans. Thomas Gilby (London: Eyre & Spottiswoode, 1963), p. 7. Such a claim has religious education implications, for on this view the passing on of revelation would seem to be more important for some learners than for others.

5. John Locke, *An Essay Concerning Human Understanding* (1690), Book Four, ch. XIX, ed. A. D. Woozley (London: Collins, 1964), p. 432.

6. Many Thomists fall into this category. For a classic account see Étienne Gilson, *The Philosophy of St. Thomas Aquinas*, trans. Edward Bullough (Cambridge: Heffer, 1924), chs. IV and V. Others accept the validity of the *a priori* ontological argument, the most clearly deductive of the theistic arguments. See Alvin Plantinga, *God, Freedom and Evil* (London: Allen & Unwin, 1975), Part II, sect. c; and the articles by Charles Hartshore and Norman Malcolm reprinted in John Hick and Arthur C. McGill, eds., *The Many-Faced Argument* (New York: Macmillan, 1967; London: Macmillan, 1968).

7. Preeminently Richard Swinburne, *The Existence of God* (Oxford: Clarendon, 1979). See also John J. Shepherd, *Experience, Inference and God* (London: Macmillan; New York: Barnes & Noble, 1975).

ments;[8] although some still allow for a sort of a "natural theology" of religious experience, arguing for a knowledge of God that is based on religious experience or intuition, rather than human reasoning. (See Chapter 6 above.)

The eighteenth-century English Deists, whose influence was felt in both France and North America, in effect amended the reason/revelation diagram because of their distrust of all appeals to revelation. In the "Age of Reason" anything that did not have its source in universal, analytic, experimental reason was suspect. These extremists of the Enlightenment rejected not only particular revelations, but also the authoritarian legislations of sovereigns and churches. Revelation (the "Book of Scripture") was for the Deists valid only in so far as it was a "republication" of the truths of natural theology (the "Book of Nature"). The category (A) truths of our diagram were rejected as superstitions. As the English Deist Matthew Tindal put it, in his *Christianity as Old as the Creation, or The Gospel a Republication of the Religion of Nature* (1730), "*Natural* Religion . . . differs not from *Reveal'd*, but in the manner of its being communicated". He argued that God must deal with human beings as rational creatures "by proposing Arguments to convince their Understandings, and influence their Wills, in the same manner as if propos'd by other Agents", so as to honor human rational accountability. Hence revelation itself must not be "arbitrary", but rather "founded on the Reason of Things". Revelation, consequently, is but "a Republication, or Restoration" of the religion of nature.[9] Because of their rejection of revelation, the Deists retained only a very watered down form of religion: thin on theology, distrustful of ritual and pietism, and reduced very largely to morality. They represented an extreme form of modernism in which all the stress is laid on reason. Despite piercing criticism,[10] Deism

---

8. See, for example, Antony Flew, *God and Philosophy* (London: Hutchinson, 1966), chs. 3-5; Anthony Kenny, *The Five Ways* (New York: Schocken; London: Routledge & Kegan Paul, 1969); John Hick, *Arguments for the Existence of God* (London: Macmillan, 1970; New York: Herder and Herder, 1971); J. L. Mackie, *The Miracle of Theism* (Oxford: Clarendon, 1982).

9. Matthew Tindal, in John Martin Creed and John Sandwith Boys Smith, eds., *Religious Thought in the Eighteenth Century* (Cambridge: Cambridge University Press, 1934), pp. 32-34. For an excellent summary study of Locke and the Deists see James C. Livingston, *Modern Christian Thought* (New York: Macmillan, 1971), ch. two. On "Enlightenment religion" more generally see Ernst Cassirer, *The Philosophy of the Enlightenment*, trans. Fritz C. A. Koelln and James P. Pettigrove (Princeton, N.J.: Princeton University Press, 1951), ch. IV and Peter Gay, *The Enlightenment: An Interpretation. Vol. 1: The Rise of Modern Paganism* (London: Wildwood, 1973), chs. 4-7.

10. Joseph Butler was historically important in challenging the position of the Deists on revelation. He pointed out that the Deist was quite happy to infer a divine author from the "Book of Nature", despite the "favoritism", inadequacy and suffering displayed in the natural order. Yet the Deist denied that scripture could have the same author *on account of* similar deficiencies in the latter text. Butler argued that Deists who accept that God's existence and nature can be proved from (ambiguous and partial) nature should also recognize that (ambiguous and partial) revelation is analogous, and therefore probably has the same author. "Now the weakness of these opinions may be shewn, by observing the suppositions on which they are founded, which are really such as these; . . . that it cannot be thought [God] would bestow a favour

has been profoundly influential in both American and English contexts.

Any Christian religious educator who follows along this road will tend naturally to engage primarily in critical Christian religious education and hardly at all in formative education, at least as far as Christian cognition is concerned. The Christian tradition really hardly needs to be passed on, according to this interpretation, for Christian belief (at least) can be recreated *de novo* by each generation, provided that its members are sufficiently skilled in intellectual argumentation. If reason can serve as a primary source of religious beliefs about God and the afterlife, then Christian religious education needs to teach *only* the skills of reasoning. The Christian learner can do the rest on her or his own. We may note that the subject-matter and method needed for this sort of religious education is almost identical with that required by a general training in rationality: it is a sort of "philosophical education". The distinctiveness of religion and religious education is therefore lost on this account of the matter.

Revelation Alone?
Other religious thinkers have entirely rejected the idea that truths about God can be discovered by human reason: redrawing our diagram without the overlap of category (B). The most influential of these is Karl Barth, whose position is grounded in the claim that reason is "fallen" and unable to find God without God's help. For Barth, the Word of God is purely a gracious gift; fallen human beings have no other capacity to know God. He argues that the unique revelation in Christ "comes to us as a datum with no point of connection with any other previous datum". According to Barth, the religious problem with natural theology is that it gives rise to human religion—the idea that we can know God by ourselves and save ourselves by our own efforts. This is the antithesis of God's way of revelation. (And for Barth natural theology is an "also" that always becomes an "only".) Barth writes: "When the Christian language speaks of revelation and God . . . it speaks of Jesus Christ. When the Christian language speaks of God it does so not on the basis of some speculation or other, but looking at this fact, this story, this person. It cannot place this fact in relationship to any system of principles and ideas which would illuminate its importance and significance; it cannot explain and establish it from any other source."[11]

upon any, unless he bestowed the same upon all: suppositions which we find contradicted, not by a few instances in God's natural government of the world, but by the general analogy of nature together." Joseph Butler, *The Analogy of Religion, Natural and Revealed, to the Constitution and Course of Nation* (1736), Part II, ch. VI, ed. W. E. Gladstone, *The Works of Joseph Butler* (Oxford: Clarendon, 1897), Volume I, p. 227. See Anders Jeffner, *Butler and Hume on Religion: A Comparative Analysis* (Stockholm: Diakonistyrelsens Bokförlag, 1966).

11. Karl Barth, "The Christian Understanding of Revelation", from *Against the Stream* (London: SCM, 1954), reprinted in John Bowden and James Richmond, eds., *A Reader in Contemporary Theology* (London: SCM, 1967), pp. 32-33. However, Barth allows for some sort of general revelation—sharply distinguished from natural theology—in the idea of lights and truths in creation: "in the gloom caused by the sin of man, there is still a measure of

Barth's religious epistemology thus relies entirely on revelation.

This sort of account of the status of revelation might be interpreted by conservatives as justifying placing most emphasis on the transmission of a primordial revelation. In reading some authors we get a strong sense of Christian religious education as the passing on of the tradition whole, or at least as the passing on of that element in the received tradition ("the old, old story", or the apostolic preaching of the Christ Event) that will evoke for the next generation a contemporary revelation of God's Word.[12] Those writers who have been particularly influenced by the kerygmatic theology of which Barth is the prime exponent are very likely to model the work of Christian religious education on the activity of preaching,[13] perhaps stressing the teacher's authenticity and dedication, or his/her witnessing and proclaiming skills as significant features. The dominant aspect of the preacher-model of Christian religious education is the preacher's role as proclaimer of the gospel to the learner. The Christian religious educator here is *keryx*: the herald of the heavenly Ruler. Johannes Hofinger writes of the Christian learner: "As God's heralds, we are to present Christian doctrine to him but not merely as something that he must 'study' and 'know'. We are to make him aware of God's personal invitation to him ... " The learner should realize that he or she is personally addressed and personally invited, not merely by the teacher, but by God.[14]

We may compare Karl Barth's definition of church proclamation: "Proclamation is human speech in and by which God Himself speaks like a king through the mouth of his herald, and which is meant to be heard and accepted as speech in and by which God Himself speaks ... "[15] This model of Christian teaching leads to a very high view of the responsibility and role of the Christian religious educator as a channel for the voice of God. However, it must be recognized (as Barth does) that it also carries with it the danger of ignoring the human contribution of the religious educator's own

brightness". Barth, *Church Dogmatics*, Vol. IV, Part 3, First Half, trans. G. W. Bromiley (Edinburgh: Clark, 1961), pp. 135-165 (quoting from p. 141).

12. See Johannes Hofinger, *The Art of Teaching Christian Doctrine* (Notre Dame, Ind.: University of Notre Dame Press, 1962); Josef Andreas Jungmann, *Handing on the Faith* (New York: Herder, 1962). Compare Harold William Burgess, *An Invitation to Religious Education* (Birmingham, Ala.: Religious Education Press, 1975), ch. II.

13. On the virtues and vocation of the true preacher see Søren Kierkegaard, *Training in Christianity*, trans. Walter Lowrie (Princeton, N.J.: Princeton University Press, 1967), p 229; Karl Barth, *The Word of God and the Word of Man*, trans. Douglas Horton (London: Hodder & Stoughton, n.d., original edition 1928; New York: Harper, 1957), ch. IV.

14. Hofinger, *The Art of Teaching Christian Doctrine*, pp. 19-20. See also *ibid.*, p. 197; Josef Andreas Jungmann, *The Good News Yesterday and Today*, trans. William A. Huesman (New York: Sadlier, 1962), *passim*; Alfred McBride, *Catechetics: A Theology of Proclamation* (Milwaukee: Bruce, 1966), p. 150; Mary C. Boys, *Biblical Interpretation in Religious Education* (Birmingham, Ala.: Religious Education Press, 1980), ch. 2.

15. Karl Barth, *Church Dogmatics*, Vol. I, Part 1, trans. G. W. Bromiley (Edinburgh: Clark, 1975), p. 52. Compare his *Church Dogmatics*, Vol I, Part 2, trans. G. T. Thomson and Harold Knight (Edinburgh: Clark, 1956), pp. 800-812.

voice.[16] But perhaps its most fundamental problem is the extent to which it implicitly bypasses the human contribution of the learner: her ability, through her own experience and reason, to make her own contribution to her own Christian learning.

This "transmission", "proclamation", "preaching" or "herald" model of Christian religious education has been extensively criticized, not only for restricting the freedom of the learner to experience and explore, but also for too narrowly confining religious teaching to the verbal, conceptual and cognitive. Certainly, Christian learning is not to be represented as a broadcast studio in which a cognitive message is transmitted by a teacher towards a passive recipient. A further danger of such a model, particularly when wedded to an interventionist-miraculous view of God's revelation, is that it will tend to underplay the significance of the learner's own behavior and the environmental variables of the learning situation, passing over this empirical knowledge and relying rather on a theological account of how God's word is ("must be") spoken and heard. The resulting pedagogy is patently inadequate as an appropriate account of the dynamics of Christian religious education.[17]

Other accounts of Christianity and of Christian religious education argue for a greater role and responsibility for the Christian learner himself in critiquing and remaking the tradition, or at the very least in responding to the old gospel in new and varied ways (see Chapter 5 above). Such accounts may still speak of "revelation", but insist that their theology of revelation "demands that the history which the teaching of revelation begins with is always the student's own history".[18] In so far as this is a recognition of the importance of the learner's own experience and her active participation in her own learning, it must be welcomed. But with these accounts we face the

---

16. Interestingly enough, Barth's "positivism of revelation" does not wed him to a defense of biblical fundamentalism, or any other propositional account of truth. Rather, for Barth, revelation comes directly from God in a hidden way that can be seen only by the eyes of faith, as God graciously communicates himself through the miracle of belief. God cannot be spoken of except in his hidden revelation in Jesus Christ, his Word. We cannot speak of God "without the veil", and therefore without the reservation of God's mysterious hiddenness, or apart from his miracle of grace. Even the Bible remains a "human document"—as fallible, uncertain and humanly relative as any other. It can only *become* God's Word in so far as God graciously allows us to hear God in it, in a divine-human encounter through the miracle of grace and the gift of faith. Barth, *Church Dogmatics*, Vol. I, Part 1, ch. I, sect. 5 and Vol. I, Part 2, ch. III, sect. 19. See also David H. Kelsey, *The Uses of Scripture in Recent Theology* (Philadelphia: Fortress; London: SCM, 1975), pp. 39-50.

17. See the critical account of such theories in James Michael Lee, *The Flow of Religious Instruction* (Birmingham, Ala: Religious Education Press, 1973), ch. 7; see also Boys, *Biblical Interpretation in Religious Education*, pp. 230-239.

18. Gabriel Moran, *God Still Speaks* (London: Burns & Oates, 1967) (= *Catechesis as Revelation*, New York: Herder and Herder, 1966), p. 54, compare p. 51. See also Moran, *Design for Religion* (New York: Herder and Herder, 1970; London: Search, 1971) and *Interplay* (Winona, Minn.: St. Mary's Press, 1981), ch. 4; Lewis Joseph Sherrill, *The Gift of Power* (New York: Macmillan, 1955), *passim*; Burgess, *An Invitation to Religious Education*, ch. IV; and *The Child in the Church* (London: British Council of Churches, 1976), p. 23.

opposite danger from that inherent in the Barthian approach: the ever-present temptation of equating revelation with "discovery as an ongoing human enterprise".[19] Defenders of the position argue, however, that this is counter-balanced by the value of their recognition of the significance of the human pole of revelation, and their acknowledgment of the importance of the learner's own religious experience and reflection.

Barth wrote in conscious opposition to Friederich Schleiermacher's "Copernican revolution in theology",[20] a move which gave rise to Liberal Protestantism but was influential across a much wider area. Schleiermacher's main theme was that religious experience (broadly conceived) was the primary datum of religion. Reacting against the treatment religion had suffered at the hands of Enlightenment thinkers, who viewed it either as a body of cosmological truths or as a piece of morality, Schleiermacher argued for a view of Christianity as a particular stream of religious consciousness in history. For him religion was piety ("feeling", "intuition", a "sense and taste for the infinite", a "feeling of absolute dependence", or "God-consciousness"). Doctrine was secondary and derivative: "Christian doctrines are accounts of the Christian religious affections set forth in speech".[21] For Schleiermacher God is directly known in religious experience. In contrast with Barth's "downward theological method", in which God is the subject of revelation rather than the object of religious experience, this is "theology from below up"—the subjective method of doing theology. Schleiermacher argues that dogmas and doctrines "that many consider the essence of religion" are all the result of "contemplation of feeling", of "reflection and comparison". "The conceptions that underlie these propositions are, like your conceptions from experience, nothing but general expressions for definite feelings. They are not necessary for religion itself, scarcely even for communicating religion, but reflection requires and creates them."[22]

But in the case of Barth and others, religious experience is rejected in that it is regarded as falling into the same category as reason when both are treated as sources of religious knowledge (natural theology). Both represent fallen humanity "writ large". Neither reason nor religious experience can deliver what they pretend to offer—a "natural" way from the human to the divine. Clearly Barth wishes to dismiss these two phenomena as sources of Christianity for theological reasons. God is utterly other, the transcendent

19. Randolph Crump Miller, *The Theory of Christian Education Practice* (Birmingham, Ala.: Religious Education Press, 1980), p. 9.

20. Karl Barth, *Protestant Theology in the Nineteenth Century: Its Background and History*, trans. Brian Cozens and John Bowden (London: SCM, 1972; Valley Forge, Pa.: Judson Press, 1973), p. 459 and ch. 11 *passim*.

21. Friederich Daniel Ernst Schleiermacher, *The Christian Faith* (1830), ed. H. R. Mackintosh and J. S. Stewart (Edinburgh: Clark, 1928; New York: Harper & Row, 1963), p. 76, compare pp. 16-18. See also Claude Welch, *Protestant Thought in the Nineteenth Century*, Vol. I (New Haven: Yale University Press, 1972), ch. 3.

22. Friederich Daniel Ernst Schleiermacher, *On Religion: Speeches to its Cultured Despisers* (1799), trans. John Oman (New York: Harper & Row, 1958), p. 87.

Creator. He is in heaven and we are on earth. Thus God can only be known through God: the human reception being through obedience, not experience. There can be no independent saving knowledge arising from any capacity of religious cognition in fallen human nature, nor any analogy of being between God and the world, because the existence of these factors would qualify the transcendence of God and allow for the possibility of human beings taking the initiative in salvation and religious knowledge.[23] This theological critique, it should be noted, is very different from the view that reason and religious experience do not *in fact*, or for philosophical reasons *cannot*, supply truths about God. But it has the same educational consequences. It leads to a Christian religious education that necessarily takes a very low view of the learner's innate potential for religious discovery. This revelational religious epistemology, we note again, has practical implications for the way in which people are taught to be Christian.

We have considered in Chapter 6 above the variety of types of religious experience, their place in Christian religious education and their epistemological implications. It is clear that Christians who give priority to veridical ("truth claiming") religious experience will emphasize the evocation of such experiences, and the learning of attitudes and dispositions that tend to predispose the learner to them. My concern here is to argue that, despite the history of distinguishing Barthian "downward", "objective" theologies of revelation from Schleiermachian "upward", "subjective" theologies based on religious experience, revelation itself can *only* be viewed as the correlate of some form of religious experience. For in order for there to be a revelation, God must do something ("unveil" or "disclose" himself) *and* human beings must experience this unveiling. One cannot have one without the other. If revelation is a source of religious belief, then so is religious experience. Those who defend a revelational theology are therefore implicitly and paradoxically taking very seriously the religious experience of those who received that revelation. The difference between this position and that of the theologians and Christian religious educators who take seriously the religious experience of *contemporary* Christians is therefore not as great as it may appear.

Theology according to Barth is knowledge following from faith: a faith-knowledge that is different in kind from any other knowledge in origin and form, particularly in being defined by obedience to the truth of the revelation in Jesus Christ. Hence it is not just speculative reason, which seeks to argue to conclusions about God, that is suspect. For Barth, intellectual exploration of Revealed Faith is only possible in the sense of our recounting and expounding it. There appears to be no room for *critical* reason here, if that implies a reason whose criteria are (at least in part) independent of the matter to which they are applied. It follows, then, that there would be no place either for any proper critical Christian religious education. According to Barth, reason can only serve the gospel by elucidating it and illustrating it according to "its own

---

23. Karl Barth, *Church Dogmatics*, Vol. II, Part 1, trans. T. H. L. Parker *et al.* (Edinburgh: Clark, 1957), ch. V, sect. 26; also *Church Dogmatics*, Vol I, Part 1, ch. I, sect. 6, p. 123.

principle of explanation". Reason cannot challenge it from any rational, nonrevelational standpoint.[24] Thus: "The necessary and fundamental form of all scriptural exegesis ... must consist in all circumstances in the freely performed act of subordinating all human concepts, ideas and convictions to the witness of revelation supplied to us in Scripture."[25] Barth is notorious for this insistence that, to quote Sykes, the "only antidote to the weakness he observed in liberal Protestantism was the vigorous exclusion from the principles of theology of any kind of independent status for human rationality or potentiality".[26] Human reason is severely put in its (limited and subordinate) place in this account of religious truth, religious knowing and religious education.

Barth's revelational theology has of course been extensively critiqued. Some regard it as overly "intellectualist", and even as identifying revelation and salvation.[27] Many philosophers of religion reject any Barthian "logic of obedience" that claims that human language can convey truth about God only in and through the obedience of faith. Thus Ferré writes: "It is impossible, ... to remain content theologically or philosophically with the divorce which obedience allows—glories in!—between the logical character of human theological discourse and the 'meaning' and 'truth' which is allegedly 'breathed into' it miraculously and independent of its nature".[28] Such critics contend that Barth's split between God and human beings, and between revelation and reason, disables our accounts of both theological understanding and Christian communication. They cannot remain content with a theory of proclamation that regards any development in the learner of critical or speculative reasoning powers, or of a disposition to religious experience, as inimical to a proper teaching of the Christian gospel. By contrast a Christian theology that allows a place, however limited, for a truly human reasoning and experiencing will also find room for them in its list of the proper outcomes and content of Christian religious education. (For further criticisms of the Barthian epistemology see below pp. 286-287. [Ch. 10])

A Reasonable Religion?

The place of reason in Christianity remains highly controversial. Those who argue that reason has a critical, clarifying and systematizing function in reli-

---

24. Karl Barth, *Church Dogmatics*, Vol IV, Part 3, Second Half, trans. G. W. Bromiley (Edinburgh: Clark, 1962), pp. 846-850.

25. Barth, *Church Dogmatics*, Vol I, part 2, p. 715, see also pp. 727-740.

26. S. W. Sykes, "Barth on the Centre of Theology", in Sykes, ed., *Karl Barth: Studies of his Theological Method* (Oxford: Clarendon, 1979), p. 46; see also Brand Blanshard, "Critical Reflections on Karl Barth", and replies by Edward A. Davey, George S. Hendry, Linwood Urban and others, in John Hick, ed., *Faith and the Philosophers* (New York: St. Martin's Press, 1966), part IV.

27. See F. Gerald Downing, *Has Christianity a Revelation?* (London: SCM, 1964), pp. 158-159, 255, 266-268.

28. Frederick Ferré, *Language, Logic and God* (New York: Harper, 1961; London: Eyre & Spottiswoode, 1962), p. 89.

gion, but that it is not to be thought of as one of the *sources* of religion, might argue that Christianity is rational or reasonable in that it accords with reason (is justifiable, rests on adequate grounds, is coherent etc.); but they would add that, like sensory knowledge, moral knowledge and so on, its origins lie elsewhere.

The use of the terms "rational" and "reasonable" as possible descriptions of religion needs some clarification. According to Patrick Burke, religion is never rational in *sense one* (but is, rather, nonrational or arational) in that "its roots do not lie at all in the activity of reasoning", but rather (he adds) in "the experience of an imperative need". He claims, however, that religion is always rational in *sense two*: in that there are always reasons and explanations, construed as understandable causes, for it. Finally, religion is variously rational (opposite irrational) in a *third sense* of the word, which according to Burke "is synonymous with 'reasonable'", "depending on the extent to which it is pervaded by reflective thought". "Rational" here means "rests on grounds, and is justifiable".[29] But what is now meant by rational in this third sense of *being in accord with reason*?

Appeals to reason may sound as if they are referring to a single, unitary, neutral tool. John Kleinig, however, contends that:

> The reification of concepts so characteristic of Western philosophy should not blind us to the fact that there is no such thing as Reason. There are simply people who think (i.e. reason), and who do this well or badly. Behind their thinking activity there lurks no parent animal "Reason", intuitively observed and self-evidently sovereign, but a set of culturally acquired and alterable standards by which that thinking activity can be evaluated. The so-called "laws of logic", perhaps the most permanent standards of rational assessment, comprise only a small part of the critical apparatus to which we appeal when making rational appraisals. Other parts are highly controversial.[30]

29. Patrick Burke, *The Fragile Universe: An Essay in the Philosophy of Religion* (London: Macmillan; New York: Barnes & Noble, 1979), pp. 82 and 83. See Macquarrie's distinction on p. 157 above, and Glossary.

30. John Kleinig, *Philosophical Issues in Education* (London: Croom Helm; New York: St. Martin's Press, 1982), p. 265. On the variety of "scrupulous thinking" shown in different disciplines see G. Ryle, "A Rational Animal", in R. F. Dearden *et al.*, eds., *Reason* (London: Routledge & Kegan Paul, 1975), pp. 40-41; also R. S. Peters, "Education and Human Development", in R. F. Dearden *et al.*, eds., *Education and Reason* (London: Routledge & Kegan Paul, 1975), pp. 123-124. "Reason" (with a capital "R") is part of what has been called "the Project of the Enlightenment" and has been subject to savage criticism in postmodernist philosophy—see Kenneth Baynes *et al.*, eds., *After Philosophy* (Cambridge, Mass.: M.I.T. Press, 1987), p. 68 and *passim*. See also Chapter 10 below, and compare Richard Rorty's (rather extreme) comment on the trial of Galileo: "We would do well to abandon the notion of certain values ('rationality', 'disinterestedness') floating free of the educational and institutional patterns of the day. We can just say that Galileo was *creating* the notion of 'scientific values' as he went along, that it was a splendid thing that he did so, and that the question of whether he was 'rational' in doing so is out of place." Richard Rorty, *Philosophy and the Mirror of Nature* (Princeton, N.J.: Princeton University Press, 1979; Oxford: Blackwell, 1980), p. 331.

Certainly the elementary rules of logical thinking, such as the laws of non-contradiction and excluded middle, will not get us very far in assessing the rationality of a religious belief, or any other belief for that matter.[31]

Such an account of the situation has profound implications for the educational enterprise, and especially for the specific activity of religious education, its justification and its content. The philosopher of education Israel Scheffler puts rationality into its proper philosophical and educational perspective for us:

> The operative principles of rational judgment at any given time are ... much more detailed and specific than a mere requirement of formal consistency. Such consistency is certainly fundamental, but the way its demands are concretely interpreted, elaborated, and supplemented in any field of inquiry or practice, varies with the field, the state of knowledge, and the advance of relevant methodological sophistication. ...
> The fundamental point is that rationality cannot be taken simply as an abstract and general ideal. It is embodied in *multiple evolving traditions* in which the basic condition holds that issues are resolved by reference to *reasons* themselves defined by *principles* purporting to be impartial and universal. These traditions should, I believe, provide an important focus for teaching.[32]

It is important to recognize that some criteria of rationality, although they are capable of application across widely different disciplines of thought and forms of life when construed in a highly *formal* way, have a radically different *content* appropriate to each different context. For example, the rational criterion of appeal to evidence, while relevant to most research and scholarship, understands testing procedures in disparate ways in different disciplines.[33] This is particularly obvious in the cases of theology and the natural sciences. Teaching people to "examine the evidence" is an activity that will be understood very differently in the two fields, as a function of the very different notions of what is meant by both examination and evidence in science and theology.[34]

Even the application of the criterion of self-consistency (noncontradiction),

---

31. While accepting with Aristotle that no one who understands the laws of logic can remain rational whilst rejecting them, Alasdair MacIntyre adds "observance of the laws of logic is only a necessary and not a sufficient condition for rationality". Alasdair MacIntyre, *Whose Justice? Which Rationality?* (London: Duckworth, 1988), p. 4; compare Aristotle, *Metaphysics*, Treatise Gamma. See also Chapter 10 below.

32. Israel Scheffler, "Philosophical Models of Teaching", in R. S. Peters, ed., *The Concept of Education* (London: Routledge & Kegan Paul, 1967), pp. 131-132.

33. Thus Peters, "Education and Human Development", p. 124.

34. See Ian G. Barbour, *Issues in Science and Religion* (Englewood Cliffs, N.J.: Prentice-Hall; London: SCM; , 1966), Part Two; Ian G. Barbour, *Myths, Models and Paradigms* (New York: Harper & Row; London: SCM, 1974); Holmes Rolston, III, *Science and Religion: A Critical Survey* (New York: Random House, 1987), ch. 1 and pp. 335-345; and above Chapter 4.

depending as it does on the actual content of the propositions that it is judging, will vary systematically from context to context. Conjunctions of belief that would properly be rejected as contradictions in commonsense language about material objects may be treated more gently in the languages of theoretical physics (where electrons are both "waves" and "particles"), and in theology (where Christ is both human and divine).[35] Christian theology, like many other comprehensive systems of thought, has developed a complex system of reasoning to enable it to cope with the complex and multifaceted nature of reality. It is for this reason that it often speaks in paradoxes: holding together apparently contradictory beliefs so as to bear witness to important, though disparate, insights into reality. (In Christian theology these paradoxes include not only the Christological paradox, but also the claims that God is both "near" and "far", both "just" and "merciful", both "Judge" and "Victim", etc.) A too pedantic and clear-cut use of reason might collapse such paradoxes and thus jettison significant illumination for the sake of a clarity achieved unnecessarily early in the exploration.[36] Paradox is particularly rife in theology because the objects of theology transcend experience and can be described only in figurative language.[37] Christian religious educators need to recognize this. It may be that literal, simplistic reasoning is easier to develop through education; but it filters out the complex discourse and metaphorical imagery on which much of religious thinking depends.

THE NATURE OF RELIGIOUS UNDERSTANDING

Wittgenstein on Reason and Religion

Some philosophers of religion have gone beyond the generally accepted principles outlined in the preceding paragraphs to develop a more extreme position, often labeled (by its critics) "Wittgensteinian Fideism". In his later philosophy Ludwig Wittgenstein radically modified his earlier "picture theory" of meaning which treated the meaning of language solely in terms of its referent (a view that was to greatly influence Logical Positivism).[38] Repenting of what he regarded as his former errors, this *later Wittgenstein* now supplemented this with an account of the meaning of a sentence in terms of the use to which it was normally put, arguing that we must not force on lan-

---

35. See William H. Austin, "Waves, Particles and Paradoxes", *Rice University Studies* 53: 2 (1967); J. Astley, "Paradox and Christology", *King's Theological Review* 7: 1 (1984).

36. This is argued by John Wisdom, *Paradox and Discovery* (Oxford: Blackwell; New York: Philosophical Library, 1965), ch. XI.

37. I. T. Ramsey and N. Smart, "Paradox in Religion", *Proceedings of the Aristotelian Society* Supp. Volume XXXIII (1959).

38. See Ludwig Wittgenstein, *Tractatus Logico-Philosophicus*, trans. D. F. Pears and B. F. McGuinness (London: Routledge & Kegan Paul; New York: Humanities Press, 1961). On the continuities and differences between the earlier and later philosophies of Wittgenstein, see David Pears, *Wittgenstein* (London: Collins, 1971), ch. 5; Anthony Kenny, *Wittgenstein* (Harmondsworth, England: Penguin, 1973), ch. 12. On Logical Positivism compare A. J. Ayer, ed., *Logical Positivism* (London: Allen & Unwin; Glencoe, Ill.: Free Press, 1959). The "later Wittgenstein" was certainly not a Logical Positivist.

guage preconceived ideas of what its meaning must be, but should rather look at the ways in which it is actually used. There are various types of language, each with its own peculiar logic (or "grammar": i.e. rules for use). These different "language-games"—"consisting of language and the actions into which it is woven"—grow out of, and define, different activities or "forms of life".[39] Wittgenstein's reason for introducing the term "language-games" seems to have been to emphasize that distinctions between sense and nonsense do not exist in abstraction, prior to and out of the context of human life, experience and language.[40] Despite some commentators, it is not clear that Wittgenstein regarded any human phenomenon on the scale of a religion as a form of life or a language-game.[41] But at least we seem to have his permission to talk of *religious* language-*games*, and perhaps religious *forms* of life. Some of these may be distinctive of religion, although they are not to be viewed as isolated from nonreligious ways of talking and behaving.

In his *Lectures and Conversations* and other writings, Wittgenstein treated religious belief as a matter of using a picture and letting it regulate one's whole life.[42] Religious belief, he argued, is not based on evidence in the same way as scientific or historical belief; it is not subject to the same criteria of reasonableness.[43] We discover this, Wittgenstein believed, by listening to the way in which religious language is actually used. Thus he recognized, in a famous phrase, "theology as grammar": in the sense that theology, like any discipline, tells us what it makes sense to say and not to say about its subject matter, "what kind of object anything is".[44] As Stuart Brown puts it: "in describing theology as 'grammar' Wittgenstein seems to be regarding it as concerned to articulate the standards of intelligibility implicit in the language of a given religion .... The point is ... that the standards which govern what it makes sense to say within a given field of discourse must be

39. Ludwig Wittgenstein, *Philosophical Investigations*, trans. G. E. M. Anscombe, Part I, paras. 7, 23, 241, 373, 563; Part II xi (p. 226); Kenny, *Wittgenstein*, ch. 9.

40. D. Z. Phillips, *Belief, Change and Forms of Life* (London: Macmillan; Atlantic Highlands, N.J.: Humanities Press International, 1986), pp. 105-106.

41. The view taken by Norman Malcolm—see his *Ludwig Wittgenstein: A Memoir* (London: Oxford University Press, 1958), p. 72. Contrast Fergus Kerr, *Theology after Wittgenstein* (Oxford: Blackwell, 1986), pp. 30-31; but see also Stewart R. Sutherland, "On the Idea of a Form of Life", *Religious Studies* 11: 3 (1975) and Cyril Barrett, *Wittgenstein on Ethics and Religious Belief* (Oxford: Blackwell, 1991), pp. 117-133. See note 53 below.

42. Ludwig Wittgenstein, *Lectures and Conversations on Aesthetics, Psychology and Religious Belief*, ed. C. Barrett (Oxford: Blackwell, 1966), pp. 53-72.

43. Thus "historical proof (the historical proof-game) is irrelevant to belief". Ludwig Wittgenstein, *Culture and Value*, trans. Peter Winch, ed. G. H. von Wright (Oxford: Blackwell, 1980), p. 32.

44. Wittgenstein, *Philosophical Investigations*, Part I, para. 373; compare his *Zettel*, ed. G. E. M. Anscombe and G. H. von Wright, trans. G. E. M. Anscombe (Oxford: Blackwell, 1967), para. 717 and *Wittgenstein's Lectures: Cambridge 1932-1935*, ed. Alice Ambrose (Oxford: Blackwell, 1979), p. 32. See also Richard H. Bell, "Theology as Grammar: Is God an Object of Understanding?", *Religious Studies* 11: 3 (1975).

sought *within* that field of discourse itself."[45]

What has been called Wittgenstein's "pedagogical turn" in philosophy,[46] whereby he draws our attention to how people learn and are taught the (often implicit) rules for the use of concepts, particularly religious concepts, is of signal relevance to religious educators. "God", "creation", "grace", "sin" etc. are concepts that are, in Dean Martin's words, "learned within the Christian community where they have instituted ruled uses". These concepts are "capacities belonging first to others and, with training, to the prospective candidate" for religious belonging.[47] This "training" comes both through processes of implicit linguistic enculturation and through more formal instructional modes whereby children, youth and adults learn to speak of religious realities correctly—which includes their using this language in the appropriate affective context. Here Wittgenstein's philosophical insights mesh with the concerns of practical Christian religious educators.

It must also be noted, however, that for Wittgenstein religion is not so much a system of knowledge as an affective, salvific way of life based on "an interpretation". So Wittgenstein argued that a religious belief could only be "something like a passionate commitment to a system of reference": "although it's *belief*, it's really a way of living, or a way of assessing life. It's passionately seizing hold of *this* interpretation." On the basis of this understanding of religion, Wittgenstein offered his own account of the nature of religious instruction. "Instruction in a religious faith, therefore, would have to take the form of a portrayal, a description, of that system of reference, while at the same time being an appeal to conscience." Wittgenstein also specified the religious learning outcomes. Religious education would result in the learners, of their own accord, "passionately taking hold of the system of reference". "It would be as though someone were first to let me see the hopelessness of my situation and then show me the means of rescue until . . . I ran to it and grasped it."[48]

It may be argued that if this account of the matter is to be accepted then

---

45. Stuart C. Brown, *Do Religious Claims Make Sense?* (London: SCM; New York: Macmillan, 1969), pp. 46-47.

46. C. J. B. Macmillan, "*On Certainty* and Indoctrination", *Synthese* 56: 3 (1983), p. 363; Wittgenstein, *Lectures and Conversations*, pp. 1-2.

47. Dean M. Martin, "Learning to Become a Christian", *Religious Education* 82: 1 (1987), pp. 96-97, 100. See also Rush Rhees, *Without Answers* (London: Routledge & Kegan Paul; New York: Schocken, 1969), pp. 125-128.

48. Wittgenstein, *Culture and Value*, p. 64; see also p. 28. Compare W. Young, "Wittgenstein and Christianity", in W. L. Gombocz, ed., *Philosophy of Religion: Proceedings of the 8th International Wittgenstein Symposium* Part 2 (Vienna: Holder-Pichler-Tempsky, 1984), pp. 154-155. The interpretation of Wittgenstein as a *thoroughgoing* expressivist in religion and nonrealist in theology is well illustrated in Don Cupitt, *The Sea of Faith* (London: BBC, 1984), pp. 213-225. It is challenged by Fergus Kerr (*Theology After Wittgenstein*, p. 129, and chs. 5 and 6 *passim*) and Cyril Barrett (*Wittgenstein on Ethics and Religious Belief*, p. 257: "Wittgenstein never said that religious belief is *nothing more than* a way of life according to a picture"; see also p. 269). Also note W. D. Hudson, *Wittgenstein and Religious Belief* (London: Macmillan, 1975), pp. 177-183; and note 58 below.

many of the conclusions drawn in Chapter 6 of the present book would be reinforced. On this account, Christian religious education, instead of concerning itself solely or primarily with passing on *theoretical* knowledge about the nature of God or God's metaphysical relationship with the universe, should concentrate rather on teaching attitudes, valuations and dispositions to see and live life in a particular way. Affective and lifestyle learning outcomes will be its primary aim, rather than anything in the cognitive domain.

After Wittgenstein

Wittgenstein's later thought has exerted considerable influence on the understanding of religion espoused by philosophers such as D. Z. Phillips, G. F. Hughes, R. F. Holland, Peter Winch, Norman Malcolm, Paul Holmer and Gareth Moore.

Some have particularly taken up Winch's comment that criteria of logic are "not a direct gift of God, but arise out of, and are only intelligible in the context of, ways of living or modes of social life". It follows, he claims, that "one cannot apply criteria of logic to modes of social life as such". Science and religion are two such modes, each with criteria of intelligibility peculiar to itself. Thus *within* science or religion actions can be logical or illogical: "in science, for example, it would be illogical to refuse to be bound by the results of a properly carried out experiment; in religion it would be illogical to suppose that one could pit one's own strength against God's; and so on". But these criteria of intelligibility do not apply *outside* these realms. "We cannot sensibly say that either the practice of science itself or that of religion is either illogical or logical; both are non-logical."[49]

Such a view has profound implications for any discussion of the rationality of Christianity, and therefore of Christian religious education. Donald Hudson comments on its implications:

Christianity is essentially rational although only *Christian* good reasons count within it. ... Reasons do not subsist *in vacuo*. They must always be moves within some language-game or other and the basic presuppositions of the game will determine in the last analysis what counts as a good reason within it and what does not. If being rational means *more* than simply having good reasons for what one says or does—if it means ... being open-minded, always ready to respond to some new reason, always subjecting the reasons one has hitherto accepted to critical re-examination—nevertheless the fact remains that what counts as a reason is determined by the language-game or form of life in which it has to play its part.[50]

---

49. Peter Winch, *The Idea of a Social Science* (London: Routledge & Kegan Paul; Atlantic Highlands, N.J.: Humanities Press, 1958), pp. 100-101.

50. W. Donald Hudson, *A Philosophical Approach to Religion* (London: Macmillan; New York: Barnes & Noble, 1974), p. 185; compare pp. 149-150.

"Wittgensteinian Fideism", in an extreme form, argues that the demand for a general justification of religious beliefs is misconceived. Treating science and religion as forms of life, it argues that they are based on fundamental pre-suppositions that are necessarily unjustifiable in other terms. They are just there, they are lived: their language-games are played. Hence their (given) forms of life may quite properly be taught and accepted.[51] There are no "reasons" for adopting a form of life: the only "reasons" are those that work for and against certain beliefs *within* a form of life. On an extreme version of this account, religion—like science—is seen as an option of faith (hence "fideism": belief based on faith, rather than rational evidence[52]). *In fine*, according to Norman Malcolm, "religion is a form of life; it is language embedded in action— . . . a 'language-game'. Science is another. Neither stands in need of justification."[53]

D. Z. Phillips discusses the implications of this position for the debate about the rationality of religion, claiming that there is no "paradigm of rationality to which all modes of discourse conform". Commentators on religion (and on religious education) need to recognize, he would argue, "the diversity of criteria of rationality; . . . . that the distinction between the real and the unreal does not come to the same thing in every context", and thus that "what 'agreement with reality' amounts to . . . is itself determined by the language-games we play and the forms of life they enter into".[54] The recognition of this situation appears to lead Phillips and others into an extreme position: a form of equation of religious understanding and religious belief, leading to the claim that "understanding religion is incompatible with scepticism".[55] For the Wittgensteinian there is no theoretical, intellectual—or

---

51. Wittgenstein, *Philosophical Investigations*, I, paras. 217, 654; II xi, p. 226; D. Z. Phillips, *Faith after Foundationalism* (London and New York: Routledge, 1988), pp. 33, 81; Brian Haymes, *The Concept of the Knowledge of God* (London: Macmillan; New York: St. Martin's Press, 1988), ch. 14. See also Ludwig Wittgenstein, *On Certainty*, ed. G. E. M. Anscombe and G. H. von Wright, trans. Denis Paul and G. E. M. Anscombe (Oxford: Blackwell, 1974), para. 559: "the language-game is . . . not based on grounds. It is not reasonable (or unreasonable). It is there—like our life."

52. The phrase "Wittgensteinian Fideism" comes from Kai Nielsen: see his "Wittgensteinian Fideism", *Philosophy* 42: 161 (1967) and "The Coherence of Wittgensteinian Fideism", *Sophia* 11: 3 (1972). Nielsen claims that D. Z. Phillips gives us "a detailed paradigmatic statement of Wittgensteinian Fideism". Kai Nielsen, *An Introduction to the Philosophy of Religion* (London: Macmillan, 1982; New York: St. Martin's Press, 1983), p. 200.

53. Norman Malcolm, "The Groundlessness of Belief", in Stuart C. Brown, ed., *Reason and Religion* (Ithaca, N.Y.: Cornell University Press, 1977), p. 156. Others prefer to say not that religion is a form of life, but that "it is impossible to imagine a religion . . . . without imagining it *in* a form of life". D. Z. Phillips, "Belief, Change and Forms of Life: The Confusions of Externalism and Internalism", in F. Crossan, ed., *The Autonomy of Religious Belief* (Notre Dame, Ind.: University of Notre Dame Press, 1981), p. 60. See note 41 above.

54. D. Z. Phillips, "Faith, Scepticism and Religious Understanding", in D. Z. Phillips, ed., *Religion and Understanding* (Oxford: Blackwell, 1967), p. 68; Phillips, *Faith after Foundationalism*, p. 55.

55. Phillips, "Faith, Scepticism and Religious Understanding", pp. 76-79. This claim is often misunderstood (understandably!). See below pp. 177-179.

hypothetical—knowledge of God. To know God, to believe in God, is to be committed to religious action. This involves using religious language with understanding (i.e. using it correctly, according to its own logic). In a notorious passage, Phillips argues that the believer must learn to use religious concepts. "What he learns is religious language; a language which he participates in along with other believers. What I am suggesting is that to know how to use this language is to know God."[56] Later he commented on this passage: "When I said that . . . I was referring to the language of worship, contemplation, and religious practices. To *use* this language is to worship, to believe in God."[57]

The Reality of God

It is clear that one reason why Phillips and some other "neo-Wittgensteinians" treat religion as radically different from science, history or metaphysics is that they see religious language as expressive of attitudes and commitments rather than descriptive of facts, and therefore "noncognitive" rather than cognitive (in the sense of fact asserting). Within it the sentence "God exists" is not a statement of fact but an expression of faith, i.e. an expression of a commitment to a certain way of life. As James Kellenberger puts it, "in essence religious belief *is* religious activity for Phillips", it is "having a way of life". Such a "believing-in" implies no believing-that God exists, for "in religious *practice* the question of God's existence does not, and cannot, meaningfully arise—there is only the use of the question to reject the religious way of life".[58] Phillips reveals his position in another comment on learning a religion. "In learning by contemplation, attention, renunciation, what forgiving, thanking, loving, etc. mean in these contexts, the believer is participating in the reality of God; *this is what we mean by God's reality.*" Underlying such a comment is the view that asking people whether they think that religious beliefs or beliefs about an afterlife are true is not the same as asking them to produce evidence for these beliefs. It is rather asking them whether they can live by them.[59]

---

56. D. Z. Phillips, *The Concept of Prayer* (London: Routledge & Kegan Paul, 1965; New York: Schocken, 1966) p. 50, compare p. 18.

57. D. Z. Phillips, *Faith and Philosophical Enquiry* (London: Routledge & Kegan Paul, 1970), p. 69.

58. J. Kellenberger, *The Cognitivity of Religion: Three Perspectives* (Berkeley: University of California Press; Basingstoke: Macmillan, 1985), pp. 11, 29, 32. See D. Z. Phillips, *Religion without Explanation* (Oxford: Blackwell, 1976), chs. 10 and 11; Rhees, *Without Answers,* pp. 119, 131-132; Don Cupitt, *Taking Leave of God* (London: SCM, 1980), especially chs. 4 and 5. Phillips writes, "'There is a God', though it appears to be in the indicative mood, is an expression of faith". Phillips, *Religion without Explanation*, p. 181, see also pp. 149-150. Kellenberger claims that Wittgenstein himself is not to be described as a religious noncognitivist (*The Cognitivity of Religion*, pp. 26-27).

59. D. Z. Phillips, *Death and Immortality* (London: Macmillan; New York: St. Martin's Press, 1970), pp. 55, 7l; compare p. 68 and Phillips, *Faith after Foundationalism*, pp. 107, 324-325. See also Stuart Brown, "Religion and the Limits of Language", in Brown, ed., *Reason and Religion*, pp. 245-247.

The implications of this position for Christian religious education are more radical than those that flow from Wittgenstein's own account of the matter. If religion is to be given this noncognitive (non fact asserting) interpretation, then Christian language about God, Jesus, the Spirit, the soul, heaven etc. is not to be construed as implying a set of beliefs-that. Religious education, on this view, even if it uses this traditional language of Christianity and teaches other people to use it themselves in prayer, worship and confession, does not have the teaching of Christian beliefs-that among its aims. It seeks, rather, the learning of Christian lifestyle and affect, *and nothing more*.

The Critical Response

Such "nonrealist" implications have been resisted by more traditional philosophers of religion who continue to understand terms such as "God" and "eternal life" as referring to extralinguistic realities, a view designated as "realist" in philosophy. For them God exists (if at all) as an entity outside of religious language, such that belief in God involves more than using religious concepts correctly and being committed to the spiritual and moral attitudes for which "God" is an appropriate symbol. Some critics of Phillips have described his noncognitive philosophy of religion as a form of "metaphysical atheism", and as "reducing God to a mere concept". "Statements which appear to be about God are in this way shown to be about believers."[60] Similar criticisms have been made of the more explicitly nonrealist religious expressivism of Don Cupitt.[61]

Other critics have argued that a good point about the context dependence of rational criteria has been done to death, at least by *some* of the neo-Wittgensteinians, resulting in an account of religious language-games/forms of life that makes them (or "it") *so* distinctive that they share *no* criteria of intelligibility and rationality with other domains of language/behavior. That, they claim, is just not true to religion,[62] or indeed to Wittgen-

---

60. Alan Keightley, *Wittgenstein, Grammar and God* (London: Epworth, 1976), p. 136; Patrick Sherry, *Religion, Truth and Language-Games* (London: Macmillan; New York: Barnes & Noble, 1977), p. 45; Roger Trigg, *Reason and Commitment* (Cambridge: Cambridge University Press, 1973), p. 35, compare p. 89. See also John Hick, "The Justification of Religious Belief", *Theology* 71: 573 (1968); Derek Stanesby, *Science, Reason and Religion* (London: Routledge, 1988), pp. 177-181; Michael C. Banner, *The Justification of Science and the Rationality of Religious Belief* (Oxford: Oxford University Press, 1990), ch. 4.

61. John Hick, "The Wider God Debate", in Michael Goulder and John Hick, *Why Believe in God?* (London: SCM, 1983), ch. 6; Fergus Kerr, "Don Cupitt's Philosophy", *The Month* 247: 1408 (1985); Rowan Williams, "'Religious Realism': On Not Quite Agreeing with Don Cupitt", *Modern Theology* 1: 1 (1984); John Bowker, *Licensed Insanities: Religions and Belief in God in the Contemporary World* (London: Darton, Longman and Todd, 1987) (= *Is Anybody Out There?*, Westminster, Md.: Christian Classics, 1988), ch. 2; Brian Hebblethwaite, *The Ocean of Truth: A Defence of Objective Theism* (Cambridge: Cambridge University Press, 1988), ch. 3.

62. Humphrey Palmer, "Understanding First", *Theology* 71: 573 (1968), p. 573; Vernon Pratt, *Religion and Secularisation* (London: Macmillan; New York: St. Martin's Press, 1970), pp. 41-45; Trigg, *Reason and Commitment*, ch. 4; Sutherland, "On the Idea of a Form of Life";

stein.[63] Despite such criticisms, students of religion may still have a lot to learn from Phillips and others, if only because we are often tempted to underestimate the differences between religion and other human activities (particularly science), and to forget that words like "rational" and "reasonable" are context dependent *at least to some degree.*[64] In any consideration of the rationality of religion and of religious nurture such a recognition is of central importance.

TYPES OF RELIGIOUS UNDERSTANDING

The Wittgensteinian Position and Religious Education

Interestingly enough, the apparent strategy of the neo-Wittgensteinians of collapsing the distinction between understanding and belief in religion has been used by one author as an argument against the possibility of teaching people about religion without teaching them to be religious. Roger Marples combines this move with the (rather un-Wittgensteinian) claim that religion has to be tested by universal criteria of rationality and fails such a test.

He begins by accepting what he takes to be the central Wittgensteinian principle that "relative to the language-game of which they form a part, grammatical claims express conceptual truths and it is for this reason that understanding them and recognising them to be true are one and the same thing".[65] (A "grammatical claim" is one based on what Wittgenstein called the "grammar" of a concept, which we noted above is the "logic" or rules of meaning implicit in the language-game that employs that concept—i.e. the rules that show us how it is to be used.[66]) Marples continues, however, by arguing that the development of such religious understanding in general education is indefensible "on the grounds that it is not morally permissible to get people to believe things unless those beliefs can be justified by appeal to universal criteria of rationality". Thus any attempt to get people to understand religion is covertly evangelistic and, from the high moral ground so frequently

---

James Richmond, "'Religion without Explanation': Theology and D. Z. Phillips", *Theology* 83: 691 (1980); Nielsen, *An Introduction to the Philosophy of Religion*, chs. 3-5 and other works cited *passim*; Joseph Runzo, *Reason, Relativism and God* (London: Macmillan; New York: St. Martin's Press, 1986), pp. 181-192; R. W. Hepburn, "Attitudes to Evidence and Argument in the Field of Religion", in Roger Straughan and John Wilson, eds., *Philosophers on Education* (London: Macmillan, 1987), pp. 140-141. Phillips himself denies that his position is "internalist" (= "all external criteria of meaning are irrelevant to religious belief") as some critics assume: see his "Belief, Change and Forms of Life", pp. 61-66, 86-90, and below Chapter 10. He argues, therefore, that the Wittgensteinian approach "has nothing to do with any attempt . . . to shield religion from criticism . . . nothing Wittgenstein says . . . . prohibits criticism of or within religious traditions". (*Belief, Change and Forms of Life*, p. 39, compare p. 41.)

63. Kerr, *Theology after Wittgenstein*, p. 31.

64. Kai Nielsen, "Wittgensteinian Fideism Again: A Reply to Hudson", *Philosophy* 44: 167 (1969), pp. 64-65.

65. Roger Marples, "Is Religious Education Possible?", *Journal of Philosophy of Education* 12 (1978) p. 87.

66. *Ibid.*, p. 82; compare above pp. 171-172.

occupied by the rational liberal educator, improper.

Marples's position may be countered by the standard arguments against the assumption that "universal criteria of rationality" will alone be able to justify our beliefs.[67] With regard to Marple's interpretation of the Wittgensteinian principle, however, we may note that Phillips at least has repeatedly denied that his own account of religious understanding and religious belief is to be taken as amounting to a claim "that religious belief can only be understood by religious believers".[68] It is certainly the case that this part of Marples's argument may be met by a Wittgensteinian distinguishing between *understanding religion through participation and advocacy* (as in religious communities) and *understanding religion through elucidation* (as in those educational communities that teach about religion). In a significant passage Phillips allows for such a distinction, adding that this sort of elucidation calls for "a sympathetic relation to religion" in the educator since "it involves unpacking the significance of values, ideals, different conceptions of worship and love, and the roles they play in people's lives". Although this is not a task confined necessarily to religious believers, it *is* confined to "those who take religion seriously, who see something in it, and respect it". This class of educators might well include someone who had come to the conclusion that religious beliefs were false, but was aware of how much was involved in appreciating the nature of religious beliefs. Yet it might well exclude some who were devout believers, "but who lacked the ability to elucidate" the nature of their beliefs. Phillips writes: "So the ability to teach in this context is not synonymous with the ability to believe; it is synonymous, however, with the ability to respect or to see something in religion". He compares this case with the ability to effect musical education, which he equates with musical appreciation. Such teaching "cannot be put in the hands of the tone deaf".[69]

It might be said that neither learner nor educator is expecting or attempting a full *participant-understanding* in teaching *about* religion, for this can only come from *using* religious language (worshiping, praying, confessing, committing oneself).[70] In such education about religion *observer-understanding*[71] (*of* participant-understanding!) is the sole goal. In religion and

---

67. See pp. 173-174 above and Chapters 4 and 10. David Attfield replies to Marples in his own paper "Is Religious Education Possible?", *Journal of Philosophy of Education* 12 (1978).

68. Phillips, *Belief, Change and Forms of Life*, p. 11.

69. Phillips, *Faith and Philosophical Enquiry*, pp. 166-167. Here Phillips is not identifying understanding and belief, but "understanding and feeling the attraction or force of religion". Kellenberger, *The Cognitivity of Religion*, p. 40. Compare Stewart R. Sutherland, "Religion and Ethics: A Survey of Recent Work by D. Z. Phillips", *Human World* 5 (1971), p. 43.

70. And it is perhaps to be *identified with* using that language in this way, as the Wittgensteinian would claim.

71. This may be described as "a cognitive process of structuring experience or data". Charles F. Melchert, "Understanding and Religious Education", in Iris V. Cully and Kendig Brubaker Cully, eds., *Process and Relationship* (Birmingham, Ala.: Religious Education Press, 1978), p. 43. See also Melchert's "What is Religious Education?", *Living Light* 14: 3 (1977), p. 352.

religious education we have to appreciate the distinction between these two very different understandings of religious understanding, distinguishing the understanding that is a part of religion from an understanding of religion.

Participants and Observers

It is clear that Phillips himself does recognize this distinction. Thus he argues that it is because religious doctrines, worship, ritual, etc. are connected with practices other than those that are specifically religious, that "it is possible to convey the meaning of religious language to someone unfamiliar with it".[72] Despite the claims often made against Phillips, he has defenses against the accusation that he has confused a participant's religious understanding with an observer's understanding of religion. He writes: "True, religious believers call obedience to God a form of understanding. It would follow that anyone who did not practise such obedience in his life, lacked *that* understanding. But a philosopher can understand what I have just said about religious understanding and give an account of how obedience to God differs from other kinds of obedience, without being a believer himself, that is, in this context, without being obedient to God."[73]

What is interesting about Marples's paper, however, is the underlying, and entirely proper, claim that a *full* understanding necessitates getting on the inside of a religion by seeing things as the religionist sees them: that is, understanding the religion's ideas, feelings and activities "as from the point of view of an adherent".[74] One does not need to tread the neo-Wittgensteinian way at all in order to argue that the greater the demand that the learner's understanding of a religion must be "just like" that of the believer, the closer education about a religion comes to education into a religion. If educationists wish to preserve *that* distinction, they will have to settle for a partial understanding which is sufficient for teaching about religion (in non-church schools or colleges),[75] but woefully insufficient for religious adherence.

The outsider's understanding can never be a full understanding—a "participant-understanding"—of what it is to be in someone else's shoes or skin. Understanding through participation is always more than understanding by nonparticipatory elucidation ("observer-understanding"). This is a truism that is not confined to understanding someone else's religion. But it is particularly pertinent when we are faced by the imaginative and affective dimensions of being religious. I noted in Chapter 6 that in the early church, Christian religious education involved "warm" rather than "cold" teaching, for early Christianity knew that no one had really learned a doctrine whose heart had not been appropriately moved by it.[76] This is a plausible position, for how can

---

72. Phillips, *Faith and Philosophical Enquiry*, p. 230.

73. Phillips, *Belief, Change and Forms of Life*, p. 12.

74. Compare Marples, "Is Religious Education Possible?", pp. 90 and 85; and A *Groundplan for the Study of Religion* (London: Schools Council, 1977), p. 22.

75. Compare Attfield, "Is Religious Education Possible?".

76. See pp. 121, 131-132. Compare John Calvin, *The Institutes of the Christian Religion*, Book One, Chapter 2. Such an understanding "includes having been initiated into the expe-

the *believer* have *fully* understood the theological doctrine of grace, or the story of the ascension, in the absence of feelings of being accepted or a desire to worship the risen Christ? The scholar's understanding of the same doctrines must include an appreciation of that connection with feelings and attitudes, and an empathic insight into these affective states, but it cannot be expected fully to include the "felt understanding" that is the prerogative of the believer. Empathy is not sympathy, which would be complete "fellow feeling". Here is one major factor pressing us to an acknowledgment of the importance of recognizing degrees of "religious understanding".[77]

Education in Religion

A somewhat different issue has been raised by those who make much of the distinction between "education in" and "education about" religion. Donald Hudson has argued that in secular educational contexts, teachers of all subjects (other than religion) engage in *both* activities. They do not only pass on a lot of information about (i.e. "teach about") mathematics, chemistry or history. They also see it as their task to get pupils to think mathematically or historically, that is to *do* these subjects rather than just learn about them in a detached way.[78] Education *in* a subject, Hudson contends, involves "initiation into the principle of procedure on which that whole discipline depends".[79] In

---

rience one understands", together with "an intellectual and emotional appreciation" of, and insight into, this experience. Craig Dykstra, "The Formative Power of the Congregation", *Religious Education* 82: 4 (1987), p. 545. On the place of "emotional" and "bodily" modes of understanding, alongside more "cognitive", "analytic" and "synthetic" ones, see Charles F. Melchert, "'Understanding' as a Purpose of Religious Education", *Religious Education* 76: 2 (1981). For an account of the place of insight and experience in understanding see Raymond Holley, *Religious Education and Religious Understanding* (London: Routledge & Kegan Paul, 1978), chs. 4 and 5.

77. See Gabriel Moran in Norma H. Thompson, ed., *Religious Pluralism and Religious Education* (Birmingham, Ala.: Religious Education Press, 1988), p. 54; Michael Grimmitt, *Religious Education and Human Development* (Great Wakering, England: McCrimmon, 1987), p. 137. Ninian Smart notes that "the concept of understanding has to do with degree: there are more or less profound, more or less superficial understandings. .... it is not an all-or-nothing-at-all matter, whereas the argument about commitment to a tradition is posed in that way". Ninian Smart, *Concept and Empathy*, (London: Macmillan, 1986), p. 224, see also pp. 197-198. For my comments on commitment see below Chapter 8. The *empathic* student of religion has been described as a "participant observer" or "watcher", who enters the world of the religious believer and yet remains detached. Alison J. H. Leech, "Another Look at Phenomenology and Religious Education", *British Journal of Religious Education* 11: 2 (1989), p 74. The "observer-understanding" referred to here is of this nature: i.e. more than the (nonempathic) understanding of a *total* outsider. See also Edwin Cox, "Understanding Religion and Religious Understanding", *British Journal of Religious Education* 6: 1 (1983) and Jeff Astley, "The Place of Understanding in Christian Education and Education about Christianity", *British Journal of Religious Education*, forthcoming.

78. W. D. Hudson, "The Loneliness of the Religious Educator", in J. G. Priestley, ed., *Religion, Spirituality and Schools* (Exeter: University of Exeter School of Education, 1982).

79. *Ibid.*, p. 26. In religion it includes teaching another person "how to think for oneself in religious terms, and how thereby to put oneself in the way of the sort of experience, or the kind of value judgments, which such thinking can generate". W. D. Hudson, "Two Questions about Religious Education", in Straughan and Wilson, eds., *Philosophers on Education*, p. 110.

the natural sciences this is the principle of natural causation (the uniformity of nature). In religion—presumably only theistic religion—it is "the principle that God exists". Just as pure science seeks to discover what natural uniformities there are, and applied science how we can act according to them; so "pure religion" is concerned to discover God's nature and will, and "applied religion" to show how we can act according to *them*. Thus, according to Hudson, "learning to think religiously is learning to explain what goes on, and to tackle what needs to be done, in the light which pure or applied religion may shed"[80]—i.e. in terms of God's existence. The existence of God and the uniformity of nature are equally fundamental to their respective disciplines. In Wittgensteinian vein, Hudson asserts that within such disciplines nothing can count against them. They are "principles of procedure": methodological rules that determine what is to count as an explanation or an experience within science or religion.[81] However, the development of both disciplines, so as to create a set of beliefs, still remains subject to criteria of rationality which include that of openness to revision by "what appears to be" good evidence.[82]

Hudson argues that the intrinsic method of a subject-area or topic (the way it proceeds) is not logically independent of its content. In consequence, learners cannot be taught how to think even about religion (or morals or politics) without being implicitly taught what to think about these subjects. He writes that "the constraints which constitute *how* to think always narrow down *what* to think". They do so "constitutively", in the sense that an educator instructing learners in a certain subject "will necessarily be channelling their attention to the content of that subject and away from that of any other". They do so "determinatively", in that educators who show their learners how to give the correct answers to questions in their subject "will necessarily be channelling their attention to those answers and away from any others".[83]

Patently this is a different sort of "teaching how" from that proposed for teaching about religion by Ninian Smart. For Smart, teaching how involves giving people the capacity to do religious studies, by giving them the capacities (skills, and empathic and appreciative sensitivities) to understand and

---

80. Hudson, "The Loneliness of the Religious Educator", p. 26.

81. Thus they reside in class (2) of Hudson's rational system of beliefs, see above pp. 57-58. A fuller account of Hudson's view of religious belief as a language-game in which the concept of God is a tacitly presupposed constitutive concept is to be found in his *A Philosophical Approach to Religion*. He argues there that belief in a caring God is an "end-point to inquiry" (p. 10). It determines what constitutes explanation and experience in religion (pp. 16-22), and it is "a commitment from which the distinctively theistic method of interpreting experience proceeds" (p. 66). Hudson identifies the "fundamental pictures which make up religious belief" with what others have called "bliks" (Richard Hare), "onlooks" (Donald Evans) and "end-statements" (Paul van Buren). Such statements of belief (about God) "embody the standard of sense and nonsense in religion" (p. 21).

82. Hudson, "The Loneliness of the Religious Educator", p. 34. See also Martin, "Learning to Become a Christian", pp. 104-111.

83. W. D. Hudson, "Trusting to Reason", *New Universities Quarterly* (Autumn 1980), p. 246.

think about religion.[84] Smart does not advocate secular education that gets people to *do religion*; but this does, at least at first sight, seem to be Hudson's intention. Or rather he advocates *doing religious thinking*, for his parallel with pure and applied science and his focus on "*thinking* religiously" indicate that the center of gravity of his account lies in the cognitive realm, rather than the affective or practical areas.[85]

In a more recent article Hudson explicitly denies that he is advocating a form of evangelism. He reiterates that "becoming educated *in* religion" means learning how to think for oneself in religious terms, but adds that he does not mean that such a person "will necessarily go on to do so with any degree of conviction or commitment". He writes that just as it is possible for those who have had a scientific education not to think scientifically about the practical problems that arise in their lives, and for those who know how to look at things in a historical perspective to feel that "history is bunk", so it is possible for some who have been taught how to think for themselves in religious terms to choose not to do so. By contrast, Hudson claims, somebody's "becoming religious" implies not only that that person is learning to think for himself/herself in religious terms, but also that she or he is "coming to do so as a committed religious believer".[86] Thus secular education could include teaching people *how to* think and act religiously, but without persuading them actually to do so. But here the parallel with scientific and historical education breaks down rather, for in these other disciplines "education in" *does* seem (a) to presuppose the value and truth of the method, and (b) to involve engendering a positive commitment to thinking scientifically and historically about the world. Both the advocates and the opponents of "religion on the curriculum" might wonder why, in the case of religion, the method should be taught at all if the teacher (and subsequently her students) are not committed to its value and the truth of its conclusions.

---

84. Ninian Smart, *Secular Education and the Logic of Religion* (London: Faber & Faber, 1968), pp. 91, 95, 97. See also R. M. Rummery, *Catechesis and Religious Education in a Pluralist Society* (Sidney: Dwyer, 1975; Huntington, Ind.: Our Sunday Visitor, 1976), pp. 158-160 and the charts comparing "teaching about", "education in", and "teaching how" on p. 157 and facing p. 166.

85. See W. D. Hudson, "Is Religious Education Possible?", in Glenn Langford and D. J. O'Connor, eds., *New Essays in the Philosophy of Education* (London: Routledge & Kegan Paul, 1973), pp. 169-173. I am sure Hudson *intends* his account to be wider than this, as he speaks of initiation into "a kind of explanation, and a form of experience". Learning to think religiously certainly involves "learning to explain what goes on" in the light of the existence of God. But it surely does not include "learning . . . to tackle what needs to be done"—for this is *acting* religiously, rather than *thinking* religiously. It only involves learning the principles of how to tackle what needs to be done. Doing religion is much wider than doing theology. See his "The Loneliness of the Religious Educator", pp. 35, 26. In another paper Hudson more clearly distinguishes the twin tasks of religious education as initiation into theology (teaching people how to do theology—i.e. "how to think and speak in terms of god") *and* initiation into devotion (teaching people to be devout—i.e. to put their trust in, and acknowledge their duty to, God). Hudson, "Is Religious Education Possible?", pp. 177-178, 183.

86. Hudson, "Two Questions about Religious Education", p. 111.

The Justification of Religious Education

What should we make of Hudson's apologia for religious education as education in religious thinking? In the context of the debate about what should be taught in secular education it could be argued that much of science and history teaching is in fact education *about* scientific and historical beliefs rather than education *into* doing science or history, and quite properly so. Scientific and historical beliefs will only be formulated within these disciplines by scientists and historians who accept their methodological rules and presuppositions and think scientifically and historically. However, to learn that water boils at 100°C under one atmosphere of pressure, or the dates of the War of American Independence, need not involve the learners in the scientific or historical thinking necessary to the discovery and defense of such statements. This may be inadequate educationally, but it is possible—and practiced. Thus, to adopt John Sealey's distinction, education offered by "educational institutions" is largely a *second order activity*. That is, much education is a matter of studying, "appreciating" and "understanding" subjects, rather than of engaging in the (*first order*) activities of writers, musicians, artists, scientists and historians. Hence students at school and college may learn to understand and appreciate literature, music—and religion, rather than to become novelists, musicians and religious people.[87]

These claims would be contended, however, by many educators. They would argue that education *does* include inducting students into the first order activities of writing (narrative essays if not novels), performing music and becoming scientists (Hudson's "thinking scientifically for themselves"— i.e. framing and testing hypotheses and the like). These processes may not be the whole of education for children, youth or adults, but they are a proper part of it. But then, if we are permitted to make our students into musicians and scientists, why can we not make them—even in secular schools, colleges and adult education programs—into religionists, or at least into theologians?

I can see no obvious *philosophical* rebuttal of this argument that on examination does not turn out to be a case of special pleading. On logical grounds the argument is won. But educational policy is not, and cannot be, decided on the grounds of logic alone. It is here that the moral and sociological dimensions should come into the picture: as they must in any justification of curriculum activity. In the context of many Western nations we simply have to say that a society that increasingly does not share the (or "one"?) fundamental principle of theism is unlikely to want its publicly funded schools and colleges to induct learners in the practice of doing religious thinking.[88] With

---

87. John Sealey, "Teaching 'About' and Teaching 'What Is' in Religion", *British Journal of Religious Education* 2: 2 (1979) p. 59; compare John Sealey "Education as a Second Order Form of Experience and its Relation to Religion", *Journal of Philosophy of Education* 13 (1979).

88. Despite Hudson: see "The Loneliness of the Religious Educator", p. 35. Hudson expresses himself much more cautiously on this topic in "Two Questions about Religious Education" (see pp. 118-120).

this subject at least, second order activity is all most people want in their public education establishments.

Theological Education

Clearly, however, what Hudson *has* offered us is an account of what it is to learn to think theologically (i.e. systematically, coherently and clearly about—and with reference to—God), and that account *is* entirely appropriate and proper in the context of confessional Christian religious education *in the church*. (Hudson calls this "thinking religiously", but religious thinking is obviously wider than theological, and even theistic, thinking.)

Just as theology has a proper part to play within Christianity, so theological education is an appropriate element within a full Christian religious education, at least for those Christians who are capable of it (see Chapter 5). While accepting that there is always a danger that theology—like Barth's natural theology—will be an "also" that becomes an "only", elbowing aside other significant contents of Christian religious education, there is an equal danger that systematic and coherent thinking about Christian truth may be unnecessarily neglected. My stress on the affective dimension of Christianity should not be taken as a denial that there is a proper place for Christian theological education within the broader category of Christian religious education. But this theological education must be *real* theological education. Hudson's arguments certainly need to be heeded by some seminaries, theological colleges and adult Christian religious educators who model themselves on the secular academy and educate their charges *about* theological scholarship rather than in theological thinking. The study of (other people's) theology is entirely appropriate in the secular university, and easily defensible as a proper subject alongside other scholarly disciplines. But it is the job of the church—its lay people as well as its ministers—to *do* theology, that is to engage in the processes and produce the products of theological thinking for themselves, and not just to read the theology of other people. The study of second-hand theology cannot be an end in itself for any Christian. It must lead to, sharpen and enliven her own theological thinking. It is said that the New Testament scholar R. H. Lightfoot was wont to rebuke his students, after they had read their essays to him, with the words: "Stop telling me what 'biblical scholars think . . . '. *Be* a biblical scholar; and tell me what *you* think." The injunction can be applied with even more force to those who "do systematic theology" by simply and solely footnoting what Schleiermacher or Barth really meant. Such activity is very valuable, of course;[89] but it is still second-hand. My account of what systematic theologians think is not my systematic theology. Doing theology *is* different from learning about it.

---

89. It is particularly valuable in secular educational contexts where theologians have to justify their work in the face of secular criticism and puzzlement. On English theological education see Stephen Sykes, "The Study of Theology in University and School", in James Barnett, ed., *Theology at 16+* (London: Epworth, 1984). See also p. 98, note 89 above.

Bernard Lonergan distinguishes two phases of theology. There is a first "mediating phase", consisting of "a theology *in oratione obliqua*" that tells what others have had to say about God and salvation. But there is also a second, "mediated phase", a "theology *in oratione recta*" in which the theologian, enlightened by the past, can no longer be content "to narrate what others proposed, believed, did", but must pronounce "which doctrines were true, how they could be reconciled with one another and with the conclusions of science, philosophy, history" and how they are to be communicated appropriately in confrontation with the problems of today.[90] In so far as theology is a proper content for it, and learners are capable of it, Christian religious education must move people on to this second phase. This will involve forming people in the skills, and motivating them for the tasks, of doing Christian theology for themselves. Only thereby will they do it for the church. There is, of course, much more to Christian religious education than this, in particular the development of affective and lifestyle processes and products. Further, the debate about how far Christian theology *is* a proper content for Christian religious education for many learners, in many contexts, is not to be prejudged one way or the other. Yet these are not excuses that should allow religious educationists to avoid reflecting on what is involved in teaching theological thinking.

---

90. Bernard J. F. Lonergan, *Method in Theology* (New York: Herder and Herder, 1972; London: Darton, Longman & Todd, 1973), pp. 133-134, 267. Compare Edward Farley, *The Fragility of Knowledge: Theological Education in the Church and the University* (Philadelphia: Fortress, 1988).

Part IV

Some Key Philosophical Issues in Christian Religious Education

CHAPTER 8

Freedom and Belief

There is a considerable literature in both philosophy and the philosophy of religion devoted to the issue of the role of the will in belief. Some have spoken of "the will to believe" and many others have assumed some volitional element in belief—particularly religious belief. It is not unusual to hear that we may in some cases have a duty to believe certain things and correspondingly not to believe others.[1] These are issues that are clearly germane to any philosophy of Christian religious education.

FAITH AND BELIEF

Before discussing the role of the will, it is necessary to take the preliminary step of clarifying the relationship of faith and belief (compare pp. 149-153). Clearly our understanding of "the teaching of faith" in Christian religious education must depend on our understanding of the nature of faith.

On the traditional Thomistic analysis—that which follows Thomas Aquinas—faith in God (*fides, credere*) is essentially a matter of having a *belief-that*, i.e. believing a proposition. It is an intellectual conviction that God exists. Aquinas contends that the person of faith must also believe other propositions about God, and publicly confess his or her beliefs.[2]

---

1. "The will to believe" is from William James. James later regretted his famous phrase, preferring "the right to believe". William James, "The Will to Believe" and "The Sentiment of Rationality", in *Selected Papers on Philosophy* (London: Dent; New York: Dutton, 1917). On the ethics of belief, see William Kingdon Clifford, "The Ethics of Belief", in his *Lectures and Essays*, Vol. 2 (London: Macmillan, 1879; New York: Macmillan, 1901), pp. 177-199, reprinted in Walter Kaufmann, ed., *Religion from Tolstoy to Camus* (New York: Harper, 1964); and William P. Alston, *Epistemic Justification: Essays in the Theory of Knowledge* (Ithaca and London: Cornell University Press, 1989), ch. 5 (see especially n. 5).

2. Thomas Aquinas, *Summa Theologiae*, 2a, 2ae, q. 1. art. 2. and q. 2. art. 2. See also John Hick, *Faith and Knowledge* (Ithaca, N.Y.: Cornell University Press, 1966; London: Collins, 1974), Introduction and ch. 1 and M. J. Charlesworth, *Philosophy of Religion: The Historic Approaches* (London: Macmillan; New York: Herder and Herder, 1972), pp. 68-69. For

Alternatively faith may be construed, on the Lutheran model, as a *belief-in* that involves both beliefs-that and trust (*fiducia*), approval and commitment. Faith understood in this way is primarily an attitude of esteeming and trusting, which cannot simply be reduced to cognitive affirmation. Thus: "belief-in is a 'pro-attitude'. One is 'for' the person, thing, policy etc. in whom or in which one believes"; and "trusting is an affective attitude".[3] The "trust" component of faith may be defined more actively as a person's acting, presumably with good purposes, on the assumption that God will do for that person what he or she wants or needs, "when evidence gives some reason for supposing that [God] may not".[4] This gives us a more active interpretation of faith, which has implications for the debate about the role of the will in faith.

As we saw in Chapters 6 and 7, it is usually taken to be the case that belief-in presupposes belief(s)-that; but modern "noncognitive" (in the sense of "non fact asserting") accounts of religious language—e.g. those of D. Z. Phillips and Don Cupitt—deny this, affirming rather that belief-in God is

---

Aquinas, belief is inferior to and incompatible with knowledge; whereas for most contemporary philosophers knowledge entails belief—see Richard Swinburne, *Faith and Reason* (Oxford: Clarendon, 1981), pp. 106-107, and above pp. 150-151. The traditional Catholic stress on the character of faith as intellectual assent (which Luther regarded as merely "historical faith") is outlined in Avery Dulles's essay in James Michael Lee, ed., *Handbook of Faith* (Birmingham, Ala.: Religious Education Press, 1990), ch. 7.

3. H. H. Price, *Belief* (London: Allen & Unwin; New York: Humanities Press, 1969), p. 452. I am unhappy with Norman Malcolm's claim that while "belief in God will involve some affective state or attitude", yet "those attitudes could vary from reverential love to rebellious rejection". Norman Malcolm, "Is it a Religious Belief that 'God exists'?", in John Hick, ed., *Faith and the Philosophers* (New York: St. Martin's Press, 1966), p. 107. I would argue that "belief-in" is normally regarded as involving *positive* attitudes. Price reminds us that there is also a "minimal or merely factual belief-in" (e.g. "believing in fairies") that *can* be reduced to belief-that (*Belief*, pp. 431-432). Others have argued that this use of "belief-in" to make a debatable, and often doubted, existence claim contributes something to its religious use. See W. D. Hudson, "Is Religious Education Possible?", in Glenn Langford and D. J. O'Connor, eds., *New Essays in the Philosophy of Education* (London: Routledge & Kegan Paul, 1973), p. 176; also J. J. MacIntosh, "Belief-in", *Mind* N.S. 79: 315 (1970), pp. 398-407. The classical Lutheran and later Protestant view of faith as trust is expounded by Alexander J. McKelway in Lee, ed., *Handbook of Faith*, ch. 8. See also John Dillenberger, ed., *Martin Luther: Selections From His Writings* (Garden City, N.Y.: Doubleday, 1961), pp. 24, 58-61. For a profound Jewish meditation on faith as trust and faith as assent see Martin Buber, *Two Types of Faith*, trans. Norman P. Goldhawk (London: Routledge & Kegan Paul, 1951). It should be said that classical Protestant dogmatics often discerns within *fides propria* (personal faith) the three elements of *fiducia* (trust in God's promises/personal commitment—the central element), *notitia* (knowledge/belief-that) and *assensus* (assent/intellectual acceptance). Compare Heinrich Heppe, *Reformed Dogmatics*, ed. Ernst Bizer, trans. G. T. Thomson (London: Allen & Unwin, 1950; Grand Rapids, Mich.: Baker, 1978), p. 530.

4. Swinburne, *Faith and Reason*, p. 115. Such a broader analysis of trust may serve as a connecting link between "faith as trusting" and "faith as doing" ("a lived life of agapé"), between "faith as a relationship to God involving knowledge, assent and trust" and a "freedom from concern for self [which] means freedom in responsible and loving action in the world". See Thomas H. Groome, *Christian Religious Education* (San Francisco: Harper & Row, 1980), pp. 57-66; Randolph A. Nelson, "Growth in Faith through Social Ministry", in Lee, ed., *Handbook of Faith*, p. 224. See also note 46 below.

essentially belief-in (i.e. commitment to) certain religious values, attitudes and ways of life, such as disinterested love. This interpretation of religion leads to a form of religious education that stresses attitudes and behavior, and places emphasis on the teaching of religious beliefs-that only as symbolic expressions for religious lifestyle and affective states.

A third form of faith is sometimes described in which there is trust, but where beliefs-that play no part. This is faith as *acting-as-if*. It involves acting on the assumption that there is a God without believing that God exists (but only that God's existence is probable, or simply possible), by doing those actions which one would do if one believed these things.[5] Louis Pojman's analysis of faith as profound *hope*, entailing belief-in the object of hope (trust) but not belief-that, is similar. "To believe that God exists is to believe that there is a being with certain necessary properties . . . But to believe-in God implies only that one regards such a being as possibly existing and that one is committed to live *as if* such a being does exist."[6] Naturally the account of belief given in this paragraph gets short shrift from many critics. As one such remarks, "If they cannot accept it intellectually, why fool around? 'As-if' religion strikes me as a self-deceptive exercise in futility."[7] Religious education that is designed to produce this sort of faith (or "hope") might have a slightly greater emphasis on producing religious beliefs-that than that oriented to noncognitive Christianity (if a belief-that God's existence is possible may be taken as a religious belief-that), but this would be much less than that of a religious education whose objectives are framed by a traditional understanding of the nature of Christianity and of faith.

John Hick espouses a rather different view of faith from any of the above, as we have seen (pp. 124-126). For him faith is the interpretative element within religious experience "by which we experience life as divinely created and ourselves as living in the unseen presence of God".[8] We shall be taking up some further implications of this account later. If adopted, it would lead us to construe religious education that leads to faith as religious education that produces a disposition to have such a religious experience.

FREEDOM AND BELIEF-THAT

Building on Pojman's terminology, we may distinguish between three positions on the relationship of the will to belief: "direct volitionalism", "non-volitionalism" and "indirect volitionalism".

---

5. Swinburne, *Faith and Reason*, p. ll6; compare Peter R. Baelz, *The Forgotten Dream* (London: Mowbrays, 1975), ch. 8, and Anthony Kenny, *The God of the Philosophers* (Oxford: Clarendon, 1979), p. 129.

6. Louis P. Pojman, *Religious Belief and the Will* (London: Routledge & Kegan Paul, 1986), p. 228. See also Swinburne, *Faith and Reason*, p. 167.

7. Kent Bach, *Exit-Existentialism: A Philosophy of Self-Awareness* (Belmont, Calif.: Wadsworth, 1973), p. 4.

8. John Hick, *The Second Christianity* (London: SCM, 1983), p. 47.

Direct Volitionalism

This view holds that we can—and sometimes should—assent to, or withhold assent from, at least some beliefs by a direct ("basic") act of the will (something we do without first doing something else)[9]. Aquinas distinguishes faith (*fides*) from scientific knowledge (*scientia*) in that in the case of faith the assent of the intellect is not wholly coerced by the object of reason or the rational evidence, but requires an additional voluntary act of the will, moved by God's grace. "The author of faith is he who produces the believer's assent to the truth declared. Mere hearing is not a sufficient cause. The assent is caused by the will, not by any necessity of reason. And therefore a preacher or herald cannot produce faith. God is the cause of faith, for he alone can alter our wills."[10] René Descartes held the even more extreme position that *all* believing is an action that we can freely decide to perform or not, in affirming or denying propositions (other than the clear, distinct and indubitable propositions about the thinking self and the existence of God).[11] On such a view we are directly responsible for our false beliefs and errors of judgment. Christian religious educators who adopt such a position will stress the learner's "own responsibility for her/his own learning" to an extreme degree, at least with regard to cognitive learning. Great weight is here being placed on the "freedom of the learner", and the responsibility of the teacher for the learner's learning will be appropriately played down.

Direct volitionalism has run foul of two strong counterarguments, however, relating to the experience and the logic of belief.[12] The first is a *Phenomenological Argument*. This claims that psychologically belief is typically a passive "happening", "event", or "effect": something caused in us, not an act chosen by us. Christians and Christian religious educators are in a good position to comment on the strength of this argument from the phe-

---

9. See Arthur C. Danto, "Basic Actions", *American Philosophical Quarterly* 2 (1965), pp. 141-148; Alston, *Epistemic Justification*, pp. 119-120.

10. (Although this is a prompting or enabling that does not remove the will's freedom and responsibility.) Thomas Aquinas, Disputations, XXVII *de Veritate*, 3, *ad* 12, trans. Thomas Gilby, in *St. Thomas Aquinas: Theological Texts* (London: Oxford University Press, 1955), p. 198.

11. René Descartes, *Meditations on the First Philosophy*, IV.

12. Pojman, *Religious Belief and the Will*, pp. 157-179. Those who deny that the will is really "free" anyway, or interpret freedom of the will as being compatible with determinism (see above p. 72), present us with different problems. If our choices and acts are not truly free, then whether or not our *beliefs* are acts of will seems a lesser concern. If our actions may be properly described as free and yet be determined (the "compatibilist" position), then it could be argued that the adjective "free" may also apply to our beliefs, but the question whether or not the will is involved in believing remains relevant. Here I assume a rather conservative notion of what constitutes freedom of the will, a view that treats the existence of free will as incompatible with determinism (the "incompatibilist" position). For some reflections on the issues involved see C. A. Campbell, *In Defence of Free Will* (London: Allen & Unwin; New York: Humanities Press, 1967), chs. I and II; Robert Young, *Freedom, Responsibility and God* (London: Macmillan; New York: Barnes & Noble, 1975); Gary Watson, ed., *Free Will* (Oxford: Oxford University Press, 1982).

nomenology of belief. We simply ask ourselves: What does it feel like to believe anything? The claim here is that it feels as though beliefs force themselves on us. Pojman writes that believing "seems more like falling than jumping, catching a cold than catching a ball, getting drunk than taking a drink, blushing than smiling". Similarly William Alston asks us to consider whether we are "so constituted as to be able to take up propositional attitudes at will" and predicts that we shall find this to be "psychologically impossible".[13]

The second argument, the *Logic of Belief Argument*, takes a different line. It is based on the premise that there is something incoherent or logically odd in the claim that one can obtain or sustain a belief in full consciousness by an act of will. The difficulty is that our control over our believing must be limited if it is to remain "believing" at all. Bernard Williams's account of the argument is often cited. He claims that it is necessarily the case that I cannot "bring it about, just like that, that I believe something". Why not?

> One reason is connected with the characteristic of beliefs that they aim at truth. If I could acquire a belief at will, I could acquire it whether it was true or not; moreover I would know that I could acquire it whether it was true or not. If in full consciousness I could will to acquire a "belief" irrespective of its truth, it is unclear that before the event I could seriously think of it as a belief, i.e. as something purporting to represent reality. At the very least, there must be a restriction on what is the case after the event; since I could not then, in full consciousness, regard this as a belief of mine, i.e. something I take to be true, and also know that I acquired it at will.[14]

According to Pojman, in standard cases of belief "A cannot both believe that *p* and that A's belief is presently caused by his willing to believe that *p*".[15] To *believe* a proposition, on the philosophical analysis of believing, is to presuppose that one has evidence for that proposition, or that it is self-evident.[16] Most philosophers would claim that religious beliefs-that must also have this nature if they are to count as beliefs. Most religious believers would agree.

Nonvolitionalism
This would be the extreme, opposite, position from that of direct volitionalism.

---

13. Pojman, *Religious Belief and Will*, p. 160; Alston, *Epistemic Justification*, p. 122.

14. Bernard Williams, "Deciding to Believe", in his *Problems of the Self* (Cambridge: Cambridge University Press, 1973), p. 148. See also Swinburne, *Faith and Reason*, pp. 25-26. The argument is not necessarily wedded to an account of truth as correspondence with the facts. But Williams's conclusions have been criticized by Barbara Winters "Believing and Will", *Journal of Philosophy* 76: 5 (1979), pp. 251-256. William Alston is also unconvinced by this argument (*Epistemic Justification*, p. 122).

15. Pojman, *Religious Belief and the Will*, p. 171.

16. On this view self-creative and self-verifying beliefs are taken to be cases of *indirect* volition (see below; also Price, *Belief*, Part II, ch. 6).

Nonvolitionalists would hold that the will *never* plays a role in belief formation.

David Hume claims (not always consistently) that assent is wholly involuntary, a matter of feeling. He writes: "belief consists merely in a certain feeling or sentiment; in something, that depends not on the will, but must arise from certain determinate causes and principles, of which we are not masters." Being "convinc'd of any matter of fact" involves our doing nothing but conceiving it, "along with a certain feeling, different from what attends the mere *reveries* of the imagination". Similarly, where "we express our incredulity concerning any fact, we mean, that the arguments for the fact produce not that feeling".[17] Belief, then, "consists not in the nature and order of our ideas, but in the manner of their conception, and in their feeling to the mind". It is "something *felt* by the mind",[18] although Hume recognizes that he is using the term "feeling" somewhat analogically here.[19]

Belief, on this view, is not the product of an active decision-process, that is of an act of will. It is rather, in Williams's words, "a passive phenomenon, something that happens to us". On such an account, according to Brümmer, "it is not possible to choose whether or not to become convinced by the evidence that one does . . . consider". Beliefs, like emotions and unlike (the usual view of) decisions, are *effects*—in this case "states of minds which are caused in us by the evidence". They are not acts.[20]

Those religious educators who take such a view of religious beliefs-that will interpret their craft appropriately. If the learner's will plays no role in the formation of his/her religious beliefs, then rhetoric about the "freedom of the learner" will need to be very heavily qualified (but see note 12). Correspondingly, religious educators who adopt such a view should recognize the heightened responsibility of the teachers for their learners' learning.

However, while a number of philosophers (including some direct volitionalists) would accept that this account fits many of our ordinary—particularly our perceptual—beliefs, they are unwilling to deny the will *any* role in belief formation. The remaining option attracts those who seek a

---

17. David Hume, *A Treatise of Human Nature*, Appendix, ed. L. A. Selby-Bigge (London: Oxford University Press, 1888), p. 624. It has been claimed that Hume's celebrated injunction that "a wise man . . . proportions his belief to the evidence" in his (later) *Enquiry Concerning Human Understanding* allows more room for an *activity* of deciding on evidence. See Section X, Part I, of the *First Enquiry*, ed. L. A. Selby-Bigge (London: Oxford University Press, 1902), p. 110; and compare Vincent Brümmer, *Theology and Philosophical Inquiry* (London: Macmillan, 1981; Philadelphia: Westminster, 1982), pp. 155-156 and Price, *Belief*, pp. 239-240. But it should be noted that Hume reiterates his point about "feeling .. which depends not on the will" in the *Enquiry* (Section V, Part II; p. 48).

18. Hume, *Treatise*, p. 629.

19. Hume speaks of a feeling of the "superior *force*, or *vivacity*, or *solidity*, or *firmness*, or *steadiness*" of an idea assented to when compared with a fictitious idea. Hence "those ideas, to which we assent, are more strong, firm and vivid, than the loose reveries of a castle-builder" (*Treatise*, Appendix, p. 629 and Book I, Part III, Part VII, p. 97).

20. Williams, *Problems of the Self*, p. 148; Brümmer, *Theology and Philosophical Inquiry*, pp. 157, 192.

middle way, especially for religious beliefs. It is the position of "indirect volitionalism".

Indirect Volitionalism

On this view the will only plays (or never plays more than) an indirect role in believing. We can on occasions obtain or sustain a belief by the indirect operation of various acts of will. These might include the selective direction or fixing of our attention, and our imagining what a situation would be like if the proposition under consideration were true. Pojman writes:

> Many of the beliefs that we arrive at are finally the results of our policy decisions. Although believing itself is not an act, our acts determine the sorts of beliefs we end up with. It is primarily because we judge that our beliefs are to some significant degree the indirect results of our actions that we speak of being responsible for them. Although we cannot be said to be directly responsible for them, as though they were actions, we can be said to be indirectly responsible for many of them. If we had chosen differently, if we had been better moral agents, paid attention to the evidence, and so forth, we would have different beliefs than we in fact do have.[21]

Such a position is a very attractive one and does not run foul of the arguments against direct volitionalism considered earlier. This is what Alston describes as our "indirect voluntary influence" over our beliefs. It is achieved either by our engaging in activities that influence our coming to a particular belief (e.g. by looking at particular evidence), or by our engaging in activities that "affect our general belief-forming habits or tendencies" (e.g. "talking myself into being less (more) subservient to authority" or "practicing greater sensitivity to the condition of other people").[22] This is the position I intend to argue for and analyze here, picking up its implications for religious belief and Christian religious education below (see especially pp. 204-218).

Price on Freedom of Belief

It may be useful at this point to look in more detail at the work of one philosopher who has made a major contribution to philosophical and religious debate about the nature of belief: Henry Habberley Price (1899-1971). Price's position clarifies a number of important aspects of the issue.

Modern philosophers usually give a dispositional analysis of belief-that,

---

21. Pojman, *Religious Belief and the Will*, p. 180. See also Brand Blanshard, *Reason and Belief* (London: Allen & Unwin, 1974; New Haven: Yale University Press, 1975), pp. 402-404; J. L. Mackie, *The Miracle of Theism* (Oxford: Clarendon, 1982), pp. 201-202 and ch. 11 *passim*. There may be other acts that we could perform to engender belief indirectly, such as taking drugs, auto-suggestion and hypnosis. These are less epistemologically desirable, but on some extreme occasions they could possibly be justifiable.

22. Alston, *Epistemic Justification*, pp. 137-138.

on which a belief is a (more or less) long term tendency to say, do or feel certain things that are occurrent manifestations of the belief.[23] Acquiring and losing a belief are acknowledged to be mental occurrences ("processes" or "happenings"), but it is argued that the belief itself is not something that happens at a particular moment.[24] While adopting this account of the matter, Price presents us with an analysis of the mental occurrence of *assent* that seems to mediate between (extreme interpretations of) the Cartesian and the Humean positions on the freedom of assent.

Price distinguishes two elements in assent (= "the taking up of an attitude towards an entertained proposition"). He calls these two components preference and confidence.[25] Confidence comes in degrees, whereas preference is all-or-nothing. In preferring a belief p to its alternatives we plump for it as at a crossroads, but we may still have various degrees of confidence about the alternative we have preferred. In an earlier paper, Price referred to preference as the "volitional", and confidence as the "emotional" factor in assent, although he described the former as only "*analogous to* choice or preference or decision".[26] Elsewhere he more clearly avers that "because of this preferential element in it, assent may look rather like voluntary choice. But the appearance is deceptive. It is not a free choice at all, but a forced one." He argues that if we are in "a reasonable frame of mind" we cannot help preferring the proposition which the evidence favors, much though we may wish that we could. ("I mean, you cannot help preferring the proposition which *your* evidence favours, the evidence *you* are at the moment attending to, though the evidence which other people have may of course be different.") It just is not in our power to avoid assenting to the proposition that our evi-

---

23. On dispositions and occurrences see Glossary and Gilbert Ryle, *The Concept of Mind* (London: Hutchinson, 1949), ch. V. Others prefer to describe beliefs as continuing "states" of a person: e.g. D. M. Armstrong, *Belief, Truth and Knowledge* (Cambridge: Cambridge University Press, 1973), ch. 2. Richard Swinburne argues that a belief is an inner attitude towards propositions, manifested in action and often evidenced by public criteria, "but which may exist independently of its manifestations". It is a mental state "of which a subject is aware or can be made aware by self-examination". It is thus not *simply* a disposition. Swinburne, *Faith and Reason*, pp. 12-18; compare R. B. Braithwaite, "The Nature of Believing", *Proceedings of the Aristotelian Society* 33 (1932/3). Price adopts a modified form of dispositionalism, helpfully describing a person's belief as "a multiform disposition" which is manifested or actualized in a person's actions and inactions, in his or her emotional states (e.g. hopes and fears), and in feelings of doubt, surprise and confidence. A belief is also expressed in a person's conscious and unconscious inferences (*Belief*, p. 294).

24. Price, *Belief*, pp. 20-25, 241-289, 296-301, 363. A rather wider account of occurrent believing is given by Timothy L. S. Sprigge in *Facts, Words and Beliefs* (London: Routledge & Kegan Paul; New York: Humanities Press, 1970), p. 175.

25. Price, *Belief*, p. 207. Such assent is to be distinguished from an "acceptance" of a proposition understood as a "policy of deeming, positing, or postulating" it (i.e. using it in one's reasoning). L. Jonathan Cohen, *An Essay on Belief and Acceptance* (Oxford and New York: Oxford University Press, 1992), p. 4. According to Cohen, belief is involuntary whereas acceptance is voluntary and culpable (see pp. 20-27).

26. H. H. Price, "Some Considerations about Belief", in A. Phillips Griffiths, ed., *Knowledge and Belief* (London: Oxford University Press, 1967), p. 45, my italics.

dence favors, nor to assent instead to some other proposition when the evidence appears to us to be clearly unfavorable to it.[27]

We cannot, therefore, directly will ourselves to believe something. But Price continues by allowing that "indirectly, though not directly, and over a period of time, though not instantaneously, one *can* voluntarily control one's beliefs—at any rate up to a point". Beliefs can be both gradually cultivated and preserved against loss, by actions that are within our free control: in particular the voluntary direction of our attention. Thus (a) we may selectively direct our attention to one type of evidence rather than another, or (b) we may fix our attention repeatedly, "on what it would be like if the proposition were true" and, indeed, act as if it were true.[28]

Activities such as these, we should note, are of considerable importance in Christian religious education, where studying the Bible, meditating on the implications of Christian doctrines, and even "role-playing the role of the pray-er" (i.e. engaging in the *overt behavior* of prayer and worship, even in an agnostic frame of mind) can lead to the evocation of appropriate beliefs. By such means people (including Christian learners) can—indirectly—voluntarily cultivate beliefs. Thus Price concludes that volitional words do apply to beliefs. Belief as a persistent state or disposition "can be acquired or abolished, strengthened or weakened", i.e. learned, by an extended course of voluntary effort, but not by any instantaneous act of the will.[29]

Price goes on to say that the notion of a duty to believe can only get a purchase with regard to these voluntary efforts, for these are the only ones that are within our power to do or not to do ("ought" in moral philosophy always implies "can"). Yet he is reluctant to say that we may ever have a *moral* duty to form or change our beliefs in these ways. Indeed, rather, we have a duty (though only a *prudential* one) to be open-minded about our beliefs, by considering the evidence for and against them as impartially as possible.[30] The indirect control that we may exercise over our religious beliefs would presumably be similarly assessed by Price. Thus, although there are educational procedures by which we may indirectly cultivate our own religious beliefs, the use of these procedures is to be judged against our prudential duty to be "open-minded" and "impartial". Those religious educators who wish to emphasize the learner's control over his or her beliefs should note that, according to this view at least, this control ought to be exercised in a rationally reflective manner. And that will not inevitably lead to

---

27. H. H. Price, "Belief and Will", in R. F. Dearden *et al.*, eds., *Reason* (London: Routledge & Kegan Paul, 1975), p. 209.

28. *Ibid.*, pp. 209, 211-212. Compare the account of faith as "acting-as-if" above.

29. *Ibid.*, p. 213; compare *Belief*, pp. 221-226.

30. *Ibid.*, pp. 213-217; *Belief*, p. 238. See also Roy Edgley, *Reason in Theory and Practice* (London: Hutchinson, 1969), pp. 95-101 and Alston, *Epistemic Justification*, pp. 139-150. But a doctor, for example, has a moral obligation to keep up with the medical literature, and "an ethic of belief may reduce to an ethic of investigation and openness to criticism". Louis P. Pojman, "On Criteria for Rational Religious Belief", in Alistair Kee and Eugene T. Long, eds., *Being and Truth* (London: SCM, 1986), pp. 412-413.

the adoption of *Christian* beliefs. We may be able to evoke beliefs by encouraging certain learner activities, but the learner's duty to engage in an impartial appraisal of the evidence related to these beliefs would appear to override, on Price's account, any religious or moral motivation for engaging in these practices. (For further reflections relevant to this issue see Chapters 4 and 5 above.)

In his Gifford lectures Price seems at first sight to give more force than the above account allows to the Cartesian emphasis on freedom of assent.[31] He chides empiricists like Hume for taking too passive a view of the mind—"as if it were half asleep all the time". We are not, he argues, always in this condition. Rather it is in our power to wake up, "to become self-conscious and clearly aware of what is going on in us" and to criticize and evaluate it: asking ourselves what reason there is for believing something we find ourselves believing. Then, Price claims, we can—at least sometimes—*decide* to give up one belief, adopt another or suspend judgment altogether. Such a decision is sometimes effective. Thus "it is as if we had the power of intervening, consciously and rationally, in our own mental processes, and of altering the course they take."[32]

This is not, however, a return to the full-blown Cartesian doctrine of freedom of assent. We cannot keep ourselves "woken up" all the time, as that rationalist philosopher assumed. Yet, Price now argues, Descartes is right in insisting that we do have the power of withholding assent if we see no good reason for assenting to a proposition.[33] This, Price claims, is a sort of rational autonomy.[34] It is more than just a matter of a belief being *my* belief, for it includes some element of conscious decision with regard to the beliefs to which we assent.

But it is not clear that Price has allowed much more room for freedom of belief here. It could be argued that this activity of "waking ourselves up" is no more than our getting ourselves into what he referred to earlier as the "reasonable frame of mind" of considering the evidence or lack of it ("no good reason"), and being open to the influence of that evidence—albeit rather late in the day and after our beliefs have already been formed in us. I contend that the argument still stands that *at some stage* in our weighing of the evidence (or recognizing the weight of the evidence, or giving weight to the evidence) this process becomes automatic and beyond our control. Both the logic and the experience of belief imply that this is the case. Despite this language of "decision", "giving up" and "adoption",

---

31. Pojman classifies the later Price as a "prominent volitionist" (*Religious Belief and the Will*, p. 146, compare p. 149), but this is surely going too far. For a more cautious assessment see *ibid.*, p. 98.

32. Price, *Belief*, p. 230. See also Stuart Hampshire, *Thought and Action* (London: Chatto & Windus; Toronto: Clarke, Irwin, 1959), p. 213. In *Belief* Price argues that Hume's analysis applies only to immediate, "automatic beliefs" which arise in us "without any previous process of questioning or deliberation or weighing of evidence" (pp. 183-184).

33. Price, *Belief*, p. 237.

34. *Ibid.*, pp. 229, 231; see below pp. 204-208 and above Chapter 4.

Price's new account does not take us much beyond the conscious techniques for affecting our believing that were described earlier, i.e. *indirect volitionalism.*[35]

Conclusion

To some extent, then, we are free to attend to evidence, and to decide to consider this evidence rather than that. In my view this would allow sufficient room to the exercise of freedom for the believer to be regarded as a free agent. Some hold this to be a necessary condition of being rational.[36] In his criticism of Kant's argument for the freedom of the will as a precondition of rational judgment, John Mackie has contended that, although a rational theoretical judgment cannot be seen by the person who makes it as having been caused *"in any of the wrong sorts of way*, that is, in ways irrelevant to the truth or justification of the belief", yet "there is no difficulty in holding a serious rational belief and at the same time seeing it as having been caused in a

---

35. Interestingly enough, in *Belief* Price still appears reluctant to describe preferential assent as a "decision". It remains "in some respects analogous" to a decision (p. 206), but he regards that as too active a word for it (p. 219—compare p. 294). In the same book Price argues that we only feel "confidence in a wider sense of feeling, in that confidence is an introspectible mental state that is "lived through" or "enjoyed" (pp. 288-289). But this is still very passive language. See above p. 196.

36. See J. R. Lucas, *The Freedom of the Will* (London: Oxford University Press, 1970), ch. 21 and references cited; Roger Trigg, *Reason and Commitment* (Cambridge: Cambridge University Press, 1973), pp. 138-145. Philosophers who defend the dualistic notion that minds and mental events constitute a radically different and distinct category from matter (including the brain) need to find good arguments against monistic views (to the effect that the mind and the brain are just two aspects of one thing) and epiphenomenalistic views (for which the mind has no causal efficacy of its own, but is a mere "epiphenomenon" of brain activity). One argument that they often offer is that epiphenomenalism and the mind/brain identity theory inevitably lead to a deterministic view of beliefs which makes beliefs unjustifiable and therefore irrational: for I only believe *p* because of factors *a* to *z*. See John Hick, *Death and Eternal Life* (New York: Harper & Row; London: Collins, 1976), pp. 116-121; Paul Badham, *Christian Beliefs about Life after Death* (London: Macmillan; New York: Barnes & Noble, 1976), ch. 8. Richard Swinburne's criticism of epiphenomenalism is more sophisticated. He claims that he is not giving "the old bad argument" against determinism, that if our beliefs (e.g. that determinism is true) are caused they are unjustified. "Rather it is the argument that insofar as our beliefs which require reasons for their justification do not have acceptance of those reasons among their causes, they are unjustified." Abandoning epiphenomenalism of beliefs, Swinburne argues that beliefs are held because of other beliefs "in virtue of the propositional content of the latter; that is, they are held in their place by states possessing intrinsic meaning, not by mere brain correlates". He contends that, because of the close connection between belief and desire, the same applies to desire. Richard Swinburne, *The Evolution of the Soul* (Oxford: Clarendon, 1986), p. 290. Such an argument distinguishes between *perceptual beliefs* ("non-reasoned responses to the environment"), which are justified by being caused by nonmental factors, and *reasoned beliefs* that require the justification of other beliefs (as causally efficacious thoughts). This second class of beliefs may be determined by "laws of thought" without being rendered irrational. These considerations are relevant to the distinction between perceptual and other beliefs referred to in this chapter and in my discussion of indoctrination in Chapter 4.

proper way".[37] But it cannot be the case that we *decide* whether or not we are to be convinced by the evidence or arguments that we do consider. This is just something that happens to us. And that is how it ought to be, else we lose the heart of the notion of "belief", and indeed of rational belief. Our beliefs are forced into us—or out of us—by their evidence, their cogency, their intuitiveness,[38] or some other "compulsive" feature. We do not choose our gods; they choose us. "We do not believe anything deliberately, intentionally or on purpose."[39]

Freedom, and therefore responsibility, is to be located primarily *between* beliefs and actions, and—very much secondarily—in our deliberations *prior* to the formation of those beliefs. It has no significant part to play at the heart of assent itself.[40] In teaching religious beliefs, therefore, we are not offering a range of options to the learner for the exercise of the learner's untrameled freedom of cognitive choice. Nor should we be seeking only to develop and strengthen the learner's volitional powers if our aim is to develop and strengthen their religious beliefs. The scope of the learner's freedom of belief in Christian religious education is a rather limited and indirect one. *In fine* the freedom that the learner can exercise is not a freedom to adopt one belief and reject another, but a freedom to engage in actions that have much more indirect, and sometimes unpredictable, consequences on her beliefs.

FREEDOM AND FAITH

All of the above, of course, applies to beliefs-that and knowledge claims about matters of fact (whether empirical or theological). Beliefs-in, however, involve more than entertaining and assenting to propositions. As we have seen, to believe in something or someone (X) usually involves more than just believing that X exists. It normally includes having a favorable attitude towards, attaching importance to, and/or trusting in X.[41] Clearly these are important elements in religious faith in God. It could be argued that it is belief-in, rather than belief-that, that is under the control of the will; and therefore that religious faith does have an irreducible voluntaristic element

37. Mackie, *The Miracle of Theism*, p. 171; compare Immanuel Kant, *Groundwork of the Metaphysic of Morals*, trans. H. J. Paton as *The Moral Law* (London: Hutchinson, 1948), ch. III.

38. The best defense of the (currently unpopular) philosophical notion of "intuition" is to be found in the works of A. C. Ewing: see his *Non-Linguistic Philosophy* (London: Allen & Unwin; New York: Humanities Press, 1968), ch. 2, and *Value and Reality* (London: Allen & Unwin; New York: Humanities Press, 1973), pp. 41-48 and ch. 6.

39. R. F. Dearden, "Autonomy and Education", in R. F. Dearden *et al.*, eds., *Education and Reason* (London: Routledge & Kegan Paul, 1975), p. 68. But compare note 60 below.

40. Compare A. Phillips Griffiths, "Reasons and Causes", in Dearden *et al.*, eds., *Reason*, pp. 194-197. Others, of course, will continue to disagree, although even they are careful to qualify the degree of control which humans have, and should have, over their beliefs. See, for example, Arthur C. Danto, *Analytical Philosophy of Knowledge* (Cambridge: Cambridge University Press, 1968), pp. 153-155.

41. See above p. 190 and note 3, and Chapter 6.

after all. If this is the case, then religious education that strengthens the learners' disposition to exercise their free will would be more relevant to the development of their *faith*.

Swinburne on Meritorious Faith

In *Faith and Reason*, Richard Swinburne adopts the view argued here that "we cannot help having the beliefs that we do at the time at which we have them" and that such believing-that cannot therefore be meritorious (praiseworthy):[42] "belief is a passive state; merit belongs only to actions".[43] But he goes on to defend a notion of *meritorious faith*. On this account meritorious faith involves the meritorious *actions* of achieving good purposes and relying on our beliefs-that: i.e. actively trusting God, being obedient to God etc.[44] Lack of faith is only culpable (blameworthy) in the case of those who have the appropriate beliefs-that about God and about our obligation to him, but do not act on them. (Culpable nonbelief is a notion with similar restrictions. Everyone is under an obligation "to pursue inquiry as to whether or not there is a God", but only the person who recognizes this obligation but does not respond to it is blameworthy.[45]) Evangelists and religious educators should note the theological implications of this view. Such a meritorious voluntary faith is a matter of pursuing the goals of religion, acting on certain assumptions. It is, therefore, *active* trust in God. Swinburne's account here is somewhat similar to accounts of faith as "primarily lifestyle", i.e. as "active faith".[46] In this sense faith can be both voluntary and meritorious. Christian religious educators who strive to develop this in their learners will inevitably and properly focus on the learners' dispositions to act (freely) in a trusting, obedient fashion on the basis of their cognitive beliefs. But they should not confuse this with a freedom of cognitive belief-that in their learners.

Newman on Affirming or Stifling Certainty

A similar emphasis may be discerned in the thought of John Henry Newman. Jamie Ferreira contends that Newman, despite appearances, adopts a highly qualified account of the role of the will in *reaching certitude* "not . . . through a choice, but . . . an active, uncompelled yet constrained recognition"—a "non-deliberate or non-intentional adherence".[47] But she argues further that Newman's main contribution to the debate may be seen in his recognition that "the will can play a role after certitude is reached", by the believer affirming or stifling that certainty.[48] Ferreira quotes Leslie Stephen

---

42. Swinburne, *Faith and Reason*, p. 109.

43. *Ibid.*, p. 116, compare pp. 86, 109.

44. *Ibid.*, pp. 118-121.

45. *Ibid.*, pp. 142; compare pp. 29-30, 102, 157, 198-199.

46. *Ibid.*, pp. 108-115; compare p. 167. See James Michael Lee, "Growth in Faith through Religious Instruction", in Lee, ed., *Handbook of Faith*, pp. 283-286, 294-302. See also note 4 above.

47. M. Jamie Ferreira, *Doubt and Religious Commitment* (Oxford: Oxford University Press, 1980), pp. 71, 75.

48. *Ibid.*, p. 73.

who notes that "to believe what we know to be certain at times even requires a kind of intellectual heroism" in the face of our own fear (for example of the jump across the precipice, or of the Inquisition) or our "mere blind sympathy with others".[49]

But this "willing as a consequence rather than a source of certainty" is in my view better expressed in terms of a believer actively relying on her beliefs, rather than by our speaking of her freely adopting an attitude to those beliefs. Alternatively, we may argue that this affirming/stifling activity is but another form of the *indirect* activity that originally lead to (involuntary) belief formation, although this time it is operating in a reinforcing— or demolishing—manner back on to the belief that has already arisen. The exercise of the will in affirming or stifling a certainty that has already developed is one example of the proper, limited, role to be ascribed to the will in religious belief and the education of religious belief.

Freedom, Attitudes and Valuations

We must return to the question of faith. I would argue that where faith is defined (in a less active fashion than that adopted by Swinburne and others) as consisting *solely* of beliefs, attitudes and valuations, it is more difficult to speak of any element of direct volition and therefore of any direct responsibility. Certainly it is not clear to what extent our attitudes and valuations are themselves under our free control.[50] Attitudes and valuations, like beliefs, are subject to change by actions that we are free to perform, and by free actions done to us by others. We may change all of them *indirectly*. But it does not seem to be the case that we can by an act of will directly add an inch to the stature of our pro-attitude towards God, or cause our trust in God to grow. Thus our account of Christian religious education can still only give a limited place to the development of the learner's free choice as far as the learners' faith, and its component attitudes and valuations, is concerned.

Hick on Faith as Experience

The will plays a major part in John Hick's well-known notion of faith, which he understands as "a *voluntary* recognition of God's activity in human history, [consisting] of seeing, apperceiving, or interpreting events in a special way".[51] Religious people experience the world *as* God's world, other people *as* his children etc. Hick claims that our cognitive freedom, which is at a minimum vis-à-vis the physical world, is at a maximum in our cognition of the religious significance of the world. We adopt "the religious mode of apperception" by an "act of will" or a "state of willingness or consent".[52]

---

49. Leslie Stephen, *An Agnostic's Apology* (New York: Putnam's Sons, 1893), p. 47; quoted in Ferreira, *Doubt and Religious Commitment*, p. 74.

50. See Chapter 6 and Chapter 9.

51. John Hick, *Philosophy of Religion* (Englewood Cliffs, N.J.: Prentice-Hall, third edition, 1983), p. 69, my italics.

52. Hick, *Faith and Knowledge*, p. 143, compare ch. 6 *passim*.

Hick also holds, however, that Jesus and other great religious leaders were subject to such powerful religious experiences that *their* freedom of belief was much more limited. "They could no more help believing in the reality of God than in the reality of the material world." Their sense of the presence of God had an "involuntary and compelling quality" akin to that enjoyed by most people only with sense experience.[53]

But Hick's distinction here is not fundamentally one that is marked by the difference between the saints and the rest of us. It is rather a distinction between (a) coming to an awareness of God, and (b) (afterwards) enjoying that experience of God (or, more accurately, that experience of the world/other people *as* God's world/God's children). Thus Hick can write that once a person has allowed himself or herself freely to become conscious of God "that experience is, at its top levels of intensity, coercive. It creates the situation of the person who *cannot help* believing in the reality of God." Therefore "our cognitive freedom in relation to God is not to be found at this point but at the prior stage of our coming to be aware of him."[54] Elsewhere Hick argues quite generally that God does not force himself upon our attention, as does our physical environment. "The individual's own free receptivity or responsiveness plays a part" in our dawning consciousness of God, even though once we have become conscious of God that consciousness may (in some cases) "possess a coercive and indubitable quality".[55] Hence our awareness of God is *coercive but not coerced*—"although the awareness of God is coercive to one who has it in the highest degree, no one is coerced into having it".[56] Thus, even if we have an "innate tendency to interpret [our] experience religiously", this can "readily be resisted or suppressed".[57]

This rather voluntarist account of faith leaves me somewhat uneasy. Does it not fall foul of criticisms similar to those voiced in my earlier discussion of freedom of belief? That is to say, can it not be argued (1) that the phenomenology of religious experience does not accord with Hick's account, and (2) that any experiences that are under our direct control are not cognitive (in the sense of veridical) "experiences"? But perhaps Hick is making a lesser claim, to the effect that we have an *indirect* control over our religious experiences. This interpretation may be seen as underlining the position already developed in this chapter. I should be willing to agree that faith interpreted as an experience, like faith as a set of attitudes, valuations or beliefs, *is* under the control of the human will, but only in an indirect and limited sense. Then

53. John Hick, *Arguments for the Existence of God* (London: Macmillan, 1970; New York: Herder and Herder, 1971), p. 112.

54. *Ibid.*, p. 114; compare John Hick, *An Interpretation of Religion* (New Haven: Yale University Press; Basingstoke: Macmillan, 1989), pp. 159-162 and 170 n. 9.

55. Hick, "Sceptics and Believers", in Hick, ed., *Faith and the Philosophers*, p. 246.

56. *Ibid.*, p. 247.

57. *Ibid.*, p. 248. Paul Helm makes some pertinent comments about Hick's account of "cognitive freedom" in his *The Varieties of Belief* (London: Allen & Unwin; New York: Humanities Press, 1973), pp. 147-154. See also Richard M. Gale, *On the Nature and Existence of God* (Cambridge: Cambridge University Press, 1991), p. 310.

the argument would still stand that we may be largely responsible for our actions but we are only very indirectly—and therefore very slightly—responsible for our faith.

I conclude that the major influences on a person's Christian religious experience lie outside that person's free control. Religious experience happens to us, affected more by influences impinging on us—including the forces of religious enculturation and intentional Christian religious education—than on the learner's own will.

FURTHER IMPLICATIONS FOR CHRISTIAN RELIGIOUS EDUCATION

It is for these reasons that the present writer cannot accept any theological or educational position that implies that religious believing or religious trusting is straightforwardly and directly culpable or meritorious. This rejection of at least some traditional accounts of human responsibility and God's judgment on it has profound implications for theology and for Christian religious education and evangelism, but I believe that it is inescapable. We just cannot help having the beliefs that we have and not having the beliefs we do not have, nor can we choose the religious attitudes and valuations that (together with those beliefs) constitute our faith or lack of it. At least we do not have *much* choice in these matters; for we can only freely choose our actions, and these actions have only an indirect effect on our believing, trusting and valuing.

We must now consider some further implications of this view for the activity of Christian religious education, broadly conceived.

Autonomy and Religion

Our discussion of the notion of freedom of assent should make us somewhat cautious of developing extreme notions of autonomy in education. R. F. Dearden has written of autonomy as the *self-determination* of what one is to think and do: a person being "autonomous" to the degree to which what that person thinks and does cannot be explained without reference to his or her own activity of mind, that is to say his or her "own choices, deliberations, decisions, reflections, judgments, plannings or reasonings".[58] This sort of autonomy excludes both (a) outward compulsion or conditioning in which other people manipulate a person's thoughts or actions,[59] and (b) addictions, psychoses or other factors internal to a person but "external to" that person's activity of mind. Dearden accepts that we do not believe things deliberately, but he does not seem to think that this fact infringes this notion of self-governing autonomy: "it is we who determine what to think or do, even if we

---

58. Dearden, "Autonomy and Education", p. 63. For a more qualified account see R. F. Dearden, "Autonomy and Intellectual Education", in his *Theory and Practice in Education* (London: Routledge & Kegan Paul, 1984).

59. On manipulation see Antony Flew, "A Rational Animal", in J. R. Smythies, ed., *Brain and Mind* (London: Routledge & Kegan Paul, 1965), pp. 118-121, 135; and below note 92.

determine it by reference to independent criteria".[60]

In educational procedures such a stress on intellectual self-confidence or autonomy is usually analyzed in terms of "asking for *reasons* as to what I ought to do, and taking it for granted that it is I who will decide the merits of the answers"; "being oneself"; "testing truth for oneself";[61] thinking for oneself,[62] etc. (See above Chapters 4 and 5.) Central to the idea of autonomy, therefore, which philosophers of education usually consider to be a good thing, is the notion of individual learners forming beliefs and making judgments for themselves on criteria that they themselves have accepted (and doing this in a *self*-critical way by keeping all these criteria under review), and acting on their decisions.[63] *A properly qualified notion of autonomy*, compatible with a denial of a direct freedom of belief, may happily embrace such phraseology. But there is a danger that the use of the language of decision and choice can easily produce an account in which a more radical freedom of belief is implied, if not directly stated.[64]   ·

It has become something of a liberal educationist's shibboleth that the autonomous person chooses for herself/himself.[65] In its original Kantian usage, "autonomy" was a feature of the will of a ("self-determined") person whose principles of action were self-originating and self-imposed. These rules were legislated by that person's own reason—rather than imposed by

---

60. Dearden, "Autonomy and Education", pp. 68-69. In a later article Dearden appears to adopt the position of indirect volitionalism, arguing that there is an ethic of belief with reference to the control we have over "giving weight to evidence or argument . . . perhaps in the face of social pressures, or the pull of one's wishes, desires and emotions". Dearden, "Education and the Ethics of Belief", in his *Theory and Practice in Education*, p. 103.

61. R. F. Dearden, *The Philosophy of Primary Education* (London: Routledge & Kegan Paul; New York: Humanities Press, 1968), pp. 46, 52-53, 57; compare p. 73. See also R. S. Peters, "The Justification of Education", in R. S. Peters, ed., *The Philosophy of Education* (London: Oxford University Press, 1973), p. 257.

62. John M. Hull, *What Prevents Christian Adults from Learning?* (London: SCM, 1985), p. 16.

63. Derek C. Meakin, "The Justification of Religious Education", *British Journal of Religious Education* 2: 2 (1979), p. 53; see also John Wilson, *Preface to the Philosophy of Education* (London: Routledge & Kegan Paul, 1979), p. 101; Harvey Siegel, "Indoctrination and Education", in Ben Spiecker and Roger Straughan, eds., *Freedom and Indoctrination in Education* (London and New York: Cassell, 1991), p. 37.

64. According to James Fowler, at the faith stage that he calls "Individuative-Reflective Faith" there is a "critical choosing of one's beliefs, values, and commitments". Fowler, *Becoming Adult, Becoming Christian* (San Francisco: Harper & Row, 1984), p. 62. It is worth mentioning here, in a book that often attempts a sort of dialogue between philosophy and psychology, that psychologists tend to use the word "choice" in a way that a philosopher would not, to describe a situation where people may do one of several different things, without any implication of freedom. See George Mandler and William Kessen in Stuart C. Brown, ed., *Philosophy of Psychology* (London: Macmillan; New York: Barnes & Noble, 1974), p. 342 and ch. 16 *passim*. See also the criticisms by Alan R. White and Les Holborrow, in *ibid.*, pp. 329-330, 332-333.

65. R. S. Peters, "Education and Human Development", in Dearden *et al.*, eds., *Education and Reason*, p. 122.

God, other people, or by inclinations essentially "other" than his or her own rational self.[66] In both its moral and intellectual designations, then, autonomy comes down to *personal choice*. Our discussion of the role of freedom in believing, however, suggests that in that phrase we should stress "personal", rather than "choice". The reason being, of course, that, at least in the case of intellectual autonomy—the "autonomy of belief"—the choice is by no means wholly a voluntary one. This "choice" is very largely forced upon us. To use the language of choice to refer to this situation, therefore, is to operate with a rather Pickwickian notion of choice. It is not, or at least not directly, a matter of our *deciding* to believe. Autonomy here can mean no more than that it is the *real I*, not-less-than-I, who comes to have a belief; and who perhaps exercises choice only at the level of choosing to examine the evidence. We may choose our path to belief; we cannot directly choose our beliefs.

It is certainly true that my authentic self may properly be said to include "having a mind of my own". This is to be understood, however, not in the sense of my choosing my beliefs, but of my choosing to perform the activity of thinking critically about my beliefs—and thus partly in terms of my capacity for the critical self-assessment of my beliefs.[67] I have argued in Chapters 4 and 5 that *in so far as I possess such a capacity, and value it*, I am not being treated fully as a person (and therefore autonomously)—by myself or by others—when my beliefs are produced or sustained in ways that bypass or disable this element. The same qualification applies to other learners also. This much can be said. In this sense autonomy is "part of what it means to be a person".[68] But we must beware of going further by giving an account of autonomy that construes it as incorporating an untrammeled cognitive freedom. That is not a possible account of what it is to believe, and therefore to know, anything; and it presents us with an unrealistic, because over-rationalistic, image of what it is to be human. Christian religious educators in particular must be very wary of unqualified rhetoric about educational autonomy, as should those engaged in a critique of secular educational theory and practice.

These comments should be taken together with the arguments presented in Chapter 5 for a *qualified* role for critical thinking and critical education. Here my concerns meet, to some extent, the criticisms that Elmer Thiessen

---

66. Immanuel Kant, *Groundwork of the Metaphysic of Morals*, ch. II; compare H. B. Acton, *Kant's Moral Philosophy* (London: Macmillan; New York: St. Martin's Press, 1970), pp. 39-44.

67. Thinking in this sense is something that a person can choose to do or not to do. "It is the *result* of this process which is not under the agent's control." R. S. Downie, "On Having a Mind of One's Own", in Roger Straughan and John Wilson, eds., *Philosophers on Education* (Basingstoke: Macmillan, 1987), p. 89. Compare John Kleinig, *Philosophical Issues in Education* (London: Croom Helm; New York: St. Martin's Press, 1982), ch. 6; and above Chapters 4 and 5.

68. Meakin, "The Justification of Religious Education", p. 54. It is also, perhaps, an expression of one's "core self"—see Arnold S. Kaufman in James F. Doyle, ed., *Educational Judgments* (London: Routledge & Kegan Paul, 1973), pp. 47-48.

makes of claims in the educational literature about the possibility and desirability of a full rational autonomy—an absolute independence of mind and unrestricted critical competence. He dismisses this as a romanticized, unrealistic ideal; adopting in its place Lawrence Haworth's account of normal rational autonomy or "critical competence"—a tradition-bound autonomy that sets realistic limits to its demands for critical reflection. Haworth, drawing on S. I. Benn, writes of the critical thinking that sets us free as "a process of examining the basis for our values and beliefs from a perspective that takes for granted the other values and beliefs we acquired as a result of growing up within a determinate culture".[69] Thiessen claims that this normal autonomy is a Christian value, whereas complete independence or perfect rationality is not even a human possibility.[70] Interestingly enough, the psychologist of religion Heije Faber uses the same phrase—"normal autonomy"—to mark his recognition, from a rather different perspective, that self-confidence and creativity can only properly develop (that is develop without turning into "perverted self-justification" and "desperate self-assertion") on the foundation of a more passive and dependent basic trust. Despite the rhetoric of some existentialist thinkers, autonomy, independence, individuality, nonconformity and self-confidence can only properly develop psychologically within the framework of, and in union with, heteronomy, dependence, communality, conformity and confidence in others. Here again the issue of autonomy is situated in the context of the balance between formative education and critical education (see above Chapter 5). A heavy qualification of the place of independence and autonomy in a properly human—and Christian—understanding of maturity and adulthood is to be found in the work of a variety of religious educators.[71]

---

69. Lawrence Haworth, *Autonomy: An Essay in Philosophical Psychology and Ethics* (New Haven: Yale University Press, 1986), pp. 3-4. See also *ibid.*, chs. 2, 11 and 12; S. I. Benn, "Freedom, Autonomy and the Concept of a Person", *Proceedings of the Aristotelian Society* N.S. 77 (1975/76), pp. 126-127. Compare John White, "The Justification of Autonomy as an Educational Aim", in Spiecker and Straughan, eds., *Freedom and Indoctrination in Education*, p. 85. A valuable critical elucidation of liberal conceptions of autonomy is to be found in Richard Lindley, *Autonomy* (London: Macmillan Education; Atlantic Highlands, N.J.: Humanities Press, 1986).

70. See Elmer J. Thiessen, *Teaching for Commitment: Liberal Education, Indoctrination and Christian Nurture* (Montreal: McGill-Queen's University Press; Leominster, England: Fowler Wright, 1993), ch. 5. I am grateful to Thiessen for the opportunity to see an early version of this excellent text and to discuss it with him. For a properly qualified notion of autonomy see also Leon McKenzie, *Adult Education and Worldview Construction* (Malabar, Fla.: Krieger, 1991), pp. 68-69.

71. For Faber's understanding of "normal autonomy" see Heije Faber, *Psychology of Religion*, trans. Margaret Kohl (Philadelphia: Westminster, 1975; London: SCM, 1976), pp. 201-202, 209-210, 217. For a critique by religious educators of the notion of maturity in terms of "autonomous independent man", see Gabriel Moran, *Education Toward Adulthood* (New York: Paulist, 1979), ch. 2; Jeff Astley, "Growing into Christ", in Jeff Astley and David Day, eds., *The Contours of Christian Education* (Great Wakering, England: McCrimmon, 1992), ch. 21. The individualism of much contemporary discussion of autonomy is also criticized by John Kleinig in his "Moral Education and the Nature of Morality", *Journal of Christian*

At this point it is relevant to observe that there are analytic philosophers who are willing to call into question those who appeal too simplistically to autonomy as a (or the) formal criterion of *morality*. Thus Anthony Quinton writes that "this criterion . . . appears to dress up a particular moral taste as neutral analysis". No doubt, he adds, there is something "supine and feeble, especially in a rapidly changing world, in the uncritical absorption of conventional moral opinions". But virtue by and large "consists of adherence to the rules one actually has, not in having rules arrived at in a particularly critical and enterprising way". Even where the rules themselves are morally intolerable, as in the case of the Nazi fanatic, this is "because of their content rather than their mode of acceptance". Like science, Quinton argues, morality is mainly taken on authority. Science and morality are social products; "all moral agents are largely consumers", beneficiaries of the moral innovations of others.[72] Educators, especially Christian religious educators, need not be ashamed of recognizing that many of our moral insights have this sort of origin. Heteronomy—and formative education—is not necessarily always a bad thing (again see Chapter 5 above).

Religious Commitment

Those who are concerned with teaching about religion in secular education make much of the distinction between the aims and objectives of this activity and those of Christian religious education. Such a distinction often revolves around the notion of religious commitment. Thus intentional Christian religious education, and cognate terms, have been defined (in contrast to teaching about Christianity) as "the teaching activity which intends to foster or deepen the commitment of those who are already believers or already inside the religious community".[73]

The word "commitment" is defined by the dictionaries as an act of binding oneself to a certain course of action. It is an act of involving and pledging oneself—especially in terms of an "engagement or involvement that restricts freedom of action". We speak, it may be noted, of committing people to prison. Such language tends to make us think of religious commit-

---

Education 72 (1981), pp. 40-45. Similarly some of those who write of religious conversion as, or involving, "self-transcendence" construe this as a surrender not of "oneself or one's personal moral autonomy", but of "one's illusion of absolute autonomy". Walter Conn, *Christian Conversion* (Mahwah, N.J.: Paulist, 1986), p. 31, compare pp. 22-24.

72. Anthony Quinton, *The Nature of Things* (London: Routledge & Kegan Paul, 1973), pp. 379-380. Compare A. H. Halsey, "On Methods and Morals", in Mark Abrams *et al.*, *Values and Social Change in Britain* (Basingstoke: Macmillan, 1985), p. 7. See below Chapter 9.

73. John M. Hull, *Studies in Religion and Education* (Lewes, England: Falmer, 1984), pp. 176-177. This is Hull's definition of "religious nurture", which for Hull is a process of education. Iris V. Cully, for whom nurture (broadly enculturation) is distinguished from education and instruction, also links it specifically with the purpose of engendering commitment. Iris V. Cully, "Christian Education: Instruction or Nurture?", *Religious Education* 62 (1967). See also Charles Melchert, "The Future of Religious Education: Commitment in Religion and Education", in Gloria Durka and Joanmarie Smith, eds., *Emerging Issues in Religious Education* (New York: Paulist, 1976).

ments primarily as involvement in ("commitment to") certain types of *overt behavior* (praying, giving alms etc.).[74] Existentialist and Wittgensteinian accounts of religion often seem to regard it solely as a commitment to a way of life. More traditional accounts of religion, however, argue that such existential commitments presupposes a commitment to certain theological *beliefs*.[75] We may speak in addition of commitment to religious *attitudes*.[76]

Shivesh Chandra Thakur defines the personal commitment that is distinctive of religion as being on three distinct, but related, levels: belief-commitments, attitude-commitments and action-commitments. On this account the language of "commitment to" is regarded as a longhand (or shorthand?) for people actually having religious beliefs and attitudes and performing religious actions. *Belief-commitments* are "beliefs-that" about God, heaven, nirvana, the Qur'ān etc. *Attitude-commitments* are sometimes regarded as following from these, although others regard them as more fundamental. Attitude-commitments include love of neighbor, together with moral and religious beliefs-in such as reverence for life and devotion to God. These account for the emotional tone that surrounds religious beliefs and practices. The third grouping, *action-commitments*, comprise the way of life of a religion—including its moral commitments (actions), ritual practices and other overt behaviors.[77] Thakur's account, which I follow here, is similar to the multidimensional account of religious commitment (in its "broadest possible conception") given by Rodney Stark and Charles Y. Glock, who discern five "aspect[s] of religious commitment":

(1) *the belief dimension* ("a certain theological outlook", maintaining "some set of beliefs");

(2) *religious practice* (ritual and devotion);

(3) *the experience dimension* (religious experiences etc.);

(4) *the knowledge dimension* (knowledge of beliefs, practices, scriptures and traditions); and

---

74. See *The Concise Oxford English Dictionary* (London: Oxford University Press, 1976), p. 203. Other personal commitments may be analogous to religious commitment in depth, but not in breadth or range—compare Ian T. Ramsey, *Religious Language* (London: SCM, 1957), pp. 28-37.

75. Brümmer, *Theology and Philosophical Inquiry*, pp. 211-213 and Trigg, *Reason and Commitment*, ch. 3. Compare also John Macquarrie, *The Faith of the People of God: A Lay Theology* (London: SCM; New York: Scribner's, 1972), p. 11, and Robert Jackson, "Commitment and the Teaching of World Religions", in Robert Jackson, ed., *Approaching World Religions* (London: Murray, 1982), p. 93. See also Chapter 6 above.

76. John Sealey, *Religious Education: Philosophical Perspectives* (London: Allen & Unwin, 1985), p. 10.

77. Shidesh Chandra Thakur, *Religion and Rational Choice* (London: Macmillan; Totowa, N.J.: Barnes & Noble, 1981), pp. 28-32, compare pp. 102-103. Belief-commitments (of a persistent nature) have been termed "convictions": see James Wm. McClendon, Jr., and James M. Smith, *Understanding Religious Convictions* (Notre Dame, Ind.: University of Notre Dame Press, 1975), pp. 7-8. Willem Zuurdeeg's account of "convictions" (he calls them "persuasions"), however, treats them as closer to attitude-commitments: see Willem F. Zuurdeeg, *An Analytical Philosophy of Religion* (New York: Abingdon, 1958; London: Allen & Unwin, 1959), ch. 1.

(5) *the consequences dimension* (effects of religion in everyday life and relationships, and in other activities).[78]
Other social scientists, however, define commitment more narrowly as an affective element.[79]

Consonant with my earlier claims to the effect that our beliefs and attitudes/emotions are not freely chosen by us in the way that at least some of our actions may be said to be, I would contend that even this broader language of commitment cannot be taken always to imply a freely chosen act. To some extent *we* choose and make action-commitments, but belief-commitments and attitude-commitments largely happen to us. We (eventually) find ourselves with them. It is only when our action-commitments *indirectly* impinge on the automatic processes that form our beliefs and attitudes that we can claim to have had any say in these cognitive and affective areas, and this sort of "intervention into ourselves" is fairly limited both in scope and effect. "Commitment" is perhaps an inappropriate word to use in analyzing religion if its etymology misleads us into treating all commitments as acts of the will over which we have direct control.

Certainly many commentators on religious education write rather too easily about people becoming "religiously committed" by choosing a religion

---

78. Rodney Stark and Charles Y. Glock, "Dimensions of Religious Commitment", reprinted in Roland Robertson, ed., *Sociology of Religion* (Harmondsworth, England: Penguin, 1969), pp. 253-261. Some commentators label this an analysis of "lived religion" or "religious living". See James Michael Lee, *The Shape of Religious Instruction* (Birmingham, Ala.: Religious Education Press, 1971), p. 11; Howard William Burgess, *An Invitation to Religious Education* (Birmingham, Ala.: Religious Education Press, 1975), p. 132. John M. Finney discerns similar "dimensions of religious commitment": i.e. "ritual commitment", "knowledge commitment", "experiential commitment", "belief commitment" and "devotional commitment". John M. Finney, "A Theory of Religious Commitment", *Sociological Analysis* 39 (1978).

79. See Hans Mol, *Identity and the Sacred: A Sketch of a New Social-Scientific Theory of Religion* (New York: Free Press, 1977), p. 216; Marie Cornwall and Stan L. Albrecht, "The Dimensions of Religiosity: A Conceptual Model with an Empirical Test", *Review of Religious Research* 27: 3 (1986), pp. 227, 229. Lee distinguishes between just having beliefs and attitudes (and performing actions), and being committed to them. Here commitment is "a feeling, a valuing . . . an affective process" that we direct towards our beliefs, attitudes and actions, or which accompanies them. James Michael Lee, *The Content of Religious Instruction* (Birmingham, Ala.: Religious Education Press, 1985), p. 133. We may compare such accounts with the Krathwohl Taxonomy where commitment is described as an intense form of conviction or involvement, a type of valuing in the affective domain. David R. Krathwohl *et al.*, *Taxonomy of Educational Objectives: the Classification of Educational Goals. Handbook II: Affective Domain* (New York: McKay; London: Longmans, 1964), pp. 149-150. This construal fits the notion of commitment to (loyalty to or faith in) a value. But religious commitment is a term that is used with a wider meaning. Those social scientists who write of commitment as "an attachment" to, for example, "a consistent line of activity", or as a "constraint of behavior", understand it more in its active sense of binding, joining or fastening on to something, than in terms of an affection or devotion. Compare Howard S. Becker, "Notes on the Concept of Commitment", *American Journal of Sociology* 66: 1 (1960). Robert Towler (following Gerhard Lenski) distinguished *associational commitment* (belonging to a church as to any club or association) and *communal commitment* (a "more total" commitment involving, for example,

or an ultimate meaning system for themselves.[80] In the area of religious beliefs and attitudes this is more of a "forced choice" than a "free" one. Most people do not in fact choose their religion, or at least not much of it. And this is simply because most religious belief- and attitude-commitments, while undeniably "owned" by people and therefore properly "theirs", are not—at least not directly—chosen or created by them.

The same may be said, of course, of more secular commitments. But religion *is* a special case. It is a special case because its belief-commitments are so wide ranging and all absorbing, and so closely tied to attitude- and action-commitments. It is a special case because its attitude-commitments well up from the very depths of what is most distinctly human about us; for religion gives us meaning, and expresses and evokes our passions (see Chapter 6). On the whole we "cannot help ourselves" in religion. Theologians who stress either God's initiative in revelation (and our passive role in its reception), or the divine prevenience in bestowing the gift of grace, should have no difficulty with these claims; nor should anyone who embraces a religious epistemology that has taken seriously an analysis of the notion of belief and the phenomenology of religious knowledge. It is the position that best fits a proper understanding of (analysis of) religion. I would go further and argue that to "choose a religion" is almost a contradiction in terms: it is *not* to be religious. Truly to believe in—as really to love—a person, or ideal or Faith is to be overtaken by it.

---

a tendency to form relationships only within one's church). He places the former in the category of "practice". Robert Towler, *Homo Religiosus* (London: Constable, 1974), pp. 129-130. In everyday parlance a focus on activity, particularly evangelistic, pastoral and prophetic activity, is often said to characterize "committed" Christians—a phrase that has been described as "the modern and revealing substitute for 'devout' Christians". John Mahoney, "Theological and Pastoral Reflections", in Mark Abrams *et al.*, *Values and Social Change in Britain*, p. 263.

80. See H. S. Elliott, *Can Religious Education be Christian?* (New York: Macmillan, 1940), p. 315; James D. Smart, *The Teaching Ministry of the Church* (Philadelphia: Westminster, 1954), p. 167; J. Gordon Chamberlin, *Freedom and Faith* (Philadelphia: Westminster, 1965), p. 155; Schools Council, *Humanities for the Young School Leaver: An Approach through Religious Education* (London: Evans/Methuen, 1969), p. 11; Brenda Watson, *Education and Belief* (Oxford: Blackwell, 1987), p. 48; V. Bailey Gillespie, *The Experience of Faith* (Birmingham, Ala.: Religious Education Press, 1988), pp. 84-86, 130-134. Despite his more sophisticated notion of what is involved in religious choice, Edward Hulmes's stress on "choosing sides" and "education in choosing" in religious education still seems to put too much stress on an individual's free act of commitment. Edward Hulmes, *Commitment and Neutrality in Religious Education* (London: Chapman, 1979), pp. 32-34, 82, 103, but also p. 64; Edward Hulmes, "The Education of Commitment", in J. G. Priestley, ed., *Religion, Spirituality and Schools* (Exeter: University of Exeter School of Education, 1982), p. 60 and *passim*; and Edward Hulmes, "A Response" to "Openness and Commitment", *Occasional Papers* 20 (Oxford: Farmington Institute, 1985). Similar criticisms apply to Michael Grimmitt's account of conscious "choosing between beliefs": Michael Grimmitt, *Religious Education and Human Development* (Great Wakering, England: McCrimmon, 1987), pp. 81-92. See also Gabriel Moran, *Design for Religion* (New York: Herder and Herder, 1970; London: Search Press, 1971), p. 2.

Christian religious education, however critical and reflective it be, may not describe itself as "successful" unless it results in such commitment. This is not a matter of "preparing for" or "allowing" Christian commitment as a later, possible, future consequence; but of commitment as an essential outcome and aim of any activity that is properly to be described as Christian religious education, and an intrinsic part of its substantive content and its structural content (procedure). Education for religious commitment is education that is intentionally targeted to teaching (facilitating) religious commitment. Both proponents and critics of such a view of Christian religious education need to reflect, in the ways suggested above, on the extent to which this does, and does not, allow for the freedom of the Christian learner.

Critical Education Revisited

But where will the liberal educationists find a place for their much vaunted "rationality" in this account? Are the doors to be opened to any and every device for engendering a passionate faith? *Après cela le déluge?* By no means. Such thin-end-of-the-wedge arguments are invariably invalid. We must identify instead a proper, qualified, and cautiously stated role for the exercise of rationality in religious belief and religious education.

The fact that we do not choose our beliefs does not mean that we cannot change our beliefs, nor that they may not appropriately be subjected to critical appraisal. Vincent Brümmer, who agrees that "it is not possible to choose whether or not to become convinced by the evidence", reminds us that it is possible to choose whether to consider or ignore such evidence.[81] These acts are open to us, and therefore may properly be prescribed or proscribed. Being rational, he argues, is a matter of adopting "an open and critical attitude towards those beliefs which we have".[82] (We recall that Price wrote of assent as the taking up of an attitude towards a proposition.) I do not accept that all attitudes, or all aspects of every attitude, are under the control of the will. But an attitude is, or includes, a disposition to act in a certain manner,[83] and we may certainly be said—on occasions—(to decide) to adopt the policy of behaving in a certain manner. Thus we may decide to look at, and look for, evidence that conflicts with the beliefs that we hold. We may search for falsifying evidence. If that is what it means to be "open-minded" and "rational", then we can decide to be rational.

I would be less happy, however, with a claim that we are free to choose whether or not to adopt a critical attitude either in the sense of a tentative, cautious view of our own beliefs, or as a pro-attitude towards "open", "critical" or "rational" believing in general (see Chapter 5). These seem to be affective elements of the person, and we do not directly choose our feelings (see Chapter 9). Critical education, in order to be successful, does not only need to give its learners the choice of adopting critical enquiry as a policy. It

81. Brümmer, *Theology and Philosophical Inquiry*, p. 157.
82. *Ibid.*, p. 194.
83. *Ibid.*, p. 104.

needs *to make them* feel tentative about their beliefs (and the advisability of this across the epistemic board is in doubt, as we saw in Chapters 4 and 5). It needs also *to evoke in them* a desire for critical exploration and critical discovery—a love of criticism. As we saw in Chapter 5, "critical rationality" is based as much on an affective stance as is any other way of life. John Haught has written of the "desire to know"—which is detached and disinterested, but not passionless or lifeless—as "the most fervent orientation in many people's lives".[84] In my experience the "disinterested love of truth" (an attraction uninfluenced by what is to the learner's own advantage and self-interest) is most likely to be exemplified by those with a real "interest" in it (in the other sense of "interest": i.e. concern, curiosity). Dispassionate (=impartial) enquiry, in so far as it is a possible and worthwhile goal, is best pursued by those with a passion for it. Critical education needs to form such a concern and such a passion. Critical education, therefore, including critical Christian religious education, needs to be formative to some extent in order to be successful.

Responsibility in Believing and Responsibility in Christian Religious Education

Indirect volitionalism implies that we have an indirect responsibility for our beliefs, not that we have no responsibility at all for them. On such a view it is possible to argue for a sort of ethics of belief, understood as a moral—or at least a prudential—requirement that we should disinterestedly seek the truth and allow the evidence full sway over our beliefs. There may be limits to such a requirement, and some of these limits may be relevant to the case of religious belief; but we surely have to begin with a presumption in its favor. On prudential and utilitarian grounds alone, one should need a lot of persuading before advocating alternative educational strategies in many areas of belief.[85] But there *are* hard cases, and "evidence" is not a neutral term. So we must be cautious here too about succumbing to educational rhetoric that will blind us to the individual and social necessity of the deep inculcation of many beliefs (see Chapter 4 and 5). The fact remains, however, that learners are only responsible indirectly for their beliefs, in that—and in so far as—they are (partly) directly responsible for choosing among the pathways that lead them to their beliefs.

One recurring problem in practical Christianity is that created by our not distinguishing the moral and spiritual issues in our knowledge of God from the epistemological ones. I should indeed be expected to trust my spouse, children, friends and colleagues (to a greater or lesser extent) to keep their promises and to behave in a certain manner. But when the believer claims to

---

84. John F. Haught, *Religion and Self Acceptance* (Washington, D.C.: University Press of America, 1980), pp. 25-26.

85. Pojman, for one, contends that "instances of justified voliting" probably are exceedingly rare (*Religious Belief and the Will*, p. 192). He is referring here to getting oneself to believe something (indirectly) where we discern that the evidence alone does not warrant it.

extend such a trust to *God*, it is not always recognized that an epistemological factor has been introduced into the notion of trust (or "faith"). I am now "trusting God *to exist*"—and to have such and such a character, and to have revealed these truths about himself—as well as myself possessing the attitudes and performing the actions that would be appropriate to such a God if he did exist. Christians of many ages and temperaments have at some time suffered guilt for their lack of meritorious "moral trust" (i.e. actively trusting God to be good: an *action* based on a *belief-in*), when their real problem has been a lack of nonmeritorious "epistemological trust" (i.e. "trusting God to exist": essentially a *belief-that*). Christian religious educators need to be aware of this problem, and of their own responsibility for explaining its nature and easing their learners' pain in this area. They should certainly be taking care not to exacerbate the situation.[86]

In his paper on "The Virtue of Faith",[87] however, Robert Merrihew Adams argues that various cognitive errors are morally culpable ("cognitive sins"), even where such cognitive failings are involuntary. He gives as examples (1) false ethical beliefs which may be the root of a blameworthy action; (2) negligent harmful false beliefs that the subject could have avoided by an indirect exercise of the will; and (3) false beliefs associated with (involuntary) bad desires and motives. Category (2) seems to me to be uncontroversial, but the other two categories are more difficult. In what sense can such beliefs be culpable if they are involuntary? Adams, a Christian, speaks of them as "sins". But the movement of his discussion is in the direction of claiming rather that they are just bad beliefs, errors or failures. If they *are* bad, then it would be better for us to be without them, and proper for us to wish to be rid of them—to "repent" of them. It may also be proper for us to be (humanly) blamed for them, for blame is a social institution designed partly to change people for the better; as such it "works" even on involuntary beliefs. But the language of sin is surely not useful here, for sin marks an action culpable before God, one that God will hold against us. "Sin" is not the right word, although the language of *fault* is appropriate.

Perhaps we make too much of responsibility, freedom and choice over beliefs *because* of a theistic framework and a particular theological heritage. Annette Baier's perceptive comments should give us pause:

---

86. The problem is exacerbated by comments like the following: "The only serious reproach that either believer or unbeliever may justly direct to the skeptic is that of declining to make up his mind in one direction or the other—that is, a moral rather than an intellectual reproach". Geddes MacGregor, "Doubt and Belief", in Mircea Eliade, ed., *The Encyclopedia of Religion*, Vol. 4 (New York: Macmillan; London: Collier Macmillan, 1987), p. 425. Compare R. W. Hepburn, "Attitudes to Evidence and Argument in the Field of Religion", in Straughan and Wilson, eds., *Philosophers on Education*, pp. 144-145 and Basil Mitchell, *The Justification of Religious Belief* (London: Macmillan, 1973; New York: Seabury, 1974), pp. 139-142. See note 91 below.

87. Reprinted in Robert Merrihew Adams, *The Virtue of Faith* (New York: Oxford University Press, 1987), ch. 1.

Belief, like feeling, is usually something which responds to reasons without any need or room for choice on our part, yet which may be criticized as unreasonable. We are thought to be at fault when our beliefs are not adequately backed by reasons, and may be at fault when our feelings are out of line with the reasons we have for feeling, just as we are usually at fault when our actions lack good enough reasons, even though we don't decide what to believe, nor what to feel, in the way we can decide what to do. The question "Am I at fault?" is not the same as the question "Did I decide wrongly?" and *only divines in disguise suppose that discernment of faults and vices is the same as judging who deserves what punishment.* We criticize people for their credulity, for their stupidity, for their sentimentality, for their hardness of heart, without any implied suggestion that they could, at will, have avoided those faults. So it is important to see that the spontaneity of feeling no more exempts feelings from criticism as appropriate or inappropriate, reasonable or unreasonable, rational or irrational, than the spontaneity of belief exempts them from such criticism.[88]

"Moral assessment", John Kincullen has said, "is not oriented toward retribution". Moral assessment has various other purposes, "for which we may need to decide what moral qualities a person has, but not whether they are innate, accidental or deliberately acquired".[89]

But Adams's paper is worth studying further, for he later gives an account of what is and what is not a part of "the sin of unbelief". "I think the sin of unbelief always involves rejection of something God has said to the sinner. Simply not believing that God exists is not the sin of unbelief, if God has never spoken to you. . . . . It is not a refusal to assent intellectually to theological truths, but a failure to trust in truths to which we do assent."[90] Adams contends

---

88. Annette Baier, *Postures of the Mind: Essays on Mind and Morals* (London: Methuen; Minneapolis: University of Minnesota Press, 1985), p. 110, my italics. But compare Alston, *Epistemic Justification*, pp. 118, 152 and see below Chapter 9. Stuart Brown regards the claim to a freedom of belief as incorporating a confusion "due to mismodelling belief upon action". He writes that it is true that if we never exercised options in what we did we would not be free in our actions, but neither would we be accountable. "It is also true that if we are to be answerable for what we have done we must have had the option of doing something else. But that is not true of belief. There is no place in talk about belief for the kind of contrast which is needed if a 'free-will' problem is to arise for it." Stuart Brown, *Religious Belief* (Milton Keynes, England: Open University Press, 1973), p. 56. We may note that even a deterministic philosopher like J. J. C. Smart is willing to accept the application of the notions of praise and blame to *human actions* as essentially "grading" activities, while he rejects the idea of judging *people* because that is dependent on a metaphysics of free will. J. J. C. Smart, "Free-will, Praise and Blame", *Mind* 70: 279 (1961); compare also L. C. Holborrow, "Blame, Praise and Credit", *Proceedings of the Aristotelian Society* N.S. 72 (1971).

89. John Kilcullen, *Sincerity and Truth: Essays on Arnauld, Bayle and Toleration* (Oxford: Clarendon, 1988), pp. 201-202. See also William Kneale, "The Responsibility of Criminals", in James Rachels, ed., *Moral Problems* (New York: Harper & Row, 1971), pp. 245-248.

90. Adams, *The Virtue of Faith*, pp. 16-17. Philosophers sometimes distinguished "unbelief" (lack of trust) from "disbelief" (cognitive doubt).

that "reasons to doubt other people's trustworthiness should sometimes be totally ignored", and "hedging our bets" on God's goodness is always a sin of unbelief (usually motivated by fear and our desire for control).[91] Although I am not totally clear as to where *Adams* is drawing the limits of the sin of unbelief, his argument seems to allow us to continue to distinguish nonculpable epistemological problems of belief (Does God exist? Has he spoken to me? What did he say?) from the moral/spiritual problem of culpably not trusting—or, better, not actively trusting—a God whose existence and revelation is accepted by the believer. Christian religious educators need to acknowledge that distinction.

Whose fault?

If we were to adopt a stronger view of freedom of belief, we might argue that the educator's responsibility is diminished to the extent that the learner's responsibility for her own beliefs increases. But on the view taken in this chapter, it would appear that the beliefs that a person ends up with are largely outside her control. That seems to put them more in the control of those who structure, facilitate and enable her learning. In Christian religious education these are her Christian religious educators, a phrase that is to be understood very broadly as including any person who affects her Christian learning, at least intentionally. To recognize that power and responsibility over other people's beliefs is not to advocate or imply an *improper* control, or any diminishment of the learner's "autonomy". It is, rather, to be realistic about what happens in the real world; and what cannot happen. To call all such facilitated-learning "manipulation", and to deny it the title "education", would be to collapse a distinction well worth preserving, and to end up with a vanishingly small constituency of proper educators and the properly educated. In a word, it would be very silly.[92]

---

91. *Ibid.*, pp. 18-20. According to Alan Goldman: "One *morally ought* to believe a principle if believing it is morally best according to moral criteria implicit in one's other beliefs. One *epistemically ought* to believe it if it entails some beliefs in that framework and is counterexemplified by none." Alan H. Goldman, *Moral Knowledge* (London: Routledge, 1988), p. 165, my italics.

92. We must be ever wary of pejorative educational words like "manipulation". The use of these words to mark certain processes often depends more on the speaker's evaluation of the result of the process than on the nature of the process itself. "The difference between 'cultivation' and 'manipulation' may be somewhat subtle, hinging on whether or not approval is given to a stipulated goal." Walter Feinberg, *Reason and Rhetoric* (New York: Wiley, 1975), p. 241. It is because people are free, unlike things and machines, that the word "manipulation" takes on a morally pernicious meaning when applied to them. Feinberg writes that when a person resists attempts to be shaped in one way or another it is because that person has already chosen an end that he or she finds incompatible with these attempts. To respect someone's choice means that, "in the absence of overwhelming reasons to the contrary", any attempt to move that person from one state to another should be "above board" and should appeal to his or her "own capacity for insight and reason" (*ibid.*, p. 242). Such a definition would not seem to be applicable to very young children (and some other learners), and needs to be developed by a fuller account of what constitutes "insight and reason". But it does help us to

Christian religious educators, indeed all educators, need to recognize their responsibility for the beliefs of those in their charge. They share that responsibility with nature and society and God, and therefore we should not blame them for everything that learners learn and believers believe. But they cannot slough off that responsibility onto the shoulders even of their adult "students" by a misapplication of the educational imperative "take responsibility for your own learning". That is not to say that learners do not have their own responsibilities. Those who emphasize the importance of human freedom and responsibility will want to say that Christian religious education does not take that freedom and responsibility away from the Christian learner. If the learner retains some freedom over against the pressures of the environment, including her learning environment, then it is possible for her *to some extent* to resist (or to open herself up to) the influences of Christian religious education. Thus she can exercise her freedom in the *indirect* ways that people can affect their own beliefs, attitudes and dispositions. To this extent her responsibility remains, and perhaps her exercise of it is to be judged not so much by its effects as by the quality and direction of its striving.

One further point: Christian religious education produces Christian learning, and Christian learning produces Christians (in the sense of people with the Christian attributes). Since we regard these outcomes as good things (for these attributes are themselves good), then we can praise or blame, rejoice or express dismay at the attributes of the learner and the Christian religious educator's role in producing them. But this is *not* the same as putting ourselves in the position that only God could occupy, and judging a Christian learner's, or a religious educator's, moral or spiritual ultimate worth. Not even divines in—and out of—disguise (see p. 215) should do that. "Judgment is mine", says the Lord.

FREEDOM OF BELIEF OR FREEDOM FOR BELIEF?

The thesis that we have only an indirect control over our beliefs, and are therefore not directly responsible for the beliefs that we have, may be resisted by those influenced by political as well as theological assumptions. Freedom is much valued in liberal democracies as a sociopolitical good, and this freedom is often thought of as including "freedom of worship" and indeed "freedom of religious belief". When these concepts are analyzed, however, both will be seen as examples of an *outer freedom*—i.e. the freedom

---

see that it is, at least in part, a fact about the (adult?) learner—about the sort of person the learner wishes to be and to become—that is the criterion that distinguishes unacceptable manipulation from acceptable forms of educational change. This is similar to the position we adopted on indoctrination and critical education (see above Chapters 4 and 5). To manipulate is to change people *against their will and desires*. But we should note that making people more critical ("more rational") could *also* fall under this definition, at least after they have achieved a certain amount of self-knowledge.

to exercise one's desires, beliefs or decisions by fully acting out behaviors that a person wishes to act out. They do not necessarily imply an *inner freedom*, in the sense of that person being either directly or indirectly in control of his or her desires, beliefs or decisions. Outer freedom is influenced by political and social events, in this particular case the enforcement of laws on religious liberty. Inner freedom, however, cannot be thus policed or imprisoned, nor can its existence be guaranteed by the absence of outer restrictions. When people claim that they value freedom (or "independence", or "free choice") highly,[93] they are talking about outer freedom: freedom from restrictions that prevent them doing what they want to do. Those who hold that their beliefs, attitudes and values are totally determined and not at all under their free control may well still value a sociopolitical environment in which they are free to express and exercise these attributes. This may be true even of those who claim that they do not have any free control over their decisions and actions. Those who hold this more extreme position may still value freedom of religious belief and freedom of worship: in the sense of an outer freedom that does not restrict the exercise and expression of their religious beliefs, attitudes and actions. People want to be free to do and say what they want to do and say, but this is irrelevant to the question as to whether their actions, desires, beliefs or attitudes are under their free control. "Religious freedom", then, is an outer freedom. It is better described as a freedom *for* (expressing and encouraging) belief (or worship), than as a freedom *of* belief.[94]

---

93. See Milton Rokeach, *The Nature of Human Values* (New York: Free Press; London: Collier Macmillan, 1973), pp. 57, 60, 76, ch. 6, and Appendix C.

94. Such freedom for belief may also be described as a freedom *from* the control of others in expressing the beliefs one has; whereas freedom *of* belief is to be interpreted as the supposed freedom *to* exercise one's own control over one's own believing.

CHAPTER 9

Education, Ethics and the Emotions

REASON AND EMOTION IN MORAL EDUCATION

Wilson on Religious and Moral Education

According to John Wilson, educating people in religion is "a matter of help-ing them to become more reasonable in the sphere of religion".[1] He argues—and I agree—that religion is particularly concerned with emotions like awe, reverence, guilt, fear and love, directed towards certain objects. Essentially it is an "emotion-based" outlook. Hence—and again I agree—a large part of education in religion is (an aspect of) "education in the emotions".[2]

For Wilson, however, this is primarily a matter of helping people "to become more reasonable in the sphere of the emotions".[3] It includes, as a cru-cial element, a sort of philosophical education directed towards *under-standing* religious emotions—for example by encouraging critical reflec-tion on the objects of the learner's worship, awe etc. and the appropriateness of such emotions.[4] Education in religion should incorporate, he adds, a more psychological education leading to increased *self-control* of religious emo-tions and secularly-oriented equivalent emotions. He describes this element as a "type of education ... more analogous to psychotherapy than to sub-ject-teaching". Yet the insight-generating analysis involved here, which is to be accompanied by the development of "skills and aptitudes in expressing and controlling emotion" and which is designed to free learners "from unconscious

---

1. John Wilson, *Education in Religion and the Emotions* (London: Heinemann, 1971), p. 1. Wilson writes from out of a British context, and largely with reference to secular school-ing. For his use of the language of "reasonableness" and "rationality" (as synonymous), see below pp. 221-222 and Glossary.

2. John Wilson, *Approach to Religious Education* (Oxford: Farmington Trust, n.d.), pp. 4-5; compare *Education in Religion and the Emotions*, p. 18 and John Wilson, "First Steps in Religious Education", in Brenda Watson, ed., *Priorities in Religious Education* (London: Falmer, 1992), pp. 11-12.

3. Wilson, *Education in Religion and the Emotions*, p. 1.

4. *Ibid.*, pp. 63-64, ch. 7.

counter-motivation", is part and parcel of an overall aim to give people "a *cognitive* grasp of their emotions".[5] This objective of understanding/control of the emotions (their "education and proper direction"[6]) is closely related to Wilson's account of *moral education*, which he defines as "education about what a person ought *overridingly* to *do*, and about what he ought to *feel*".[7] Indeed, according to Wilson, religious education is largely a part of this wider enterprise.

Wilson's account of moral education involves him in identifying the *moral components*—that is attributes that mark out the reasonable, morally educated person—which moral education seeks to develop. Wilson's view that his versions of religious education and moral education do not involve the inculcation of a particular religion or morality,[8] and are therefore appropriate in secular education, is dependent on his claim that these components "represent all the qualities which are logically required for having the right emotion directed towards the right object"[9] and (in the case of morality) "can be derived from what one means by 'morality'".[10] On this account even students in a secular school can quite properly be educated into the methods of (rationally) being moral and of (rationally) being religious.

But what Wilson says of this group of learners is relevant to moral education and religious education within a Christian context also, i.e. for Christian religious education. Most Christian religious educators would not wish to subordinate this enterprise to that of moral education, but would recognize that in one sense or another Christian religious education incorporates (Christian) moral education. Some will emphasize solely the formative nature of this moral education, in forming Christian moral attitudes and virtues and informing Christian conscience. Others would also place stress, some of them far more stress, on the development of critical reflection on received Christian morality and on the learner's own moral decisions. For both groups, Wilson's account—and the following response to it—may be instructive.

Many of Wilson's moral components[11] are "attainments" or "abilities": e.g.

---

5. Wilson, *Approach to Religious Education*, p. 12, compare p. 14; *Education in Religion and the Emotions*, Appendix VI, especially p. 244, and "First Steps in Religious Education", p. 20.

6. Wilson, *Education in Religion and the Emotions*, p. 17.

7. *Ibid.*, pp. 162-163.

8. Compare Wilson, *Education in Religion and the Emotions*, p. 186; *Approach to Religious Education*, p. 3; John Wilson, *Approach to Moral Education* (Oxford: Farmington Trust, 1967), pp. 3-4; John Wilson *et al.*, *Introduction to Moral Education* (Harmondsworth, England: Penguin, 1967), pp. 26-28.

9. Wilson, *Approach to Religious Education*, p. 5; compare *Introduction to Moral Education*, p. 218 n. 2.

10. Wilson, *Approach to Moral Education*, p. 6; *Introduction to Moral Education*, p. 77.

11. See Wilson *et al.*, *Introduction to Moral Education*, pp. 192-203; *Education in Religion and the Emotions*, p. 261; *Approach to Religious Education*, p. 5; *Approach to Moral Education*, pp. 4-7; John Wilson, *Moral Education and the Curriculum* (Oxford: Pergamon Press, 1969), pp. 2-8; John Wilson, *Moral Thinking* (London: Heinemann, 1969), pp. 50-70; John Wilson, *The Assessment of Morality* (Windsor, England: NFER, 1973), pp. 38-40, ch. 5; John Wilson,

the mastery of relevant knowledge of the consequences of actions or the know-how of social skills (Wilson calls this "GIG"), the awareness of one's own and others' feelings ("EMP"), and the ability to prescribe action for oneself for the right reasons ("DIK"). These are all fairly unexceptionable as "nonpartisan" rational learning outcomes. One component, "PHIL", is perhaps more problematic in this respect. "PHIL" is an attitude of respect or concern for others based on "the ability to identify with other people, in the sense of being such that other people's feelings, wants and interests actually count or weigh with one, or are accepted as of equal validity to one's own".[12] In some of his writings, Wilson has distinguished three elements in PHIL:[13] (a) having the concept of a person—a *belief* that others count; (b) having *feelings* that support the principle that others count; and (c) performing the appropriate *actions* that use this principle.[14]

In much of Wilson's account the words "rational" and "reasonable" are used interchangeably, as they are by many philosophers, to describe beliefs and actions that are justifiable because well grounded. In this sense rational or reasonable *people* are those who base their beliefs (and actions) on good evidence and argument ("have good reasons"), and rational or reasonable *emotions* are those that are directed towards their proper objects and have cognitive components (factual judgments and related factual evaluations) that are in this way well grounded.[15] The philosopher's other sense of "rational", however, connoting an origin in the activity of reasoning,[16] is also relevant to Wilson's account: for underlying much of Wilson's work is the attempt as far as possible to derive morality from reasoning.

A Teacher's Guide to Moral Education (London: Chapman, 1983), Appendix I; John Wilson, *A New Introduction to Moral Education* (London: Cassell, 1990), ch. 8. We should note that of Wilson's moral components EMP and KRAT (see note 30 below) are described as "*particularly* relevant to the emotions, and hence to religious ... 'outlooks'" (*Education in Religion and the Emotions*, p. 162, compare "First Steps in Religious Education", p. 13).

12. Wilson, *Approach to Moral Education*, p. 4.

13. Wilson, *Education in Religion and the Emotions*, p. 261; *A Teacher's Guide to Moral Education*, p. 136. Elsewhere Wilson claims that PHIL involves a *belief* which "should normally go along with an emotion or *feeling*—that of respect for, or caring about, other people— and the two merge into an attitude adopted towards them". He adds that "the person with PHIL must feel sufficiently to act on his belief in equality, but need not feel more"—as, for example, an intense feeling of love or altruism (*Moral Education and the Curriculum*, pp. 2-3). See also Richard Pring, *Personal and Social Education in the Curriculum: Concepts and Control* (London: Hodder & Stoughton, 1984), pp. 29-30.

14. Sometimes (c) is expressed less actively by Wilson, as "claiming to use this concept [of a person] in an overriding, prescriptive, and universalized .... principle". John Wilson, "Philosophical Difficulties and 'Moral Development'", in Brenda Munsey, ed., *Moral Development, Moral Education and Kohlberg* (Birmingham, Ala.: Religious Education Press, 1980), p. 226. See also Wilson, *The Assessment of Morality*, pp. 41-50 and *A New Introduction to Moral Education*, pp. 134-139.

15. Wilson *et al.*, *Introduction to Moral Education*, pp. 51, 92-99, 116, 123; see also *A New Introduction to Moral Education*, pp. 96, 114.

16. See Glossary, pp. 294-295.

Hare on the Nature of Morality

Following Richard Hare,[17] Wilson argues that morality—in order to be morality—must be both universalizable ("impartial as between persons" in morally identical situations), and also prescriptive (prescribing the same maxims for others). According to Wilson this *involves* taking other people's interests into account, for this is a corollary of being willing to apply one's moral principles to other people. Wilson writes: "In making moral judgements, we consider other people as being on an equal footing with ourselves: what goes for us, goes for them too, and vice versa." Without this, morality and the formulation and use of interpersonal rules could not get started. Wilson argues further that if a person's moral opinions have to prescribe conduct for others as well as for that person himself/herself, the implication is that the person concerned regards these others as equals: "one might think that he could not advance these opinions with any show of reason, or with much chance of success, unless he so regarded them".[18] In this way Wilson sometimes strives to show that rational morality, considered in formal terms rather than in terms of content, *necessarily* involves PHIL.[19] He argues that "reasoning itself implies a kind of embryonic morality, inasmuch as anything that could count as a reason must be impartial as between one person and another", and further that "not just *anything* can count as a reason".[20]

Hare himself pulls more out of the concept of rationality than this, and Wilson's arguments on occasion seem close to Hare's position. Hare argues that universal prescriptivism is "a formal foundation" for a particular moral view: i.e. preference utilitarianism, the view that actions are right in so far as they provide people with what they prefer to have and prevent them having what they prefer not to have. Hare claims that in searching for conduct that we can prescribe universally in a given situation, "we find ourselves bound to give equal weight to the desires of all parties (the foundation of distributive justice); and this, in turn, leads to such views as that we should seek to maximize satisfactions". The basis for this claim is that if my action is going to affect the interests of a number of people, and I ask myself what course of action I can prescribe universally for people in just this situation, "then what I shall have to do, in order to answer this question, is to put myself imaginatively in the place of the other parties". Standing in the shoes of each per-

---

17. R. M Hare, "Universalisability", *Proceedings of the Aristotelian Society* 55 (1954-55), pp. 304-312 and *Freedom and Reason* (London: Oxford University Press, 1963) especially part I; compare also his *The Language of Morals* (London: Oxford University Press, 1952), *passim* and *Essays on Religion and Education* (Oxford: Oxford University Press, 1992), *passim*.

18. Wilson *et al.*, *Introduction to Moral Education*, p. 77.

19. *Ibid.*, pp. 93, 99. In later works Wilson notes that this is not so much a *logical* derivation as a "phenomenological" one relating to "how human beings think ... when they satisfy their desires". John Wilson, *A New Introduction to Moral Education*, pp. 97-98; Wilson, *A Preface to Morality*, pp. 45, 53-58.

20. Wilson *et al.*, *Introduction to Moral Education*, pp. 104, 105. Compare Wilson, *A Preface to Morality*, p. 37 and ch. 4.

son in turn, I must ask how much I want to have this or to avoid that. Now if I want to give equal weight to the interests of each of them, Hare asks "what can I possibly do except advocate that course which will, taken all in all, least frustrate the desires which I have imagined myself having? But this (it is plausible to go on) is to maximize satisfactions."[21]

A Critique

It would appear, however, that such considerations go beyond what is demanded by the logic of universal prescriptivism, which is itself based on the formal properties of words like *right* and *wrong*. They go beyond it to embrace questions about what it is psychologically (i.e. empirically) possible for people to desire. The *formal* requirement of universalizability needs to be combined here with an appeal to inclination and interest, wants and desires, in order to produce such a moral *content*.[22] John Mackie has argued that there are three different kinds or stages of universalizability, of which only the first (the ruling out of numerical differences between one individual and another) can be argued to be a logical thesis. The others (putting oneself in another's place, and taking account of people's different tastes and ideals) cannot. However, all three are needed to create utilitarianism, and even in the case of the first stage Mackie argues that "the principle that actions are to be guided by judgements which pass the test" of universalizability is itself "a substantive practical principle . . . a demand for a certain sort of fairness".[23] The route from the logic of universal prescriptivism to adopting the ideal of distributive justice involves more than rational reflection. Keith Ward has similarly argued that Hare's universalizability principle is not so much a matter of logic as "something more like a substantive principle of 'fair play'"—"treat people impartially and equitably"—which "is just one possible prescription among others, and . . . cannot be inflated into a criterion of morality".[24]

Geoffrey Warnock was among the first to criticize Hare on the grounds that we cannot by the argument from universalizability "be constrained to attach *much* weight, if any, to the interests of others", for in fact we may be entirely ready to concede that these others are not morally required to attach much weight, if any, to our own interests. This is true, he claims, however intense-

---

21. Hare, *Freedom and Reason*, p. 123; see also Hare, *Essays on Religion and Education*, pp. 175-177. Compare Wilson, *A Preface to Morality*, pp. 47-60.

22. The debate is surveyed in W. D. Hudson, *Modern Moral Philosophy* (London: Macmillan; Garden City, N.Y.: Anchor Books, 1970), pp. 189-192, 227-231, 311-329. We may note that Hare argues that the inclinations of others do not always count in morality, e.g. in matters of ideals. Compare Hare, *Freedom and Reason*, pp. 149-154; see also his *Essays on Religion and Education*, pp. 94, 123, 170.

23. J. L. Mackie, *Ethics: Inventing Right and Wrong* (Harmondsworth, England: Penguin, 1977), pp. 83-98; see also Peter Singer, *Practical Ethics* (Cambridge and New York: Cambridge University Press, 1979), pp. 204-208.

24. Keith Ward, *Ethics and Christianity* (London: Allen & Unwin; New York: Humanities Press, 1970), pp. 40, 43.

ly we may dislike it when, "in the competitive free-for-all, it happens that [we come] out on the losing side". This being the case, the requirement of universalizability "appears, whether in theory or in practice, to set almost no limit to the practical judgments which *can* be consistently made and maintained" by sane people. If so, he concludes, as a weapon of moral argument it does not "carry much fire-power".[25] In a similar vein, Don Locke has criticized universalizability, and Lawrence Kohlberg's closely related criterion of reversibility of moral judgments, as insufficient to guarantee "a unique, correct and rationally acceptable answer to every moral problem". And Bernard Williams has summed up this side of the debate by claiming convincingly that in ethics "there is no route to the impartial standpoint from rational deliberation alone".[26]

Geoffrey Warnock has elsewhere developed the more radical argument that reason alone cannot be our general rule and guide in everything ethical because it is *possible* to hold "without gross defect of reason, that morality is actually a *bad thing*". Against those philosophers who maintain that morality must have an irresistible claim upon rational acceptance, Warnock—while accepting that "moral reasons really are reasons, and could not rationally be denied to be so"—contends that this does not take us very far. In any "full-blooded 'acceptance' of morality", he argues, "a great deal more than this is involved". "In short: while a rational being, merely *qua* rational, may possibly be obliged to concede that what moral argument adduces as reasons really are reasons, I do not see that he can be obliged to concede—could not rationally deny—that morality really 'works', so to speak, as it is supposed to work, or that, in the balance with other reasons for and against doing things, moral reasons must be accorded very great or preponderant cogency." Such a person may really see what morality is, but think that there is not much in it. Warnock contends that we are unavoidably involved here with issues as to what is true, and what is to be valued, "and while not all opinions on these matters may be equally tenable, or reasonable, or uneccentric, these are issues on which rational beings may rationally differ". If this is so, then recognition of "the moral law" as the main effective determinant of practical judgment and action "cannot be forced, so to speak, *a priori* upon rational beings".[27]

---

25. G. J. Warnock, *Contemporary Moral Philosophy* (London: Macmillan, 1967), pp. 45-46. See also C. C. W. Taylor's "Critical Notice of R. M. Hare's *Freedom and Reason*", in G. Wallace and A. D. M. Walker, eds., *The Definition of Morality* (London: Methuen; New York: Barnes & Noble, 1970).

26. Don Locke, "A Psychologist Among Philosophers: Philosophical Aspects of Kohlberg's Theories", in Sohan Modgil and Celia Modgil, eds., *Lawrence Kohlberg: Consensus and Controversy* (Lewes, England: Falmer, 1985), pp. 31-38 (quotation from p. 37); Bernard Williams, *Ethics and the Limits of Philosophy* (Cambridge, Mass.: Harvard University Press; London: Collins, 1985), p. 70, see chs. 4 and 5 *passim*.

27. G. J. Warnock, *The Object of Morality* (London: Methuen, 1971), pp. 159, 163-164; contrast Wilson, *A New Introduction to Moral Education*, p. 89 (but see also pp. 115-116) and Hare, *Essays on Religion and Ethics*, pp. 173-177 (but see also pp. 208-211).

Rationally, then, we do not *have* to recognize morality. Rather we recognize it when we "come to *want to*", for example when we want another person's suffering not to happen. "Thus, it is possible for a person to want to be moral; and a person is moral, by and large, exactly in proportion as he really wants to be so." According to Warnock, the essence of the remedy for human ills is "not in reason; it is in non-indifference".[28] And that is surely a feature of human affectivity: our being *moved* by the suffering of others. Here we discover once more an argument for the centrality of the affective. We also find an antirationalist argument to the effect that "reason alone" cannot get us very far in life—in this case in the moral life; nor can it provide us with all we need or want in education—especially not in moral education and any moral education component of Christian religious education.

Education in Morals and the Emotions—Within Reason Alone?

Wilson's PHIL appears on occasion to take us beyond purely rational expressions of the notion of universalizability to a moral "attitude" or "feeling" of concern, which leads not only to ("actions" of) "justice" and "giving others their rights", but even as far as "benevolence, love, altruism".[29] Here we do not just have a formal condition for rational morality, but part of the content of a particular type of morality. On the one hand such considerations seem to open Wilson to the charge that he is advocating the inculcation of a particular morality, and a particular set of emotions, in his account of secular schooling.[30] But second, and more central to our concerns, these discussions illustrate the limitations of trying to produce an education in morals or religion within the limits of reason alone. When *reason* speaks of "taking other people into account" (because "what is right for one is, other things being equal, right for another"[31]), it is not prescribing universal benevolence or perhaps even universal justice, for to do so would be to go beyond what is necessary, at least as a *logical* consequence of the nature of moral judgment alone. Morality, however, *is* concerned with these things.

Certain writers on moral education have criticized what they believe to be the implications of Wilson's position for what constitutes rational moral education. Francis Dunlop draws on the example of King David's action vis-à-vis Uriah the Hittite (see 2 Samuel 11). This, Dunlop claims, was "all too rational":

---

28. Warnock, *The Object of Morality*, pp. 165-166. Also note Bernard Williams, *Morality* (New York: Harper & Row, 1972; Cambridge: Cambridge University Press, 1976), pp. 25-26. Here, and in the arguments following, see also Anthony O'Hear, *Education, Society and Human Nature* (London: Routledge & Kegan Paul, 1981), pp. 126-135.

29. Wilson, *Education in Religion and the Emotions*, p. 261. However Wilson draws back a little from this elsewhere: see note 13 above.

30. One of his moral components (KRAT) is described in an early source as including "actually having the right feelings/emotions" (Wilson, *Approach to Religious Education*, p. 5), although education of the emotions involves more than that (see *Education in Religion and the Emotions*, pp. 244-250). See also *Introduction to Moral Education*, p. 65; *Education in Religion and the Emotions*, p. 171.

31. Wilson, *A Teacher's Guide to Moral Education*, p. 29.

In so far as the action is defective, it is not *reason* that he lacks . . . so much as justice and integrity; the only adequate characterization of it is that it was evil. To suggest *simply* that it was irrational is to suggest either that David was stupid or silly, and made some rather feckless technical mis-calculation, or that his action was incomprehensible. But clearly this sort of "rational evil"—far removed from fecklessness—is all too easily under-stood.

Dunlop reckons that such attempts to interpret morality in terms of ratio-nality refuse to attend to "the basic moral fact of our awareness of obligation and to start from this datum". Mary Warnock similarly criticizes Wilson's position for being too abstract, focusing too much on a methodology of rational moral thinking rather than on certain "qualities of character" that we want for ourselves and our children.[32]

But Wilson's account of the nature of morality does take note of such criticisms. His more recent work in particular develops his earlier recogni-tion of the limitations of a formal and conceptual methodology.[33] It shows that Wilson is aware of the "limitations that apply to any formal system that attempts to bind individuals into the public mode", and of the fact that a conceptualizing (and "consistent and reasonable") creature will not *inevitably* endorse a search for satisfaction that subscribes to "the principle that wants or needs in general ought to be satisfied". Wilson writes:

> There are some severe limitations on reason as an inducement to enter the public form. First . . . it is not clear that one ought always to be consis-tent or impartial or reasonable, if it does not always pay; and second, a per-son's desires may be so weak that, though he may be brought to be rea-sonable and to universalise, he has nothing much to be reasonable and universalise *with*. It is, I think, fairly clear even in advance that much more needs to be said about the notion of a person's *attachment* to other people, not just about the logical network which he must accept if he is to be reasonable.[34]

In a significant passage, Wilson recognizes "a sort of vicious circle":

> We want wicked and selfish people to take other people seriously; to do that, we want them to consider the logic of the moral concepts; to do *that*, we want them to ask questions and have some commitment to rea-

---

32. Francis Dunlop, "Form, Content and Rationality in Morality and Moral Education", *Proceedings of the Philosophy of Education Society of Great Britain* XI (1977), pp. 93-94; Mary Warnock, *Schools of Thought* (London: Faber & Faber, 1977), pp. 130-136. See also Meriel Downey and A. V. Kelly, *Moral Education: Theory and Practice* (London: Harper & Row, 1979), pp. 118-119, and Pring, *Personal and Social Education in the Curriculum*, pp. 72 and 79.

33. Wilson *et al.*, *Introduction to Moral Education*, pp. 105-107.

34. Wilson, *A Preface to Morality*, p. 58, other quotes from pp. 56-57.

son in general; but that, finally, involves that they take other people seriously. For reason is essentially dialectic: it involves listening to other people's views and answering them, joining and competing with them in the search for truth. A child could not learn how to think (or even to talk) if he did not experience this process, as mediated to him by adults. Unless he trusts other people and takes them seriously, he cannot learn to reason. Everything, therefore, turns ultimately on whether it is better for him to face the world or not, better to do business with reality or retreat from it. The quick answer to this is that it is better for him if he can love the world and feel at home in it; otherwise the inevitable fact is that he will not and cannot face it—and there is no kind of logical reasoning that has any claim upon him.[35]

This by no means implies a moral education within the bounds of reason alone, but one that recognizes the centrality of attachment and feeling.

It is appropriate now to turn to Wilson's discussion of the education of the *emotions*. We may readily agree that he is right to lay stress on the role of rational appraisal in the targeting of emotions like awe, reverence, fear and love (using "rational/reasonable" in the sense of "agreeable to reason", "well-grounded", "sensible"). But here too, at the center of his analysis, there may lurk the danger of yielding too much territory to the forces of rationality—in this case in the theater of operations of the emotions.[36] We may argue that good reasons can be found for recognizing limits to the rational appraisal of the emotional life, as well as for refusing to interpret morality—and moral education—primarily in terms of the development of rational understanding.

To take a rather obvious point first. Reason, as we shall see, may be allowed considerable scope in assessing the rationality of emotions through its role in appraising the rationality of the beliefs that in some sense undergird them. But these are judgments about the orientation (or targeting) of the emotions. Indeed they are particular judgments based on particular emotions. This sort of rational appraisal can have little to say when confronted with the more basic question as to whether it is a good thing to have these particular emotions at all. Some emotions (e.g. fear and parental love) have an obvious biological utility, but this is not true of all of them. How do we judge whether or not to develop these other emotions in those whom we educate?

To be totally without emotion, we may reasonably claim, would be a bad state of affairs. Ronald Hepburn writes: "The person who lacks emotional energy is like a ship that cannot be manoeuvred because it is becalmed or

---

35. *Ibid.*, pp. 73-74.

36. But we should note that Wilson does recognize that being reasonable is "as much an 'affective' as a 'cognitive' matter", at least in the sense that we recognize unreasonableness in people as much by their behavior and feelings as by their powers of ratiocination. John Wilson, "Rationality and Moral Education", *Proceedings of the Philosophy of Education Society of Great Britain* XI (1977), p. 101.

because its engines have failed. 'Free choice', in a minimal sense, is still possible (the rudder itself can be moved); but it is not efficacious."[37] Such a person would not even be a moral being, for, in the words of another philosopher, "there is no morality where there are no feelings".[38] (See below pp. 243-248.) Despite the risks we run in having emotions, including the risk of these emotions being or becoming irrational, we would not be human without them.

That which applies to emotions in general may also apply to particular emotions. It *is* possible to argue that it is a good thing—intrinsically and/or instrumentally (as leading to human flourishing for themselves and others)—for people to have certain emotions. This is a value judgment, and one that lies at the heart of many educational agreements and disagreements, not least in Christian religious education. It is a judgment about the sort of people we ought to be and to become, and the sort of people we ought to educate into being. Reason alone cannot adequately guide value judgments, for reason alone is blind in this area. In the end, appeal must be made to a vision: a vision which is in part a claim about which emotions are of moral worth in a person. As one religious educationist has put it: "moral people are people who can see and do see".[39] Christian moral theology and ethical thinking offers just such a vision of values, against which all attempts at Christian moral education may be assessed. Therefore it is not by any means unarguably the case that we should only educate people to love "wisely". We need also—and first—to educate them to love. Sometimes, perhaps, it might even be permissible to educate them to love "too well", for that may possibly be an essential element in all real loving. Certainly Christian religious education may only properly be designated as such when it seeks to facilitate the learning of a version of universal altruism, i.e. self-giving Christian *agapé*, in Christian learners.

Educators, including Christian religious educators, are often guilty of encouraging and inducing emotions without any concern for questions of reasonableness. This is dangerous, and often counter-productive. Yet we must not allow the pendulum to swing too far in the opposite direction. The "rhetoric of reason" can produce a similarly unbalanced response. A stress on "reasonableness" and "rationality" with regard to the emotions can lead to a resurgence of a Passion versus Reason model of human nature that can quickly lead on to a dehumanizing educational approach. There is something disturbing about people being educated to target their emotions "rationally", to adjust them "appropriately" to their objects, and to exercise self-

---

37. R. W. Hepburn, "The Arts and the Education of Feeling and Emotion", in R. F. Dearden *et al.*, eds., *Education and Reason* (London: Routledge & Kegan Paul, 1972), p. 99.

38. H. H. Price, *Belief* (London: Allen & Unwin; New York: Humanities Press, 1969), p. 424.

39. Craig Dykstra, *Vision and Character* (New York: Paulist, 1981), p. 49; see also Stanley Hauerwas, "Character, Narrative, and Growth in the Christian Life", in James Fowler and Antoine Vergote, eds., *Toward Moral and Religious Maturity* (Morriston, N.J.: Silver Burdett, 1980), p. 472.

control (presumably on the basis of this reasoning), *if* these acts are seen to be opposed to, and fundamentally to constrain, their human emotions. Should the end result of such reflection be that the racist argues herself out of her racism, and the hopeless lover from his hopeless loving, then the end may seem to justify the means. But the same means may be used—for reason is a two-edged sword—to create an inhuman, calculating sort of emotional response, or a person who is unwilling to commit herself in love to anyone or in devotion to any cause, because "nothing is (rationally) worth it". Doubtless this would be to misunderstand and misapply the careful thinking of Wilson and others, but such abuse of the work of educationists is not unusual in the practice of education. At a popular level these risks *are* run, sometimes even by Christian religious educators.

All love, and most commitments, go "beyond the evidence" (in the sense of empirical data or inferential argument) in some way or another; not "unreasonably beyond", perhaps, but our personal life hardly gets started until we act "despite the appearances". The logic of certain key terms both in personal relationships and in the Christian tradition is such that extreme open-mindedness, tentativeness and critical rationality are inimical to their development. Examples would include "trust", "love", "commitment", "hope" and "faith". "Belief that goes beyond the evidence" is often regarded as quite proper, and indeed as essential, in interpersonal relationships, both for understanding and for trusting other people.[40] Love, like religion, often seems too resistant to falsification to be rational, but it is a mark of true personal commitments that they are in this way tenaciously held. "She loves me" and "God loves me" are propositions that are not appropriately given up at the first sign of conflicting evidence, from flying crockery or disappointed prayer. If "cold reason" is too cold to grasp this leap of the moral and religious imagination beyond the facts-as-they-seem, then it must be transcended. Christian religious education must be wary of contexts and processes that depend on such low temperatures, for they can serve only a small part of its aims.

We do need to reason about our emotions, to reflect on the beliefs and evaluations underlying them and the evidence relevant to such cognitions. Our emotional life needs this rational support and direction. But it cannot survive on this alone. Reason cannot, and must not, replace the passions. Sometimes, surely, we are at our most Christian—and indeed our most human—when we *do* love "too well", "against all reason" and "despite the evidence". The mother who alone believes in her son's innocence may be being very irra-

---

40. Robert M. Adams, *The Virtue of Faith* (New York: Oxford University Press, 1987), p. 14. The contribution of "self-fulfilling beliefs" to personal relationships and religion is also worthy of some reflection. If I bring up my child to believe that people love him (often despite the evidence) he will take the step of risk and form relationships with them, and love may be engendered. If I bring him up to trust people, some of them at least will become trustworthy by thus being trusted. There are great dangers here, of course. But most educators and parents would claim that the risks are worth taking, and some religious educationists might claim that there are close parallels here with learning to love and trust God. See Price, *Belief*, Part II, ch. 6.

tional. But isn't she being a mother? It is only with the help of a corrupt Hebrew text that Job can cry, "Though he slay me, yet will I trust in him" (Job 13:15, K.J.V.). Yet it may be just that sort of response that marks out those who know true religion—and true love. Christian moral and emotional education cannot rely on "reason alone", *if* our criteria of reasonableness of morality and the emotions precludes such learning outcomes. (For further discussion, see below pp. 232-235, 237-241, 254-256.)

Formative and Critical Education and the Emotions

Educational processes—in the broad sense of "education" that we have adopted in this book—may arouse and evoke all sorts of emotions, and not just "rational" ones (in the sense of emotions whose cognitive components are rationally justifiably). The same can be said, *a fortiori*, of Christian religious education. Formative education helps to mold people's affective life, forming their emotions. It can be judged on the grounds of the rationality of the emotions so formed (in the sense given) and their moral worth, as well as on the morality of the educational processes involved. Critical education of the type Wilson and others advocate will help learners to reflect critically on their emotions, thus allowing their rationality to be assessed (as their moral worthiness or their appropriateness should be assessed on other criteria). But such a critical education is parasitic on people having emotions at all, and indeed on their having their own specific emotions. Here again critical education presupposes formative education. Those who approve of emotions a, b and c usually claim that education in the broad sense may quite properly induce such emotions (perhaps even nonrationally?), as well as encouraging us to reflect on them rationally.

David Cooper writes as follows, in response to R. S. Peters's account of the education of the emotions as a "thoroughly cognitive" endeavor that changes emotions by means of changes in belief. "In some cases, surely, the more vital task would be to put someone in the way of those experiences—musical ones, say—which might elicit feelings of which [the learner] had hitherto been incapable." Cooper adds that if "educating the emotions" were to be defined solely in cognitive terms, then eliciting feelings (say) through musical experience would not belong to it. But the question would then arise (for the secular and the religious educator) whether *education* of the emotions in this limited sense is the educator's main task.[41]

This general discussion may be given a particular perspective in the light of the concerns of the Christian religious educator. For if the "evocative-education" that is being argued for here is a proper part of secular educational activities, it has an even more central part to play in the value-laden, character-directed formation of persons that is a major feature of Christian religious edu-

---

41. David Cooper, *Authenticity and Learning* (London: Routledge & Kegan Paul, 1983), p. 65. Compare R. S. Peters, "The Education of the Emotions", in Dearden *et al.*, eds., *Education and Reason*, pp. 84-89.

cation. Indeed I have argued in Chapter 6 that Christian religious education is perhaps *primarily* a matter of forming "Christian attitudes" and "Christian emotions".

Such a viewpoint is somewhat akin to that of Craig Dykstra, whom I quoted earlier (p. 228). Dykstra criticizes Lawrence Kohlberg's "juridical ethics" for placing a premium on "human capacities for analytical reasoning, disinterested judgment, decisiveness of will, and rational discourse".[42] Dykstra argues, against such a view, that "a person's morality cannot be summed up in the decisions one makes and the justifications one gives for those decisions. Most of what constitutes a person's morality refers to basic attitudes toward life and the underlying vision of reality that provides the foundation of these attitudes."[43] This is to espouse a "visual ethics", in which "action follows vision; and vision depends on character—a person thinking, reasoning, believing, feeling, willing, and acting as a whole". In this context the sources and justifications of decisions and actions "are not abstract, impersonal, universal principles", but a vision of life "that issues from the quality of consciousness and character of particular moral persons and communities". This ethic sees moral actions as responses to what we see: a "truthful seeing" that involves the formation of a particular character.[44] Hence, as one moral philosopher recognizes, "The most a moral philosopher can do is to paint a picture of various types of life ... and ask which type of life you really want to lead". He adds that the type of life we most want to lead will depend on the sort of people we are.[45] This is surely at the heart of *Christian* religious and moral education.

---

42. Dykstra, *Vision and Character*, p. 8. Compare Carol Gilligan, *In a Different Voice* (Cambridge, Mass.: Harvard University Press, 1982), ch. 2. It should be noted that Kohlberg regards "cognition" and "affect" as different aspects of the same mental event, so that "the development of mental dispositions reflects structural changes recognizable in both cognitive and affective perspectives". Lawrence Kohlberg, "Stages of Development as a Basis for Moral Education", in Munsey, ed., *Moral Development, Moral Education and Kohlberg*, p. 40. However, it is the cognitive component that Kohlberg stresses. See Lawrence Kohlberg, "Stage and Sequence: The Cognitive-Developmental Approach to Socialization", in David A. Goslin, ed., *Handbook of Socialization Theory and Research* (Chicago: Rand McNally, 1969).

43. Dykstra, *Vision and Character*, p. 21. Dykstra appeals for support to Iris Murdoch's stress on a person's "total vision of life" which is "the texture" of a person's being—see her "Vision and Choice in Morality" in Ian Ramsey, ed., *Christian Ethics and Contemporary Philosophy* (London: SCM; New York: Macmillan, 1966) and *The Sovereignty of Good* (London: Routledge & Kegan Paul; New York: Schocken , 1970), ch. 1.

44. Dykstra, *Vision and Character*, p. 59. Stanley Hauerwas comes to a similar conclusion: "Morality cannot be separated from moral persons so that it can be learned independent of them, but rather requires learning to be as they are". Stanley Hauerwas, "Character, Narrative, and Growth in the Christian Life", p. 445. Compare also Stanley Hauerwas, *The Peaceable Kingdom: A Primer in Christian Ethics* (Notre Dame, Ind.: University of Notre Dame Press, 1983; London: SCM, 1984), chs. 2 and 3.

45. P. H. Nowell-Smith, *Ethics* (Harmondsworth, England: Penguin, 1954), p. 319; compare Hare, *The Language of Morals*, p. 69. Hence: "differences of opinion concerning any matter of vital importance spring from differences of constitution". Samuel Butler, *The Way of All Flesh* (London: Marshall Cavendish, 1987, first edition 1903), p. 326.

EMOTIONS, ETHICS AND PERSONS

Reason and Feeling: A Holistic View of Persons

Mary Midgley is a philosopher who has written extensively of the complex nature of human beings, the role of feeling as constitutive of that nature, and the need to recognize the proper and appropriate (and limited) role of reason with regard to such a nature. Her position, and that taken by an increasing number of philosophers, is sympathetic to a holistic view of the learner as a person who does not easily split into cognitive and affective, or reasoning and passionate, parts. Such a view will be welcomed by those who advocate a holistic view of the Christian learner and of Christian religious education.

Midgley argues that at birth we are not blank paper, "but complex beings with an emotional constitution which we very much need to understand better. We have a nature as well as a history."[46] Midgley rejects the personification of "Reason" as an opponent of "Feeling" and a governor of "a chaotic alien tribe of Passions or Instincts", preferring a more holistic view of human beings and of the structure or constitution of human nature,[47] which includes the structure of our feelings and instincts and "indicates the good and bad for us".[48] Further, "our emotional constitution is not revealed by logic. It is a very large and general empirical fact." Any attempt to reduce morality to "its minimal logic" that pays no attention to our human emotional constitution is reductive—"illicit nothing-buttery."[49]

In *Beast and Man* Midgley develops her argument at length.[50] Reason does indeed have a part to play as our own organizing, reflective, choosing activity, which grows out of and completes "a natural balance of parts". Rationality is not "opposed to our nature, but continuous with and growing out of it". Our need for some form of rationality (and speech and culture) is natural to us. But this means "that facts about our other needs, about our whole system of needs, have to come in to determine what sort of culture, what rational way of life, can suit us. Our full emotional nature determines our aims, as well as the formal, structural characteristics."

46. Mary Midgley, *Biological and Cultural Evolution* (Tunbridge Wells, England: Institute for Cultural Research, 1984), p. 15.

47. Mary Midgley, *Beast and Man: The Roots of Human Nature* (Ithaca, N.Y.: Cornell University Press, 1978; London: Methuen, 1979), pp. 256, 258, 260 and *Heart and Mind: The Varieties of Moral Experience* (New York: St. Martin's Press, 1981; London: Methuen, 1983), ch. 1. See also G. Ryle, "Can Virtue be Taught?", in Dearden *et al.*, eds., *Education and Reason*, pp. 52-53.

48. Midgley, *Beast and Man*, p. 75, see also pp. 76, 82, 260-261. Annette Baier has commented on the limited nature of the spectrum of our emotions, a fact that supports our sense that we are in "bondage" to them. (We can attempt to produce complete lists of our feeling-possibilities, but not of our actions or beliefs.) Annette Baier, *Postures of the Mind* (London: Methuen; Minneapolis: University of Minnesota Press, 1985), pp. 123-124.

49. Midgley, *Heart and Mind*, p. 17, see also pp. 47-48.

50. *Beast and Man*, ch. 11, quotations following are from pp. 321, 281, 280.

Therefore, Midgley argues, the form of rationality appropriate to human beings with their natural needs, feelings and emotions cannot be a simple-minded reason. Simple schemes of thought are rational only when they fit the phenomena, but human needs are actually very complex. Hence "any system of thought that is to organize them must admit their complexity". For Midgley "reason and feeling are aspects of all our motives", they are both central aspects of what it is to be human. Thus they have to work together, to "fit" each other:

> Reason does not develop as a neutral, computerlike, technological device, detached from all aims. Form is not a colonial import, to be stamped on brute matter. The only picture that makes evolutionary sense is the Aristotelian one where matter fits its form—not the Platonic one where matter is bare negation, surd, irrational, resistant, indeed the root of all evil. The structure of feeling demands a corresponding structure of thought to complete it. The reason of a social species is not programmable in just any direction. It arises as an aspect of stability and friendliness.

In short, reason radically divorced from the emotions is no longer human, and therefore no longer reasonable.

Midgley is here advocating a holistic view of persons that is of signal importance in any account of the nature and role of reason in morality and moral education, and therefore in Christianity and Christian religious education (see Chapters 6 and 7 above). In her essay "The Objection to Systematic Humbug" she takes the discussion further. Our need for coherence, "for the unity of the personality", indicates the conceptual continuity between action, thought and feeling, of "our inner and our outer lives", and is itself a function of a powerful feeling for unity and order. This feeling (or "wish" or "motive"), Midgley argues, is—paradoxically enough—what is meant by reason in phrases like "what reason demands" or "losing one's reason". Rationality or reasonableness cannot here merely be intellectual consistency, nor the fact-finding ability which is all that David Hume took it to be (hence, notoriously, his assertion that "'Tis not contrary to reason to prefer the destruction of the whole world to the scratching of my finger").[51] Such accounts suggest a picture of Speculative Reason as a slave or secretary situated outside the committee room in which the Passions are arguing. Having provided them with factual data, Reason sits—with "nothing to act on"—"waiting to be told what to do". Midgley offers an alternative scenario. Reason (*practical* reason) is not an inactive secretary, but the chair of the meeting or "more plausibly the whole well-ordered gathering": "the core of the personality, the central I, the subject who owns 'the passions' as his attributes . . . but who is more than these attributes, and can . . . to some extent arbitrate between them". It is this subject that feels, thinks *and* acts.

On turning to Kant's elevation of the *will*—which for Kant has uncondi-

---

51. David Hume, *A Treatise of Human Nature*, Book II, Part III, Section III, ed. L. A. Selby-Bigge (Oxford: Clarendon, 1888), p. 416.

tional value and is defined as good in so far as it is rational—over human affection (accidental, contingent, having only a conditional value), Midgley observes that it makes little sense to praise will divorced from feeling. She asks what sort of a good will would it be that existed "quite independent of affection for anyone"? For a rational creature to be a social creature it has also to be "a creature with affections". But the rejection of this sort of abstraction cuts both ways. Feeling divorced from will is mere passive sentimentality. Values such as real affection or love have "to include steady, rational good-will". Thus "feeling has its active, deliberate side".

All of this underlines a holistic view of persons in which thought, feeling and action are "conceptually, not contingently, connected" as aspects of one person or, better, of that one person's conduct. In both philosophical and psychological analysis, it is "no use trying to unscrew the outside from the inside of the teapot". This position also suggests that a moral education—and therefore a full Christian religious education—cannot be directed to "the Reason" or "the Will" alone, or even to "the Passions" alone. Such education must involve an education of the will, moral reason and passions together: by facilitating self-knowledge and hard thought (particularly about our feelings), by advocating and encouraging a directing of the learner's attention to moral considerations and empirical facts, by evoking and developing certain feelings and attitudes themselves (e.g. sympathy for others and a passion for justice), and by encouraging on occasion an acting-as-if that may result in the learner, for example, coming to love those towards whom she has been taught to act lovingly.[52] This is a *practical* moral (and religious) education that recognizes *practical reason*.

In advocating a "rational romanticism" the philosopher Robert Solomon also argues against the division of the human soul into Reason and Passion, the one at war against the other. According to Solomon, objective reasoning is a *particular* form of reason, free of personal values and passions. It has its place, but it is not the whole of reason. Solomon argues that reason, viewed more broadly, remains subjective and personal: not a different, nonpassion-al, "faculty" directed against the passions, but rather "the articulate expression and expansion of the passions themselves". "Reason is nothing other than perspicacious passion."[53] Although we may be unable to accept fully Solomon's account of what constitutes an emotion (see below pp. 252-254), his stress on the nature of reason as *our* (and therefore our "passionate") reflecting is more holistic, and therefore more human, than most post-

---

52. Midgley, *Heart and Mind*, ch. 7. The quotations are from pp. 86, 88, 89, 94, 95, 102. For Kant on the will and human affections see his *Groundwork of the Metaphysics of Morals*, trans. H. J. Paton as *The Moral Law* (London: Hutchinson, 1948), ch. I.

53. Robert C. Solomon, *The Passions* (Notre Dame, Ind.: University of Notre Dame Press, 1983), pp. 120-121; compare p. 414. The claim that Western philosophy understands reason as male—well documented in Genevieve Lloyd, *The Man of Reason* (London: Methuen; Minneapolis: University of Minnesota Press, 1984)—may be relevant here. See also Carol McMillan, *Women, Reason and Nature* (Oxford: Blackwell; Princeton, N.J.: Princeton University Press, 1982).

Enlightenment accounts of rationality.

A similar view is taken by John Macmurray. For Macmurray reason is the "capacity to behave in terms of the nature of the object . . . , our capacity for objectivity".[54] But this account is not in disagreement with that of Solomon, for "objectivity" here is a matter of corresponding to and apprehending reality, and that is the function of emotion.[55] Rather more extremely, Macmurray sees reason as "primarily an affair of emotion", to be distinguished from that "derivative and secondary" process of the intellect, intellectually reflective reason or "rationality of thought".[56] The intellectual mode of reason is "a determination of the World-as-means" and is essentially concerned with generalization. But the "emotional mode of reflection" is equally an activity of learning, although its concerns are different: "it moves towards a greater particularization of the representation; and by this it expresses a valuation of what is represented as an end in itself".[57] This focus on intrinsic value is one that we shall pick up later.

All these holistic analyses of what it is to be a person closely parallel the holistic account of what it is to be a Christian person adopted in Chapter 6, and provide a necessary broadening and qualification of the place of reason in Christianity and Christian religious education discussed elsewhere in this book. Although Christian religious education can by abstractive thought distinguish cognitive and affective components, it cannot teach one in splendid isolation from the other. Nor should its exponents be divided simplistically into those who seek to make Christians (more) rational and those who want to make them (more) emotional. The warfare between reason and the emotions, with educators and educationists drawn up on two opposing sides in defence of one or the other, needs must declare a truce. We *can* have both. In order to be human and Christian we must have both.

The Philosophical Analysis of Emotion

As we saw in Chapter 6, contemporary philosophers (along with some psychologists) tend to adopt some form of "cognitive theory" of the emotions. On this view, some cognition (factual judgment) is regarded as a constituent element of an emotion, along with or including an evaluative component, and some would add an "appetitive" (= want or desire) component.[58] George Pitcher uses the portmanteau term *apprehension* to cover a number of "modes

---

54. John Macmurray, *Reason and Emotion* (London: Faber & Faber, 1962), p. 19.

55. *Ibid.*, pp. 43, 49. See above p. 148.

56. *Ibid.*, p. 26; compare pp. 75, 211.

57. John Macmurray, *The Self as Agent* (London: Faber & Faber, 1957), pp. 198-199.

58. See William Lyons, *Emotion* (Cambridge: Cambridge University Press, 1980), chs. 2, 4, and 5; R. S. Peters, "The Education of the Emotions"; Wayne Proudfoot, *Religious Experience* (Berkeley: University of California Press, 1985), pp. 83-118. For accounts by recent psychologists of a cognitive theory of the emotions, see Andrew Ortony *et al.*, *The Cognitive Structure of Emotions* (Cambridge: Cambridge University Press, 1988). See also Gordon W. Allport, *The Individual and His Religion* (New York: Macmillan, 1950), pp. 17-20 and George Mandler, *Mind and Emotion* (Malabar, Fla.: Krieger, 1982), pp. 67, 105-107, 149-152. In this text I shall be concentrating on the philosophical literature on emotion.

of awareness" that involve an element of factual judgment giving rise to belief, imagining, thinking, knowing etc.[59] He argues that the *evaluation* component of an emotion, in favor of or against what is evaluated, "requires some 'cognition', . . . some apprehension, on the part of the person who makes the evaluation".[60]

The existence of these elements in an emotion explains both how an emotion can have an object, and how it can be judged reasonable (in the sense of justifiable and well grounded) or unreasonable. Thus an emotion is unreasonable if it incorporates an unreasonable apprehension—e.g. a false belief. My anger with my son is unreasonable if he did not break the window; my reverence for God is unreasonable if God does not exist. But evaluations (and desires) may be regarded as unreasonable too, as is evidenced in the emotions containing them: such as violent anger over my son's "barbaric" untidiness, hatred or contempt at the sight of any "disgusting" human nakedness, or fear that includes a desire to avoid a "dangerous" situation that cannot in fact possibly harm me.[61] Clearly such evaluations are to be judged on the basis of evaluative norms for which it is not as easy to get agreement as it is with cognitions. Our grounds for making judgments of "reasonableness" are not as "objective" in these cases. It has been argued, however, that although there clearly are elements that can differ between societies, "there are natural and indeed logical limits to the range of what objects given emotions can take, and what emotions a human being is expected to feel or, alternatively, to dispense with".[62]

Educators in the tradition of "liberal education" (see Chapter 3) are happy to speak of educating a person's emotions—rather than just *training* them— with regard to their cognitive element, claiming with R. S. Peters that here "we speak of 'education' because of the work that has to be done on [a learner's] beliefs".[63] Thus with regard to the examples of unreasonable emotions given above, we may envisage educational techniques that would make me more

---

59. G. Pitcher, "Emotion", in R. F. Dearden *et al.*, eds., *Reason* (London: Routledge & Kegan Paul, 1975), p. 228; compare p. 224.

60. *Ibid.*, p. 227. See Lyons, *Emotion*, pp. 77, 208. Both Pitcher and Peters call the evaluative component of an emotion a cognition; see also Anthony Kenny, *Freewill and Responsibility* (London: Routledge & Kegan Paul, 1978), p. 46. Lyons is more of a philosophical purist in his use of language: "to evaluate is not to gain knowledge but to relate something already known and perceived to some rating scale" (*Emotion*, p. 59, also pp. 73, 77; but compare p. 62).

61. Pitcher, "Emotion", pp. 231-232. See Peters, "The Education of the Emotions", p. 86; Lyons, *Emotion*, pp. 65-66, 72-73, 78, 95.

62. Bernard Williams, "Morality and the Emotions", in his *Problems of the Self* (Cambridge: Cambridge University Press, 1972), p. 225.

63. Peters, "Education as Initiation", in Reginald D. Archambault, ed., *Philosophical Analysis and Education* (London: Routledge & Kegan Paul; New York: Humanities Press, 1965), p. 99; compare Peters, "The Education of the Emotions", pp. 86-87; also Ryle, "Can Virtue be Taught?", pp. 53-54, and the work of John Wilson (see above). See also Robert C. Solomon, "Emotions and Choice", *Review of Metaphysics* 27: 1 (1973), pp. 40-41 and *The Passions*, p. 197.

reasonable or rational in my emotional life by encouraging me, doubtless in the best open-minded educational manner, to change my beliefs and/or the evaluations arising from them. Christian religious education should certainly adopt such techniques.

But are there limits to such rational persuasion?[64] In addition to those limits outlined earlier in this chapter, rational persuasion—and education—is limited if, as some philosophers seem to think, *certain* emotions need not have or do not have grounds, and are not therefore open to appraisal by standards of appropriateness.[65] As such standards do not apply to these emotions, they are not to be judged "unreasonable" or "irrational" on the sort of criteria that may appropriately be used in other cases. They are rather, in one sense, nonrational or arational states. They might be regarded, in Peters's words, as "just one of those things to which human beings are subject".[66]

(Being in) love is regarded by some as such an emotion.[67] Christians often speak of Christian religious education as providing people "with a context for falling in love with Christ", and religious conversion as "other-worldly falling in love".[68] Of course, as Dwayne Huebner has reminded us, "love is

---

64. It has been argued that persuasion is rational when it is the case both (a) that reasons, facts or arguments are the agent of persuasion, and (b) that these reasons, facts or arguments are "to the point". J. N. Garver, "On the Rationality of Persuading", *Mind* 69: 274 (1960), p. 170.

65. Solomon suggests a different sort of limit to the power of reflection to change our emotions. To change our emotions we need more than insight, we also need a commitment to action—mainly through the *expression* of our emotions. Solomon, *The Passions*, pp. 421-422, compare pp. 424-425. See Irving Thalberg, "Emotion and Thought", in Stuart Hampshire, ed., *Philosophy of Mind* (New York: Harper & Row, 1966), pp. 209-210. Educators will recognize here the relevance of claims that people can act themselves into different ways of feeling. See Jeff Astley, "Growing into Christ", in Jeff Astley and David Day, eds., *The Contours of Christian Education* (Great Wakering, England: McCrimmon, 1992), pp. 317-318; James Michael Lee, *The Content of Religious Instruction* (Birmingham, Ala.: Religious Education Press, 1985), pp. 253-257.

66. R. S. Peters, "Reason and Passion", in Dearden *et al.*, eds., *Reason*, p. 68. Wilson himself acknowledges the limited extent to which we may criticize the lover as "unreasonable or misguided". Wilson, *A Preface to Morality*, p. 93.

67. Love, of course, has many dimensions. In ordinary language, psychological analysis and theological discussion it incorporates active good will and other particular ways of behaving. It is sometimes described as an emotion—either a basic emotion or a mixed emotion derived from two basic emotions. See Ortony *et al.*, *The Cognitive Structure of Emotions*, chs. 1 and 8, and Robert Plutchik, "Emotions: A General Psychoevolutionary Theory", in Klaus R. Scherer and Paul Ekman, eds., *Approaches to Emotion* (Hillsdale, N.J.: Erlbaum, 1984). At other times love is referred to as a disposition, virtue or attitude. Our interest here is in its affective dimension and its evaluative component.

68. John H. Westerhoff, III, *Living the Faith Community* (San Francisco: Harper & Row, 1985), p.98; Bernard J. F. Lonergan, *Method in Theology* (New York: Herder and Herder, 1972; London: Darton, Longman & Todd, 1973), p. 240, see also pp. 105-106, 270, 283. Similarly James Fowler writes: "Conversion means a recentering of our passion. It is a falling in love with . . . God". James W. Fowler, *Becoming Adult, Becoming Christian* (San Francisco: Harper & Row, 1984), p. 140. Walter Conn explores this theme in depth in his *Christian Conversion: A Developmental Interpretation of Autonomy and Surrender* (Mahwah, N.J.: Paulist, 1986), see pp. 23, 31, 134-150, 224-228.

a sticky wicket in educational circles".[69] If this is true of love *simpliciter*, how dare we risk drawing any educational conclusions from the phenomenon of "falling in love"? Yet of all human phenomena this seems closest to the religious impulse, a fact which demands that we consider it more closely.

Pitcher writes: "If Paul loves Suzy, there seems to be no clear sense in which his love might be called reasonable or unreasonable, rational or irrational and so on. . . .". The reason for this is that evaluations made by someone in love are "in a manner of speaking, indefensible: for in them, something is deemed good in itself". A person in love wants, for example, to be with his or her beloved; and wants this simply because the lover enjoys the company of the beloved for its own sake. There is no reason for it, the lover just wants to be with the beloved. Pitcher goes on to argue that this explains why a person's love of another, like a preference about ice cream, "cannot be adjudged reasonable or unreasonable" for it includes evaluations for which there can be "neither standards of criticism nor justifying reasons".[70] William Lyons comments on this passage that a lover does not love for reasons "because, if by 'reason' we mean a consideration which, if put to anyone, or at least almost anyone, would count for him, it is a category mistake to ask for reasons in such a case". In the case of love there are no "good reasons or real reasons". Only "private and personal" reasons could be given for the "rating or evaluative process" in emotions like love. This being so, Lyons continues, it might be useful to build on Pitcher's insight by making a distinction between an "appraisal" (a nonobjective, arational rating) and an "evaluation" (an objective, rational rating). Armed with this distinction he writes that "the evaluative aspect of certain emotions, such as love and hate, resembles more an exercise of unreasoning taste than of reasoned evaluation", and hence they should be termed appraisals rather than evaluations.[71]

Let us return to Pitcher's "something . . . deemed good in itself". We may

---

69. Dwayne Huebner, "Religious Metaphors in the Language of Education", *Religious Education* 80: 3 (1985), p. 466.

70. Pitcher, "Emotion", pp. 232-233; compare Peters, "Reason and Passion", p. 68. Similarly the sixteenth century Michel de Montaigne writes: "If I were pressed to say why I love him, I feel that my only reply could be: 'Because it was he, because it was I'". See his essay "On Friendship", quoted in Oswald Hanfling, *The Quest for Meaning* (Oxford: Blackwell, 1987), pp. 113-114. It may be argued, however, that the wants entertained by the lover can be adjudged reasonable or irrational (as in "blind infatuation") on the basis of our judgment as to whether the lover's beliefs about the beloved (she is "kindly", "good company" etc.) are well founded or not. See Gabriele Taylor, "Love", *Proceedings of the Aristotelian Society* LXXVI (1975/76). Yet surely the lover finds his beloved to have these qualities *because* he loves her.

71. Lyons, *Emotion*, p. 80. Pitcher denies that such an analysis applies to hate (see "Emotion", p. 223). Other philosophers agree that "we allow that people may love whatever they choose, . . . we do not as a rule speak of justification in this case". Mary Warnock, "The Justification of Emotions", *Proceedings of the Aristotelian Society* Supp. Volume XXXI (1957), p. 57. Warnock adds that we are more ready to criticize hatred as unjustified. This position is developed by A. C. Ewing, who adds "mild liking" to love as examples of cases where it "does not seem to the point to talk of the justification of emotions" (*ibid.*, p. 67).

contrast such an intrinsic good with the notion of an instrumental good.[72] The latter is good *for something*, and there is the possibility of considerable agreement in such a designation because it hinges on empirical questions of cause and effect. Has my enemy's behavior really done this to me? Have my friend's actions really had that effect? But it should be noted that instrumental goods are parasitic on intrinsic goods. And here the notion of appraisal/evaluation is shown to presuppose moral and nonmoral values. Something can be good (or evil)-as-a-means (i.e. has "extrinsic value") only if something else can be properly said to be good (or evil)-as-an-end in itself (i.e. has "intrinsic value", or—as some would prefer to say—"is a value").

It is now possible to develop further the discussion on evaluation and valuation introduced above (pp. 144-146). We can produce intersubjectively agreed, "rational" criteria for assessing what is to be considered instrumentally good. But what sort of justifying reasons could there be for intrinsic goods? "Why do you want to be with her?" "Because I do." This is an "ultimate" desire.[73] In the case of love we are faced by what Lyons calls a "private or personal reason", the rating scale used is "of a very personal and subjective sort". We find little (but we do find something) that is "objective" about it. We only agree up to a point as to what is—i.e. what we find to be, or rate as—"lovable", or even "desirable". (In this area, we may add, most people would admit that relativism *is* allowed to rule—compare Chapter 10 below.) There is much more common agreement as to what is to be evaluated "harmful", at least in the sense of dangerous-and-to-be-feared. Yet Lyons argues that even the rating of a situation as dangerous is done "with a personal twist", for it is seen as threatening me or to those close to me, "where I am the final arbiter of whether it is really threatening or not". A good proportion of fears are thus rated by others as phobias.[74]

We should note the inevitable gap between the factual claim (belief) and the evaluation raised on its foundation, for the latter is "a specific way of viewing the object". It is a disposition to evaluate, appraise or judge the object, that is to take a particular view of it in relation to one's own needs, interests or values. The evaluation is not logically tied to the belief in the sense that the former inevitably follows from the latter.[75] Only a firm—or rash?—belief in common sense, or "normal" human nature, or rationality will enable us to leap over the gap between the two without any qualms, dismissing those

---

72. See John Hospers, *Human Conduct* (New York: Harcourt Brace Jovanovich, 1972), part 3.

73. Roy Edgley, *Reason in Theory and Practice* (London: Hutchinson, 1969), pp. 159-163. John Wilson also notes that we often "do not know why we love this or that person or thing or activity" (*A Preface to Morality*, p. 91). He endorses the view that love is in many ways like religious commitment, in which similarly "different people attach themselves, or find themselves attached, to various objects of worship". But, Wilson adds, we need to make people more aware of their predispositions to love and worship, and "[match] them up to particular objects which can in reality satisfy them" (*ibid.*, p. 94).

74. Lyons, *Emotion*, pp. 59, 60.

75. *Ibid.*, pp. 77, 58, 86-87.

who evaluate things differently as "neurotic".[76]

So our discussion of the place of evaluation in emotion raises both the issue of value relativism, and that of valuing in general. The educator and the Christian religious educator must face some difficult questions: "Why do you (don't you) value—ascribe worth to or recognize the worth of—happiness, courage, duty, truth, justice; Arian features and the taste of peanut butter; power and fame; Jesus's character or the Kingdom of God?" Can it be that the answer in the end is always just: "Because I do (or don't)"? Some things are valued in and of and by themselves: not (or not just) as means to other goods, but as intrinsic goods. Are we to argue that the only possible answer to requests for reasons justifying these valuations is a personal one: "Because *I* do"?[77] It may be that I belong to a group that shares my valuation of such things, so that I can say "because *we* do".[78] Often that group will be so wide as to exclude only the "neurotics", but that should not blind us to the apparently thoroughly personal focus of such valuations, and the consequent plausibility of some form of value relativism. Solomon convincingly argues that what is included in *our* world but absent from *the* world is value, and adds that "the *source* of these values is the passions".[79] It is certainly not a pure, passionless objective or empirical reason that directs our actions and gives meaning to our life. Here lies the truth behind Hume's famous but misleading words: "It appears evident that the ultimate ends of human actions can never . . . . be accounted for by *reason*, but recommend themselves entirely to the sentiments and affections of mankind, without any dependance on the intellectual faculties".[80]

The implications of all this for Christian religious education should be clear. The teaching of Christian ideals, moral and spiritual values, attitude-virtues etc. is not to be justified by some rational appraisal of these learning outcomes, for ultimately they do not stand in need of, and cannot have, any such rational justification. On the view expressed here, the quest for a Christian religious education that will educate people into a "wholly rational adoption" of

---

76. Lyons argues that it is because an emotion such as fear is tied to a more or less objective evaluation that we dismiss someone who is afraid of flies as "neurotic", i.e. as having an irrational and persistent fear which conflicts with the (our) "commonsense" evaluation of its object (*ibid.*, p. 78).

77. This claim has been extended very widely—to life itself. Thus: "We do not remain alive *because* we judge that life is good—or for any other reason". "The desire to cling to life is one that exists in us independently of reason." "We do not desire [life] for a reason . . . but *that* we desire it is a reason for holding on to it . . . " (Hanfling, *The Quest for Meaning*, pp. 77-78).

78. Quinton points out that most agreed value judgments in fact "are just what they would be if to ascribe value to something were to assert that it is such as to give satisfaction to people in general in the long run". Anthony Quinton, *The Nature of Things* (London: Routledge & Kegan Paul, 1973), p. 366. See below p. 241.

79. Solomon, *The Passions*, pp. 67-68.

80. David Hume, *An Enquiry Concerning the Principles of Morals*, Appendix I, ed. L. A. Selby-Bigge (Oxford: Clarendon, 1902), p. 293. Hume uses "reason" here in a very broad sense to cover both inference and apprehension of objective facts. See Alan H. Goldman, *Moral Knowledge* (London: Routledge, 1988), pp. 55-61, and p. 233 above [Midgley p. 17 MS].

Christian values (on what grounds, one might ask?) is clearly a quest for an illusion. Values do not have that nature, and they cannot be taught in that way. Christian religious education must rather—and can only—produce a love for them. It must evoke feelings. This does not exclude its allowing a real place to rational reflection on those feelings; but reason can play no greater a role than that. Too much Christian religious education, particularly of adults, devotes itself entirely to cognitive, rational reflection on Christian values. If, as I have argued, such reflection is largely irrelevant as far as the recognition of intrinsic value is concerned, it is not surprising that it is impotent to effect religious change. In this area Christian *religious* education must primarily be an induction into religious feeling.[81]

Ethical Theories and their Educational Significance

But the account of valuation given above needs to be challenged. Many would argue that it confuses two different species of value. Thus it is said that the difference between the intrinsic goods desired by the lover (or the peanut butter eater), and the intrinsic goods valued by the moral (and religious?) man or woman, is that the latter are regarded as things that everyone *ought* to value. Moral valuation is a puzzling phenomenon and moral philosophy has come up with many different theories as to its nature. Serious students of moral education, and of religious education when it is seen to include moral education (as in Christian religious education), need to reflect on the nature of moral judgment.

On the view of ethics known as *intuitionism*,[82] moral judgments convey information ("moral facts"), but are different in kind from other judgments. On this account moral values are facts (but "non-natural" facts, not empirical facts) that are known by some kind of moral "insight", "vision" or non-inferential intuition. Correct moral judgments should be accepted by all, it is claimed, because they properly represent objective moral facts. Ethical *naturalism* (or descriptivism)[83] is a similar theory to the extent that it agrees that the value of something is an objective characteristic, but naturalism regards this as a consequence of certain natural or empirical features of that situation (e.g. "institutional facts", human wants and needs, "human flourishing") rather than of some mysterious non-natural feature. Intuitionism is now generally discredited. It has been criticized for assimilating ethical truths to necessities and for failing to explain their link with practical considerations; but some form of naturalism remains attractive to many contemporary philosophers. Others, however, reject this theory as not taking

---

81. See for example, Morton Kelsey, *Can Christians Be Educated?* (Birmingham, Ala.: Religious Education Press, 1977), ch. 6.

82. A view espoused, for example, by W. D. Ross in *The Right and the Good* (London: Oxford University Press, 1930); compare W. D. Hudson, *Ethical Intuitionism* (London: Macmillan; New York: St. Martin's Press, 1967).

83. See G. J. Warnock, *Contemporary Moral Philosophy*, ch. VI; W. D. Hudson, ed., *The Is-Ought Question* (London: Macmillan, 1969; New York: St. Martin's Press, 1973), parts Three and Four; Quinton, *The Nature of Things*, ch. 12.

seriously enough the fact-value dichotomy.

Christian religious educators are likely to be more sympathetic to a *super-naturalistic ethics*. This would defend moral objectivity by appealing to nonempirical, "supernatural" moral facts (ideals) that are identified with the will of God.[84] I would claim that such a position needs to be more grounded in the human pole of morality than many of its defenders allow, and needs to answer the basic question: do we not obey God because *we* recognize God's laws as "just" and "right"? This may involve a conflation of supernaturalism with a form of (created) naturalism.

Moral educators and Christian religious educators who are influenced by the three different accounts of morality given above will focus their attention on different objectives. Intuitionistic educators would concentrate on developing moral intuition (so-called moral "experience"), presumably relying on traditional accounts of how such moral disclosures may best be evoked, and such moral intuitions trained. Naturalistic educators would focus on passing on the received moral language of a culture (for those of a Christian persuasion, the culture of the church), with its in-built moral valuations. Whereas supernaturalistic educators would major on proclaiming the will of God, as expressed in classic and contemporary revelations about the "divine law". Or, if they espoused a different view of revelation, they might aim to evoke a contemporary discernment of God's will in ways that might be similar to the techniques of their intuitionist colleagues.

However, many philosophers do not believe that the (apparent) fact-value gap can be bridged by reducing values to facts, or deriving them from facts, in the ways suggested by these three theories. On the widely influential philosophical view of ethics known as *prescriptivism*,[85] the essence of moral discourse is that it is prescriptive: i.e. it entails imperatives. In saying that I "ought" to do something, x, that the action is "right" and its consequences "good", I am implicitly telling both myself and you to do x. If and when you sincerely accept my moral judgment on this matter and are able to act upon it, you will do x. That is what moral language *means*. Such a judgment, as we have seen, is said to be "universalizably" prescriptive—so in making the judgment I am implicitly telling *everyone* that they ought to do x under the same ("morally identical") circumstances. In doing so I am not stating moral facts. I am rather prescribing moral actions and similar moral attitudes in others.

This is an attractive explanation of what is going on when people judge morally. It relates valuation to prescription by bridging the gap with the notion of preference: I *prefer* action x on moral grounds, and therefore command you to do likewise. But it has been criticized for a number of reasons, not least the difficulty of giving an account of moral judgments that are in the past tense. It is also said to suffer from the basic weakness of conflating

---

84. Ward, *Ethics and Christianity*, chs. III and IV; see also G. F. Woods, *A Defence of Theological Ethics* (Cambridge: Cambridge University Press, 1966), chs. 5 and 6.

85. As developed by R. M. Hare. See the account given earlier in this chapter (pp. 222-223).

personal preference and moral (or other) valuation. In Bernard Williams's words "there is always room for any given person's choice not to be directly related to the way in which that person sees the merits of the thing", and "you can distinguish between thinking that a given item is good of its kind and liking, wanting or choosing that item".[86]

Prescriptivism is a *noncognitive account* of moral language, using that phrase once again to connote "neither true nor false" because "non fact asserting". (On this usage, statements of fact are cognitive utterances; whereas commands, recommendations, exclamations, and expressions of feeling and attitude are noncognitive.) According to prescriptivism, ethical utterances prescribe a particular sort of conduct, and thus can be neither true nor false. But as they are also universalizable—in ways that judgments of gustatory taste, some (but not all) aesthetic judgments, and many judgments of "lovableness" are not—they do not function in a merely individual, private or subjective fashion. On the other hand, prescriptivism is by no means a fully fledged objectivist theory of moral judgments, as is naturalism and all theological accounts of ethics. It does not imply any "objective ethical prescriptivity".[87]

The educational implications of presciptivism have already been outlined at the beginning of this chapter, in describing John Wilson's account of moral education. While not ignoring the development of the range of skills and capacities needed in order to be a "morally educated person", adherents of this position tend to lay considerable stress on rational reflection on the meaning of moral language and on the implications of rational morality.

Of the various accounts of moral language, the one that most appeals to me is the rather earlier view usually referred to as *emotivism*,[88] although I prefer the subtler version of it that has been variously described in philosophical circles as *the attitude theory*, the "attitudinist thesis", or the "approval" or "attitudinarian" analysis. Such accounts give a more central place to moral feelings and attitudes in their analysis of ethical judgments. They recognize that moral judgments are used to express (and not just report on) the feelings of speakers about the situations with which they are faced, in particular their feelings of approval or disapproval, or—on the attitude theory—their pro- or con-attitudes (which may be more than feelings alone). On this view, when we describe things as *morally* good or bad we are expressing an attitude of approval or disapproval towards them, and stimulating those attitudes in others.

One of the standard criticisms of simple emotivism is that it depends on a causal theory of "emotive meaning" that is implausible, in that in asking for

---

86. Williams, *Ethics and the Limits of Philosophy*, p. 125.

87. The phrase is from John Mackie. He adopts a position of "moral scepticism" which admits that "a belief in objective values is built into ordinary moral thought and language", but holds that "this ingrained belief is false". Mackie, *Ethics*, pp. 48-49.

88. See Charles L. Stevenson, *Ethics and Language* (New Haven: Yale University Press, 1944); compare J. O. Urmson, *The Emotive Theory of Ethics* (London: Hutchinson, 1968).

the meaning of a speaker's utterance we are not looking for an answer in terms of psychological causes and effects, for that is not a proper answer to a question about linguistic meaning. But the more sophisticated attitude theory of ethics, which refers to "valuational meaning" rather than "emotive meaning", can meet this criticism.[89] On such a view, all value statements express attitudes, and moral statements are simply a subclass of these expressing "more strident attitudes" that are "ways of being in favour of or against types of behaviour with a degree of force which makes us wish disfavoured actions discouraged by some kind of social sanction".[90] Such attitudes are not true or false in the way that beliefs are (in the sense of conforming—or failing to conform—to facts). But attitudes often appear to be opposite and incompatible, and thus can be treated rather like beliefs.[91] These approvals/disapprovals, it has been claimed, are (or contain) feelings that have an action-guiding character, for it is part of the meaning of the words "right" and "wrong" that "we are moved to do the action to which the word 'right' is applied, and we are *moved* to abstain from doing the action to which the word 'wrong' is applied".[92] Thus when we learn how someone feels about a form of behavior—and who could dispute that this is a major part of moral education and of Christian religious education?—we are in some sort of way being told what to do ourselves. An element of prescriptivity is thus incorporated into this account, and this is a function of the *logic* of moral words, and not just of the *psychological* effects of their use.

Attitudes, and therefore expressions of attitude, can properly be said to be inconsistent with one another in much the same way as beliefs and disbeliefs, because they have logical properties that are analogous to those which assertions have. My being in favor of A is inconsistent with your being against A in a sense that results from the inconsistency between the existence of A (which I am "for") and its nonexistence (a state of affairs of which you approve).[93] Thus, although attitudes are logically independent of factual statements and therefore there can be no formal, logical inconsistency between them (this preserves and underlines the fact-value distinction), yet we can rationally discuss and evaluate attitudes. It may be claimed, then, that one should strive "to organize one's mental stance towards the world so that it is consistent and comprehensive": consistent in that its elements do not frustrate one another, and comprehensive in that it "covers one's stance to as wide as possible a range of phenomena". Such a "mental stance" in a rational person should exclude inconsistent attitudes, that is attitudes for which

---

89. See T. L. S. Sprigge, *The Rational Foundations of Ethics* (London: Routledge & Kegan Paul, 1988), ch. III. Sprigge does not go all the way with the attitude theory, but regards it as "illuminating" and as having "real merits" (p. 76).

90. *Ibid.*, p. 61.

91. See Charles L. Stevenson, *Facts and Values: Studies in Ethical Analysis* (New Haven: Yale University Press, 1963), pp. 3-9, 26-30, and Essay VII passim.

92. Price, *Belief*, pp. 416-417.

93. *Ibid.*, pp. 402-412. Compare and contrast Vincent Brümmer, *Theology and Philosophical Inquiry* (London: Macmillan, 1981; Philadelphia: Westminster, 1982), pp. 112-117.

"there are circumstances in which they *cannot* . . . both be fully actualised in feeling and action".[94] The nature of moral judgments is such that, unlike mere taste preferences, they express my desire for a "world" that is not just a private world, but includes you and impinges on you. If the world I yearn for is incompatible with the world you yearn for, we may properly disagree in our moral judgments.

These insights allow the attitude theory of ethics to defend itself against another standard criticism of emotivism, that it undermines the notion of disagreement and argument in ethics.[95] So on this account, just as with the prescriptive view of ethics, we may claim that *moral* judgments are prescriptive and universalizable in a way that most prudential or aesthetic judgments are not. Peanut butter preferences are thus distinguishable from moral preferences.

This account of the matter may be reflected in a type of moral education that focuses primarily on the formation of appropriate moral attitudes (see Chapter 6 above), yet allows a place for *some* element of rational reflection and moral debate. It is this view of Christian moral education whose implications I intend to develop in the rest of this chapter.

It may still be asked, however, on what these "prescriptive and universalizeable" moral judgments are *based*. What is the reason for them? *Why* should we take up such moral attitudes? For it is always possible to argue for a logical gap between belief and attitude (at least when we chose the linguistic expression of both very carefully): a gap that is bridged only by our moral valuation and commitment.[96] It seems to me that there remains only one answer to such questions. Surely *in fine* approvals and disapprovals are just things we feel,[97] as are likes and dislikes. This may be claimed even when the nature and strength of that feeling gives them a prescriptive, universalizable character that makes them more "objective", at least in the sense of "intersubjective", and less "personal". We just feel certain things ("values") to be intrinsically good; we just approve of them. For such approvals there could be no "justifying reasons". Reason has its proper place in ethics, as in religion, but it must learn its place. It cannot go everywhere and do everything. It can, of course, very helpfully analyze and evaluate the instrumental goods of our personal and social lives. Reason can (sometimes) show us whether this course of action will lead to our flourishing, or to the greatest happiness of the greatest number, or not. Reason is our only tool in judging the consequences of our own and other's behavior. Reason can also help to lead us to adopt a consistent and comprehensive set of moral attitudes, and one that bears some proper relation to (but is not strictly logically implied by) factual statements about the world. But it cannot show us which things are intrinsically

---

94. Sprigge, *The Rational Foundation of Ethics*, p. 68.

95. See Stephen Toulmin, *The Place of Reason in Ethics* (Cambridge: Cambridge University Press, 1968), pp. 32-33; Goldman, *Moral Knowledge*, p. 66-67.

96. Stevenson, *Ethics and Language*, ch. VII; Urmson, *The Emotive Theory of Ethics*, ch. 7; Hudson, *Modern Moral Philosophy*, pp. 118, 145-146.

97. Price, *Belief*, pp. 417, 419, 424. Certainly "there can be no value without sentience, without emotion and desire". Quinton, *The Nature of Things*, p. 373; compare *ibid.*, pp. 360-361.

good, good in and of themselves (happiness, doing one's duty, honesty, knowledge?). To put it rather rashly: only *we* can do that, and we do it on the basis of what (how) we *feel*.

This interpretation certainly denies that there is any objective moral truth in the usual sense, while allowing reason a function in the moral life. The ethical attitudinist contends "that the basic idea of 'good' and 'bad' and of all value, arises . . . from what feels good or bad to us". But many, including Timothy Sprigge from whom this quotation is taken, would go on to say that "this good and bad which is demoted to the role of what only feels so is ultimately the value which is really there in the world", a world that contains "intrinsically prescriptive features". These value properties possess a necessary effect on the will of those who know them. They are really only there as qualifiers of consciousness—"since they consist in the various ways in which things feel good or bad to sentient beings".[98]

The logical implications for moral education and Christian religious education of Sprigge's view, and of the more thoroughgoing attitude theory, are similar. In both cases there would be a focus on getting people to "recognize value", which itself is largely a matter of aiming to influence the way learners feel about things (or, to put it differently, the way things feel to the learner). If education can change people's feelings and attitudes, both by exposing them to "values" or "valuable states", and by methods that are independent of such values, then education can change people's valuing. Again we come back to the claim that affective education is more than an education *about* the affections, and may properly involve facilitating a learner's own feeling-(and therefore valuing-) states. Religious education, I would argue, is very largely precisely that sort of enterprise, for religion is very largely a celebration and expression of a particular set of values. Christian religious education is that species of religious education that involves value changes that may properly be described as changes in a "Christian" direction, i.e. the adoption and deepening of "Christian values".

However, both emotivism and the attitude theory are usually regarded as open to the criticism made of prescriptivism above, i.e. that they fail to distinguish between an individual's attitudes and that person's assessment of the merit of the object or situation to which that attitude is directed. Sprigge's position seems to offer one solution, which may be particularly attractive to the theist. But it is a solution that does not seem to explain the variety of human valuation and leaves us with a puzzling ontology. In order to meet the criticism more realistically I would argue that the attitude theory, while capturing well the underlying basis of ethical discourse and thought, needs to be supplemented by some reference to what is more than an individual's preferences, prescriptions, emotions or attitudes, even when they are of a moral nature. This "more than" element will point us once again, as it did in our consideration of rationality in Chapter 7, to the social dimension of life—in this case of our

---

98. Sprigge, *The Rational Foundation of Belief*, p. 81. See also Hilary Putnam, *Reason, Truth and History* (Cambridge: Cambridge University Press, 1981), pp. 167-173.

moral life. One condition of the proper use of an ethical concept, it has been said, is "a matter of belonging to a certain culture".[99]

I made the claim above, with reference to the location of responsibility for the recognition of value, that "only *we* can do that, and we do it on the basis of what (how) we *feel*". It is time now that I placed as much emphasis on the "we" as I have already put on the "feel". Ethical obligation is what it is partly because of the existence of *agreed social norms* of what is good and right. Ethics is personal (because affective) *and* social. It is to this social dimension that we must now turn. As we do so the reader should keep in mind the implications for a Christian moral education for which the social dimension is the Christian community, its culture and its moral norms. It is the church, after all, that is the educational context of Christian moral education.

Some philosophers have tried to rescue notions of ethical objectivism, not by locating the objectivity of ethics in either an empirical or a supernatural world, but by situating it in the "world" of social constructs. It is these constructs that are passed on by formative education, or (less often) engendered by a more critical persuasive re-formation of values.[100] Alan Goldman's subtle account of moral knowledge develops from a particular understanding of Hume's feeling-analysis of moral judgments, as reports on feelings that would arise in an informed, impartial and consistent—i.e. "rational" valuator.[101] In developing this "relational view" in a relativist direction, so as to accommodate disagreements between rational valuators, Goldman claims to show that "the main constraints on moral judgment become those of consistency and avoiding factual errors". But these constraints, he claims, are better captured in the final ethical theory I shall consider: a nonrealist, *coherentist theory of ethics*.

Such a view is nonrealist (in a technical, philosophical sense) in that the truth of moral judgments is not independent of people's moral beliefs. It is coherentist in claiming that "the truth of moral judgments lies in their coherence within a moral framework".[102] It is argued that this position fully allows for our sense of the "objectivity" of morals, in that moral obligations exist independently of any particular believer's beliefs that they do. They exist as a function of the moral norms of that person's social groups or (more precisely) of a single moral framework—i.e. "a coherent set of moral judgments that might be endorsed by a rational individual or group".[103] This is, of course, a *relativist* coherentism that admits "that what is right in relation to one moral framework may not be right in relation to another".[104] As we shall

---

99. Williams, *Ethics and the Limits of Philosophy*, p. 144.

100. See Sabina Lovibond, *Realism and Imagination in Ethics* (Oxford: Blackwell; Minneapolis: University of Minneapolis Press, 1983), sections 28-35.

101. Goldman, *Moral Knowledge*, pp. 68-90. The quotation in the next sentence is from p. 89. This may be regarded as a form of "descriptivism" (see above p. 241).

102. *Ibid.*, p. 134.

103. *Ibid.*, p. 144.

104. *Ibid.*, p. 153.

argue below and in Chapter 10, such a relativist position can still allow for genuine disagreement, argument and rational resolution of (ethical) disputes. To anticipate that account somewhat, if such disputes are within the same moral framework, then argument is entirely proper. If the dispute is with someone who espouses alien standards, then the reasoning will have to be based on some (smaller) core of shared principles or limited to assumptions common to all beliefs, moral standards, agreed standards of rationality or fact, or merely pragmatic considerations, unless it leads to a "conversion" of one of the participants.[105] For these and other reasons, Goldman regards coherentism as a "cognitive" (truth asserting) account of ethics, which allows for proper "moral knowledge". (In Christian religious education this may be described as "Christian moral knowledge".)

Interestingly enough, however, this attempt to go beyond emotivism and its near relations to a more objective account of morality based on a recognition of its external source in the norms of those groups in which individuals interact, concludes with a recognition that "we must settle for a justification of moral norms in terms of their vital social and psychological functions". Goldman continues: "our motivation to obey them must derive from common sources: self-interest and our feelings for others. We must hope that these other-regarding feelings are reinforced by moral norms themselves."[106] Therefore the coherentist position, which clearly allows full scope for the passing on of ethical norms both through enculturation-type and through more intentional educational processes, also recognizes the relationship of such norms to human feelings. It thus must also recognize the role of the formation of emotions in moral (and therefore religious) education, and the "attitudinist" moral educator may borrow something from its resources.

We may conclude, with Bernard Williams, that "the preservation of ethical value lies in the reproduction of ethical dispositions".[107] Passing on the norms themselves is important because they incorporate the social, inter-subjective component of morality. But it is not enough on its own, and this is just as true when the norms concerned are those of Christian morality. Underlying these Christian norms, and undergirding our motivation to adopt them, we find once more a set of shared attitudes, dispositions and emotions that constitute the Christian character. Christian moral education may then be seen largely as a matter of forming people in the Christian character.

However we analyze the nature of morality and moral education, I contend that affect remains in a central place. Christian moral education cannot be properly understood without reference to the formation of the Christian affections (again see Chapter 6 above).

---

105. *Ibid.*, pp. 154-157.

106. *Ibid.*, p. 178. See also Williams, *Ethics and the Limits of Philosophy*: "social or ethical life must exist in people's dispositions" (p. 201); "people's dispositions . . . . are the ultimate supports of ethical value" (p. 51).

107. Williams, *Ethics and the Limits of Philosophy*, p. 51.

FURTHER EDUCATIONAL IMPLICATIONS

Education for Moral Conversion

It is human valuations, and their related pro- or con-attitudes, that lie at the basis of all moral judgments. We can live in societies because we share many of these judgments. We share them because we live in societies. Much of our language has such agreed valuations built-in ("deception", "generosity", etc.).[108] Within a shared "form of life" (including those incorporated in the Christian life) these language-games are played, and there is room for a considerable measure of rational debate and rational agreement as to whether certain acts are right or wrong. Where we agree on standards we can argue to a conclusion. But this happy fact should not blind us to the social context of agreed norms that integrates our individual felt valuations, nor to the less happy fact that the really serious moral disagreements cannot be resolved in this fashion. Moral dilemmas often arise because our society, embracing as it does different forms of life and traditions of moral reflection/valuation, recognizes intrinsic goods that can come into conflict (e.g. "general happiness", "honesty", "preserving life" and "respect for persons"). And "the problem with value-issues of this kind for the educator, is not that concepts like truth and rationality are inapplicable but that their application does not provide him with grounds for supporting the truth or rationality of one position *rather than* the other."[109]

With regard to these situations, I find myself in agreement with the position of John Elliott on value education in public ("state") education:

> Although it makes no sense to suggest that value-issues of this kind must be capable of being resolved in a rational way, this does not rule out the possibility of a consensus in judgements, which is based on more than a conventionalist acceptance of other people's beliefs. But any such resolution *must* proceed on the basis of reflective discussion on the different points of view at stake. Such an activity opens a disputant to the possibility of coming to accept his opponents' standards as a source of over-riding reasons . . . He simply comes to view a situation in a rather different light.[110]

Elliott can think of no better way of describing this than as a "conversion": a change of view which is "neither rational nor irrational" but rather "non-rational".[111] Such an illuminating vision involves a shift in loyalties between

---

108. Hare, *The Language of Morals*, part II.

109. John Elliott, "Neutrality, Rationality and the Role of the Teacher", *Proceedings of the Philosophy of Education Society of Great Britain* 7: 1 (1973), p. 55.

110. *Ibid.*, p. 61 ("reflective discussion" here is concerned with *understanding* the valuational standards of disputants, and is different from the "argumentative discussion" that is concerned with *defense and criticism* of judgments and assumes that rational consensus is possible).

111. *Ibid.*, Charles Bailey argues that such a limitation on reason would imply that we should "remain in doubt" on these matters, not that we should decide nonrationally. See his

forms of life and procedures of moral valuation. This account corresponds with the "visual ethics" that was described earlier.

I would argue that fundamentally this vision is very often a matter of our coming to feel differently, and thus that affective change lies at the core of this sort of moral education. It helps us to "see differently", almost "to see different things". And if this is true even of public education, it is certainly true of the moral education that forms a component part of any full Christian religious education. All really effective Christian religious educators ensure that people begin to look at life in a different way, as the Old Testament prophets and sages facilitated a different theological and moral way of viewing the world, and as Jesus encouraged his disciples to see, for example, that the widow's mite was a giving greater than that of anyone else. This is *education for conversion*: the overturning of values that is at the heart of the Christian gospel, and therefore at the heart of the communication of the Christian faith. We best "catch" this vision, popular claims notwithstanding, when we are "taught" it: using the broad understanding of Christian teaching that has been adopted in this book. This is the claim at the heart of those accounts of Christian religious education that argue for a central place for conversion to the Christian Way, in particular to the Christian way of seeing and valuing. In order to "have the eyes and ears of Christian faith", it is often said, "transformations, reorientations of life, conversions are necessary". Much Christian religious education is directed to precisely this end: to a "recentering of our passion".[112]

Even where rational assessment has a greater contribution to make in moral education, in school or church, in investigating the rationality of the *beliefs* that are components of and are otherwise relevant to emotions, its role is not always straightforward. For some of these beliefs are not straightforward empirical beliefs about the existence and behavior of persons or other entities in the world; but rather cosmic, metaphysical or transcendent beliefs about the nature of reality as such. If we come to believe that all things are illusory or transient, that all hearts are corrupted by original sin, or that God exists, then our assessment of the rationality of certain emotions should be different.[113] But such metaphysical beliefs cannot them-

---

"Neutrality and Rationality in Teaching", in David Bridges and Peter Scrimshaw, eds., *Values and Authority in Schools* (London: Hodder & Stoughton, 1975), pp. 129-132. But that would be to give up life in favor of an over-emphasis on reason. For a detailed account of the role of tradition in moral reasoning, and a defence of a notion of rational conversion in this context, see Alasdair MacIntyre, *Whose Justice? Which Rationality?* (London: Duckworth; Notre Dame, Ind.: University of Notre Dame Press, 1988), and below Chapter 10.

112. The quotations are from John H. Westerhoff, III, in John Ferguson, ed., *Christianity, Society and Education* (London: SPCK, 1981), p. 192, and James W. Fowler, in *Becoming Adult, Becoming Christian*, p. 140. See also Craig Dykstra, "The Formative Power of the Congregation", *Religious Education* 82: 4 (1987).

113. Hepburn writes of religious or metaphysical views seeking "to mediate and control emotions directed at nature as a whole—nature as divine handiwork, or as ominous and inhospitable". Here are emotional "seeings-as" of cosmic scope and immense complexity. See Hepburn, "The Arts and the Education of Feeling and Emotion", p. 95, also Peters, "Reason and Passion", pp. 67-68.

selves be easily assessed by reason, as we have seen (see especially chapter 4 above).

Freedom and the Emotions

A further point must be made about freedom and the emotions. The claim that we are free to choose our emotions, presumably on the basis of their rationality, seems even more bizarre than the claim that we choose our beliefs (see above Chapter 8). To some extent we may adjudge our emotions reasonable, and therefore as justified; but we do not adopt them on the basis of this judgment. We just have them; they happen to us. Thus Lyons argues that we cannot grieve on demand ("though on demand one might be able to induce grief"), for "having an emotion is not engaging in an activity and so is not the voluntary mobilising of anything as a means to this activity". Rather emotions are complex items "involving beliefs, evaluations, wants and physiological reactions to these" and "believing that something is true, evaluating in a particular way, and wanting something in particular are not things which can be done on demand".[114]

Lyons goes on to point out that we can of course exercise some sort of *indirect* control over our emotions by manipulating our environment, by reflecting on the rationality of our emotions, by self-deception or selective memory recall, by acting out behaviors that express certain emotions and by stifling other actions, or by expressing or curbing the expression of the emotion.[115] In so far as such actions are under a person's free control—and we may note how affective Christian learning may arise along these lines—then that person can be held to be partly responsible for the emotions that he has.[116] But this is only an indirect control, and an indirect responsibility, similar to the sort of control we have over our beliefs.[117] It should not obscure the central point that the emotions are mostly passively experienced. (For a psychologist's comment see note 127.)

Bernard Williams notes, against Kant's insistence that this fact renders emotionally governed action morally worthless (*because* not free), that we should not dismiss as hastily as Kant does the "vital contribution to the notion of moral sincerity" that is contributed by the element of passivity, the "sense in which moral impulses prompt us and courses of action are impressed on us". In an argument that closely follows the pattern of his argument against freedom of belief that we outlined in Chapter 8, he claims a certain resemblance between moral and factual conviction, suspecting it to

---

114. Lyons, *Emotion*, p. 181.

115. *Ibid.*, ch. 13; compare M. Black, "Reasonableness", p. 55, and G. Pitcher, "Emotion", pp. 236-237, in Dearden *et al.*, eds., *Reason*.

116. And therefore, under certain circumstances, he may be regarded as being blameworthy. We may still "find fault" with a person's feelings and beliefs, even though people do not decide what to feel or believe—see above p. 215.

117. Descartes takes a similar view of the passions, in marked contrast to his account of beliefs. See Chapter 8 and Anthony Kenny, *Action, Emotion and Will* (London: Routledge & Kegan Paul, 1963), pp. 8-9.

be true of moral, like factual, convictions that we cannot take seriously their profession if their professors claim to have *decided* to adopt them. I concur with Williams that the idea that people decide to adopt their moral principles is false, "a psychological shadow thrown by a logical distinction"; and further that if someone did claim to have done this, we would be justified in doubting his or her veracity or the reality of the moral principles so adopted.[118] Our ethical insights, along with—because, arguably, a function of—our emotions, mostly happen to us. They are forced into us, or out of us. We may "selectively direct our attention", engage in rational reflection, or indulge in various other activities—including educational activities, and our beliefs, evaluations and emotions may change as a result. But this is all the choice that we have in the matter.[119]

If this is the case, then the implications for educators drawn in the earlier chapter on freedom of belief apply here also. Our learners are not directly responsible for their emotions (or valuations or attitudes). As educators—and particularly as Christian religious educators—it may be that we carry a greater responsibility than they do for these learning outcomes. However mature these learners may be, and however much we want to develop their autonomy and independence of us and of the tradition we pass on, their adoption of these moral and religious learning outcomes remains beyond their direct control. It is something that largely happens to them, partly through the processes of education. Thus Christian religious educators have an even more influential position than we have noted so far.

Of course one can always find dissentient voices in philosophy, and in the debate over choice and the emotions one of the most articulate of these is that of Robert Solomon. Solomon takes the line that "emotions are judgments, and judgments are actions", and hence that "we choose an emotion much as we choose a course of action", although "non-deliberately", hastily and without careful consideration.[120] In his very valuable study of "The Myth and Nature of Human Emotion", Solomon adds his voice to those who attack the idea of the passions as animal, irrational intrusions into rational human lives. This is the "myth of passivity" in which we "suffer" our passions and "submit" ourselves to them. Against this view, he argues both that our passions (emotions, moods and desires) constitute our lives and provide them with meaning *and* that they are under our control. He claims that the passions are in essence rational because they are themselves interpretative judgments. They

118. Williams, "Morality and the Emotions", p. 227, compare p. 223. "Ethical conviction, like any other form of *being convinced*, must have some aspect of passivity to it, must in some sense come to you." Williams, *Ethics and the Limits of Philosophy*, p. 169.

119. See Hepburn, "The Arts and the Education of Feeling and Emotion", pp. 95, 98-99, 106 and note 127 below.

120. Solomon, "Emotions and Choice", pp. 32-33, 20, 40. Paul Holmer distinguishes "passions" (long-term, "held in place by resolutions and avowals") from "emotions" (short-term, "usually produced by external circumstances"). The latter are seldom voluntary, unlike the former. Paul L. Holmer, *Making Christian Sense* (Philadelphia: Westminster, 1984), pp. 42, 92.

are strategies—always intentional, but not always deliberative—with which we structure our world so as to maximize our dignity and self-esteem. The (intentional) objects of emotions[121] are objects in the world experienced through our concerns and values. Emotion is often associated with feeling, but "feeling is the ornamentation of emotion, not its essence". For Solomon, then, an emotion is an active self-involved, intense evaluation of what happens, rather than a passive response to it. It is for these reasons, Solomon claims, that emotions are so dependent on our opinions and beliefs. And it is for these reasons that he sides, as he puts it, with traditional Christianity and against Nietzsche and Jung, by asserting the voluntariness of the emotions. "What one 'feels' is what one chooses and accepts", by adopting a certain attitude; "our passions are our own *doings*, and thus our own responsibility".

Solomon claims that if emotions *were* essentially feelings, sensations, or occurrences, then they would be neither reasonable nor unreasonable. But since they are acts, they can properly be assessed in this way. We work ourselves up to being angry by judgments we make about the world (in this case the "judgment of accusation"). *These* interpretative judgments *are* "deliberative". Even falling in love is "not a matter of 'falling' at all, but of choice". "Love is a set of constitutive judgments to the effect that we *will* see in this person every possible virtue, ignore or overlook every possible vice." Thus Solomon urges us to develop a conception of *"rational passions".*[122] On this view our emotions in the end are "a bit of philosophy", based on beliefs and evaluations and subject to criteria of judgment.[123] The implications of such a position for Christian religious education are clear: education of the emotions becomes largely a matter of education (cognitive and rational in content and method) directed towards the formation of, and reflection on, these judgments, as well as towards the learners' exercise of their freedom of belief.

We have already recognized the importance of the cognitive element in emotions and discussed the status of their evaluative components. I would argue that Solomon's account—although full of insights in his account of the status of the passions in life and his detailed analyses of particular emotions—is fundamentally flawed with regard to the status he gives to their interpretative element. In particular, I am unable to follow him in treating such evaluations as free acts—things that we do (see above Chapter 8). In the end such a disagreement can only conclude with a phenomenological appeal to our experience of having emotions. Emotions may indeed be *indirectly* changed, often laboriously and very incompletely, by actions that we perform; but they do seem to be things that essentially "happen to us". The contrast

---

121. On the objects of emotions, see Kenny, *Action, Emotion and Will*, ch. 9 and J. R. S. Wilson, *Emotion and Object* (Cambridge: Cambridge University Press, 1972), chs. IV-IX.

122. Solomon, *The Passions*, quotations are from pp. xvi-xvii, 158, 191, 22, 25, 162, 199, and 431; also Robert C. Solomon, "The Logic of Emotions", *Nous* 11 (1977), pp. 46 and 48. See also Robert C. Solomon, *Love: Emotion, Myth and Metaphor* (Garden City, N.Y.: Doubleday, 1981), pp. 201-203, 212-213.

123. Solomon, *The Passions*, pp. 252, 262. For this reason there is a proper "logic" of the emotions.

between the accounts given by Pitcher and Solomon of "falling in love" (see above p. 238) will perhaps provide the crucial texts for the reader's own decision on this issue. I would argue that educators, including Christian religious educators, need to recognize that all claims about the control that our learners have over their emotions must be heavily qualified.

In all fairness to Solomon, however, it should be said that *some* of his accounts of the voluntary nature of our emotions do come close to the idea of the indirect control over our (essentially involuntary) emotions described by other philosophers. Thus: "We cannot simply have an emotion or stop having an emotion, but we can open ourselves to argument, persuasion and evidence".[124] I am very ready to accept, with Midgley and Mary Warnock, that "it is often perfectly possible, given time, to rouse oneself to genuinely like and mind about people"; and that one method of emotional education is "the method of teaching people *how to behave*" since "acting the part of the generous, the good loser, may bring you nearer to the character you are pretending to be".[125] I also agree that we have the power, to some extent, of opening or hardening our hearts—particularly by letting situations "speak to us".[126] But these represent only an indirect control over the affections.[127] This is, however, of some significance for the Christian religious and moral educator, who will work to encourage the learner to exercise what control she has over her affections in a particular way, so as to achieve a particular (Christian) end. The religious educator will thus work with the learner for her affective change (as well as for her cognitive change). But this is *not* the same as the claim that the learner can directly control, and is therefore herself directly responsible for, her feeling life through the exercise of her will.

Education and Emotion: Concluding Remarks

Many philosophers of education recognize among the aims of all education (and therefore of secular education) the importance and appropriateness of

---

124. Solomon, "Emotions and Choice", p. 40.

125. Midgley, *Heart and Mind*, p. 97; Mary Warnock, "The Education of the Emotions", in David E. Cooper, ed., *Education, Values and Mind* (London: Routledge & Kegan Paul; New York: Routledge, 1986), pp. 180-181. Warnock appeals to Aristotle's suggestion that the beginner in virtue must imitate the virtuous, for only through such practice can anyone acquire a disposition to virtue. She adds "and so it may be with feelings" (p. 181).

126. Francis Dunlop, *The Education of Feeling and Emotion* (London: Allen & Unwin, 1984), p. 109.

127. For some psychological accounts of these indirect methods of controlling emotions, see the comments by Howard Leventhal and Robert I. Levy, in Scherer and Ekman, eds., *Approaches to Emotion*, pp. 285-288 and p. 408. The regulation of confrontations with emotional events, of appraisals (which "can be modified . . . by selective attention and self-serving cognitive activities"), and of emotional urges and overt responses are considered in detail by Nico H. Frijda in *The Emotions* (Cambridge: Cambridge University Press, 1986), ch. 8. Frijda significantly comments, "emotions are handled. *Handling* has overtones of involving voluntary action . . . That is not what is meant. Regulation of emotion is not always voluntary; it mostly is not. The stance taken towards one's emotional experience or response is mostly involuntary, and so are the reactions instigated by that stance" (p. 402).

forming attitudes, character dispositions and moral virtues: i.e. of the inculcation or molding of character.[128] Moral education, they thus remind us, is not
just the education of moral thinking. Similarly, we may argue that Christian
religious education seeks to educate people not only to know (and understand
and reason about) the truth, nor just to do the truth, but also—in
Kierkegaardian terms—to "be the truth".[129] The espousal of such a person-
making aim can only be defended on the basis of ethical claims about what
are the intrinsically valuable ("truthful"?) states of the human personality, and
about the components of human fulfillment. Christian theology and Christian
ethics have much to say on these subjects; more, certainly, than "mere reason" has to offer us.

When John Macmurray writes of the "education of the emotions" he certainly means something more than rational reflection on them, although that
aspect is by no means ignored. For Macmurray "the education of our emotional life is primarily an education of our sensibility". This involves our
experiencing the world for its own sake, without any ulterior purpose—an
"emotional knowledge" of the world as it is, through soaking ourselves in the
life of the world about us. It is a "training in the capacity of sensitiveness to
the object", "the cultivation of a direct sensitiveness" to the reality of the
world. This experiencing-for-the-sake-of-experiencing, Macmurray claims,
is a matter of aiming at William Blake's "refinement of sensuality". We may
also relate it to Simone Weil's account of "attention" in academic study and
religious devotion.[130] It is *education for seeing*.

Others have drawn similar parallels in the more explicitly religious domain.
John Herman Randall compares the work of the artist with that of the religious
educator (here the "prophet" and "saint") whose religious symbols evoke
an emotional response that makes us see reality differently:

> The work of the painter, the musician, the poet, teaches us how to use
> our eyes, our ears, our minds, and our feelings with greater power and skill.
> It teaches us how to become more aware both of what is and of what
> might be, in the world that offers itself to our sensitive receptivity. . . . .
>
> Is it otherwise with the prophet and the saint? They can do something
> to us, they too can effect changes in us and in our world. They too can teach
> us something, about our world and about ourselves. . . . . They enable us
> to see and feel the religious dimension of our world better, the "order of

---

128. Compare John White, *The Aims of Education Restated* (London: Routledge &
Kegan Paul, 1982), pp. 126-127; Wilson *et al.*, *Introduction to Moral Education*, pp. 168-
176.

129. See Søren Kierkegaard, *Training in Christianity*, trans. Walter Lowrie (Princeton,
N.J.: Princeton University Press, 1941), p. 202.

130. Macmurray, *Reason and Emotion*, pp. 34-35, 37, 44, 46, 71. Simone Weil writes of
the "attention" which, with its quality of openness, underlies both true academic study and true
prayer. See her essay "Reflections on the Right Use of School Studies with a View to the
Love of God", in Simone Weil, *Waiting on God*, trans. Emma Craufurd (London: Collins,
1959), pp. 66-76.

splendor", and of man's experience in and with it. They teach us how to find the Divine; they show us visions of God.[131]

In his account of affective education, Francis Dunlop stresses the importance of facilitating the growth of the "'structure of human feeling' (which largely constitutes human nature)". This will involve, among many other educational strategies, the provision of "a suitable environment for the unfolding of the affective aspects of the person", and (sometimes) the eliciting and encouraging of "new impulses and feelings". Education may properly include, then, teaching learners "how to feel". Changing people's beliefs-that alone is not enough; educating emotions must involve a change of "feeling-awareness". Bearing in mind the earlier discussion in this chapter of the social dimension of moral education, it is interesting to note that Dunlop adds that educating emotions too must be a communal thing, a "shared feeling-awareness". Indeed he argues that our sense of community is based on "shared feeling-responses". Without them community is impossible; and education—and (we might add) Christianity—is "impossible without community".[132]

Here then are other examples of an education of the emotions that involves developing and changing the emotional experience that children, youth and adults have and undergo. It is about changing and evoking emotions, and not just getting the learner to *think about* them.[133] Incorporating the appropriate content, we may adopt it as a significant feature of the activity we have called Christian religious education.

---

131. John Herman Randall, *The Role of Knowledge in Western Religion* (Boston: Starr King, 1958), pp. 128-129. It is only honest to point out that Randall is a noncognitivist in religion, and that for him the "Divine" has only a symbolic reality (see *ibid.*, pp. 103-122, 141-142).

132. Dunlop, *The Education of Feeling and Emotion*, ch. 5, quotations are from pp. 87, 88, 91, 97, 98 and 105.

133. It has been claimed that "if it be true that emotion needs to be disciplined by thought, it is just as true . . . that thought needs to be disciplined by emotion". A. Victor Murray, *Education into Religion* (New York: Harper; London: Nisbet, 1953), p. 101.

CHAPTER 10

Relativism, Religion and Education

INTRODUCTION

In his outspoken critique of contemporary American education, *The Closing of the American Mind*, Allan Bloom claims: "There is one thing a professor can be absolutely certain of: almost every student entering the university believes, or says he believes, that truth is relative. . . . . Relativism is necessary to openness; and this is the virtue, the only virtue, which all primary education for more than fifty years has dedicated itself to inculcating."[1] Bloom is referring here to a rather vulgar, facile, "late adolescent" relativism which lacks philosophical or psychological depth. Nevertheless he has put his finger on a supremely important problem. In any view of philosophy and of education in general, and in our consideration of the philosophy of religious education in particular, no debate is as central as that between—to present it in its extreme form—the relativist and the absolutist.

THE PROBLEM OF RELATIVITY

The Origins of Relativity

It is important to distinguish, as far as is possible, the philosophical debate about *relativism* from the issue of *relativity*. All educators, including religious educators, need to reflect on the state of mind, attitudes and emotions that accompany the learner's recognition of the *variety* of human interpretations of reality, and the variety of the values that people hold. This is the "Problem of Relativity". It is a recognition of *plurality* or, as some would say, of *pluralism*[2]—of the fact that people think differently. This may come both to those who espouse one of the philosophical positions that may be described

---

1. Allan Bloom, *The Closing of the American Mind* (Penguin: London; New York: Viking Penguin, 1987), pp. 25-26; compare pp. 34, 39-40.
2. I am using these terms simply to describe the situation in which there is a variety of different beliefs: compare below note 28.

as relativism, and to those who reach no such philosophical conclusions and perhaps engage in no philosophical reflection at all. Relativity raises profound issues for the practice of education in general and Christian religious education in particular, and is important as a prolegomenon to a more thoroughgoing philosophical examination of relativism itself. The problem of relativity calls for the analytic enquiry of the philosopher, not least because it is the natural starting point for practical educators in considering the "Problem of Relativism".

In the history of ideas, the eighteenth-century Enlightenment is often seen as a time when the variety of religions and worldviews came home to Westerners for the first time. The philosophers of this period usually responded to this disclosure by appealing to a rather abstracted, culture-free notion of rationality: a critical reason that was thought to be above, and hence able to judge, particular knowledge claims of particular communities (see above Chapter 7). This "solution" to the problem of relativity still has its advocates today, as does that propounded by those heirs of the Enlightenment with a particular interest in the variety of religions who explicitly advocated a relativism of truth claims.[3] A second great irruption of the problem of relativity arose in the early years of this century in response to the disillusionment with absolutist views produced by people's experience of the "Great War" of 1914-18, and the decline of social and intellectual traditions that came after it.[4]

Fowler on Relativity

As with many intellectual changes that we can identify in social history, a similar "recapitulation" may be traced in the development of the individual. For many people the discovery of variety and the sense of what Karl Barth called "the accursed relativity of every merely human possibility"[5] is a highly significant, and often traumatic, event in their life histories. This aspect of the problem of relativity is well captured in the writings of James Fowler. His research into "faith development"—a term that he uses to denote the development of an individual's way of knowing, valuing and responding to her "ultimate environment" (that which she takes to be ultimate)—makes reference to a number of faith stage changes which have implications for a study of the problem of relativity. Before examining these we should note that Fowler's account should be seen in the light of his reaction to the work of the theologian H. Richard Niebuhr, who had shown him "that relativity need not lead to relativism, but that all of our constructions of meaning, all our worldviews are in some sense relative to the ground of being and meaning".[6]

---

3. See, for example, G. E. Lessing, *Nathan the Wise*, trans. William A. Steel (London: Dent; New York: Dutton, 1930).

4. Compare Karl Mannheim, *Ideology and Utopia: An Introduction to the Sociology of Knowledge*, trans. Louis Wirth and Edward Shils (London: Routledge & Kegan Paul, 1936; New York: Harcourt Brace, 1956), part II.

5. Karl Barth, *The Epistle to the Romans*, trans. Edwyn C. Hoskyns (London: Oxford University Press, 1933), p. 255.

6. Quoted in Craig Dykstra and Sharon Parks, eds., *Faith Development and Fowler* (Birmingham, Ala.: Religious Education Press, 1986), p. 4.

Fowler's claim to have escaped relativism, which he defines as the view that "religious claims and experience have no necessary validity beyond the bounds of the communities that hold them",[7] need not concern us. There are many references in his writings to the nature of transcendent Reality— of the ultimate "Oneness" that underlies our plural, many-sided experience;[8] but he does not present philosophical arguments to substantiate these onto- logical claims, nor any explicit defenses of the implied epistemological posi- tion that knowledge claims and truth transcend particular perspectives. All we have is Fowler's recognition that his stance on the particular point considered here is based on a "theological grounding"—i.e. a particular metaphysical view of Reality.[9]

However, Fowler's work is more illuminating of the problem of relativi- ty. Fowler acknowledges that a recognition of relativity is a potent force in the development of human faith. Thus in moving from "Stage 3" (the "Synthetic-Conventional Stage" in which a person's meaning and valuing is obtained second-hand from a range of significant others) to "Stage 4" (the "Individuative-Reflective Stage" when the individual "chooses" or "decides for herself" what sort of worldview and value system she will adopt) a per- son may first experience the unsettling "vertigo of relativity".[10] Psychologically she has "left home",[11] usually physically and geographically, but more impor- tantly existentially and emotionally—even if she still remains living with mother. She has jumped out of the all-enveloping culture and is poised like a fish out of water, recognizing for the first time that her life up until now has been immersed in this particular medium and stream,[12] and able for the first time to identify a number of alternative bodies of water—and indeed even more alien environments. Those religious educators and pastors who are

7. James W. Fowler, *Stages of Faith: The Psychology of Human Development and the Quest for Meaning* (San Francisco: Harper & Row, 1981), p. 15.

8. See James Fowler, "Faith Development Theory and the Aims of Religious Socialization", in Gloria Durka and Joanmarie Smith, eds., *Emerging Issues in Religious Education* (New York: Paulist, 1976), p. 204; also *Stages of Faith*, p. 198.

9. James W. Fowler, "Dialogue Toward a Future in Faith Development Studies", in Dykstra and Parks, eds., *Faith Development and Fowler*, p. 284.

10. See Peter L. Berger, *The Social Reality of Religion* (Harmondsworth, England: Penguin, 1967) (= *The Sacred Canopy*; Garden City, N.Y.: Doubleday, 1967), p. 186. Compare: "For the true believer or the believer in truth, the endless erring of signs, which issues in the radi- cal relativity of meaning, brings nauseating vertigo. It seems that the only cure for this disease is the certainty that truth promises." Mark C. Taylor, *Erring: A Postmodern A/theology* (Chicago: University of Chicago Press, 1984), p. 176. But, Taylor adds, "since appearances are always appearances of appearances, truth can never be pinned/penned down".

11. Fowler, *Stages of Faith*, p. 177. See also Romney M. Moseley, David Jarvis and James W. Fowler, *Manual for Faith Development Research* (Atlanta, Ga.: Center for Faith Development, 1986), pp. 113, 133.

12. The metaphor, in its undeveloped form, is from George Santayana—see *Stages of Faith*, pp. 161, 177. Fowler writes of "experiences or perspectives that lead to critical reflec- tion on how one's beliefs and values have formed and changed, and on how 'relative' they are to one's particular group or background". James W. Fowler, "Perspectives on the Family from the Standpoint of Faith Development Theory", *Perkins Journal* 33: 1 (1979), p. 12.

involved with first year college students will recognize the condition, at least in those students who have not been "cured" of the vertigo before they have properly experienced it by a too early inoculation with the serum of "easy relativism". It often shows itself in a syndrome of acute, even chronic, disease: a sense of untargeted anxiety deriving from the recognition that "everyone thinks something different".[13]

The response to the vertigo of relativity, particularly for the religiously inclined, can be a rapid conversion to one particular set of beliefs and values. Conservative Christians, arguing an absolutist position, may welcome such a response, for if there is One Truth and One Ideal we should embrace it as quickly as possible. But whose view is this: the teacher's (which makes this a Stage 3 response) or the learner's (at Stage 4)? Christian learners can easily get stuck in a transitional stage between Faith Stages 3 and 4 if they attempt to cope with relativity by strengthening their reliance on external "faith authorities" while at the same time they are developing a new power of critically distancing themselves from their previous value system. It is only when they begin truly to "think for themselves" that the movement to Stage 4 is complete.[14]

But Stage 4 is not the end of the matter for some people. Fowler argues that the individual who has adopted a particular worldview for himself may find as he develops that this becomes more open—more "porous and permeable"[15]—in a fifth stage of "Conjunctive Faith". Now the person begins to recognize again, although perhaps less traumatically this time, that truth is many faceted and is to be found in a variety of places. Conjunctive faith is a way of meaning-making that recognizes "the relativity of place, language and culture of its own apprehensions in faith" and thus "learns to bring a principled openness to encounters with the strange truths of other religious and cultural traditions". This is related to what Fowler calls the "epistemological humility" of this stage.[16] While arguing that Stage 5 relativity is the recognition of the relativity of religious traditions "to the reality to which they mediate relation", Fowler asserts that Stage 5 overcomes the dizziness of relativity by a "radical openness to the truth of the other" that is made possible by "its confidence in the reality mediated by its own tradition".[17] Unlike Stage 4, where "ideological purity and consistency are major concerns, as is defending one's own ideologically held perspective against the threat of relativity",[18] open-endedness and mutuality is now the mark of the person's new balanced or inclusive faith. "This embracing of multiple meanings and per-

---

13. The emotional impact of "the loss of assumed certainty" is well described in Sharon Parks, *The Critical Years: The Young Adult Search for a Faith to Live By* (San Francisco: Harper & Row, 1986), pp. 24-26, 51-53.

14. Fowler, *Stages of Faith*, p. 179.

15. *Ibid.*, p. 198.

16. James W. Fowler, *Faith Development and Pastoral Care* (Philadelphia: Fortress, 1987), pp. 72-73.

17. Fowler, *Stages of Faith*, pp. 186-187

18. Moseley *et al.*, *Manual for Faith Development Research*, p. 148.

spectives, and the attempt to hold these in critical tension without reductionism is a key characteristic of Stage 5. . . . . The individual. . . . does not reject this plurality as a source of confusion nor seek to reduce it to a simpler scheme, but will embrace this feature of reality as a possible source of deeper understanding, allowing reality to present different aspects of itself to awareness."[19] This is not the simple view "that affirms that one belief is as good as another",[20] but a more sophisticated, complex view that finds (a multilevel) truth in many unexpected places, and is open to conversion to that truth wherever it is discerned. Thus Fowler's final stages of faith development (for this is even more markedly shown in the rare Stage 6) represent a living-with and learning-from relativity.

Here we have a most powerful and insightful account of how people cope with the problem of relativity as they develop. It is of considerable relevance to the practical concerns of the Christian religious educator.

Relativity and Christian Religious Education

The "pluralization of consciousness" in which an "outer plurality is matched by an inner plurality" is a major element in the modern psyche. According to John Hull such an "inner fragmentation" may show itself in the variety of roles that an individual must adopt in both private and public spheres. It is also expressed in the various kinds of consciousness, "worlds of meaning" or convention matrices that we adopt in our lives. It is through reflection on this inner pluralism that "we may be able to relativize the modernity which had previously seemed absolute or taken-for-granted, thus introducing an awareness of pluralism".[21]

Hull argues that creating an awareness of relativity is one of the most important outcomes of adult education, and that it is particularly important in the field of adult Christian religious education. Hull is more sympathetic than many religious educators to the strategy of introducing Christian learners to a sense of relativity, arguing that we should seek not the expulsion of pluralism but its "transformation . . . into a higher unity" where plural ideologies and consciousnesses may be mutually interrelated and recognized as a plurality "in contrast to and in relation with that which is One and Undivided".[22] Although the more philosophical aspects and implications of these processes are left undeveloped, we have here an important voice raised in commendation of the educational value of a recognition of *relativity*, particularly in Christian religious education. If the world of experience *is* actually plural, and people *do* think differently (and have done so down the ages of Christian tradition), then Christian learners need to face this fact and

---

19. *Ibid.*, p. 153.

20. *Ibid.*, p. 172.

21. John M. Hull, *What Prevents Christian Adults from Learning?*, (London: SCM, 1985), pp. 27-34 (quotation from p. 27); see also pp. 194-195. Compare Peter L. Berger *et al.*, *The Homeless Mind: Modernization and Consciousness* (New York: Vintage Books; Harmondsworth, England: Penguin, 1974), pp. 62-77, pp. 102-103.

22. Hull, *What Prevents Christian Adults from Learning?*, pp. 33-34. See above Chapter 5.

come to their Christian understanding and commitment *through* it. The awareness of plurality/relativity, and the way in which the Christian learner learns to make sense of this phenomenon, is clearly of signal importance for Christian religious education. At a certain stage, according to Gabriel Moran, "religious education is a process of de-absolutizing answers, even the best of religious answers that can be learned in school".[23]

Claims like these are strengthened by Walter Conn's assertion that "adult knowing appreciates the relativity of context: historical, political, social, cultural, personal", as well as by Robin Gill's recognition of Christian pluralism and his apologia for a "relational" understanding of the Christian faith.[24] Such accounts, and the understanding of Christian religious education to which they lead, are clearly informed by a particular interpretation of the nature of Christian truth. However, not everyone will respond to the problem of relativity in this way. How we respond to that problem, and how we help those whom we teach to respond to it, may in the end depend very much on where we stand on the even more fundamental issue of the problem of *relativism*. It is to this that we must now turn.

THE PROBLEM OF RELATIVISM

The debate over relativism is arguably the most significant intellectual issue in the recent history of ideas and in contemporary philosophical debate. It has profound implications for both theology and Christian religious education. Most Christian religious educators and theologians are very wary of relativism, but I wish to argue that a *properly qualified* relativism is less avoidable, more defensible—and less destructive—than is often thought.

The fact that people disagree about truth and value is a very important fact, and I have acknowledged that how they cope with this should be an important concern of any serious Christian religious education. This problem of relativity has philosophical implications when it leads to, or is compounded with, philosophical claims. But we must clearly distinguish at the outset between an empirical, descriptive thesis about the actual diversity of human thought ("different people think differently"), and a philosophical (epistemological) claim about the nature of truth ("truth is relative"). It is this second thesis that constitutes relativism proper.

Types of Relativism
In much of the account that follows I shall draw on the exposition and defense of relativism and religious relativism presented by Joseph Runzo in his

---

23. Gabriel Moran, *Religious Education Development: Images for the Future* (Minneapolis: Winston, 1983), p. 204.

24. Walter Conn, *Christian Conversion: A Developmental Interpretation of Autonomy and Surrender* (Mahwah, N.J.: Paulist, 1986), p. 56; Robin Gill, *Competing Convictions* (London: SCM, 1989), pp. 11-12, and Part Three *passim*.

Reason, Relativism and God.[25] Runzo has brought some useful order to the incipient chaos of many debates about relativism by distinguishing different types of relativistic thesis. Runzo defines *relativism* as "any epistemological position which holds or entails that the correctness or incorrectness of judgments about matters of truth or value varies with which individual, or set of individuals (such as a society or the whole human race) is making the judgment". He adopts, as do many others, the more descriptive term *cognitive relativism* for this epistemological position, defining it thus: "truth is relative to the cognitive element [concepts, beliefs, laws of logic, etc.] which the mind brings to experience".[26] As we shall see, Runzo also recognizes both a distinction *between* cognitive relativism (which he accepts) and a stronger (and implausible) relativist view that he calls *epistemological relativism*; and also a distinction *within* cognitive relativism between a (plausible) socially-defined *conceptual relativism* and an (implausible) individualistic *subjectivism*. It is the form of cognitive relativism that he calls conceptual relativism that Runzo expounds and defends.

Runzo underlines the claim already made above that these epistemological positions are to be distinguished from the philosophically much less significant set of views that find their natural home with the social sciences rather than in philosophy, and offer an account of the diversity of beliefs and thoughts ("relativity") rather than of the relativism of truth. These include assertions of situational relatedness (truth or value is relative to a particular situation),[27] and of the diversity of apparently incompatible beliefs and worldviews (*pluralism*[28]). This latter diversity may be explained in terms of dif-

---

25. Joseph Runzo, *Reason, Relativism and God* (New York: St. Martin's Press; Basingstoke: Macmillan, 1986).

26. *Ibid.*, pp. 27, 35.

27. *Ibid.*, p. 26. Runzo accuses Troeltsch and Lonergan, among others, of using "relative" in this "trivial and uninformative sense" (see also p. 70 n. 9). See Ernst Troeltsch, *The Absoluteness of Christianity and the History of Religions*, trans. David Reid (Richmond: John Knox Press, 1971; London: SCM, 1972), pp. 66-71, compare ch. 3; Bernard Lonergan, *Doctrinal Pluralism* (Milwaukee: Marquette University Press, 1971), p. 10; but contrast Bernard Lonergan, *Insight: A Study of Human Understanding* (New York: Philosophical Library, 1958), pp. 342-347.

28. "Pluralism" seems to be used by Runzo here simply as a description of the plural nature ("plurality") of any society in which there is a variety of worldviews (sense 1). By contrast, "pluralism" is often used by others to indicate (sense 2) a political/social, or (sense 3) an intellectual/theoretical unity that embraces this variety. Thus Lee writes of religious plurality as "merely the coexistence of the whole range of religious worldviews", whereas for him pluralism denotes "intermingling, cooperation, or joint activities" (sense 2). James Michael Lee, "The Blessings of Religious Pluralism", in Norma H. Thompson, ed., *Religious Pluralism and Religious Education* (Birmingham, Ala.: Religious Education Press, 1988), p. 59, compare *ibid.*, pp. 10-11. Similarly Kenneth Leech distinguishes a merely *plural* society ("containing a variety of ethnic and religious groupings") from a *pluralist* society "which has accepted its new character". Kenneth Leech, *Struggle in Babylon* (London: Sheldon, 1988), p. 126. See also Lesslie Newbigin, *The Gospel in a Pluralist Society* (London: SPCK; Grand Rapids, Mich.: Eerdmans, 1989), p. 14. John Hick describes his own view that the range of world faiths "constitute different conceptions and perceptions of, and responses to, the Real from with-

ferences in culture (*cultural relativism*), historical background (*historicism*), form of life/"language-game", ideology, or dominant "paradigm" of reasoning or action.[29] These descriptions of diversity (what has been called "mere sociological relativism") may give rise to an epistemological account of the relativism of truth ("normative relativism"), but they do not necessarily imply such an account.[30]

A final and very important distinction must be made between cognitive relativism (the view that truth is relative) and *value relativism* (the view that values are relative). For those who believe that ethical, and perhaps aesthetic, language is cognitive (that is "fact asserting"—i.e. it can be either true or false), the option is open to be either an absolutist or a relativist about these value truths. But many philosophers in recent years have given accounts of ethical and aesthetic language that imply that such discourse does not make assertions that can be either true or false ("cognitive utterances") but rather expresses the speaker's feelings or her commitment to a particular way of life, and/or is used to persuade others to adopt a particular policy of action. Such "noncognitive" analyses provide examples of ("pure"?) value relativism. In Chapter 9 I have analyzed some of these noncognitive accounts of ethical language and commented on their implications for Christian religious education and its dimension of moral education.

The Origins of Relativism

The philosophical debate about relativism is a very ancient one. Plato defended the absolutist position against the relativist claims of Sophists like Protagoras who asserted that humanity was "the measure of all things", and that any given thing "is to me such as it appears to me, and is to you such as it appears to you".[31] Focusing on a related Platonic theme, Richard Rorty has averred:

in the different cultural ways of being human" as "the pluralistic hypothesis"—i.e. sense 3. See John Hick, *An Interpretation of Religion* (London: Macmillan; New Haven: Yale University Press, 1989), p. 376 and Gavin D'Costa, *Theology and Religious Pluralism* (Oxford: Blackwell, 1986), ch. 2. However, Hick elsewhere uses "pluralism" in sense 1, referring to the "pluralistic religious life of humanity" (*An Interpretation of Religion*, p. 249). Here others would prefer the adjective "plural". For the debate about the significance of different understandings of pluralism in education, see David Day, "Agreeing to Differ: The Logic of Pluralism", in Frank Coffield and Richard Goodings, eds., *Sacred Cows in Education* (Edinburgh: Edinburgh University Press, 1983).

29. *Reason, Relativism and God*, pp. 10-11, 33 and 58. Historicism probably represents the intellectual origin of much contemporary relativism. It is the view that historical periods differ radically one from another, and can only be understood in their own terms (Karl Popper calls this "historism"). For Dewey's critique of absolutism and his recognition of "historic relativity", see John Dewey, *Philosophy of Education* (Totowa, N.J.: Littlefield, Adams, 1958), pp. 12-13, 135-137.

30. This nomenclature is used by Ernest Gellner: see his *Legitimation of Belief* (Cambridge: Cambridge University Press, 1974), p. 48. For another classification of types of relativism see Alvin I. Goldman, *Epistemology and Cognition* (Cambridge, Mass.: Harvard University Press, 1986), pp. 69-72.

31. Plato, *Theaetetus*, 152a, trans. G. M. Cornford in E. Hamilton and H. Cairns, eds., *The Collected Dialogues of Plato* (Princeton, N.J.: Princeton University Press, 1961), p. 856.

"The urge to say that assertions and actions must not only cohere with other assertions and actions but 'correspond' to something apart from what people are saying and doing, has some claim to be called *the* philosophical urge".[32]

The modern philosophical debate on relativism, however, at least in some of its most powerful redactions, can be traced back to the influence of the great Enlightenment philosopher, Immanuel Kant. Although Kant himself cannot be characterized as a relativist,[33] in advocating his "Copernican revolu-

---

For Plato's responses see sections 170-179. For a critique of Plato's position here see Paul Feyerabend, *Farewell to Reason* (London: Verso, 1987), pp. 42-62.

32. Richard Rorty, *Philosophy and the Mirror of Nature* (Oxford: Blackwell; Princeton, N.J.: Princeton University Press, 1980), p. 179.

33. In a closely argued monograph Terry Godlove challenges the "framework model" in which different (religious) traditions represent alternative conceptual frameworks or ways of looking at the world. In particular he contends the identification of Kant as the founding father of this position. See Terry F. Godlove, *Religion, Interpretation and Diversity of Belief* (Cambridge: Cambridge University Press, 1989). Kant's theory is not relativistic, Godlove claims, because the categorial constraints on our experience do not arise from our "subjective constitution". The necessity attaching to the categories and forms of receptivity are, rather, independent of the psychological subject, being *a priori* presuppositions or conditions of any and all empirical knowledge. See Immanuel Kant, *Critique of Pure Reason* (1787), trans. Norman Kemp Smith (London: Macmillan, 1933), A56/B81, p. 96; B167-168, pp. 174-175. This is the sense in which the categories are "objectively valid"—as "formal conditions for the possibility of experience in general" (Godlove, *Religion, Interpretation and Diversity of Belief*, p. 28). Such "transcendental constraints" determine "not merely something about *us* (what we are equipped to recognize), but rather something about *the world* that affects us (what is really and not merely absolutely possible)" (*ibid.*, p. 34, compare p. 37). We can only encounter objects necessarily in conformity to these *a priori* constraints. There may be other sentient and comprehending beings, with forms of receptivity different from our own—alien beings that encounter an eight-dimensional world, for example. Such beings are not self-contradictory. But their conceptual apparatus would not be "conceivable and comprehensible to ourselves" and "would not belong to [our] experience—the only kind of knowledge in which objects are given to us" (Kant, *Critique of Pure Reason*, A230-231/B283, pp. 249-250). Such alien understandings could not exist in our world, for that world is constrained by our transcendental equipment. This equipment is necessarily common to all human conceptual frameworks. For Kant, then, it constitutes a species-wide "schema" of a very general sort (Godlove, *Religion, Interpretation and Diversity of Belief*, pp. 120-121, 135). By contrast, the conceptual schemas referred to by relativists are less fundamental, less widespread, and do not operate as necessary *a priori* conditions of experience and knowledge. The relativists' accounts, unlike that of Kant, also distinguish neutral formless data ("content") from the interpretative grids or frameworks ("schemas") through which the data is perceived (compare *ibid.*, pp. 52, 57, 59, 74, 78, 89-92). For Kant, it has been said, "the interpretative grid or order of concepts that we must use is single" (for him there can be only one such grid), absolutely *a priori*, necessary and universal—in a word "compulsory". But for relativists, interpretation is as plural and historical-cultural as language, necessity is often "only conventional", and "there are many ways of world-making". Don Cupitt, *Radicals and the Future of the Church* (London: SCM, 1989), pp. 85-86 and *Creation out of Nothing* (London: SCM; Philadelphia: Trinity Press Intenational, 1990), pp. 29-30, 56-60, 67-68. Kant's treatment of objectivity suffers, one of his commentators has argued, from this "considerable limitation, almost, it might be said, .. handicap" of not referring to "the *social* character of our concepts". P. F. Strawson, *The Bounds of Sense* (London: Methuen, 1968), p. 151. Taking these arguments into account, it must be admitted that Kant's "fathering" of relativism is on the wrong side of the counterpane.

tion in philosophy" he sought to make his readers recognize that much that used to be naïvely regarded as part of the nature of things did in fact belong to the experiencing, thinking self. In essence relativism builds on this inward shift of the "locus of cognitive validation" to our cognitive apparatus, so that "the world is seen *within* knowledge, and not the other way round".[34] Just as Copernicus had argued that the "apparent movement" of the sun was caused by the "actual movement" of the observer on earth, so Kantian philosophy attributes to ourselves certain features that had previously been attributed to independent reality, by detailing a whole range of elements in the make-up of the experiencing and knowing mind that act as irremovable spectacles through which, and only by means of which, we can have experience and knowledge of the world. The lenses of these spectacles constitute our cognitive powers by which we organize the data given by our sense organs. These forms of sensibility (space and time) and "categories of the understanding" (concepts of substance, causality and interaction) are *a priori*—prior to experience—and constitute universal and invariable modes of perception and necessary conditions for human knowledge. Intelligible experience requires the operation of these cognitive processes. The world can only be known under such conditions, "schematized" by the mind as a world of causal interaction of concrete substances in space and time. Our perceived world is thus, in part, our own construction. The objects of our experience and knowledge must be such that our faculties can be employed in experiencing and knowing them.[35]

In this way Kant allows for his famous distinction between the ever mysterious "noumenal" reality of things-as-they-are-in-themselves and the "phenomenal" realm of things-as-they-appear-to-us: "this object as *appearance* is to be distinguished from itself as object *in itself*".[36] This is a distinction that may be described—very loosely—as being between the objective, unknowable world and the subjective world of the knower. It is apposite to comment here that Kant's position does not commit him to *nonrealism*: the view that there is no "real" world outside the minds and experiences of human beings. Thus Kant writes: "in order that something can appear to be outside

---

34. Gellner, *Legitimation of Belief*, pp. 28-29.

35. Kant, *Critique of Pure Reason*, "Transcendental Doctrine of Elements", especially pp. 65-91, 102-175, 180-187; Immanuel Kant, *Prolegomena to Any Future Metaphysics*, ed. and trans. Lewis White Beck (Indianapolis: Bobbs-Merrill, 1950), First and Second Part of "The Main Transcendental Problem", pp. 28-74. The literature on Kant's epistemology is vast. Comparatively straightforward accounts of a very difficult thinker are to be found in Geoffrey Warnock's essay in D. J. O'Connor, ed., *A Critical History of Western Philosophy* (New York: The Free Press; London: Collier-Macmillan, 1964) and in S. Körner, *Kant* (Harmondsworth, England: Penguin, 1955; New Haven: Yale University Press, 1982). For a more detailed account of Kant's epistemology see Strawson, *The Bounds of Sense*, and Paul Guyer, *Kant and the Claims of Knowledge* (Cambridge: Cambridge University Press, 1987). We should note that Kant applied this epistemology to our experience and knowledge of the external world but *not* to our experience/knowledge of God. For Kant, God was an inferred not an experienced reality—a postulate of the rational moral life. (See above Chapter 6 note 81.)

36. Kant, *Critique of Pure Reason*, B69, p. 88.

us, there must really be something outside us, though not constituted in the way we have the representation of it, since other kinds of sense could afford other ways of representing the same thing".[37] Kantianism, and some forms of relativism (as we shall see), are compatible with some forms of realism; but they are incompatible with a *naïve realism* that would treat our language and theories as accurate, literal pictures of the real.[38] Both Kantianism and relativism, however, have also been interpreted in a nonrealist ("idealist" or "instrumentalist") way.[39]

The influence of Kantianism on philosophy and theology has been immense. On these grounds alone it deserves the attention of the Christian religious educator. It has also had a profound impact on cognitive psychology, in that major figures such as Jean Piaget and Lawrence Kohlberg have taken up Kant's basic premise that the human mind and its structures act upon the knower's world to give it form, extending this insight in their schemes of cognitive developmental psychology.[40] Such accounts provide, in a modi-

---

37. Immanuel Kant, *Reflexionen*, 6312, *Akademie* edition, volume 18:612-3, quoted by Guyer, *Kant and the Claims of Knowledge*, pp. 324-325. See Runzo, *Reason, Relativism and God*, pp. 59-60.

38. We may compare A. F. Chalmers's account of "unrepresentative realism", whose theories do not describe the world as it really is but "successfully come to grips with some aspect of the world". He regards this position as relativism with an objectivist thrust. See A. F. Chalmers, *What is this Thing called Science?* (Philadelphia: Open University Press, 1982), ch. 14. See also Roy Bhaskar's defense of "epistemological relativism . . . [as] the handmaiden of ontological realism" in his *A Realist Theory of Science* (Atlantic Highlands, N.J.: Humanities Press, 1978), p. 249. For more full-blooded defences of realism against its critics, see Roger Trigg, *Reality at Risk: A Defence of Realism in Philosophy and the Sciences* (Towota, N.J.: Barnes & Noble; Brighton, England: Harvester, 1980) and William Outhwaite, *New Philosophies of Social Science: Realism, Hermeneutics and Critical Theory* (Basingstoke: Macmillan; New York: St. Martin's Press, 1987).

39. Note that Kant describes himself as both a "transcendental idealist" and "an empirical realist": *Critique of Pure Reason*, A370, p. 346. Idealism holds that reality is essentially mental ("ideas"), whereas instrumentalism argues that reality claims are to be construed merely as instruments for predicting observable phenomena. Interestingly, Richard Rorty's contentious claim to have avoided relativism is based on his giving up dependence on the concept of an uninterpreted reality—the World as Thing-in-Itself. "Given the dogma of a dualism of scheme and reality, we get conceptual relativity, and truth relative to a scheme. Without the dogma, this kind of relativity goes by the board" (*Philosophy and the Mirror of Nature*, p. 310, compare p. 325). See also Paul Feyerabend, "Realism and the Historicity of Knowledge", *The Journal of Philosophy* 86: 8 (1989).

40. Thus it has been claimed that "Kant's broad theme, recognising the mind's own positive contribution to the character of its perceived environment, has been massively confirmed as an empirical thesis by modern work in cognitive and social psychology and in the sociology of knowledge" (Hick, *An Interpretation of Religion*, p. 240). See Jean Piaget, *Six Psychological Studies* (New York: Random House, 1967); Lawrence Kohlberg, "Stage and Sequence: The Cognitive-Developmental Approach to Socialization", in David A. Goslin, ed., *Handbook of Socialization Theory and Research* (Chicago: Rand McNally, 1969), ch. 6. See also Moran, *Religious Education Development*, chs. 3 and 4; and Ken Richardson and Sue Sheldon, eds., *Cognitive Development to Adolescence* (Hove, England: Erlbaum, 1988).

fied form, major elements of James Fowler's scheme of faith development, which has been so influential in religious education and pastoral practice. Christian religious educators may already be influenced by a Kantian perspective in other areas, without necessarily being conscious of it. Thus the fundamental Kantian view of the mind as playing an active role imposing organizing forms and categories on data, so as to enable and create perception and knowledge, underlies very many other perspectives in individual and social psychology. These "interactionist", "constructivist" or "schematized" theories have been influential in forming the understanding of many practical religious educators. In their own ways, they may provide pathways to the problem of relativism that are less direct—but in the end as well-trodden—as those laid by philosophical theologians who invoke Kant as one of the founding fathers of their theological relativism.[41] Kant may not have been a relativist himself, but his influence has certainly moved others towards relativism.

Another major influence on contemporary relativism is the American tradition of pragmatism, classically represented by William James and more recently by philosophers such as Willard Van Orman Quine and Nelson Goodman.[42] The philosophy of the later Wittgenstein is also regarded by many as entailing relativism,[43] and has certainly been a profound influence in that direction for many philosophers.

Runzo on Relativism

Kant's thesis entails then that what we can know is determined by how we can know things, all human perception and knowledge being structured by the conceptual structure that our minds brings to experience, and the phenomenal world being "precisely a world which the percipient's conceptual schema makes possible".[44] According to Runzo, these claims, *supplemented by the non-Kantian claim that there exist distinct and incompatible conceptual*

---

41. Such as John Hick—see his *An Interpretation of Religion*, pp. 133, 240-249, 373-376, and Don Cupitt—see his "Kant and the Negative Theology", in Brian Hebblethwaite and Stewart R. Sutherland, eds., *The Philosophical Frontiers of Christian Theology* (Cambridge: Cambridge University Press, 1982).

42. See William James, *Selected Papers on Philosophy* (London: Dent; New York: Dutton, 1917), chs. X and XI; Nelson Goodman, *Ways of Worldmaking* (Indianapolis: Hackett, 1978). Quine regards himself as a relativist with regard to language, but an absolutist "on questions of truth and reality". W. V. O. Quine, "Relativism and Absolutism", *The Monist* 67: 3 (1984), p. 295. For a survey of the recent philosophical debate on relativism, see John Passmore, *Recent Philosophers* (London: Duckworth, 1985), ch. 5.

43. See A. C. Grayling, *Wittgenstein* (Oxford: Oxford University Press, 1988), pp. 104-109 and above Chapter 7. Wittgenstein famously remarked that "if a lion could talk, we could not understand him". Ludwig Wittgenstein, *Philosophical Investigations*, trans. G. E. M. Anscombe (Oxford: Blackwell, 1968), p. 223. Cyril Barrett claims, however, that Wittgenstein "was no more a relativist than any reasonable person can avoid being", and adopted only "a mild and moderate relativism". Cyril Barrett, *Wittgenstein on Ethics and Religious Belief* (Oxford: Blackwell, 1991), pp. 258, 161.

44. Runzo, *Reason, Relativism and God*, p. 61.

schemas,[45] together constitute conceptual relativism. Conceptual relativism (the "social" form of cognitive relativism) is simply the view that truth is relative to such schemas (cognitive structures or systems of ideas); and thus that if a proposition is true it is only true for a particular group of people, relative to a specific set of schemas, which partly constitute their phenomenal world. On this view there are no "neutral" facts, independent of minds, that can be read off the world. All perceiving is "theory-laden". Further there is no single correct set of facts representing *the* facts, for facts about reality are relative to the conceptual schemas of different perceivers.

More precisely, Runzo specifies three principles that make up the argument for (his understanding of) conceptual relativism: an argument relating both the relativity of truth and the relativity of the real to conceptual schemas.[46] *The Diversity Principle* (an empirical claim) asserts that there exist "distinct and mutually incompatible world-view conceptual schemas", each delineating a set of possible "world orders" (phenomenal worlds) in the sense that a schema in part determines what can be a fact about reality. *The Dependency Principle* (an epistemological claim about truth) holds that "the truth of any statement, *P*, depends, in part, on the conceptual

---

45. See note 33 above and Brian Hebblethwaite, *The Ocean of Truth* (Cambridge: Cambridge University Press, 1988), pp. 74-75. "Schemas" seems to be preferred to "schemata" by Runzo and others as the plural of schema. In Kantian philosophy a schema is a rule for the production of images (e.g. of a "circle" or a "dog"), linking concepts to particular perceptions (circles or dogs). In the case of a schema of a category of the understanding, however, it "determines the temporal conditions under which [the category] is applicable to objects of experience in general" (Körner, *Kant*, p. 72). The list of such universal *transcendental* schemas includes number, degree of intensity, permanence in time, etc. In this chapter, however, "schema" is a less technical term with a wider connotation and a narrower application. Runzo uses the term "schema" (or "conceptual schema") to refer to part or whole of the cognitive element or system of ideas that we bring to experience. It consists primarily of "concepts, their interrelationships, persistent beliefs, and the laws of logic" (*Reason, Relativism and God*, p. 30). Runzo's use of "schema" is thus also a rather broader understanding of the term than that adopted in developmental psychology and cognitive science. For Jean Piaget a schema was essentially a sensori-motor schema—a skill or basic pattern of adaptational action that constitutes a basic structural unit of intelligence (exemplified in the infant by grasping, sucking, etc.). This is a concept clearly related to the individual's picture of the world. See Charles Taylor, "What is involved in a Genetic Psychology?", in Theodore Mischel, ed., *Cognitive Development and Epistemology* (London; New York: Academic Press, 1971). Cognitive science has developed the notion along these lines. Thus for Michael Arbib a schema, as "the basic functional unit of action and perception", is a structure for recognizing things that enables one to behave appropriately towards them—a sort of internal model of the world. Michael A. Arbib, *In Search of the Person: Philosophical Explorations in Cognitive Science* (Amherst: University of Massachusetts Press, 1985), pp. 36-44, 47. Schemas therefore provide our "partial knowledge of reality" (*ibid.*, p. 24; compare p. 94). Arbib thinks of a person as having many different schemas in any given situation (pp. 13, 42-44), but schemas that are held in common together constitute the culture (or "social schema") which is learned by each individual (pp. 18-19, 22, 54, 58). It is this broader view of a "great schema" or "network of schemas"—which Arbib identifies with an ideology or symbol-system (pp. 47-48, see also p. 103)—that lies closest to how Runzo uses the term, especially when he writes of a "world-view schema".

46. Runzo, *Reason, Relativism and God*, pp. 57-63; see also pp. 131-132, 136-138.

schema from within which *P* is formulated and/or assessed".

Many conceptual relativists satisfy themselves with some version of these two principles. Runzo takes relativism further, however, adding *The Pluralist Ontology Principle*. This extends relativism to embrace a relativism of reality rather than just of truth, and expresses the conviction that there is more than one adequate account of reality as judged by the usefulness of such accounts in ordering experience. It claims that each conceptual schema which delimits a set of possible world orders delimits an actual world ("and no two schemas delimit identical actual worlds"). Here "actual world" comprises the phenomenal reality perceived by a schema's world order (a "subjective" world) *together with* the noumenal reality (the "objective" world). For the consistent relativist, then, there is not "one reality" but a plurality of actual worlds. This third principle thus captures the view that "'thinghood' is inherently relativistic", being dependent on the way *we* define and describe things.

This version of relativism clearly does not imply the philosophical position of nonrealism, which claims that no "real" world (or God) exists outside the experience of an experiencer.[47] Nor does it imply—which comes to the same thing—that the world, or God, is entirely a product or projection of the minds of human beings. As Ninian Smart notes, in response to the writings of Peter Berger and others, "a thing can be a human fact without being a human product"; hence "it is not . . . up to the scientist alone but to nature as well to determine the shape and the progress of science".[48] (The same point is made, *mutatis mutandis*, with regard to religion.) Relativism need not commit the relativist to the claim that what is real is *entirely* constituted or "constructed" by human perceiving.

Christian religious educators are often said to help their learners to undertake the task of "meaning-making", using the Christian schemas from the tradition as raw materials. These learners are being helped to construct their actual worlds in a particular way. On the view being expounded here, they are not creating experience or reality "out of nothing", but re-constituting experience of a reality that is already there. (The same should be noted of the psychologist of religion's "constructivist" claim that Christians "create" an ultimate environment encompassing, and encompassed by, God.) Christian religious educators who facilitate their learners' powers of (Christian) "worldmaking" may be described as being "co-creators" with God, or agents of "world transformation, rather than world creation", or by some other language that distinguishes their role, and that of their learners, from God's prerogative of *creatio ex nihilo*.

---

47. Many philosophers, however, deny that realism and relativism are compatible: see, e.g., John Skorupski, *Symbol and Theory: A Philosophical Study of Theories of Religion in Social Anthropology* (Cambridge: Cambridge University Press, 1976), Appendix: "Relativism and Rational Belief"; and Bernard Williams, "The Truth in Relativism", *Proceedings of the Aristotelian Society* N.S. LXXV (1974-75), p. 227.

48. Ninian Smart, *The Science of Religion and the Sociology of Knowledge* (Princeton, N.J.: Princeton University Press, 1973), pp. 78, 80, compare p. 90; see also Berger, *The Social Reality of Religion*, pp. 95-96.

It has been argued that the terminology of "meaning systems" is preferable to that of "worldviews" or "belief systems", the terms usually used in these discussions, in that the idea of a worldview "implies that individuals are amateur philosophers, an assumption compatible with the Enlightenment image of humanity. The concept of meaning system necessitates no such assumption. . . . . Meanings evoked by symbols occur at the emotional and volitional levels as well as the cognitive level."[49] For similar reasons ("it is far from the feel of praxis and of faith, or the smack of sacrament or angst"), Smart regards worldview only as the "least bad" English word.[50] Thus, although the account of relativism given in this chapter is described as an account of *cognitive* relativism, for which *truth* is relative to the *cognitive* concepts, beliefs etc. that we have, this should not lead us to focus only on thinking and conceptualization. It must be remembered that cognition never occurs in isolation from affect and that the worldviews discussed here represent an abstraction of the cognitive dimension from a multifaceted "meaning system" (see Chapter 6). The distinction between "*my* world" and "*the* world", therefore, must also be worked out in terms of my emotions and valuations, for it is not improper to claim—with Robert Solomon—that "it is the passions that provide the structures of my world".[51] Many religious educators would be sympathetic to such an "affective relativism" or "emotive relativism" (and perhaps to a related aesthetic or even moral "value relativism"), while denying a full cognitive relativism. If my arguments in Chapters 6 and 9 about the significance of affect in Christianity and Christian religious education are accepted, this sort of *affective relativism* may be far more relevant to the religious educator than any species of cognitive relativism. My point here is merely that affective relativism must also be recognized as a constant companion to, or aspect of, any form of cognitive relativism.

Objections to Relativism

In his discussion of relativism Runzo gives an account of the standard objections to such a position. As religious educators frequently dismiss cognitive relativism on the basis of an uncritical assessment of these objections it is important to subject them to some analysis. We may classify them as follows, indicating in each case Runzo's counter-arguments.

The first is the familiar "self-stultifying" argument. The most frequently met criticism of relativism is that it destroys itself. A total relativism would

49. Robert Wuthnow, "Two Traditions in the Study of Religion", *Journal for the Scientific Study of Religion* 20: 1 (1981), p. 24. For this wider, nonlinguistic, understanding of "meaning", see above Chapter 6.

50. Ninian Smart, *Concept and Empathy* (New York: New York University Press; Basingstoke, England: Macmillan, 1986), p. 74, also p. 82.

51. Robert C. Solomon, *The Passions* (Notre Dame, Ind.: University of Notre Dame Press, 1983), p. 68; compare p. 194. The schemas of cognitive psychology also have an affective dimension, see David S. Heywood, "Revelation and Christian Learning" (Ph.D. dissertation, University of Durham, England, 1989), chapter 3.

undermine its own claim: relativism could only *be* true for the person who held it to be true. According to Runzo, the appropriate response to this criticism is to recognize the distinction between two levels of discourse. Philosophers frequently distinguish first-order statements referring to states of affairs *in* an object language (what the philosopher Rudolf Carnap called "material-mode discourse") as being radically different from second-order statements *about* that language (Carnap's "formal-mode discourse"—not talk about x, but "talk about talk about x"). Runzo argues that cognitive relativism is to be understood as a view about the nature of the truth of *first-order* statements.[52]

However, there exists a more extreme form of relativism which holds that second-order statements also are relative truths. Runzo describes this as "epistemological relativism", and agrees that this version probably is incoherent. It would appear that the view that *all* truth is relative *is* self-stultifying, for—as Runzo argues—rational discourse depends on certain assumptions, including the assumption that the canons of rationality (second-order statements) are not mere relative truths. But one can be a consistent relativist while restricting one's relativism to first-order statements, and therefore excluding reference to metalogical and metalinguistic statements. One would then be a relativist about truth (i.e. "most" truth), while holding, for example, that the law of noncontradiction is *absolutely* true, as essential to rational discourse as such. Rationality does seem to demand this sort of *qualification of relativism*.[53] Much discussion about relativism construes it in its

---

52. Runzo, *Reason, Relativism and God*, p. 39. The general claim that self-referential arguments are invalid has been met by some philosophers by attempts to distinguish different levels of language and types of truth, and by advice to exercise caution when faced with self-inclusive classes (classes that are members of themselves). See A. N. Whitehead and Bertrand Russell, *Principia Mathematica* (Cambridge: Cambridge University Press, 1910), Vol. 1, pp. 60-65; David Pears, ed., *Russell's Logical Atomism* (London: Collins, 1972), pp. 118-128; J. L. Mackie, "Self-refutation—a Formal Analysis", *The Philosophical Quarterly* 14: 56 (1964).

53. Runzo, *Reason, Relativism and God*, p. 43, compare pp. 183-184, 220. See Kai Nielsen, *Contemporary Critiques of Religion* (London: Macmillan; New York: Herder and Herder, 1971), ch. 5. The flouting of the law of noncontradiction is surely *the* test. One cannot present a case in a consistent or coherent form, so as to be open to consideration by others, without it. Stephen Toulmin, *The Uses of Argument* (Cambridge: Cambridge University Press, 1958), pp. 25-26. See also pp. 56-57 and 169-170 above. A standard criticism of relativism is that some criteria of rationality are "universal", in being "relevantly applicable to all beliefs", and not restricted to particular contexts. Steven Lukes, "Some Problems about Rationality", in Bryan R. Wilson, ed., *Rationality* (Oxford: Blackwell, 1979); see also F. C. White, "Knowledge and Relativism I", *Educational Philosophy and Theory* 14 (1982), pp. 7-8. The very formulation of a relativist position seems to depend on the nonrelative validity of certain other concepts, including certain notions of causality. See also Bernard Williams, "The Truth in Relativism", pp. 215-217. We may compare the distinction between "hard-perspectivism" (which Louis Pojman rejects) for which "reason can only have intramural significance", and "soft-perspectivism" which recognizes "something like a core rationality common to every human culture" and where reason also has an *inter*mural use. Louis P. Pojman, *Religious Belief and the Will* (London: Routledge & Kegan Paul, 1986), pp. 197-198. On the distinction between hard-perspectivism (with its implication of incommunicability) and the more "qualified relativism" of soft-perspectivism (which "permits rational assess-ment" while recog-

unqualified form: dismissing it at a stroke, and consequently ignoring the insights it can bring to an understanding of religion and of religious education. This is a mistake.

A more sophisticated version of the first argument must now be countered, however, for the absolutist could reformulate the self-stultifying criticism at the level of third-order statements (statements about second-order statements) by asking, for example, "Is the claim that we ought to be cognitive relativists merely relatively true?". Perhaps this is the nub of the whole criticism. But in framing it has the critic of relativism allowed the relativist *any* answer? Such questions seem to try to escape all conceptual schemas; and the whole point of the relativist's claim is that one cannot "assess a theory's validity apart from any schema".[54] For the relativist, third-order questions are neither true nor false, they can only be judged on pragmatic grounds (such as expediency, parsimony, comprehensiveness, etc.). Modern philosophy has seen a resurgence of pragmatism, and this is often accompanied by a willingness to embrace some form of qualified relativism.

A more everyday criticism of relativism is the argument that it inevitably leads to skepticism and moral anarchy, making truth an arbitrary matter of what people think, and conflicting viewpoints "equally right".[55] This criticism is a common feature of popular objections to relativism from the pens of educationists and religious apologists. Runzo allows that one type of cognitive relativism probably does fall victim to this criticism. This is solipsistic "subjectivism"—the view that truth is relative to each *individual's* schema. But this is a misunderstanding of the nature of concepts as *social* constructions. According to Runzo, the relativist can still talk of "objective" truth claims provided that they are subject to "trans-schema" ("interschema") rational check-

---

nizing that the same events "can have diverse meanings") see Van Austin Harvey, *The Historian and the Believer: The Morality of Historical Knowledge and Christian Belief* (New York: Macmillan, 1966; London: SCM, 1967), ch. VII.

54. Runzo, *Reason, Relativism and God*, p. 47. Similarly Jack Meiland, "Bernard Williams' Relativism", *Mind* 88: 350 (1979). White rejects the refutation on the grounds that only the non-relativist is "likely to accept that a claim intended to be universal in its application cannot be relative in its truth" (White, "Knowledge and Relativism I", p. 5). Some relativists are willing to accept "that relativism is true, relativistically". Thus Don Cupitt, *Life Lines* (London: SCM, 1986), p. 205; contrast his earlier *The Leap of Reason* (London: Sheldon, 1976), ch. 5. In a later work Cupitt argues, in the postmodernist style, that the position of relativists is paradoxical "only because we haven't yet got the new vocabulary that we are going to need". Don Cupitt, *The Long-Legged Fly* (London: SCM, 1987), p. 89, also p. 33. Defenders of this view often appeal to the wiles of "rhetoric" as more appropriate to the justification of relativism than the philosopher's preferred "position-" accounts, which are inevitably framed in the language of objectivist epistemologies. See Feyerabend, *Farewell to Reason* p. 83; also G. H. R. Parkinson, "Humanistic Education: Some Philosophical Considerations", in Roger Straughan and John Wilson, eds., *Philosophers on Education* (Basingstoke, England: Macmillan, 1987).

55. Roger Trigg, *Reason and Commitment* (Cambridge: Cambridge University Press, 1973), ch. 1; K. R. Popper, *The Open Society and its Enemies*, Vol. II (London: Routledge & Kegan Paul, 1962), pp. 369, 387; Hilary Putnam, *Reason, Truth and History* (Cambridge: Cambridge University Press, 1981), p. 54. See also Brenda Watson, *Education and Belief* (Oxford: Blackwell, 1987), pp. 24, 29.

ing procedures within the given sociohistorical culture.[56] Thus Runzo can refer to the "objectivity" of monotheism, not implying that there is any one standard of truth, but that monotheism is subject to rational "checking procedures which are applicable across both theistic and a-theistic schemas" (examples would include considerations of coherence, comprehensiveness, proof etc.). Conceptual relativism, understood as the claim that truth is relative to the conceptual schema *of a society*, does not fall at the hurdle of this criticism; for on this view "truth is relative to a broader, *public standard*, a standard of social parameters", and this provides a public check against our believing just anything we want. This takes us a *very* long way away from a relativism that assumes (as Brenda Watson, along with many educationists, assumes it assumes) "that no-one *can* know" and which "therefore is not concerned about evidence at all".[57] We may note again the significance of the social context of epistemology, and the way in which this fits such emphases as the social context of theology, the place of the church in Christian believing, and the faith-community approach to Christian religious education with its stress on the *corporate* formation of Christian identity and the Christian worldview.

Another, related, objection to relativism is the claim that on the relativist's view a statement about one "world" cannot mean the same as a statement about another "world", and therefore that trans-schema communication and dispute is impossible. But again Runzo, unlike some advocates of the "incommensurability" and "untranslatability" of conceptual schemas, cultures and languages, argues that there is sufficient overlap between differing schemas—and therefore of "actual worlds"—to allow for such communication. It is the *totality* of people's schemas, and their corresponding actual worlds, which are incompatible; individual statements and constituent elements of people's schemas and worlds can be similar and even identical. It

---

56. Compare Wittgenstein's critique of the notion of a private language in his *Philosophical Investigations*, pp. 92-97. See Runzo, *Reason, Relativism and God*, pp. 214-216 (the quotation that follows is from p. 215).

57. Watson, *Education and Belief*, p. 33; compare Runzo, *Reason, Relativism and God*, pp. 49-50, 56. Pragmatic philosophers, who construe objectivity as intersubjectivity, admit that "our only usable notion of 'objectivity' is 'agreement' rather than mirroring". Rorty, *Philosophy and the Mirror of Nature*, p. 337, compare p. 367. Compare Strawson, *The Bounds of Sense*, pp. 151-152. Jean-Francoise Lyotard calls this consensus the "culture of a people", see "The Postmodern Condition", in Kenneth Baynes *et al.*, eds., *After Philosophy: End or Transformation?* (Cambridge, Mass.: MIT Press, 1987), p. 79. Richard Rorty writes, "To say that someone is bringing in 'subjective' considerations to a discussion where objectivity is wanted is, roughly, to say that he is bringing in considerations which the others think beside the point." Rorty, *Philosophy and the Mirror of Nature*, pp. 338-339. In the same place Rorty acknowledges another sense of subjective as "'a product only of what is in here' (in the heart . . .)"—i.e. "emotional" or "fantastical". For a radical defense of the social nature of objectivity—"all that is objective is the competitive activity of knowing, the rules of the game, and the method of scoring successes over one's competitors"—see David Bloor, "A Sociological Theory of Objectivity", in S. C. Brown, ed., *Objectivity and Cultural Divergence* (Cambridge: Cambridge University Press, 1984), quotation from p. 239.

is this acknowledgement that can save relativism from the isolationism of the claim that only those who share my worldview can understand or criticize my position. This is a popular ploy in religion, and in some accounts of religious education that have been influenced by Wittgenstein; but it cannot be supported. Runzo is not therefore defending here the views, to quote another scholar, of "relativist fideists who refuse to agree even to engage in conversation with those who don't accept their faith commitments"[58] (see Chapter 7). Radical Wittgensteinian fideism needs to be qualified just as much as does unreformed, naïve relativism before it can serve the interests of the Christian religious educator.

A final objection to relativism is that the relativist's wedding of phenomenal reality and conceptual schemas results in absurd claims, such as that no dinosaurs could exist before human minds formed a conception of them. But Runzo denies that relativism has any such implication, its point is only that for us to speak about things that existed before we did "we must speak from our own conceptual perspective".[59]

Along these lines Runzo is able to combat the arguments against (a suitably qualified) relativism, and therefore to contend that it is more plausible to hold "that there is no single, adequate way of conceiving of the 'facts' about reality", than that there can only be "one set of facts about the One Reality".[60]

The Wider Debate and Its Implications

Defenses of relativism usually focus on the social dimension of criteria of truth and rationality: the claim that knowledge must always have a "conventional character". This position has also been labeled *finitism*. Barry Barnes writes: "Finitism denies that inherent properties or meanings attach to concepts and determine their future correct applications; and consequently it denies that truth and falsity are inherent properties of statements. 'True' and 'False' are terms which are interesting only as they are used by a community itself, as it develops and maintains its own accepted patterns of concept application."[61] In nonrelativistic usage "reason" is often taken to be cognition

---

58. T. W. Tilley, "Incommensurability, Intratextuality, and Fideism", *Modern Theology* 5: 2 (1989), p. 88. See Runzo, *Reason, Relativism and God*, pp. 55, 63-64, 190-192, 209. Compare also Grayling, *Wittgenstein*, pp. 107-108. Tilley embraces *contextualism* which "recognizes that our basic agreements and the disagreements which make them possible shift with the positions from which, the purposes for which, and the audiences to which, we speak": p. 89. Different paradigms are incommensurable but comparable (pp. 93-94). This is clearly close to Runzo's form of *qualified relativism*. A trenchant critique of the fideism that often accompanies extreme relativism (i.e. the replacement of rational justification of belief by subjective commitment or "faith") is offered by William W. Bartley, III, *The Retreat to Commitment* (La Salle, Ill.: Open Court, 1984), especially pp. 73-75, 259-260. See also Putnam, *Reason, Truth and History*, ch. 5 and note 53 above.

59. Runzo, *Reason, Relativism and God*, p. 243.

60. *Ibid.*, p. 48.

61. Barry Barnes, *T. S. Kuhn and Social Science* (New York: Columbia University Press; London: Macmillan, 1982), quotations from pp. 27, 22; see also p. 67. The work of Thomas

and inference that has no social component, a view that he describes as "an intolerably individualistic conception". For Barnes (an extreme relativist), "the entire framework wherein the reasonable and the social stand in opposition must be discarded". This includes those theories of knowledge that are "morality plays set in a Manichaean cosmos" where the forces of light (experience and reason; with truth, validity, rationality and objectivity) battle it out with opposed and irreconcilable forces of darkness (culture and authority; supported by custom, convention and dogma). Barnes insists that there is nothing to be said in favor of this mythology. "Culture and experience interact at all times as knowledge grows; they operate symbiotically, as it were, not in conflict."[62]

The contrasting individualistic, "objectivistic view of knowledge", represented by much traditional epistemology, is regarded by many as fundamentally dehumanizing. Thus the sociologist of education Geoffrey Esland writes of it that it "ignores the intentionality and expressivity of human action and the entire complex process of intersubjective negotiation of meanings. In short, it disguises as given a world which has to be continually interpreted."[63] Again Christian religious educators will recognize in these writers a focus on the role of society and culture that is at least sympathetic to certain aspects of their own views on Christian enculturation within a community and to the claim that Christian truth is social truth, a truth that belongs not to individuals but to the church. The implications for their work are considered in more detail later (pp. 285-289).

Nonrelativists accept that it is this social element that is the central plank of relativism, in particular the part played in such views by the notion of social agreement. Roger Trigg argues that any theory that emphasizes "above all else the importance of some kind of agreement inevitably leads to relativism", for it suggests that "truth is not dependent on what is the case, but on what people think is the case".[64] This claim is at the center of the controversy over relativism. Critics of relativism and of the "sociology of knowledge"[65] frequently express the need "to delineate a concept of rationality

---

Kuhn on the operation of science has been a major influence in the development of relativism. For Kuhn, "there is no standard higher than the assent of the relevant community". His position is fundamentally relativist, although he has denied this and his later work presents a more qualified thesis. Thomas S. Kuhn, *The Structure of Scientific Revolutions* (Chicago: University of Chicago Press, 1970), quotation from p. 94; see also *ibid.*, pp. 206-207 and his papers in Imre Lakatos and Alan Musgrave, eds., *Criticism and the Growth of Knowledge* (Cambridge: Cambridge University Press, 1970) and T. S. Kuhn, *The Essential Tension* (Chicago: University of Chicago Press, 1977).

62. Barnes, *T. S. Kuhn and Social Science*, p. 22. See also his *Scientific Knowledge and Sociological Theory* (London: Routledge & Kegan Paul, 1974).

63. Geoffrey M. Esland, "Teaching and Learning as the Organization of Knowledge", in Michael F. D. Young, ed., *Knowledge and Control* (London: Collier-Macmillan, 1971), p. 75.

64. Trigg, *Reason and Commitment*, p. 26; compare Trigg, *Reality at Risk*, ch. 5.

65. The sociology of knowledge represents a many-faceted industry of scholarship that often presents epistemological claims enmeshed with claims of a more descriptive, empirical nature. For a brief survey by authors who try to bracket the epistemological questions and regard

which is socially blind".[66] Keith Dixon argues that relativism may be refuted "if it can be shown that enquiry into human action presupposes a universal principle of rationality".[67] This would include assumptions about what counts as an intelligible account of human action and about what counts as a legitimate (for Dixon, broadly scientific) explanation of behavior, and a commitment to the significance of the reasons for people holding beliefs. The relativist needs some such framework for his or her own concept of explanation, to arbitrate between the variety of internal explanations offered by the variety of definers of reality. I have noted this requirement in the *qualification* of relativism described above (pp. 272-273). Yet Dixon notes that such a framework is highly formal and does not define a specific set of categories, a specific delineation of rationality. He admits that the fact remains that "the concept of rationality is . . . a categorical form whose substance is essentially contestable" (as we saw in Chapter 7 above).[68] But he insists that this position still forbids the view that all categories of thought are relative to cultural consensus.

The reader may wonder whether this admission by a defender of nonrelativism does not allow some of the relativist's army to push their way in at the back door, after having been so strenuously excluded from the front. This must particularly be a danger when relativism is qualified to allow some absolute truths within its weaponry. Is there then *that* much difference between "true relativism" and a perspectival, socially-contextualized analysis of rationality and truth? Perhaps religious educators will need to look elsewhere for the decisive refutation of relativism.

Ernest Gellner's breezy critique ignores the usual criticism of the self-contradictory nature of the doctrine on the interesting grounds that "making an exception on one's own behalf . . . is the professional ailment of philosophies, and is virtually written into the terms of reference under which they work"![69] Gellner prefers to base his criticism on the claim that the relativist's recipe is "empty": that relativism is a signpost pointing nowhere (or everywhere), for "to work . . . relativism requires the existence of identifiable 'cities'" or given units of identity. "The recipe is, roughly, when in Rome, do (and above all, think) as the Romans do. . . . . [But] in the world as it now is,

---

the sociology of knowledge as concerning itself "with whatever passes for 'knowledge' in a society, regardless of the ultimate validity or invalidity (by whatever criteria) of such 'knowledge'", see the "Introduction" to Peter L. Berger and Thomas Luckmann, *The Social Construction of Reality* (New York: Penguin, 1967), quotation from p. 15. A still useful survey of the classical texts of the sociology of knowledge is provided by Robert K. Merton, *Social Theory and Social Structure* (New York: Free Press, 1968), chs. XIV and XV. Philosophers often reject the social scientists' account of a sociology of knowledge, arguing that it can only provide a sociology of *beliefs* (see above pp. 150-151).

66. Keith Dixon, *The Sociology of Belief* (London: Routledge & Kegan Paul, 1980), p. 5; compare pp. 34, 40.

67. *Ibid.*, p. 52.

68. *Ibid.*, p. 60.

69. Gellner, *Legitimation of Belief*, p. 49.

there simply are no 'Romans' and no 'Rome'."[70] It may be that Gellner is here arguing against forms of relativism that (unlike Runzo's position) understand different schemas as nonoverlapping and utterly incommensurable. But even a more qualified version of relativism seems to need actual examples of societies, cultures, forms of life or traditions that incarnate their own distinctive norms of truth and rationality. Gellner contends, however, that these do not (now) exist. They have disintegrated—probably, one may argue, through various forms of ideological evangelism, acculturation and education.

This is an interesting move, and pertinent to our concerns. Even if relativism were (theoretically) true, might it now be (practically) useless, or at least increasingly so? Educators rightly have practical utility as a prime concern, and this should be true of religious educators also. More to the point, does the plausibility of relativism actually depend on the formal nature of its articulation? It is nonrelativists, rather than relativists, who tend to appeal to actual examples of different societies and their standards of rationality and truth. Critics of relativism often argue that, where it counts, these different societies are actually operating with the *same* standards. We may need to dig more deeply than our usual superficial survey of cultures to find this. Cultures often appear to differ in their ways of thinking and arguing, when "deep down" there is fundamental agreement on canons of rationality and evidence (and, indeed, of moral truth). Some would argue that the Christian worldview is not distinctively different from others with regard to these standards. The more agreement there is, the more redundant the relativist's critique appears to be. It cannot be denied that a particular form of rationality (broadly "scientific" and "Western") seems to be slowly conquering the world. If its territory becomes species-wide, perhaps there will be no more "Romans". But I would argue that a qualified relativism may find enough disagreement to mount its critique even then.

The Transcending of Relativism

I turn now in this study of the arguments for and against relativism to an account of Alasdair MacIntyre's analysis. It is a balanced and perceptive discussion of the issues involved, and one that may offer education a significant role in the "transcending" of relativism.

In his paper "Relativism, Power and Philosophy", MacIntyre remarks on the perennial nature of the relativism debate: "relativism, like skepticism, is one of those doctrines that have by now been refuted a number of times too often. .... Genuinely refutable doctrines only need to be refuted once".[71] The

---

70. *Ibid.*, pp. 48-49. See also his *Postmodernism, Reason and Religion* (London: Routledge, 1992), especially pp. 57-72.

71. Alasdair MacIntyre, "Relativism, Power and Philosophy", reprinted in Baynes *et al.*, eds., *After Philosophy*, quotation from p. 385. Richard J. Bernstein similarly ponders on the persistence of the relativism debate in his *Beyond Objectivism and Relativism: Science, Hermeneutics and Praxis* (Oxford: Blackwell; Philadelphia: University of Pennsylvania Press, 1983), Part One. His own proposal for transcending both relativism and "objectivism" draws

problem is that of the cultural boundary situation: the situation of the bilingual speaker communicating with his own family/village on the one hand, and the outside world on the other, at a particular point in time (e.g. Ireland in 1700, or South America in the sixteenth century). In such circumstances *parts* of each language are genuinely untranslatable into the other because of their cultural differences. Situations like this have faced educators down the ages, as they speak out of one culture to another. They are not unknown to Christian religious education, particularly in its evangelistic mode. MacIntyre argues that the situation is one of a choice "not only between languages but between two mutually incompatible conceptualizations of natural and social reality". Further, this is not only a choice between two mutually incompatible sets of beliefs "but one between sets of beliefs so structured that each has internal to it its own standards of truth and justification". Such a situation, MacIntyre insists, excludes the possibility of appeal "to some neutral or independent standard of rational justification to justify the choice of one set of beliefs, one way of life, one linguistic community rather than the other".[72]

These two communities are talking about the same thing, but their conceptualization of it is different. "There is no access to any subject matter that is not conceptualized in terms that already presuppose the truth of one set of claims rather than the other." MacIntyre regards this situation as supportive of a defensible version of relativism. We may note that intercommunity agreement is here an agreement over subject-matter, and not necessarily over the meaning of propositions about that subject-matter. The rot sets in earlier than some critics of relativism assume.[73]

Such a relativism, MacIntyre argues, cannot be refuted. *It can, however, be transcended.* It can be transcended by a sort of "conversion experience" in which one partner in the debate is changed. It has already been claimed that this is a type of experience that can properly arise in educational contexts. In Chapter 9 it was suggested as a possible goal of moral education and of Christian religious education in certain situations. MacIntyre claims that we are *not* all imprisoned within our own particular standpoints, but that this claim may only be made if our tradition embodies a concept of rationality that requires a readiness to accept "a possible future defeat of the forms of theory and practice in which it has up till now been taken to be embodied within our own tradition, at the hands of some alien and perhaps even as yet largely unintelligible tradition of thought and

---

on recent discussion in hermeneutics. His stress on the importance of "practical rationality" and "dialogical communities" finds an echo in some of MacIntyre's main themes.

72. MacIntyre, "Relativism, Power and Philosophy", pp. 393-394. Feyerabend writes, "relativism .... is not about concepts ... but about human relations. It deals with problems that arise when different cultures, or individuals with different habits and tastes, collide" (Feyerabend, *Farewell to Reason*, p. 83).

73. Compare, for example, W. Newton-Smith, "Relativism (philosophy)", in W. F. Bynum *et al.*, eds., *Dictionary of the History of Science* (London: Macmillan; Princeton, N.J.: Princeton University Press, 1981), pp. 369-370.

practice".[74] In other words, our concept of rationality must recognize the rational inadequacies of our tradition from our own point of view, and the possibility of our transferring our allegiance to a very different tradition.

This is really only an extrapolation from what goes on in those many conversations and discussions in which we are really open to conversion to the views of another.[75] It is surely a limiting case of what Fowler and Hull have recognized as part and parcel of certain developmental stages and (even?) of a certain type of (Christian religious) education. A "self-critical", "open" rationality can, as it were, save us from ourselves. Through it we can escape the imprisonment of our reason. I suspect, however, that this sort of rationality will in fact look very different from that espoused by those philosophers of education who see themselves as heirs of the Enlightenment and champions of omnipotent "Reason", while failing to recognize the particularity of their own assumptions about rationality. It is far more "open"—and risky—than that.

In his *Whose Justice? Which Rationality?*, MacIntyre develops in great detail the historical and social contextual character of the principles of theoretical and practical rationality—the "conception of rational enquiry as embodied in a tradition".[76] He argues that the strongest appeal to date to the existence of a tradition-independent rationality is to be found in that saintly and seductive product of the Enlightenment—liberalism. But this, he asserts, is a fallacious appeal. I hope to have shown this myself in some small way in this text, with reference to some of the more theoretical aspects of the educational dimension of the liberal tradition. The failure of the liberal's claim, MacIntyre contends, provides us with the strongest reason for denying that there is some neutral court of appeal for decision between rival traditions;[77] for what would count as a satisfactory solution, and the reference-standards by which different solutions are to be evaluated, also differ radically from tradition to tradition.[78]

It might appear to follow from this that no tradition can claim rational

---

74. MacIntyre, "Relativism, Power and Philosophy", p. 409. Compare Bartley's comment—after claiming to have defeated "the only powerful argument on behalf of scepticism, fideism, and relativism"—"I want to hold myself open to the despair of reason, in case the argument should lead somewhere different tomorrow. Thus the pancritical rationalist may hold his practice of reasoning and obeying logic—just like everything else—open to comprehensive criticism and rejection." Bartley, *The Retreat to Commitment*, p. 260; but contrast W. D. Hudson, "Learning to be Rational", *Proceedings of the Philosophy of Education Society of Great Britain* XI (1977), pp. 43-44, and Karl-Otto Apel, "The Problem of Philosophical Foundations in Light of a Transcendental Pragmatics of Language", in Baynes *et al.*, eds., *After Philosophy*, especially p. 265.

75. Feyerabend goes so far as to say that even "speaking a language or explaining a situation . . . means both *following* rules and *changing* them" (Feyerabend, *Farewell to Reason*, p. 270).

76. Alasdair MacIntyre, *Whose Justice? Which Rationality?* (Notre Dame, Ind.: University of Notre Dame Press; London: Duckworth, 1988), p. 7, compare p. 390.

77. *Ibid.*, ch. XVII, compare p. 393.

78. *Ibid.*, p. 348, compare p. 350.

superiority over any other, each tradition (e.g. each intellectually coherent and distinctive version of Christianity) having its own view of what constitutes rational superiority. This view would lead to a thoroughgoing relativist position—which MacIntyre interprets as a denial that *rational* debate between, and rational choice among, rival traditions is possible. But MacIntyre now argues that such a position is misconceived, and represents a misunderstanding of the type of rationality possessed by traditions.

To argue this case, MacIntyre begins by distinguishing "warranted assertibility", which is always local to particular standards then and there prevailing, and "the concept of truth", which by contrast is timeless—true of all possible times and places. He claims that it is in its use of this concept of truth that a tradition, knowingly or not, "confronts the possibility that at some future time it will fall into a state of epistemological crisis", involving a dissolution of that tradition's historically-founded certitudes. Such crises can only be resolved by the invention or discovery of new concepts and theories, which are at the same time shown to be continuous with the conceptual and theoretical structures that went before. If it is part of the relativist's thesis that each tradition, "since it provides its own standards of rational justification, must always be vindicated in the light of those standards", then here at least "the relativist is mistaken". At the point of epistemological crisis, the adherents of a tradition may "encounter in a new way the claims of some particular rival tradition". They now come for the first time to understand the beliefs and way of life of this other tradition, and in order for this to happen they have to learn "the language of the alien tradition as a new and second first language". In this way a thoroughgoing relativism, which would argue that there is "no good reason to give one's allegiance to the standpoint of any one tradition rather [than] to that of any other", is shown to be inadequate. For in situations of epistemological crisis a tradition can change by recognizing the rational superiority of another tradition. I would call this a *rational conversion experience*. It is the possibility of this happening, McIntyre asserts, that "gives point to the assertion of truth and provides assertions of truth and falsity with a content which makes them other than even idealized versions of assertions of warranted assertibility".[79]

One critic (Ian Markham) contends that MacIntyre does not give an adequate *description* here of religious traditions (except for liberalized traditions). But he accepts MacIntyre's position as a prescriptive claim as to how traditions *ought* to develop. Interestingly enough for our concerns, Markham writes that the only hope for the success of MacIntyre's liberalized "Tradition-Constituted Enquiry" (overagainst the powerful success of fundamentalist-type traditions with their "closed account of disagreement") lies in *education*. Not only is it education "which may provoke the sensitivity to the inadequacy of these closed accounts". It is also "education which alone can pro-

---

79. *Ibid.*, pp. 364, 362, 365-366. We may note that Cyril Barrett argues that, as Wittgenstein admits the possibility of such a conversion, he was not an "extreme relativist". Barrett, *Wittgenstein on Ethics and Religious Belief*, p. 157.

vide the context for the learning of [a] second first-language, and genuine dialogue". Thus, paradoxically enough, MacIntyre may be viewed as an advocate of a very liberal view of education, albeit (I would add) a much more sophisticated, self-critical and defensible view than the one we often hear.[80] Is it not indeed an extreme form of the tamer species that we have earlier called *critical education*? Certainly the problem of relativism arises most potently in contexts of practical education—including Christian religious education (and evangelism). Perhaps it can only be fully met ("transcended") by this recognition of the possibility of a radical "conversion" of our rationality. In which case even Christian religious education must allow for this, and allow too that *some* situations of Christian religious education may actually lead to such a radical rational conversion.

McIntyre has shown us that in order for us to be able to claim truth we should allow that we *might* be converted out of that truth—even out of our understanding of what "true" means—and come to "see things differently" (even reason).

How does this account relate to the earlier discussions in this book of indoctrination and formative/critical education (Chapters 4 and 5)? It would appear that formative induction into a tradition *in principle* needs to allow for the possibility of the development of an epistemological crisis within that tradition that might result in its adherents undergoing conversion to (some aspects of?) a very different tradition of rationality and/or valuing. This principle extends to the (or, better, a) Christian tradition. It follows, MacIntyre claims, from a tradition's use of the concept of truth. That concept is being badly abused or misunderstood where a tradition is not open to its own reformation—albeit as a limiting case, and only through a revolution of thinking and valuing provoked by an epistemological crisis. If a tradition properly understands the implications of its use of the concept of truth then it (i.e. the tradition as a whole) may acknowledge openly the possibility of such future revolutionary rational change. This acknowledgement might well impact on the particular form of (say) formative Christian religious education in which it engages, and its relationship to the dimension of critical Christian religious education.

But I would claim that this represents no more than a minor qualification to the position advocated earlier about the need for, and balance between, these two species of education in the teaching of Christianity. It is only a minor qualification for two reasons. The first is that this openness to change is a function of the tradition and its transmission considered *as a whole*, and not of an isolated element of educational content or procedure. The tradition-as-a-whole may witness to the possibility of such a future radical change, but each individual learner or educational act need not reflect this. The second reason is that, although an acknowledged openness to possible future change is patently built-in to the scientific tradition, yet "normal science" passes

---

80. Ian Markham, "Faith and Reason: Reflections on MacIntyre's 'Tradition-Constituted' Enquiry", *Religious Studies* 27: 2 (1991), p. 267.

on its tradition largely by formative educational methods which, while they allow for occasional radical scientific revolutions, do not—and cannot—have a nature that is oriented to these unpredictable future outcomes. Religious traditions need not be treated more strictly than scientific traditions in this respect.

It is appropriate to add that those Christian traditions that do *not* openly acknowledge the possibility of such a radical self-transcendence do not thereby escape from the implications of the concept of truth that they use, nor from the implications of MacIntyre's argument. Concepts have logical implications whether they are admitted or not. Obviously such a tradition will not modify its formative (or critical) educational procedures to allow for such a change. Perhaps it ought to, as Markham suggests. If it were fully clear, self-reflective, and honest about its use of the concept of truth, perhaps it would. But then it would already have become a different sort of tradition.

Truth: Immanent and Transcendent?

Notions of truth and criteria of rationality exist within languages as *norms*. They indicate how we should think, rather than just describing how we do think. Truth is often therefore described as "objective": it is the case whether people believe it or not. Trigg comments: "Truth is in the mind of the thinker, according to the subjectivist, or arises from the collective agreement of a society, according to the relativist. The objectivist, on the other hand, holds that truth is a goal which we aim at but do not necessarily reach."[81]

It must be acknowledged that there is something genuinely human in viewing truth in this (objectivist) fashion. The related commitment to the quest for rationality—"the attempt to restore intellectual order by the sustained application of simple, delineated, lucid principles"—has been described by others as "absolutely essential for our life".[82] Educationists will recognize the force of this position. A similar normative notion of truth lies at the basis of Hilary Putnam's argument against relativism, or rather against any unqualified relativism that holds that there are *no* standards of rationality that transcend cultural communities. He argues for the transcendent, "regulative" role of reason: "consensus definitions of reason do not work, because consensus among grownups *presupposes* reason rather than defining it". Putnam argues that reason is "both transcendent and immanent", with the consequence that philosophy, "as culture-bound reflection and argument about eternal questions, is both in time and in eternity. We don't have an Archimedean point; we always speak the language of a time and place; but the rightness and wrongness of what we say is not *just* for a time and a place." Elsewhere he insists that "what the relativist fails to see is that it is a presupposition of thought itself that some kind of objective 'rightness' exists".[83]

---

81. Trigg, *Reason and Commitment*, p. 4; compare Dixon, *The Sociology of Belief*, p. 77, Trigg, *Reality at Risk*, pp. 195-196.

82. Gellner, *Legitimation of Belief*, p. 22.

83. Hilary Putnam, "Why Reason Can't be Naturalized", in Baynes *et al.*, eds., *After Philosophy*, pp. 235, 242; Putnam, *Reason, Truth and History*, p. 124. On Putnam see Passmore, *Recent Philosophers*, pp. 104-107.

It is not irrelevant to note that similar objectifying impulses arise in axiology (the study of values), particularly with regard to ethical values. Plato's "realism", that is his belief in a transcendent realm of Forms or Ideas where exist the models of mundane goodness, truth, beauty (and people, chairs and triangles), is a very powerful expression of this impulse.[84] We must recognize, however, that the normative, ideal nature of values is not to be understood without *some* reference to the human beings who do the valuing. Even theists who wish to appeal to a realm of "objective values" coextensive with the Divine Will need to see this. *To have* norms of goodness, truth and rationality is *to be committed* to behaving and thinking in a certain way, and *to commend* such behavior persuasively to others.[85] These are things that *we* do. We do them because *we* believe in these norms.

We have seen in Chapter 9 how moral and religious education is relevant to the process of changing people's valuations. At the heart of relativism there lies a similar recognition of the human component of truth and rationality. The question is whether relativism can also give an adequate account of the transcendent, normative element in the functioning of truth and reason, which might imply a similar view of the function of education in changing people's truth claims. Such an account would be broadly similar to the one articulated by MacIntyre. A self-reflective, qualified relativism may well be able to embrace it, accepting the possibility of its own transcendence. It would be a sort of "temporary" or "normal relativism".

It is certainly the case that relativism needs to be a qualified relativism if it is to survive the arguments of its critics. It can only do so by being willing to operate on a "mixed economy" of relative and absolute truths. Relativism also needs to recognize the wide overlap and agreement (perhaps sometimes species-wide, à la Kant) among human beings in very many elements of their conceptual schemas, while stressing that *some* people (and all lions, earthworms, aliens?) "see things differently". It needs to specify, more often than it does, what *practical* difference relativism makes, unless it wishes to restrict itself to articulating—as does so much philosophy—a theoretical dilemma that makes no difference "on the ground". Thus armed, I believe that relativism can provide a powerful analysis of what we mean by "truth", and a valuable prolegomenon to any study of how, through formative education and critical education, schemas may be passed on and changed. It can therefore also explain why these processes form such a crucial part of Christian religious education.

Even in its most attenuated form, even when it has suffered its severest savaging at the hands of its critics, relativism still teaches us one lesson that must not be unlearned. That lesson is that we cannot climb out of our minds, our skins, (even) our cultures so as to reason and discover truth using sterile instruments of rationality that have dropped down from heaven "untouched

---

84. See Plato's *Phaedo*, *Republic*, and *Timaeus*.
85. Vincent Bümmer, *Theology and Philosophical Inquiry* (London: Macmillan, 1981; Philadelphia: Westminster, 1982), chs. 7 and 8. See Chapter 9 above.

by human hand" and untainted by human thinking.[86] Paul Feyerabend writes: "What the early Western rationalists did invent was not argument, but a special and standardised form of argumentation which not only disregarded but explicitly rejected personal elements. In return, the inventors claimed, they could offer procedures and results that were valid independently of human wishes and concerns. . . . this claim was mistaken. The human element was not eliminated, it was only concealed."[87] The only criteria of truth and rationality that we have are those forged in the furnaces of *human* society. The educator knows that, however holy they are, we learned them at a human knee. Relativism shares this humility, and recommends a proper modesty in intellectual intercourse.[88] As we have seen, this is not the only way of learning true humility in matters rational and religious (thus, for example, nonrelativists may accept that *ultimate* truth is in practice unattainable). But it is one way. Is it a proper road for Christian religious educators to travel? Those who do travel this way will, at the very least, be forced to take full account of the human perspective of truth claims in those educational practices that seek to "change people's beliefs".

Further Implications for Christianity and Christian Religious Education

I would argue that Christianity and Christian religious education, which naturally tend towards an absolutist position, need to learn as much as they can from the debate about relativism. One such lesson is about certainty and commitment.

Runzo distinguishes what he calls "personal-absolute truth" from strictly absolute truths (in an epistemological sense). A personal-absolute truth is one that is foundational to a person's worldview and appears "to be absolute from the perspective of the person who holds the relevant schema".[89] According to Runzo, such a truth can properly—and *rationally*—be treated as if it were absolute, but its status is actually relative to the conceptual schema adopted. This distinguishes it from strictly absolute truths, which are true within any possible schema (e.g. laws of logic). The existence of these personal-absolute truths helps to explain why philosophical relativism does not necessarily lead to religious skepticism. It is both natural and *rational* for a monotheist to hold his or her worldview with absolute commitment. Thus, the relativist may claim, the absence of epistemological absoluteness does not

---

86. See Rorty, "Pragmatism and Philosophy", p. 33, also p. 54.

87. Feyerabend, *Farewell to Reason*, p. 87.

88. *Ibid.*, pp. 17, 274, 277, 305, 317. Paul Feyerabend is an extreme, anarchistic, "anything goes", democratic relativist, with a self-confessedly "irresponsible way of talking". See Passmore, *Recent Philosophers*, pp. 112-114. But perhaps I may be allowed to hide in this footnote my recommendation that anyone who wants to experience the full vigor of radical relativist evangelism should seek out his writings first. For a nonrelativist's appraisal of what is right (and wrong) about relativism, see John Wilson, *A New Introduction to Moral Education* (London: Cassell, 1990), pp. 46-48.

89. Runzo, *Reason, Relativism and God*, pp. 155, 220-221.

forbid an absolute commitment arising from faith.[90]

But the argument needs to go one stage further, for we may argue that what we have in religion is a *psychological* notion of absoluteness which is not be confused with an *epistemological* construal of the term. Relativism recognizes this. Runzo claims that although the truths of faith are indeed relative, there is a quite proper "life-transforming absolute commitment" which is "the *absoluteness* of faith".[91] We may compare the comments of Robert Adams: "the certitude of faith has much more to do with confidence, or freedom from fear, which is partly an emotional state, than it has to do with judgments of certainty or great probability in any evidential sense".[92] Christian religious educators who adopt a relativist viewpoint may strive quite as much as their absolutist colleagues to facilitate the growth of an absolute faith in this sense.

Thus, even if Christian theists were to be denied absolute theological truths, relativists might allow them an absolute faith, for more than one reason. The relativist's adoption of the conceptual schema/way of life that is religion is permitted to be as passionate and committed as any one else's. To recognize that epistemological absolute truths are not available here does not reduce the believer to uncommitted skepticism. The quest for absolutes, along with the notorious (and philosophically suspect) quest for certainty, *may* be a journey that has no possible end, as the relativist claims. In which case it would be better to light what candles we do have and embark on a road that is going somewhere, rather than to sit cursing the darkness daunted by the prospect of an unending journey to an illusory—or at least doubtful—philosophical utopia.

Christians sometimes tend to be unrealistically reluctant to make do with what they have. They are always claiming what cannot be had. Thus absolutist theologians like Karl Barth appear to fall into the trap either of absolutizing their personal (and therefore relative?) professions of faith or of making *real* revelation (in which God becomes known *by humans*) an impossibility.[93] I would argue that relativism, or at least some form of perspectivism, as an articulation of our unavoidably *human* situation, cannot be entirely discounted in our knowledge of God without making the miracle of faith an utter anomaly that completely changes the one in whom it is wrought. A revelation to humans that turns them into something other than humans has

---

90. *Ibid.*, pp. 221-222. See also Barrett, *Wittgenstein on Ethics and Religious Belief*, pp. 161-162.

91. Runzo, *Reason, Relativism and God*, p. 223, compare p. 233. See also Fowler, *Stages of Faith*, pp. 208-209 and Dean M. Martin, "Learning to Become a Christian", *Religious Education* 82: 1 (1987), pp. 110-111.

92. Robert M. Adams, *The Virtue of Faith* (New York: Oxford University Press, 1987), p. 18; see also Barrett, *Wittgenstein on Ethics and Religious Belief*, p. 179.

93. Compare Runzo, *Reason, Relativism and God*, p. 235 and ch. 5; see also above Chapter 7. Runzo himself allows a "qualified absolutism" in which God's own schema may be viewed as "supervenient", providing the final standard for the human mind. God's revelation manifests the mind of God, but *our knowledge* of that revelation is relative (*ibid.*, pp. 224-225).

failed as a revelation to humans. (In any case, a theology that is concerned with *human* salvation, and therefore with human needs and purposes, needs to give full weight to the *relative pole* of humanity if only in order to provide a proper account of God's salvific activity, and therefore of God.[94]) Whatever else it affects, I would contend, a dose of relativism should prevent the Christian religious educator from succumbing to the all too prevalent theological disease of over-presumptuousness.[95]

Are there other implications of relativism for Christian religious education? For all educators the problem of *relativity* is an important issue. Whatever the content being taught, the Christian learner faces the challenge of an actually or potentially vast variety of viewpoints—a variety of "truths". Even if she comes to believe that there is one set of absolute truths underlying this variety, she must still learn how to cope with this variety herself, how to relate to other people of different persuasions, and how to educate others to live in a world of relativity.

Not every educator sees tolerance as a virtuous educational outcome, and even those liberal educators who do so regard it implicitly place limits on the range of toleration. (Thus educators who wish to promote tolerance of faiths such as Islam often do not extend that tolerance to embrace traditional Muslim views on the status of women or, indeed, the authority of the Qur'ān.) But even those Christian religious educators who practice educational separation and adopt a policy of protecting the learner against heterodox opinion still need to give their learners the intellectual skills and—equally important—the psychological strengths to cope with an extramural world where the dizziness of relativity is an ever present danger. Advocates of the "total world" of the fundamentalist Christian school or college do not seem to be aware of this. After leaving its walls behind, will such Christian learners be able to cope with the problem of relativity? And will they be able to recog-

---

94. See above Chapters 6 and 7. This is to build on the classical theological distinction between God-as-he-is-in-himself (God's absolute, immanent or intransitive attributes), and God-as-he-is-towards-us (God's relative, emanent or transitive attributes), where the "towards-us" relationship may be understood in terms of divine grace and salvation, as well as revelation. See Martin Luther, *The Bondage of the Will*, X and Thomas Aquinas, *Summa Theologiae*. II, II, q. 1, art. 2. For a soteriological relativism that judges religious mythologies in terms of their "practical truthfulness" and "soteriological alignment with the Real", see Hick, *An Interpretation of Religion*, p. 375. For Gordon Kaufman's more epistemological distinction between the (inaccessible) "real God" and the "available God" ("a particular imaginative construct" in terms of which we think of and worship God) see Gordon D. Kaufman, *God the Problem* (Cambridge, Mass.: Harvard University Press, 1972), ch. 5 and (more radically) The *Theological Imagination: Constructing the Concept of God* (Philadelphia: Westminster, 1981), ch. 1. These theological issues are surely of key significance for the content of Christian religious education.

95. See Runzo, Reason, Relativism and God, p. 138. McKenzie (who rejects the label of relativist) notes that "other-accepting worldviews" value humility in the sense of "the simple realization that no individual can achieve a perfect understanding of the world of which he or she is a part". Leon McKenzie, *Adult Education and Worldview Construction* (Malabar, Fla.: Krieger, 1991), p. 69, compare pp. 106-107.

nize, enjoy and learn from the individual social values on offer from relativity?[96]

Christian religious educators—like all educators in our culture—are educating people to live in the larger society of an increasingly plural state. Even moral relativists have to face the task of morally educating people for responsible citizenship in such a world. A part of that task, it has been said, remains that of "uncovering all the shared values that are embedded in our common life as a diverse people", as well as equipping our learners with the skills to negotiate moral choices in the arena of conflicting values.[97] The dethroning of absolutism does *not* mean that "anything goes", or that "nothing matters" in education.

For those who are wedded to a relativist view, teaching and learning will be seen as "the *inter-subjective* construction of reality",[98] in the context of which the particular worldview is passed on, critiqued, amended, adopted and utilized. The Christian religious educator who adopts relativism will view education into the Christian worldview in a similar fashion. But need this be reflected in her actual educational practice? Relativism is the theoretical interpretation or framework into which she will fit her view of Christianity, but this may not show in the results of her actual teaching. If that is the case, then the learning outcomes of the Christian relativist will be identical with those of the Christian absolutist (whose own position similarly "may not show").[99] This is a logically and morally coherent position. No one teaches everything they believe. However, the religious educator who is persuaded of the relativist's position *might* regard the development of relativism as itself one of the proper learning outcomes of his educational practice.

Perhaps Allan Bloom's students have gone through such an intentional educational process. The account that he gives, however, seems to suggest that theirs is an intellectually (and psychologically) superficial relativism which they have just "picked up": certainly it seems to be an unreflective—and therefore unqualified—relativism. I deprecate this position quite as much as Bloom does, agreeing with M. A. B. Degenhardt that "relativism must be rejected in those naïve and uncompromising forms which preclude any rational exploration and comparison of moral differences and any advance in

96. Alan Peshkin thinks not, and fears that their minds may be closed to the cultural riches that flourish in open, plural cultures; as well as to the "critical attributes of healthy democracies" such as dissent and compromise (essential in any "diverse, complex society"). Alan Peshkin, *God's Choice: The Total World of a Fundamentalist Christian School* (Chicago: University of Chicago Press, 1986), pp. 286, 296.

97. Lonnie D. Kliever, "Moral Education in a Pluralistic World", *Journal of the American Academy of Religion* 60: 1 (1992). On the existence of such shared values across cultures and subcultures, see Lawrence Kohlberg, "Stages of Moral Development as a Basis for Moral Education", in Brenda Munsey, ed., *Moral Development, Moral Education, and Kohlberg* (Birmingham, Ala.: Religious Education Press, 1980), pp. 33, 36, 73.

98. Esland, "Teaching and Learning as the Organization of Knowledge", p. 78.

99. For example, the Christian relativist can still teach her pupils an "absolute faith" along the lines adumbrated on pp. 285-286 above.

moral understanding".[100] "Unqualified relativism", it should be agreed by both philosophers and psychologists, is a position that is—and should be— "difficult to sustain over time".[101]

In the case of those students who are capable of reflection, and whose fulfillment lies in its exercise, to encourage the development of an intellectual position that remains at a precritical level of consciousness is to have failed educationally. This is as true of the development of relativism as of anything else. Further, qualified relativism, as we have seen, does not eschew rationality, commitment or the hard work of the justification of beliefs. It is the *beginning* of an intellectual journey; not a comfortable, off-the-road resort reserved for intellectual holidaymakers. Relativism may be wrong. It certainly can be disturbing. But reflective, grown-up relativism is never a charter for philosophical drop-outs. Naïve relativism should be rooted out, and our learners should not be allowed to "get away with it". But what of *qualified* relativism? Those who are persuaded of it may indeed teach it, I would claim; but they will have to take the greatest care in selecting the proper educational processes (and learners?) so as to avoid misunderstanding. Relativism is very easily misunderstood. But then so is Christianity.

Christian religious educators certainly need to understand relativism better. They also need to do so more sympathetically. There *is* a lot of relativism about, of an increasingly sophisticated nature. There will be more, even in the churches. As MacIntyre says, it can be transcended but not easily refuted. Even if we reject it in the end, we need to take it more seriously than we do. It will not go away by being called names.

---

100. M. A. B. Degenhardt, "The 'Ethics of Belief' and Education in Science and Morals", in Leslie J. Francis and Adrian Thatcher, eds., *Christian Perspectives for Education: A Reader in the Theology of Education* (Leominster, England: Fowler Wright, 1990), p. 236.

101. Parks, *The Critical Years*, pp. 49-50, 101-103.

A Select

Glossary of Philosophical Terms

a posteriori
describes statements or concepts that can be known to be true (or false) only by reference to the evidence of experience.

a priori
describes statements or concepts that can be known to be true without reference to experience.

basic action
an action that we perform directly, and not by means of performing another action.

basic statement
indubitable statements, expressing immediate experience, that are claimed to be the basis of the rest of our empirical knowledge.

behavior
usually "overt behavior"—publicly observable actions that a creature actively performs (see p. 118, note 20).

belief
the state of holding a proposition to be true (belief-that), or of believing-in (committing oneself to and/or trusting) a person or principle. See pp. 149-153.

Cartesian
describing the philosophy of René Descartes.

category mistake
confusion caused by saying something about a topic from one category (type) that only makes sense when applied to subjects in a different category.

causation
the relation between two events or states of affairs such that (normally) the first is necessary or sufficient (or both) for the occurrence of the second.

cognition/cognitive
in philosophy and psychology, denotes mental processes (or the product of those processes) that are connected with understanding and knowledge—e.g. "thinking", "conceiving", "reasoning". Philosophers, however, are more likely to use the word "cognitive" in another (although related) sense, as descriptive of utterances that are either true or false (i.e. "factual" or "truth claiming"). This is in contrast with *noncognitive* utterances which are neither true nor false (e.g. commands, recommendations, exclamations, expressions of feelings and attitudes) or noncognitive experiences that do not give rise to factual claims about the truth or existence of anything.

concept
that which enables us properly to understand and use a piece of language.

confirmation
a weak form of verification, showing that something is more probable than not.

connotation (verb: connote)
(usually) the definition of a term: i.e. what it "means" linguistically, what it signifies.

contingent
(*of propositions*)not necessarily true, not true by definition; (*of entities, events*) not having to exist or to occur.

criterion
(usually) something which shows conclusively whether a word is used correctly or a thing exists. (*For Wittgenstein*) something that is necessarily evidence for something else—see p. 118, note 20.

deduction
inference (reasoning) in which the conclusion is logically implied or entailed by (i.e. logically follows from) the premises on which it is based.

denotation (verb: denote)
that which a term refers to, and to which it can be correctly applied.

disposition (dispositional)
a tendency, inclination or capacity to do something.

dualistic
an adjective describing the twofold nature of reality or of an aspect of reality (e.g. in the claim that substances are either mental or material).

empirical
a statement ("factual claim" or "truth claim") that can be verified, confirmed or shown to be false by reference to experience.

empiricism
the view that all knowledge (or all knowledge about facts) is derived from experience—usually restricted to sense experience.

epistemology
the branch of philosophy concerned with knowledge claims: i.e. what can be known and our ways of securing and justifying knowledge.

existentialism
a philosophical position that stresses the unique significance of concrete human existence and free acts.

fact
something existing in the world that makes a (factual) statement true, or a true proposition. "Factual" sometimes covers false statements and may contrast with "fictional" *or* "conceptual". Sometimes it is used of what *is*, in contrast with human values (what ought to be).

fallacy
a formal mistake in an argument, or a false assumption.

fideism
the view that religious knowledge (or other kinds of knowledge) rests on premises accepted on faith and cannot be established by rational means.

form/Form
(*for Plato*) Forms or Ideas are the independently existing, eternal essences that serve as models for things in the world. *For Aristotle* these "universals" (general qualities) only exist in combination with matter in particular things in the world.

implication/entailment
the logical relationship between two propositions in which one could not be true and the other false. It allows us to deduce the truth of one from the other.

incorrigible
describes a statement that someone cannot be in error in believing or disbelieving.

indubitable
describes a statement that a person cannot rationally doubt or reject.

induction
inference in which the conclusion is made more probable by the premises, but is not certainly derived from them.

inference
the process of reasoning from one set of propositions (premises) to another (conclusion).

instrumental value ("extrinsic value")
the value something has as a means to something intrinsically good.

intrinsic value
the value something has on its own account, as something worth pursuing in and of itself.

intuition
direct awareness (knowledge) of a thing or a truth without any need for inferential ("discursive") reason.

language-game
(*for Wittgenstein*) a rule-governed language practice, see p. 171.

metaphysics
a speculative inquiry making very general claims about Reality as a whole, and assertions about matters beyond the range of the senses (the "meta-empirical").

model
(*in philosophy of religion and philosophy of science*) a situation, word or phrase that we understand, which is used to describe something that we understand less well.

monistic
an adjective describing the single nature of Reality or a reality; the view that there is only one type of substance (especially denying the existence of both matter *and* mind).

natural religion/theology
knowledge about God that may be attained by human reason alone, without divine revelation

naturalism
the theory that reality is understandable without reference to the supernatu-

ral. (*In ethics*) the view that value words are definable in terms of neutral factual statements.

noncognitive
see cognitive.

occurrence (occurrent)
a particular episode, event or act.

ontological argument
an argument attempting to prove the existence of God from an analysis of the concept of God.

ontology
the study of being or existence as such.

paradox
an apparent contradiction.

performative
a description of speech acts that "do" something other than stating (e.g. warning, promising, baptizing).

positivism
an extreme form of empiricism holding that experience alone is the proper source of knowledge, and that metaphysical speculation must be rejected.

postmodernism
an intellectual and artistic position that rejects a "modernism" based on a particular (humanist) value framework, and which advocates instead a more eclectic and relativistic approach to truths and values.

premise (premiss)
a proposition on which the conclusion of an argument is (partly) based.

prescriptive
prescribing a moral maxim, attitude, or definition to others.

proposition
whatever is expressed by an indicative sentence.

rational/reasonable
1. rational may mean established through reason alone (*opposite nonrational or arational*)
2. rational (*opposite irrational*) is also used as synonymous with "reasonable",

implying well grounded or justifiable (= having good reasons). See p. 168.[1]
3. rational may also mean "capable of reasoned thinking".

rationalism
a position that appeals to reason (or reason alone) as the source of, or justification for, knowledge.

realism
the doctrine that objects exist independently of being thought of or perceived (hence "theological realism" is the belief that God exists independently of human experience or language). (*For Plato*) the view that universals (general properties) are real objects: see form/Form.

revealed religion/theology
knowledge about God that only arises from a particular divine revelation and (usually) cannot be attained by unaided human reasoning.

sense datum/sensum
the content of a sense experience or sensing ("perception").

solipsism
the theory that I alone exist.

speech act
the act of uttering language and doing things "in" and "by" such utterances (e.g. stating, requesting, promising, persuading, frightening).

theism
usually used for *monotheism*: belief in one eternal God, creator and preserver of the universe.

---

1. For the use of "reasonable" and "rational" as synonyms with the sense of "sensible", "sane", "having sound judgment", "agreeable to reason" (opposite "irrational" rather than "arational") see C. T. Onions, ed., *The Shorter Oxford English Dictionary*, Vol II (Oxford: Clarendon, 1973), pp. 1750, 1758. See also Robert J. Ackermann, *Belief and Knowledge* (Garden City, N.Y.: Doubleday, 1972), pp. 9-10, 33; Roy Edgley, *Reason in Theory and Practice* (London: Hutchinson, 1969), pp. 53-54. Some have distinguished (a) irrationality from (b) unreasonableness on the grounds that (a) is a matter of behaving or arguing without concern for reasons or by reference to irrelevant reasons (or in the face of conclusive evidence against something or complete lack of evidence for it), while (b) is marked rather by an appeal to *weak* reasons that are insufficient to justify the behavior/argument (and/or by ignoring strong reasons against it). See Robin Barrow and Ronald Woods, *An Introduction to Philosophy of Education* (London: Methuen, 1982), ch. 5, especially p. 86; R. S. Peters, "Reason and Passion", in R. F. Dearden *et al.*, eds., *Reason* (London: Routledge & Kegan Paul, 1972), p. 66, compare pp. 74-75.

transcendent
that which "goes beyond": usually used of what is beyond sense experience, human knowledge or the empirical world.

transcendental argument
(*in Kant*) an argument that shows that a proposition must be assumed to be true if some experience, reasoning or discourse is to be possible.

universalizability
the principle that particular moral judgments may or should apply to anyone in similar circumstances. See pp. 222, 242.

utilitarianism
the ethical theory that the rightness/wrongness of an action (or rule) is to be assessed by the goodness/badness of its consequences (particularly in promoting happiness).

valid (opposite: invalid)
a description of an argument in which the conclusion follows deductively from the premises. *Or* meeting the proper standards for an argument.

verifiable
can be shown to be true (or false).

verification
the act of showing something to be true.

voluntarism (voluntarist)
any theory that gives considerable significance to the human will.

volition
an act of will.

Index of Names

297

Index of Subjects